CHAPTER 47

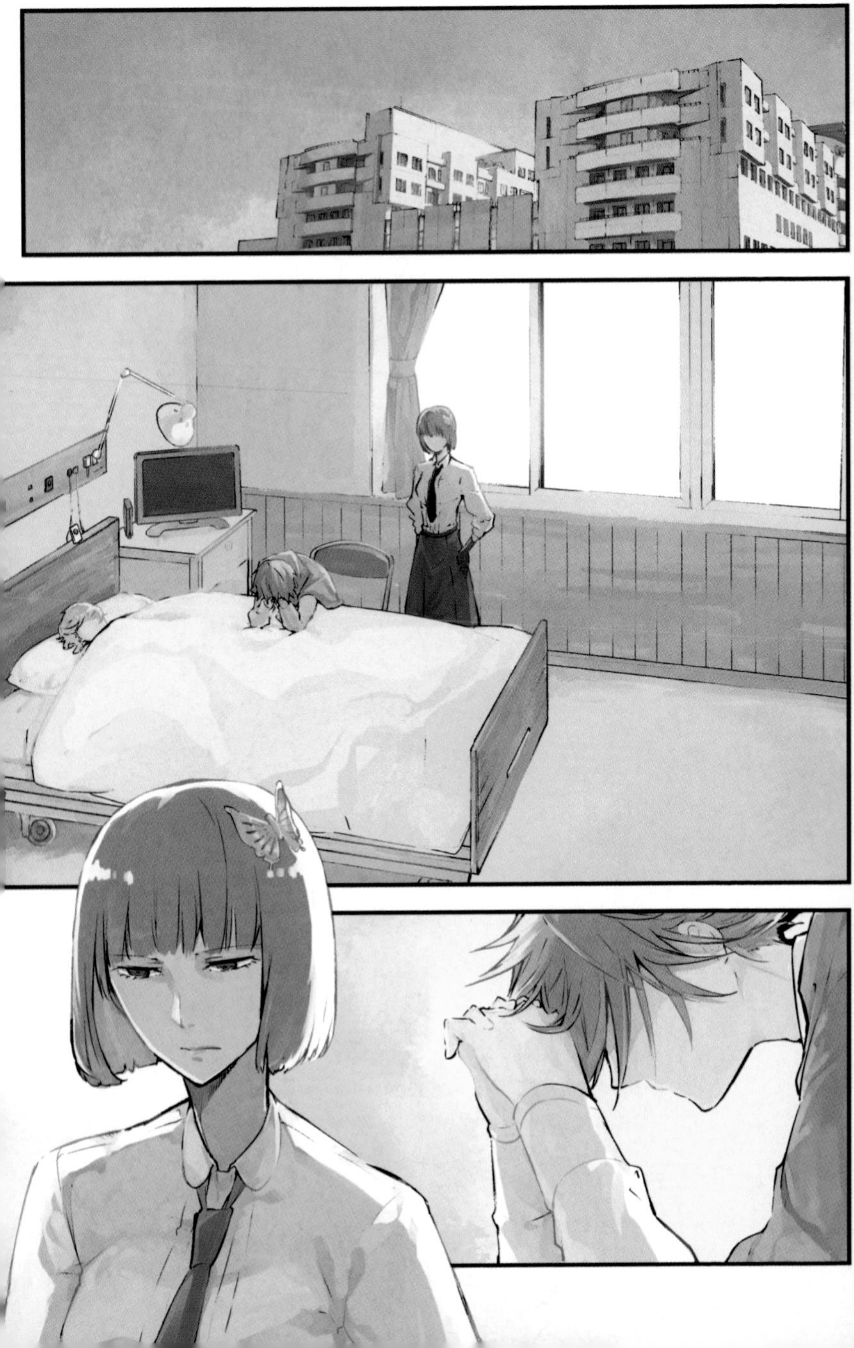

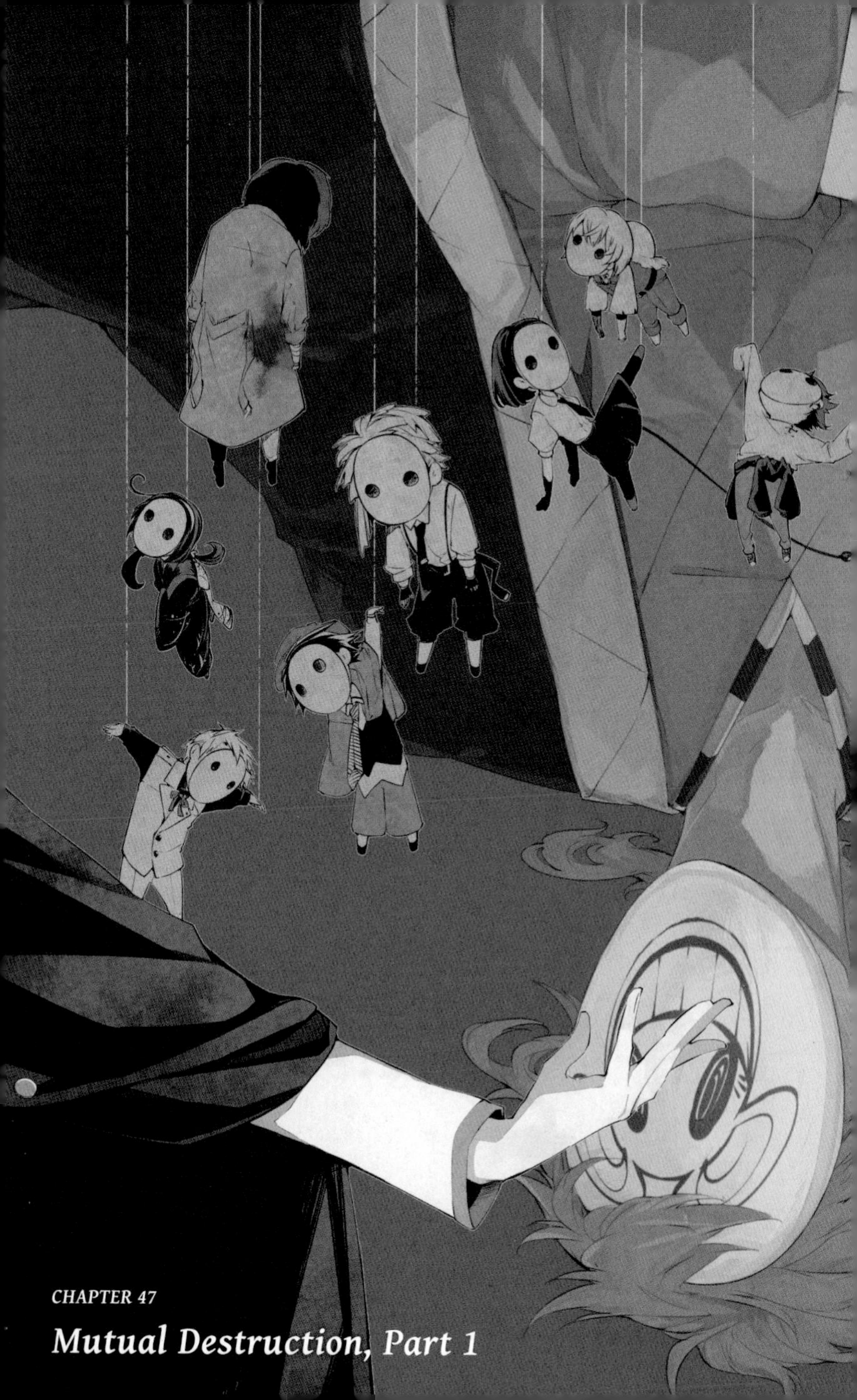

CHAPTER 47

Mutual Destruction, Part 1

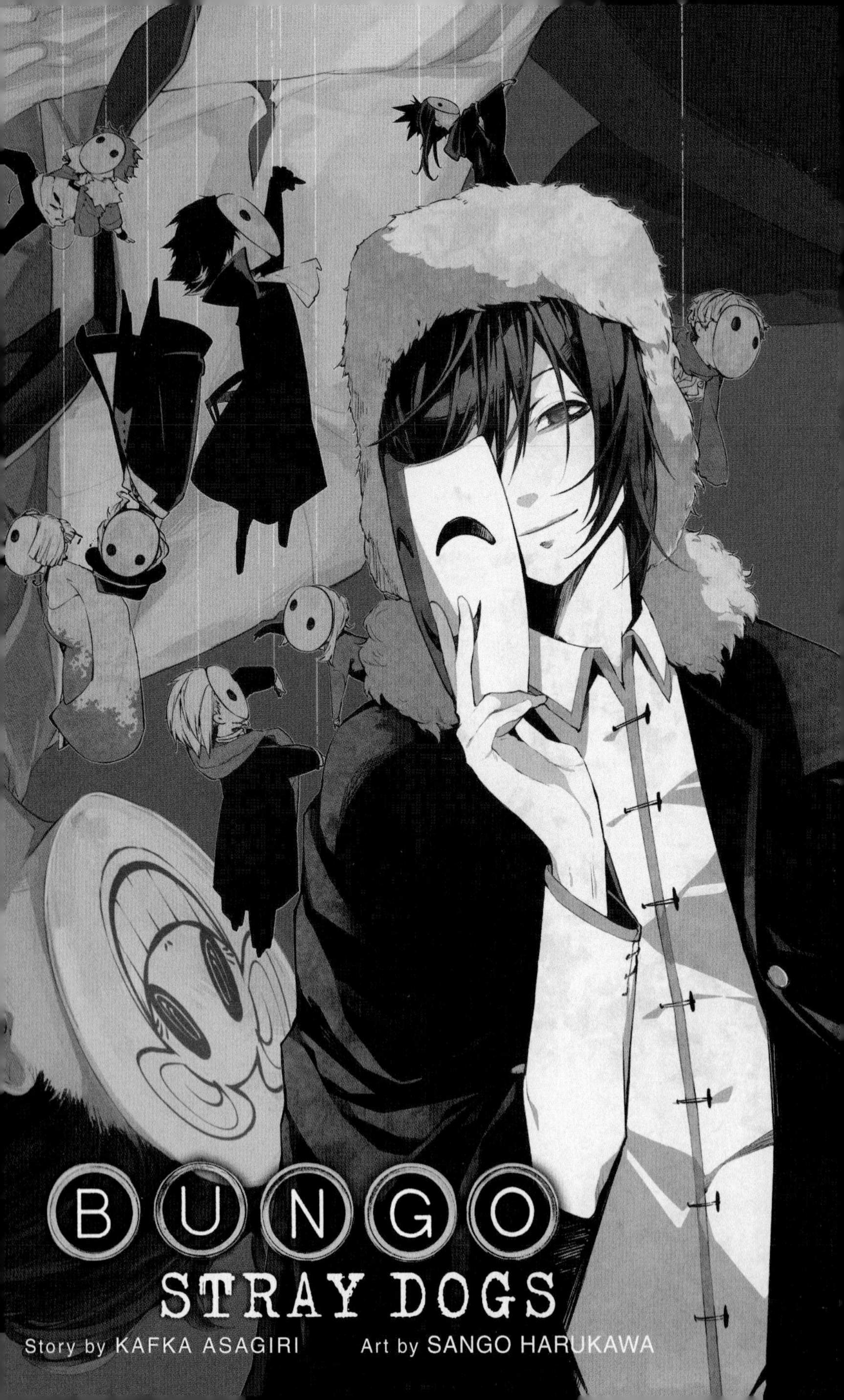
BUNGO
STRAY DOGS
Story by KAFKA ASAGIRI
Art by SANGO HARUKAWA

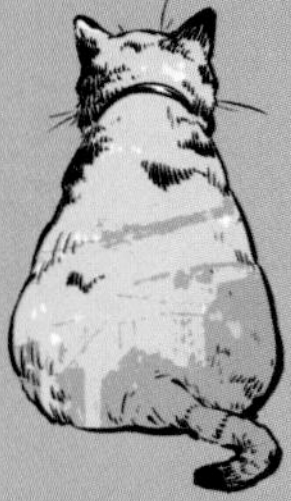

TABLE of CONTENTS

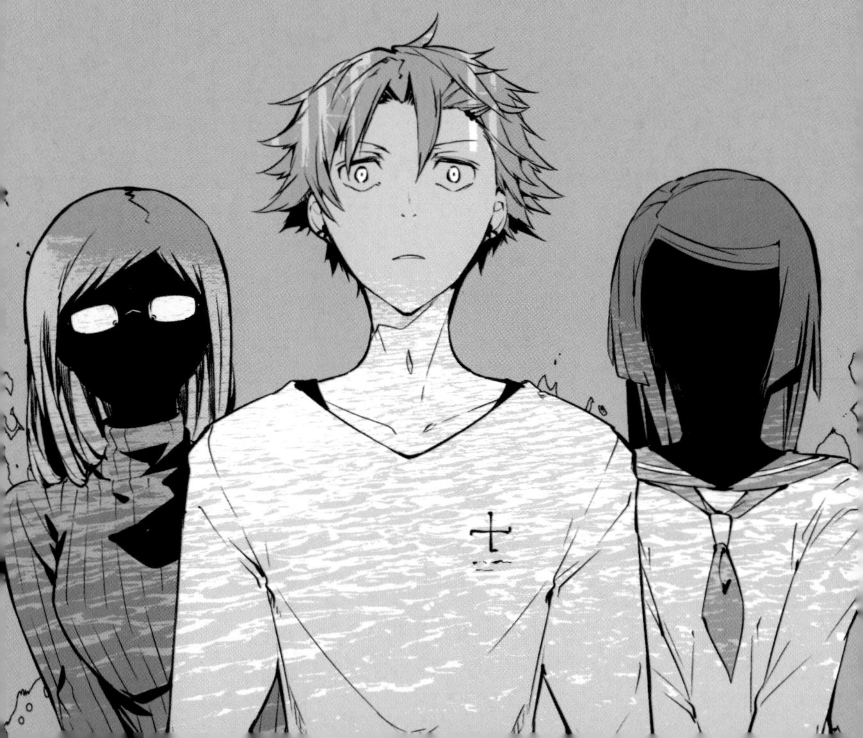

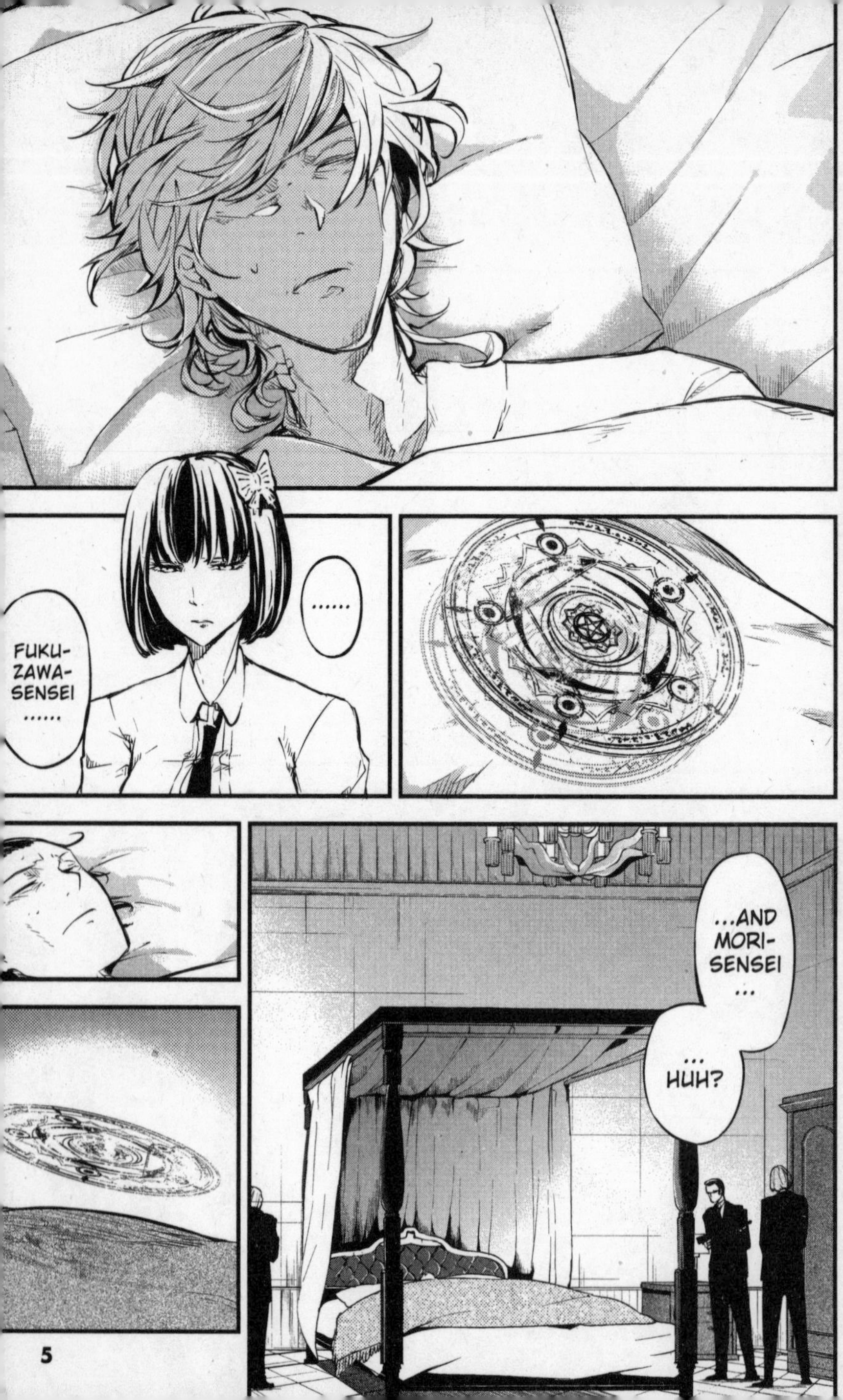
......
FUKUZAWA-SENSEI ......
...AND MORI-SENSEI ...
... HUH?

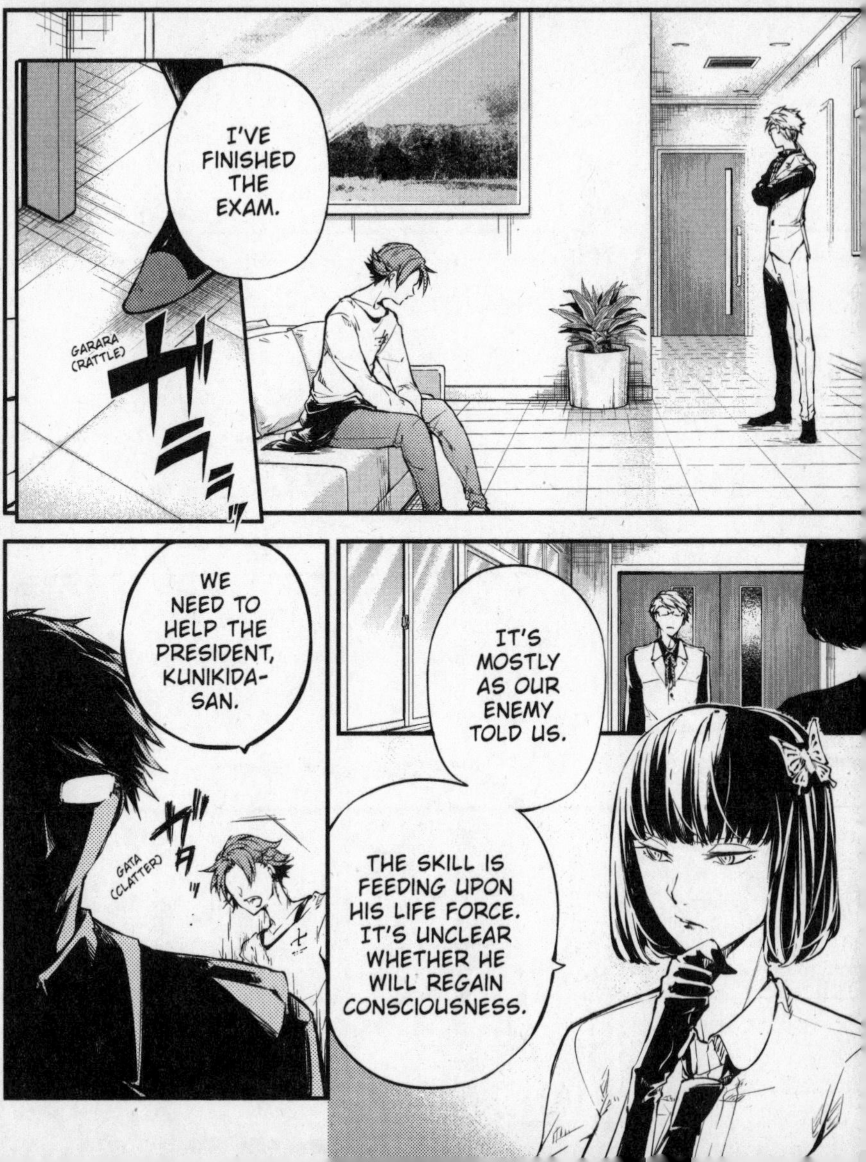
I'VE FINISHED THE EXAM.
GARARA (RATTLE)
IT'S MOSTLY AS OUR ENEMY TOLD US.
THE SKILL IS FEEDING UPON HIS LIFE FORCE. IT'S UNCLEAR WHETHER HE WILL REGAIN CONSCIOUSNESS.
WE NEED TO HELP THE PRESIDENT, KUNIKIDA-SAN.
GATA (CLATTER)

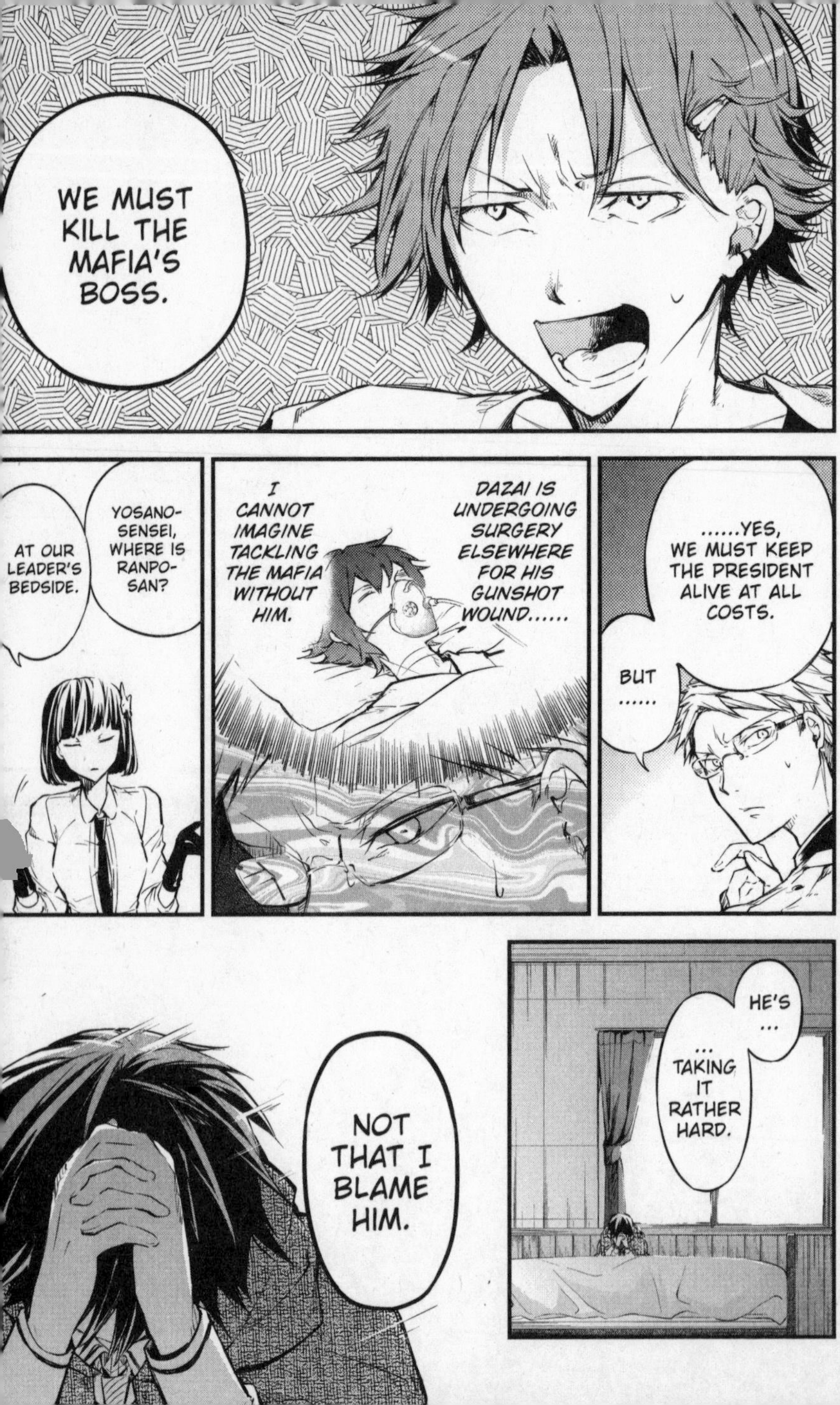
WE MUST KILL THE MAFIA'S BOSS.
......YES, WE MUST KEEP THE PRESIDENT ALIVE AT ALL COSTS.
BUT ......
DAZAI IS UNDERGOING SURGERY ELSEWHERE FOR HIS GUNSHOT WOUND......
I CANNOT IMAGINE TACKLING THE MAFIA WITHOUT HIM.
YOSANO-SENSEI, WHERE IS RANPO-SAN?
AT OUR LEADER'S BEDSIDE.
HE'S ...
... TAKING IT RATHER HARD.
NOT THAT I BLAME HIM.

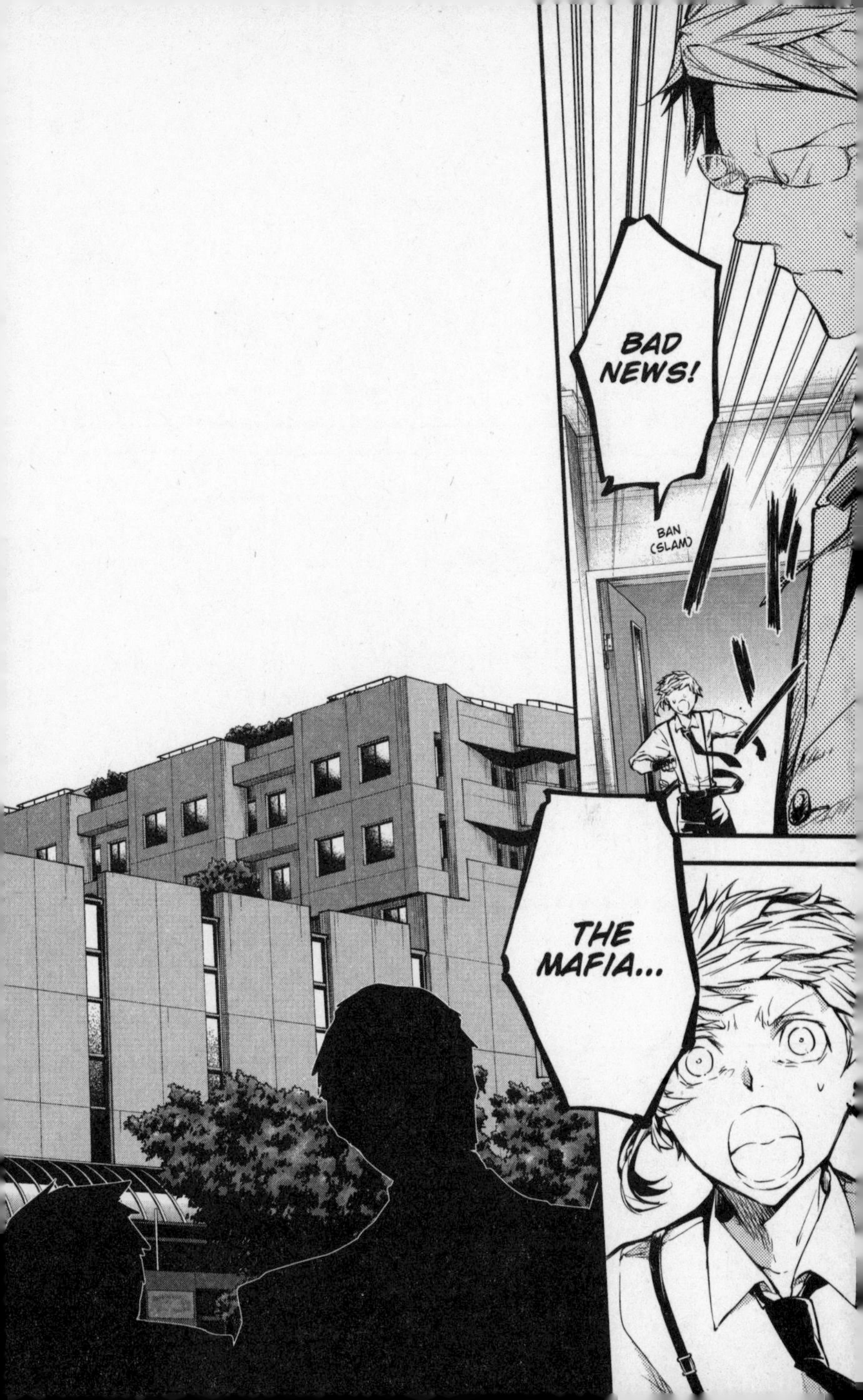
BAD NEWS!
BAN (SLAM)
THE MAFIA...

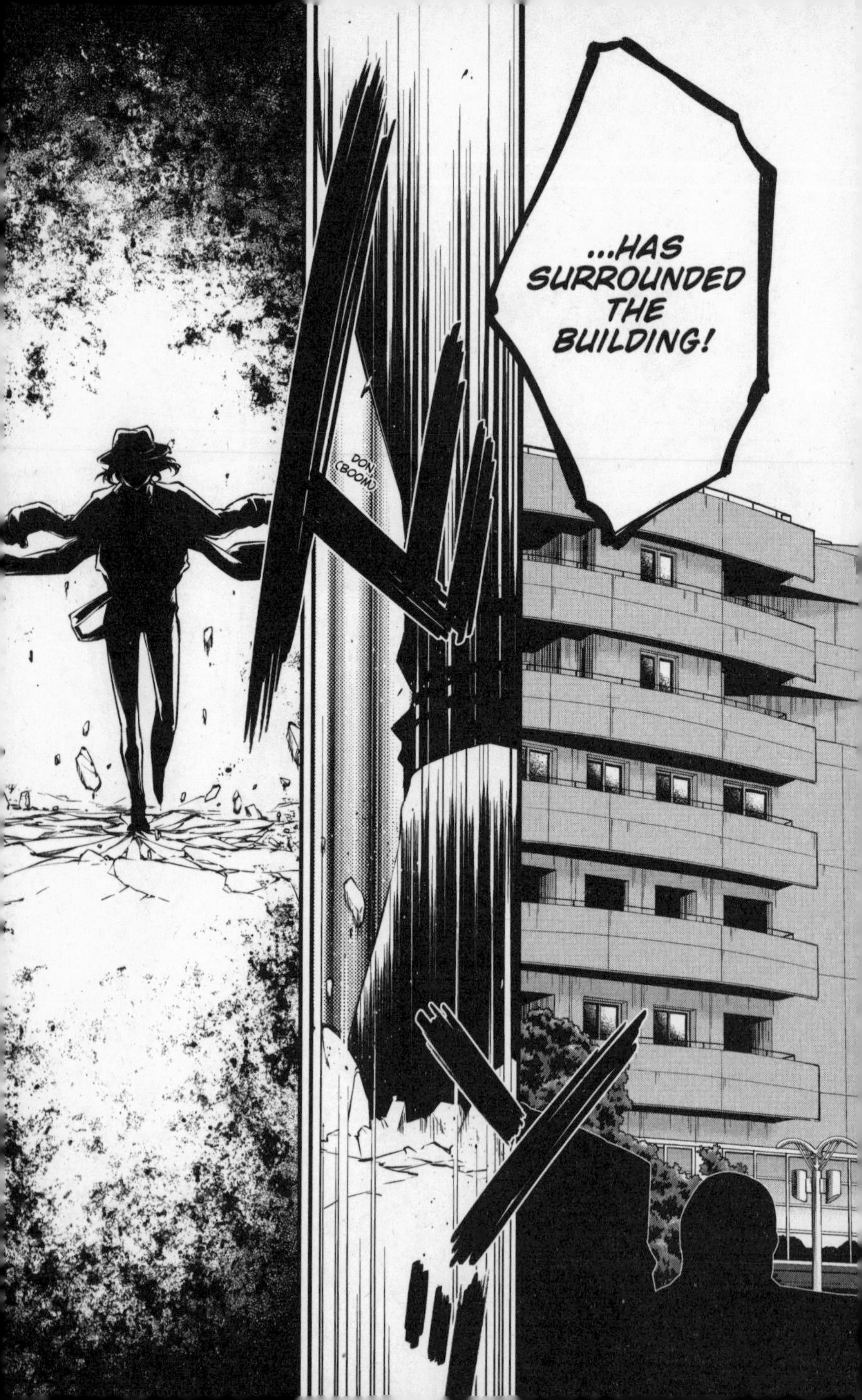
...HAS SURROUNDED THE BUILDING!
DON (BOOM)

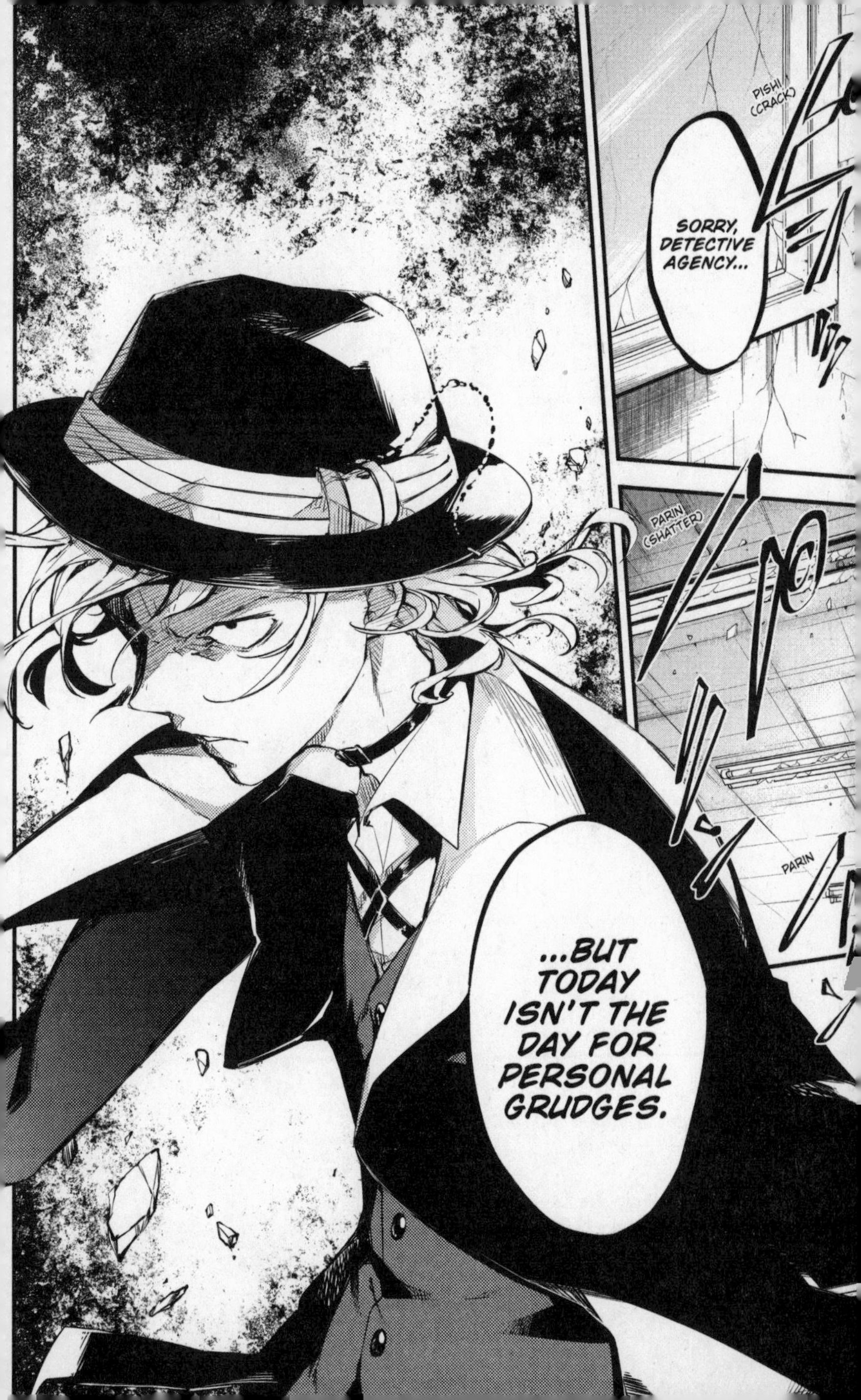
PISHI (CRACK)
SORRY, DETECTIVE AGENCY...
PARIN (SHATTER)
PARIN
...BUT TODAY ISN'T THE DAY FOR PERSONAL GRUDGES.

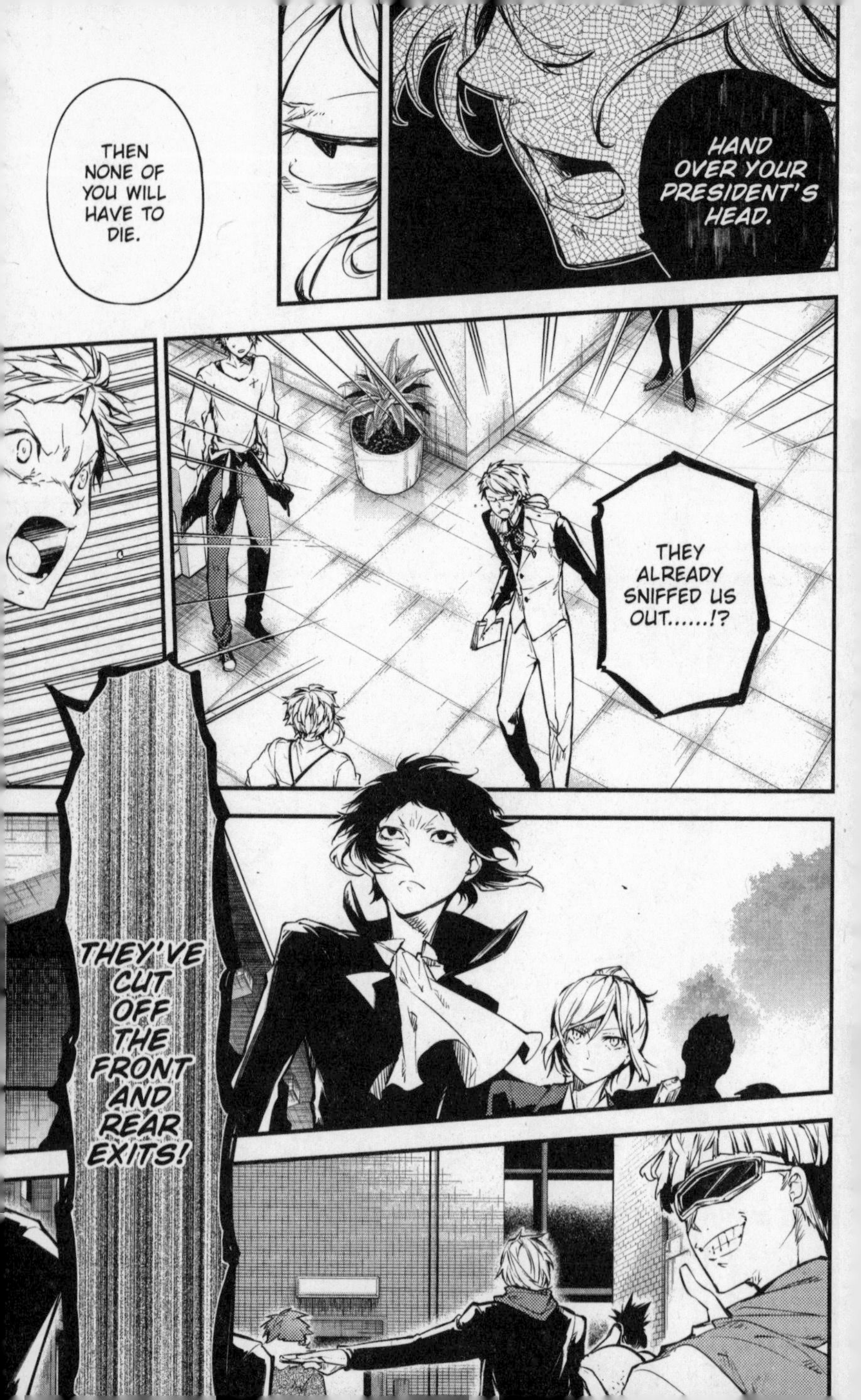
HAND OVER YOUR PRESIDENT'S HEAD.
THEN NONE OF YOU WILL HAVE TO DIE.
THEY ALREADY SNIFFED US OUT......!?
THEY'VE CUT OFF THE FRONT AND REAR EXITS!

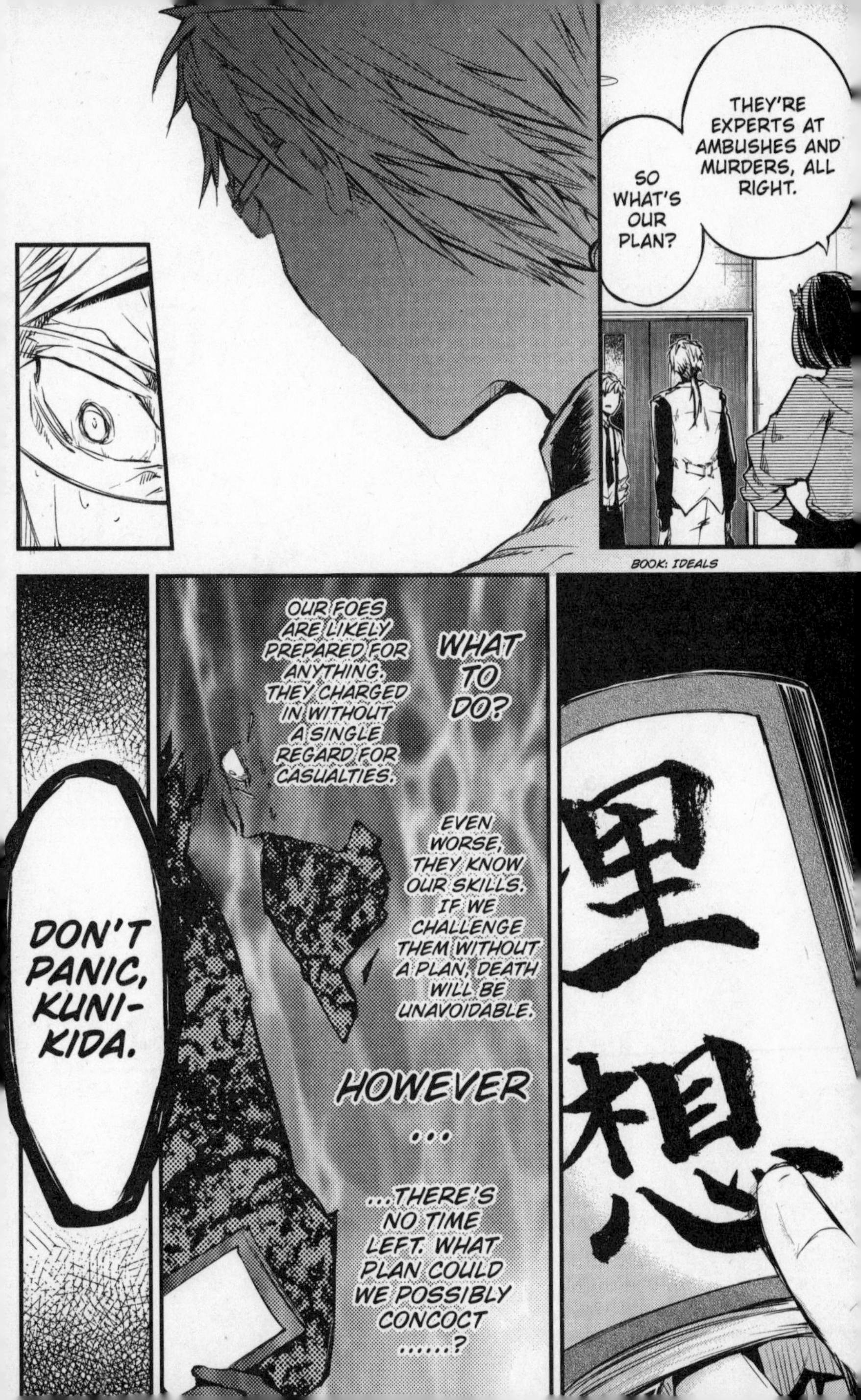
THEY'RE EXPERTS AT AMBUSHES AND MURDERS, ALL RIGHT.
SO WHAT'S OUR PLAN?
BOOK: IDEALS
WHAT TO DO?
OUR FOES ARE LIKELY PREPARED FOR ANYTHING. THEY CHARGED IN WITHOUT A SINGLE REGARD FOR CASUALTIES.
EVEN WORSE, THEY KNOW OUR SKILLS. IF WE CHALLENGE THEM WITHOUT A PLAN, DEATH WILL BE UNAVOIDABLE.
HOWEVER...
...THERE'S NO TIME LEFT. WHAT PLAN COULD WE POSSIBLY CONCOCT......?
DON'T PANIC, KUNI-KIDA.

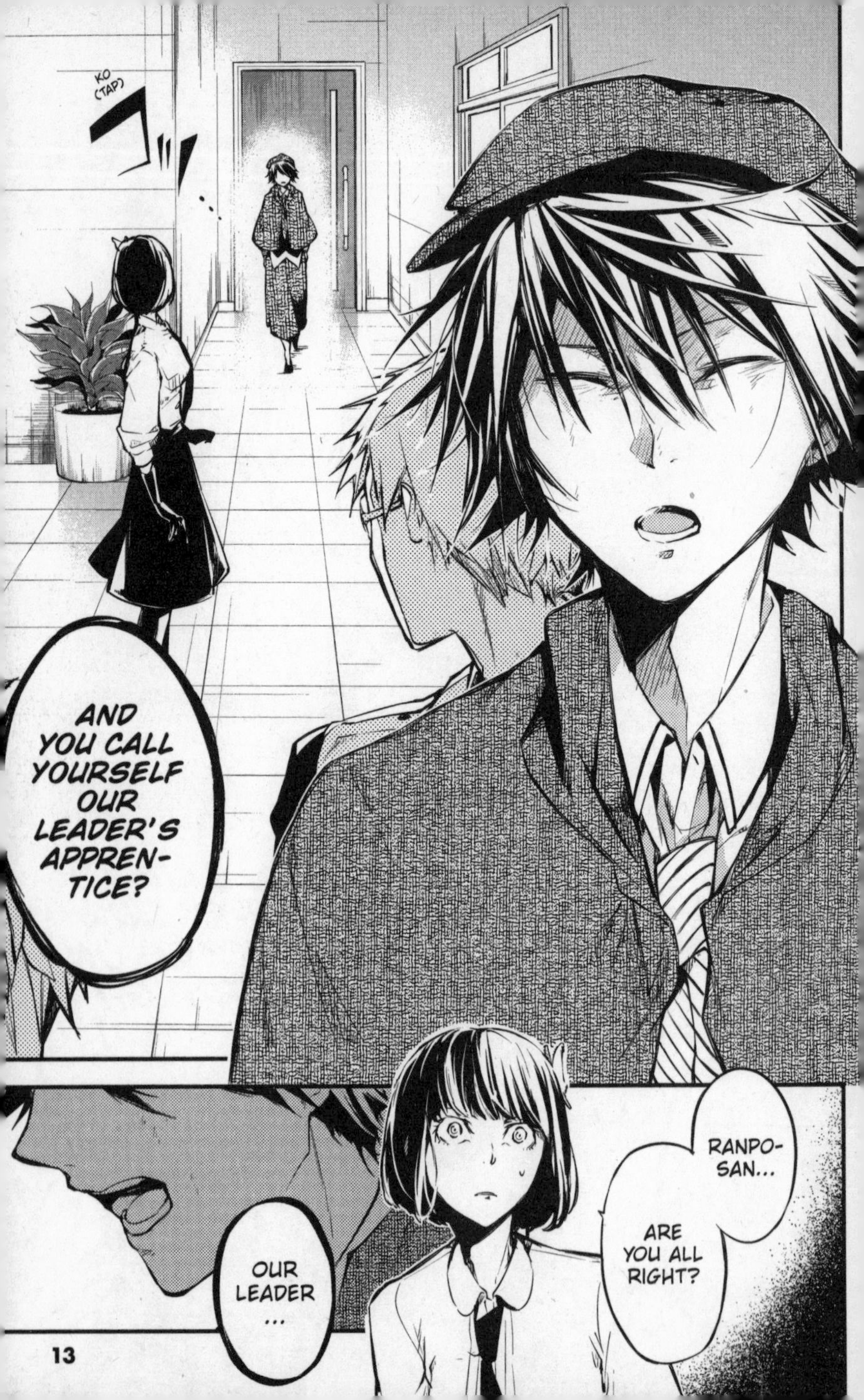
KO (TAP)
AND YOU CALL YOURSELF OUR LEADER'S APPREN-TICE?
RANPO-SAN...
ARE YOU ALL RIGHT?
OUR LEADER ...

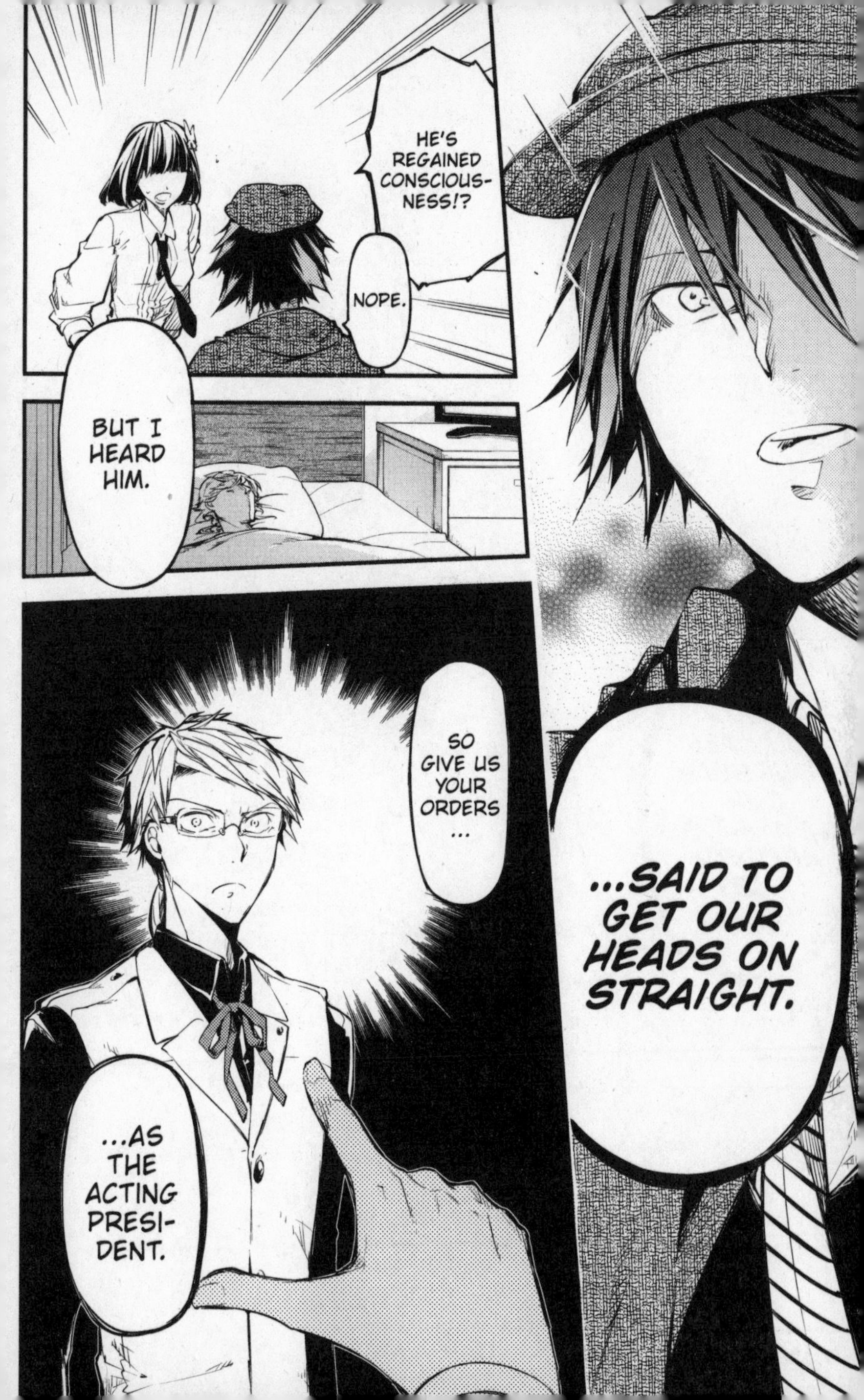
HE'S REGAINED CONSCIOUS-NESS!?
NOPE.
BUT I HEARD HIM.
...SAID TO GET OUR HEADS ON STRAIGHT.
SO GIVE US YOUR ORDERS ...
...AS THE ACTING PRESI-DENT.

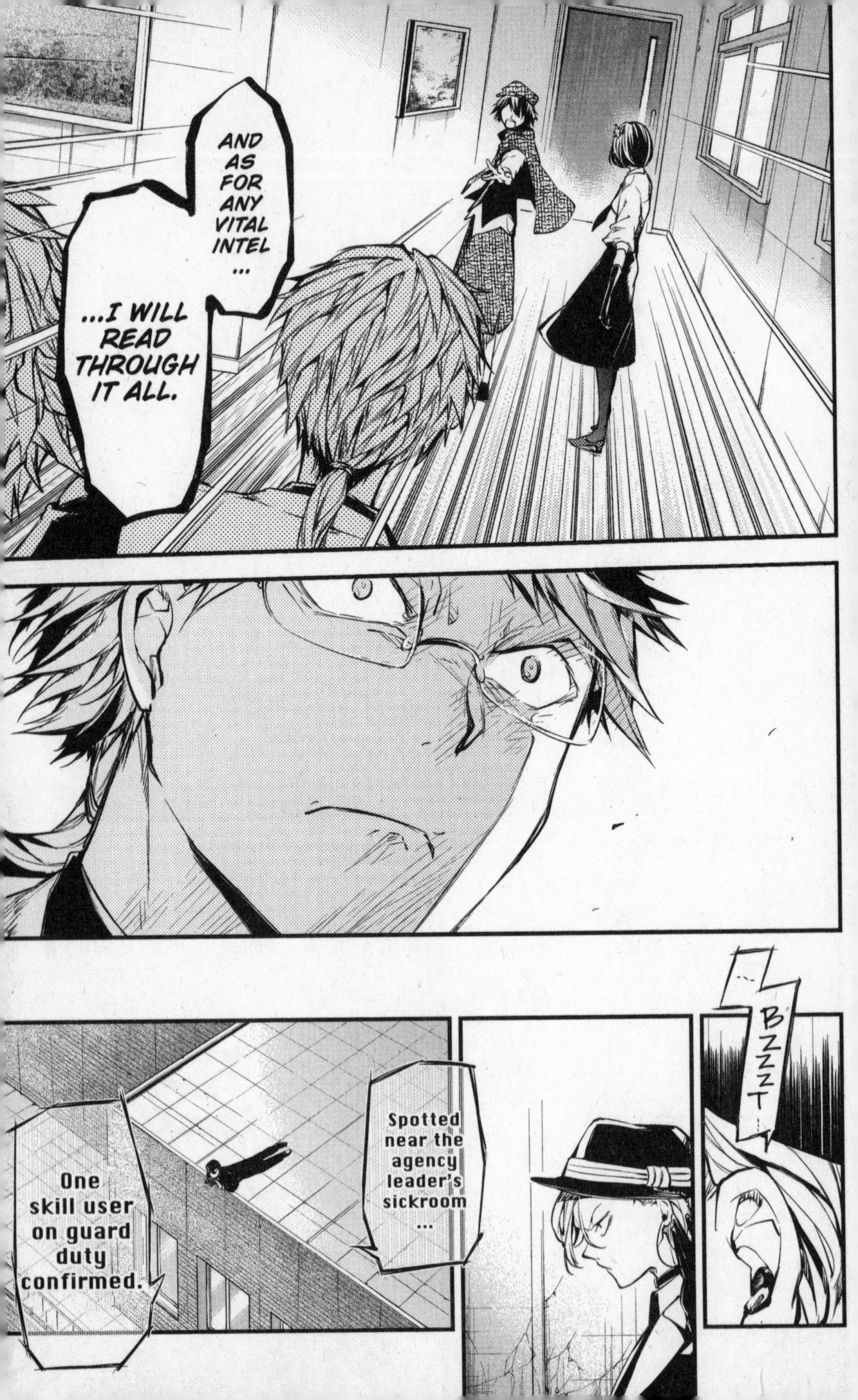
AND AS FOR ANY VITAL INTEL ...
...I WILL READ THROUGH IT ALL.
...BZZZT...
Spotted near the agency leader's sickroom ...
One skill user on guard duty confirmed.

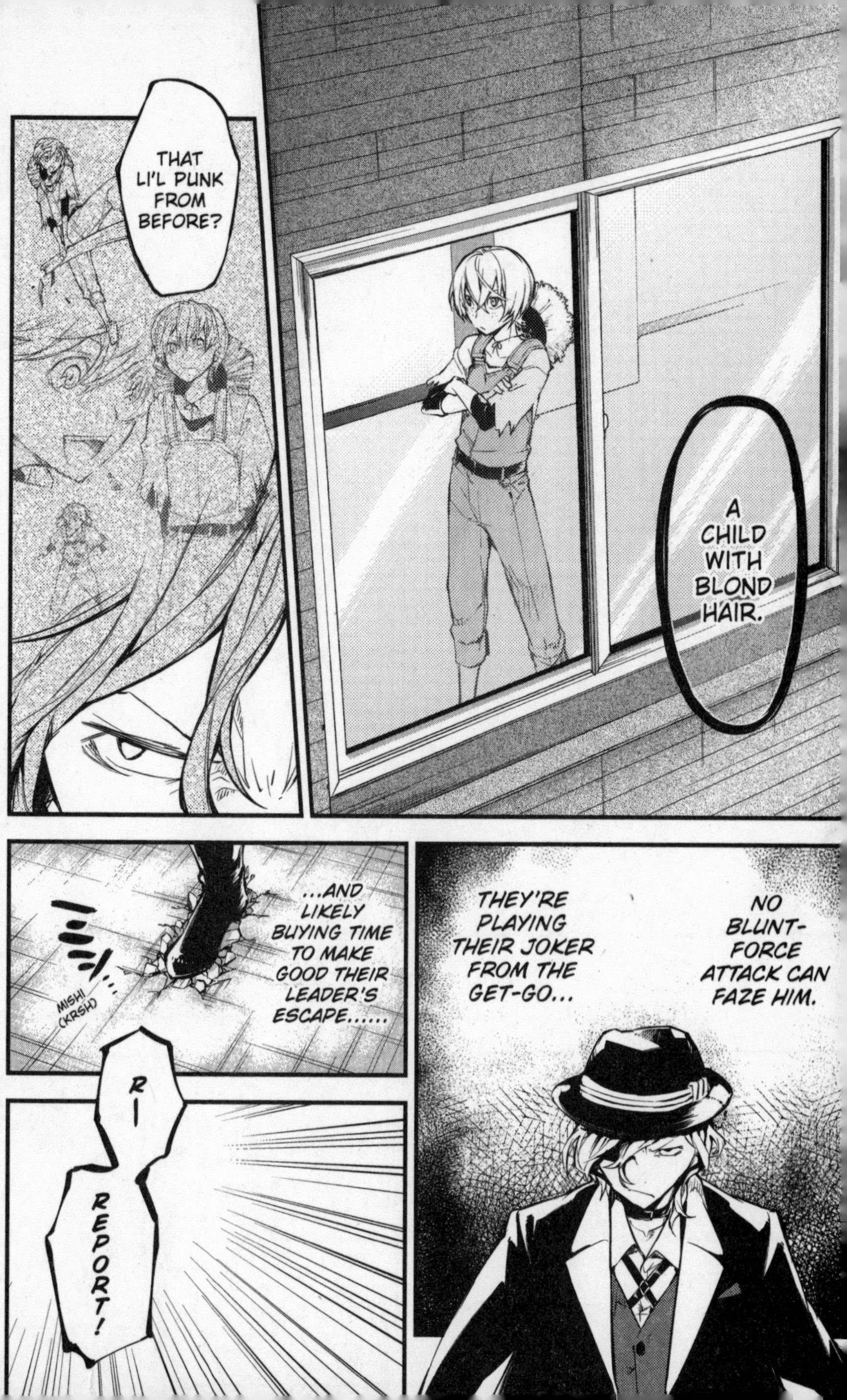
A CHILD WITH BLOND HAIR.
THAT LI'L PUNK FROM BEFORE?
NO BLUNT-FORCE ATTACK CAN FAZE HIM.
THEY'RE PLAYING THEIR JOKER FROM THE GET-GO...
...AND LIKELY BUYING TIME TO MAKE GOOD THEIR LEADER'S ESCAPE......
MISHI (KRSH)
R—REPORT!

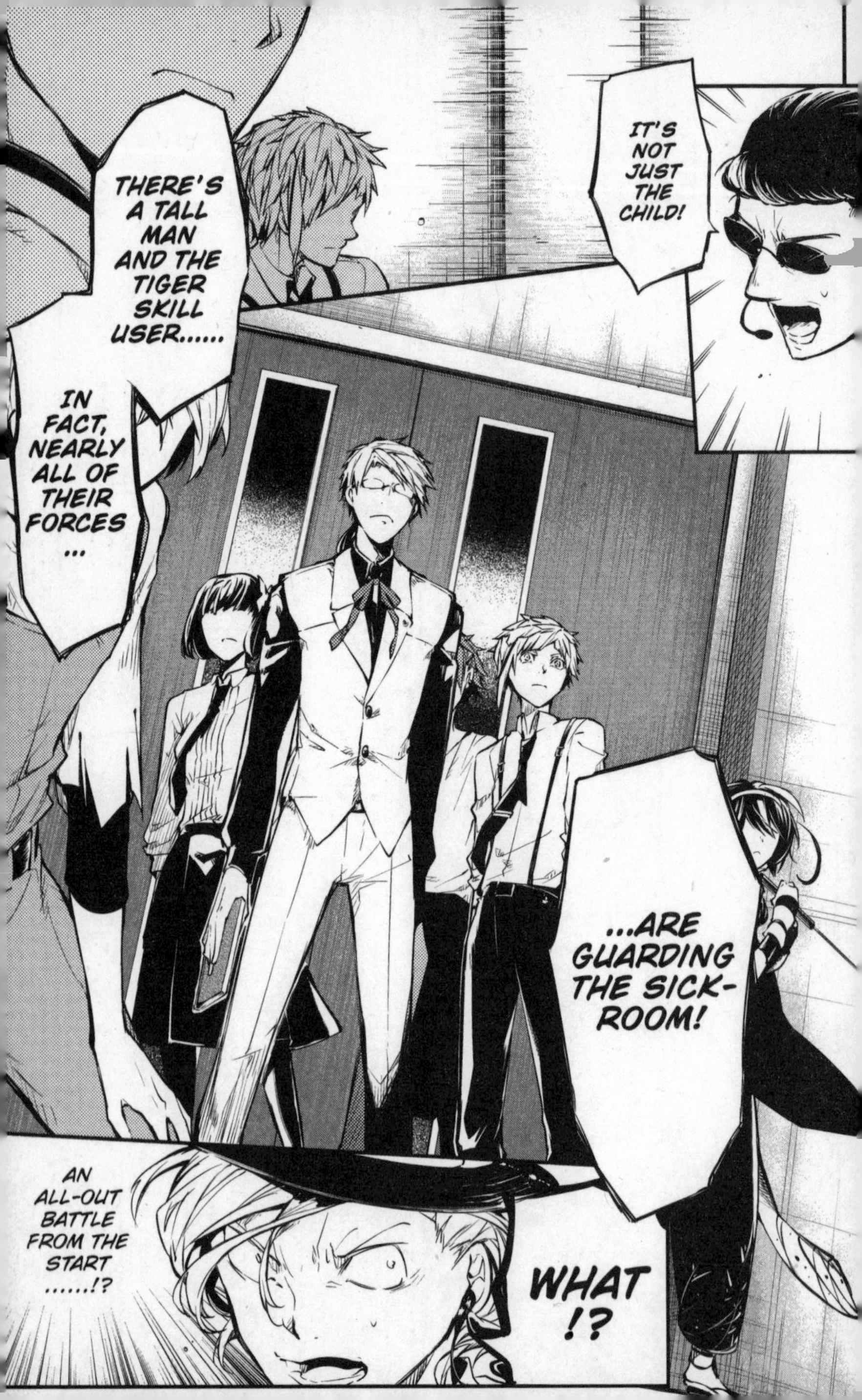
IT'S NOT JUST THE CHILD!
THERE'S A TALL MAN AND THE TIGER SKILL USER......
IN FACT, NEARLY ALL OF THEIR FORCES ...
...ARE GUARDING THE SICK-ROOM!
WHAT!?
AN ALL-OUT BATTLE FROM THE START ......!?

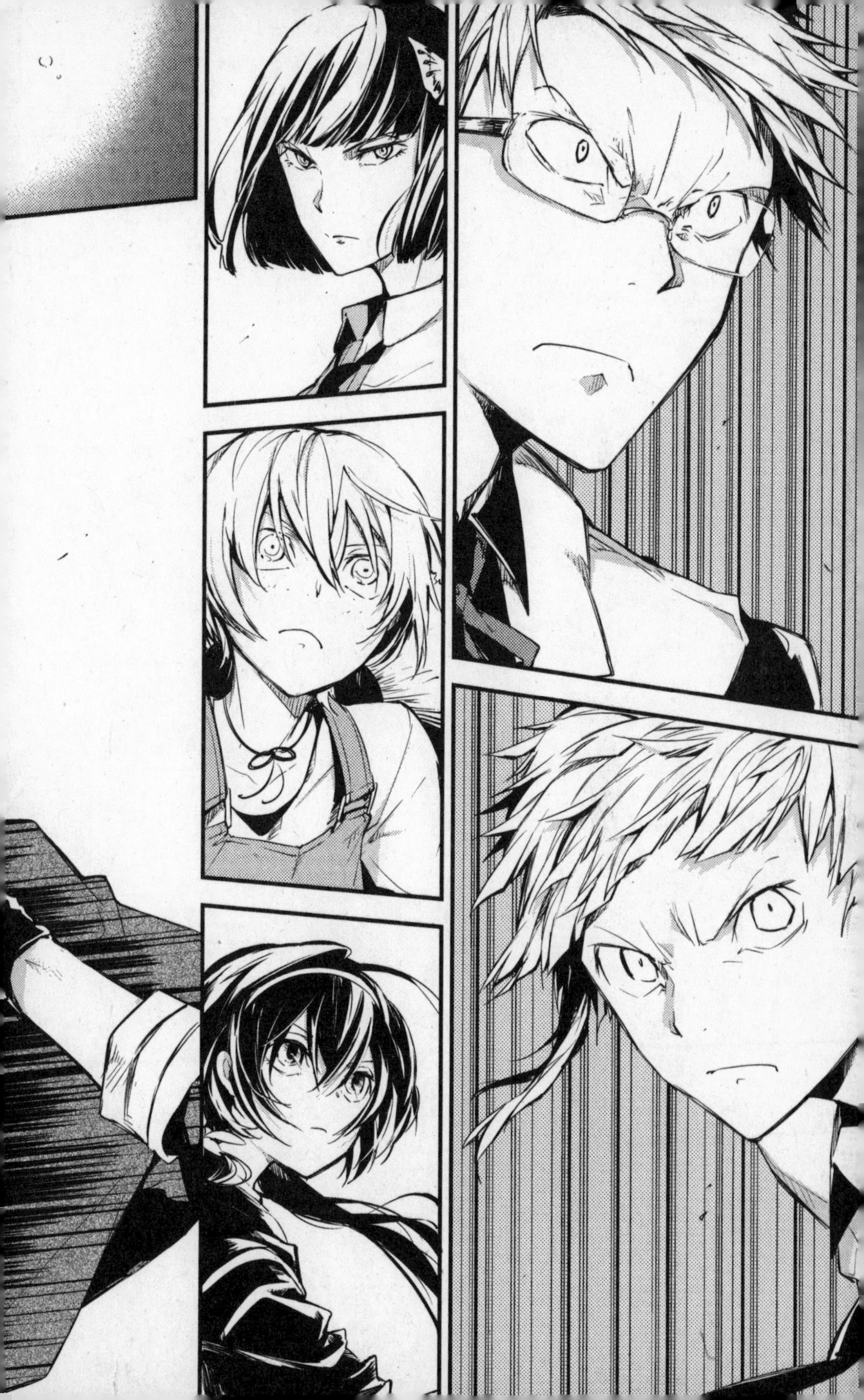

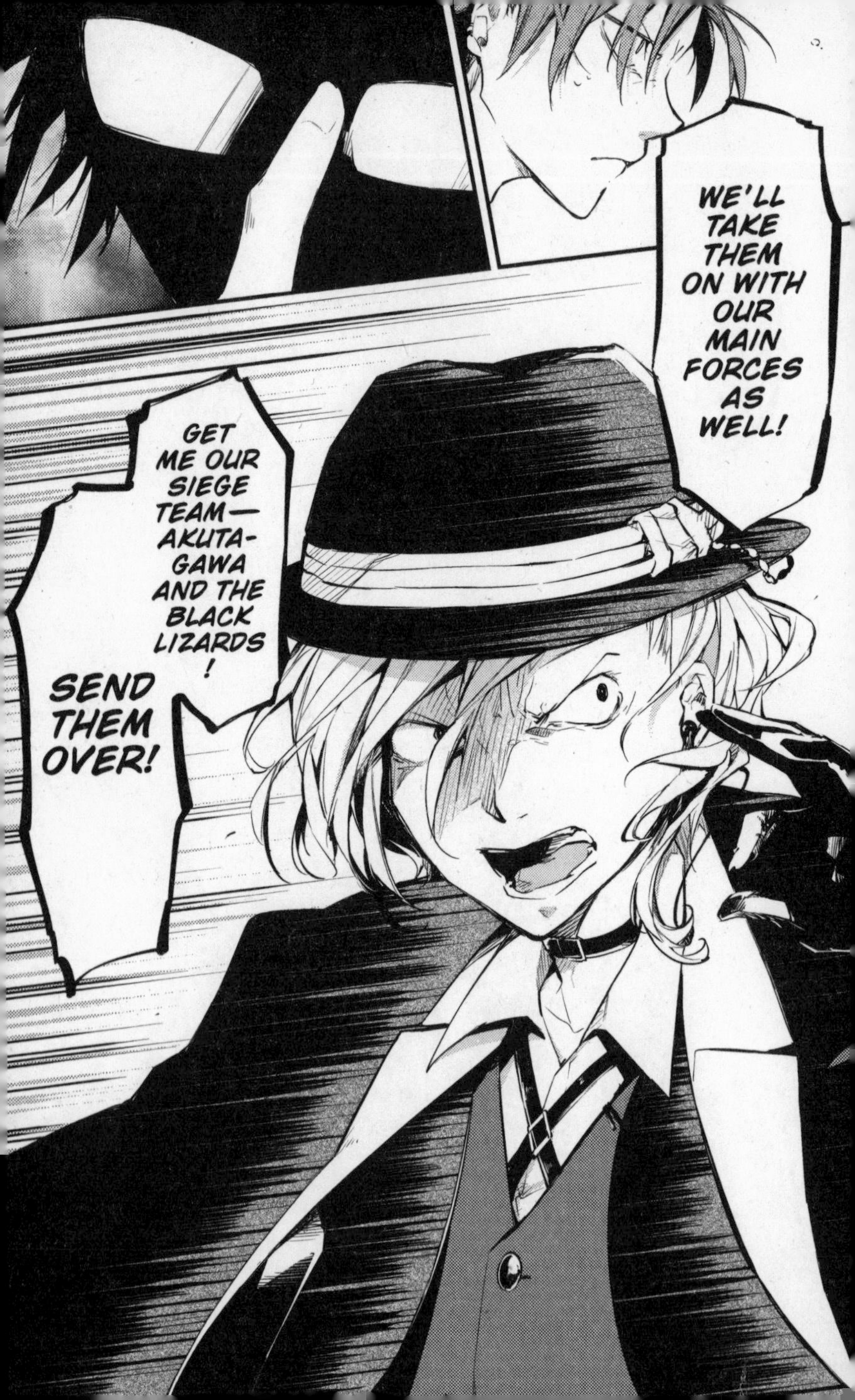
WE'LL TAKE THEM ON WITH OUR MAIN FORCES AS WELL!
GET ME OUR SIEGE TEAM—AKUTA-GAWA AND THE BLACK LIZARDS!
SEND THEM OVER!

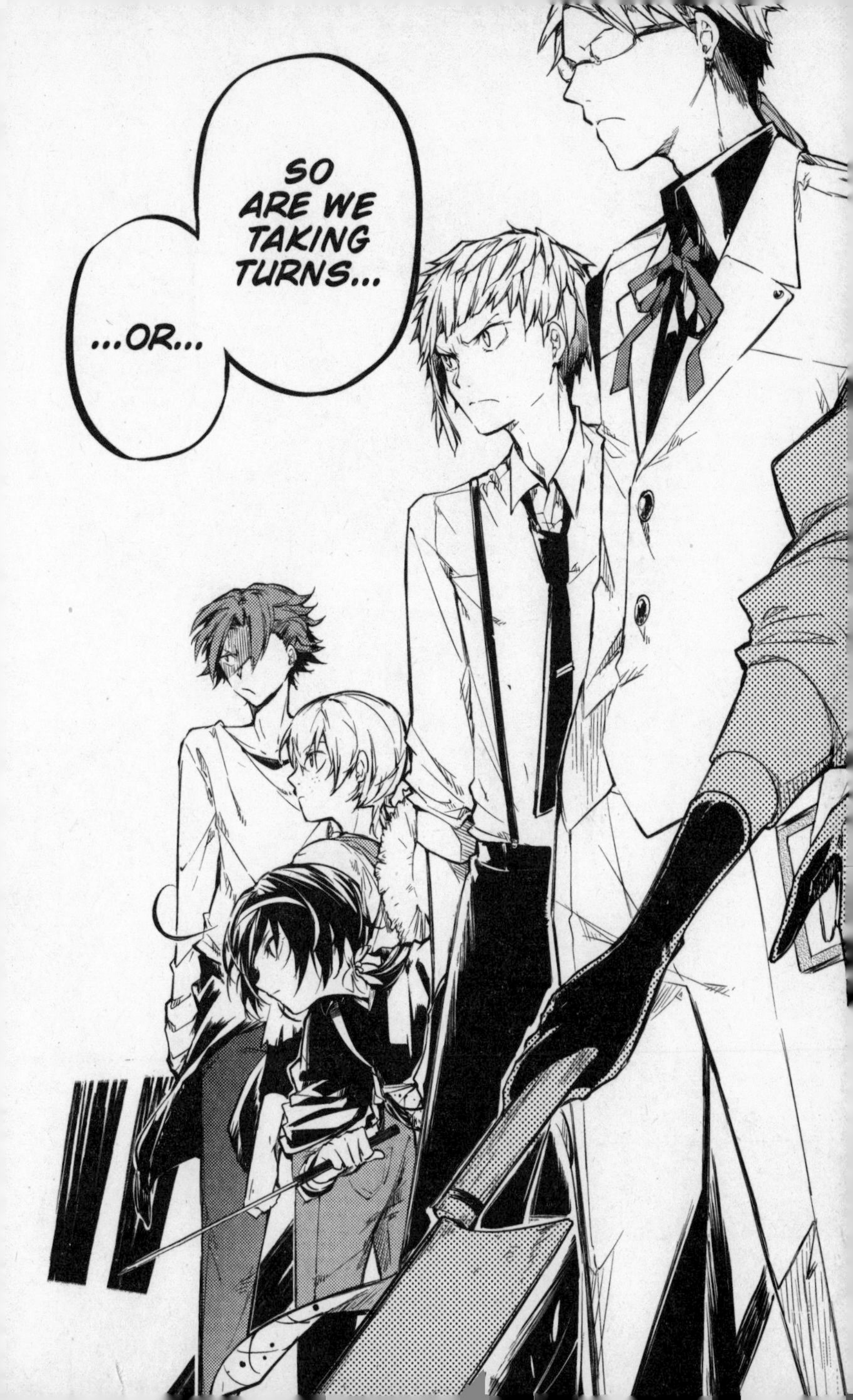
SO ARE WE TAKING TURNS...
...OR...

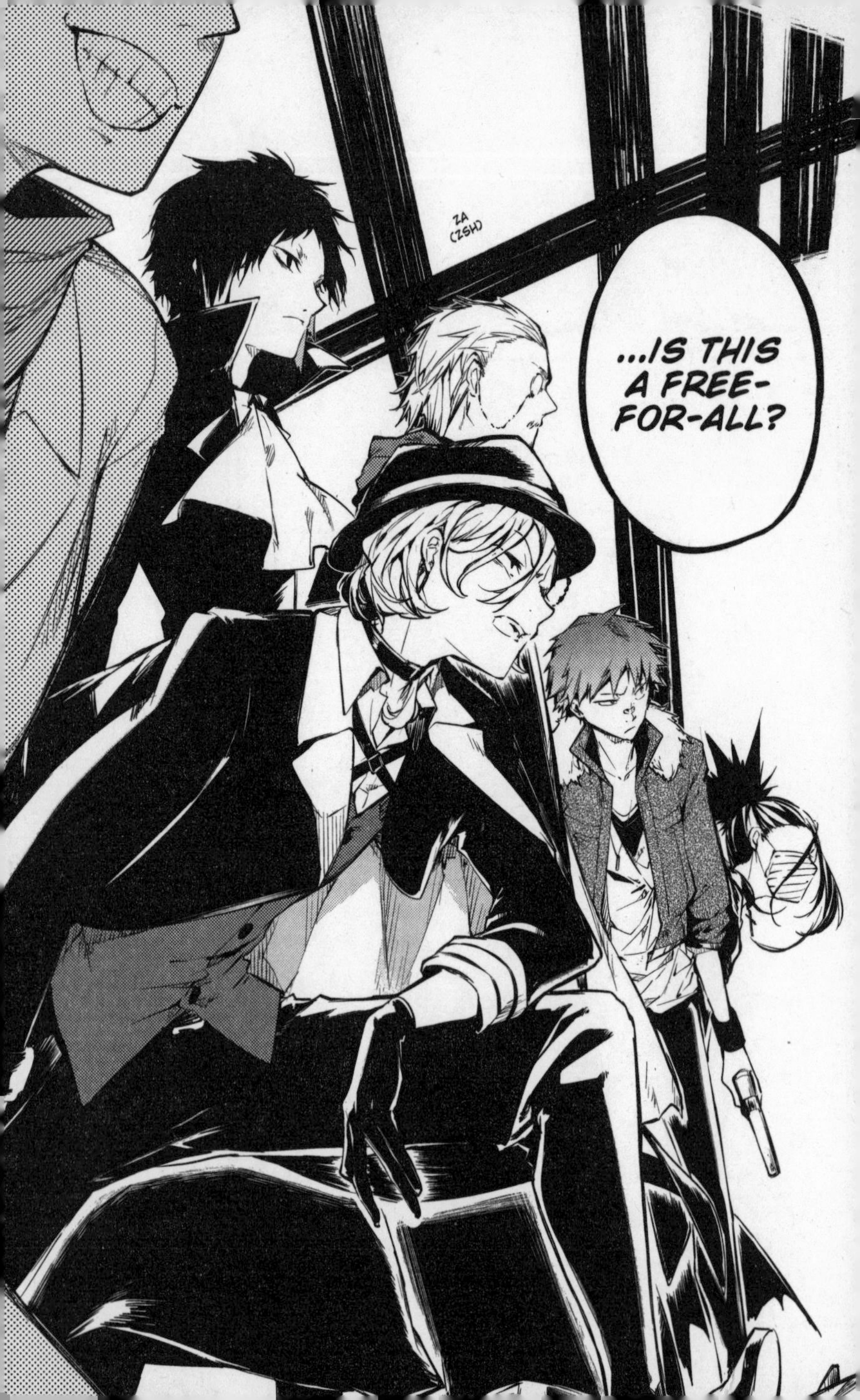
...IS THIS A FREE-FOR-ALL?
ZA (ZSH)

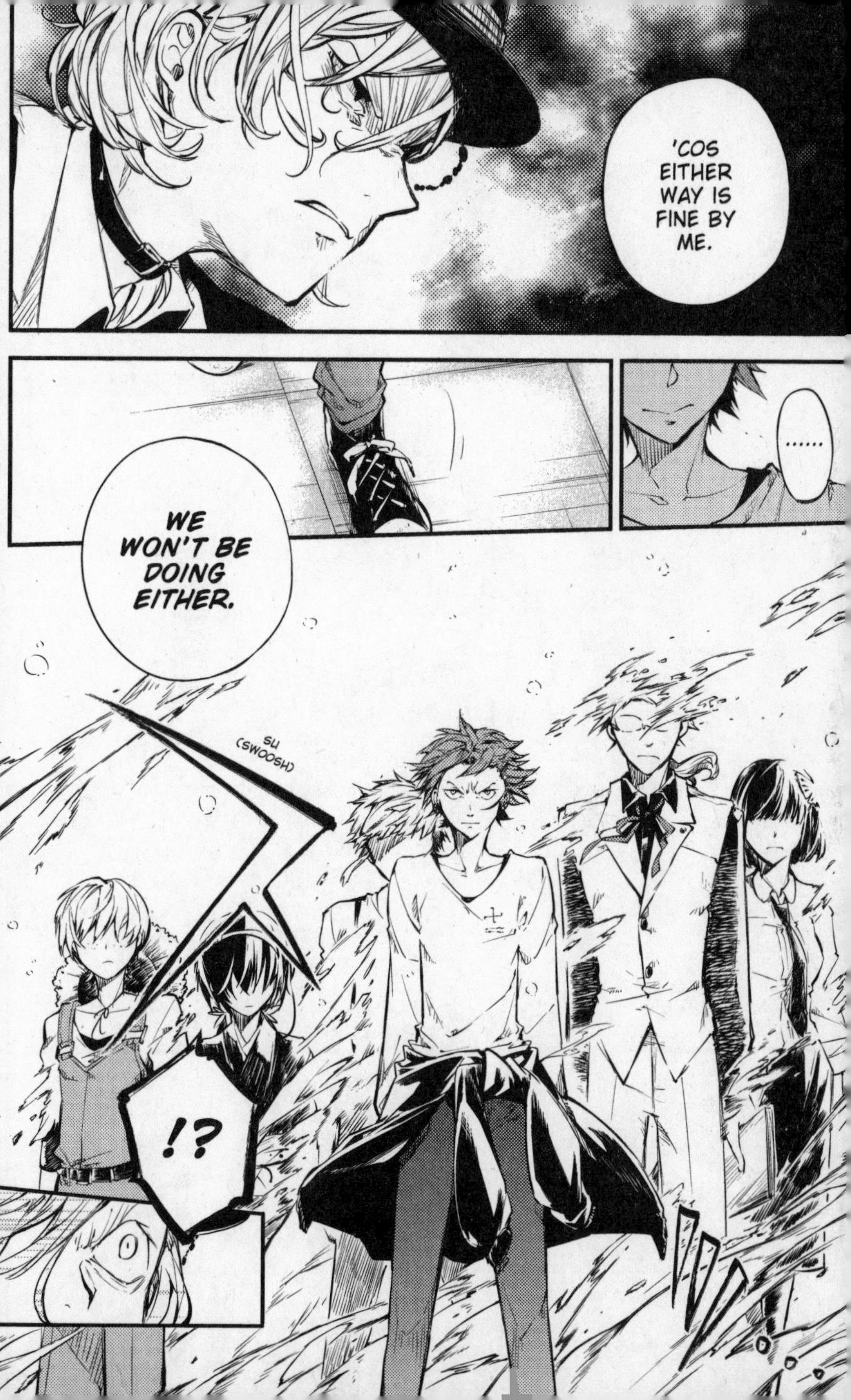
'COS EITHER WAY IS FINE BY ME.
......
WE WON'T BE DOING EITHER.
SU (SWOOSH)
!?

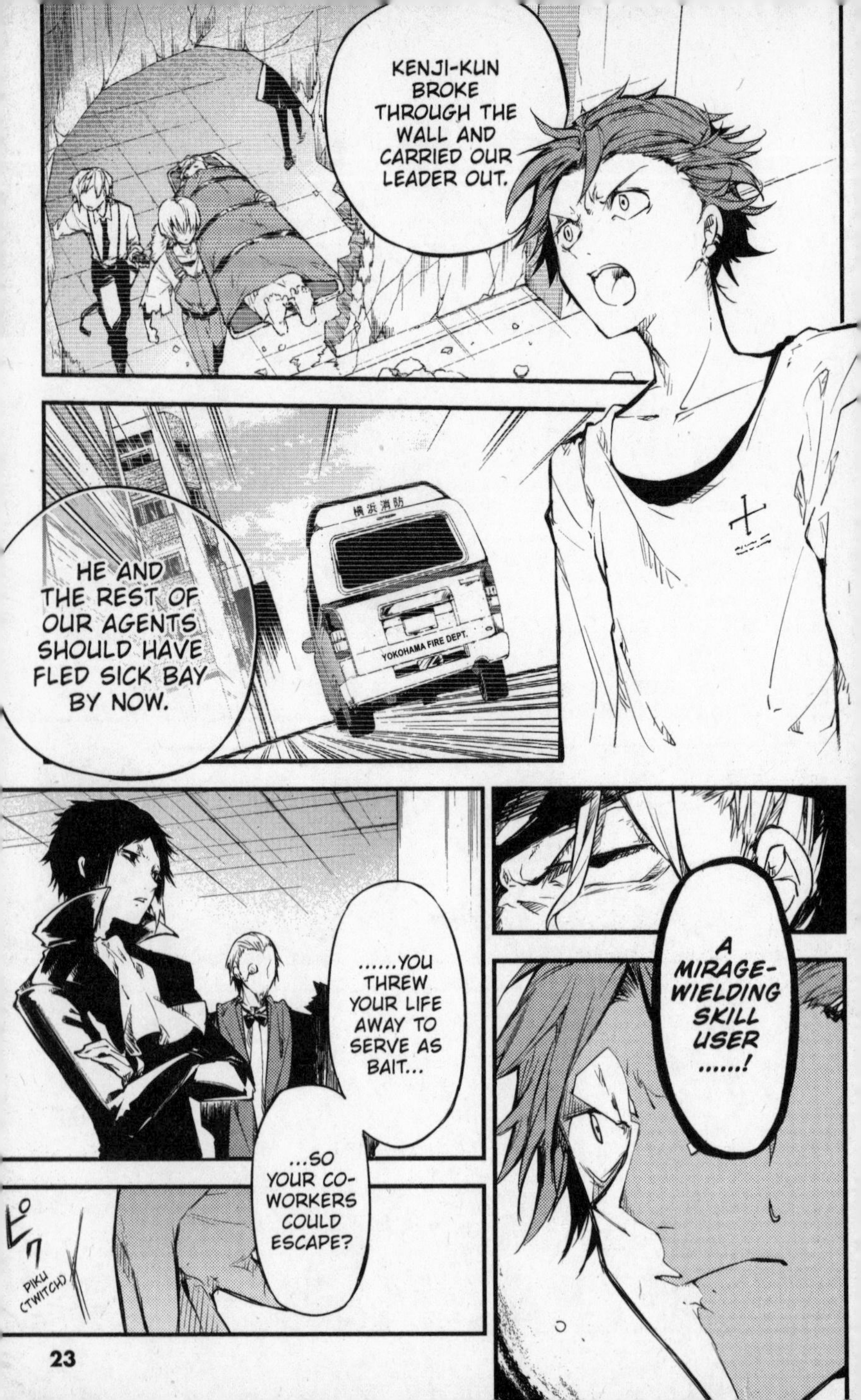
KENJI-KUN BROKE THROUGH THE WALL AND CARRIED OUR LEADER OUT.
HE AND THE REST OF OUR AGENTS SHOULD HAVE FLED SICK BAY BY NOW.
横浜消防
YOKOHAMA FIRE DEPT.
A MIRAGE-WIELDING SKILL USER ......!
......YOU THREW YOUR LIFE AWAY TO SERVE AS BAIT...
...SO YOUR CO-WORKERS COULD ESCAPE?
PIKU (TWITCH)

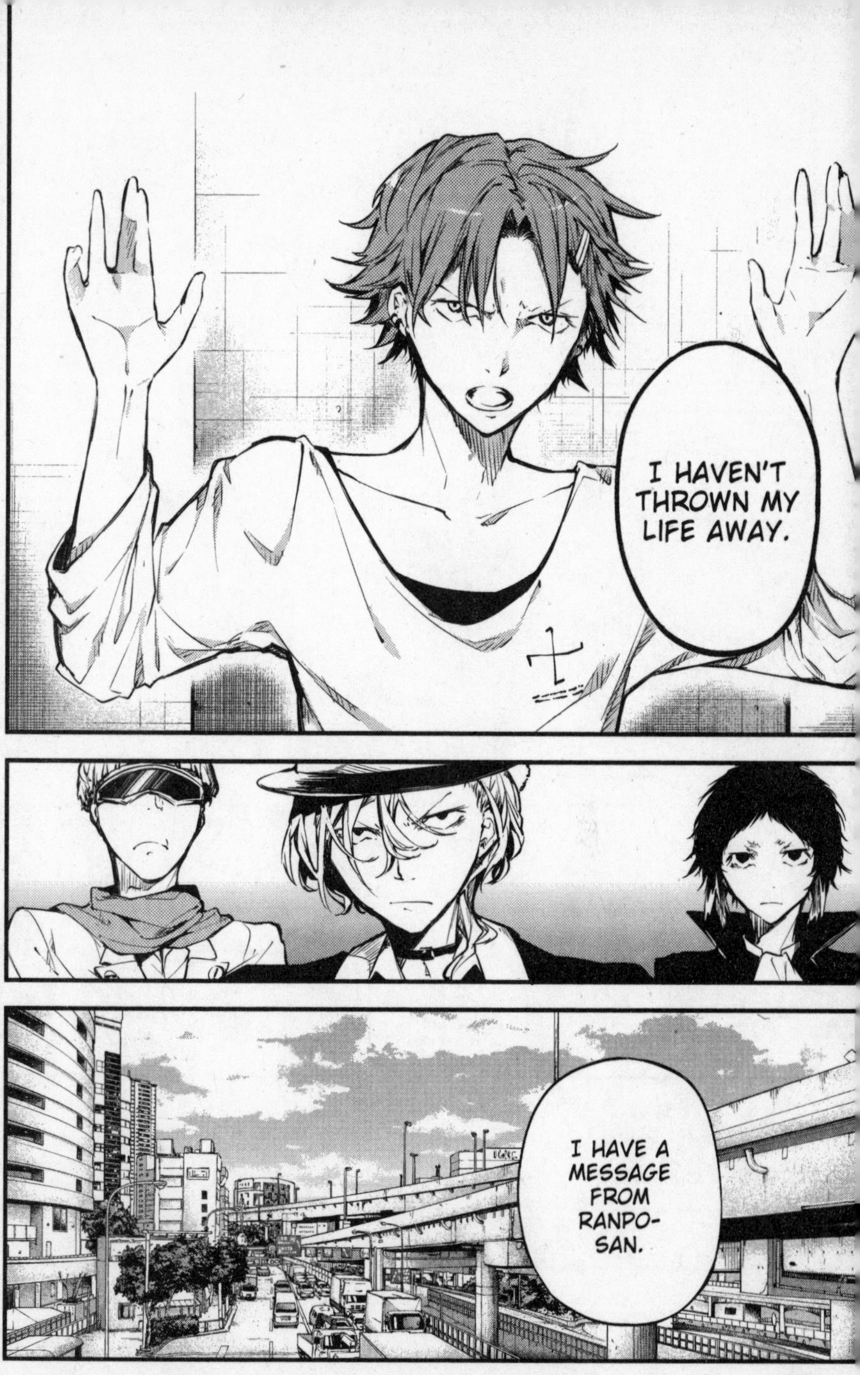
I HAVEN'T THROWN MY LIFE AWAY.
I HAVE A MESSAGE FROM RANPO-SAN.

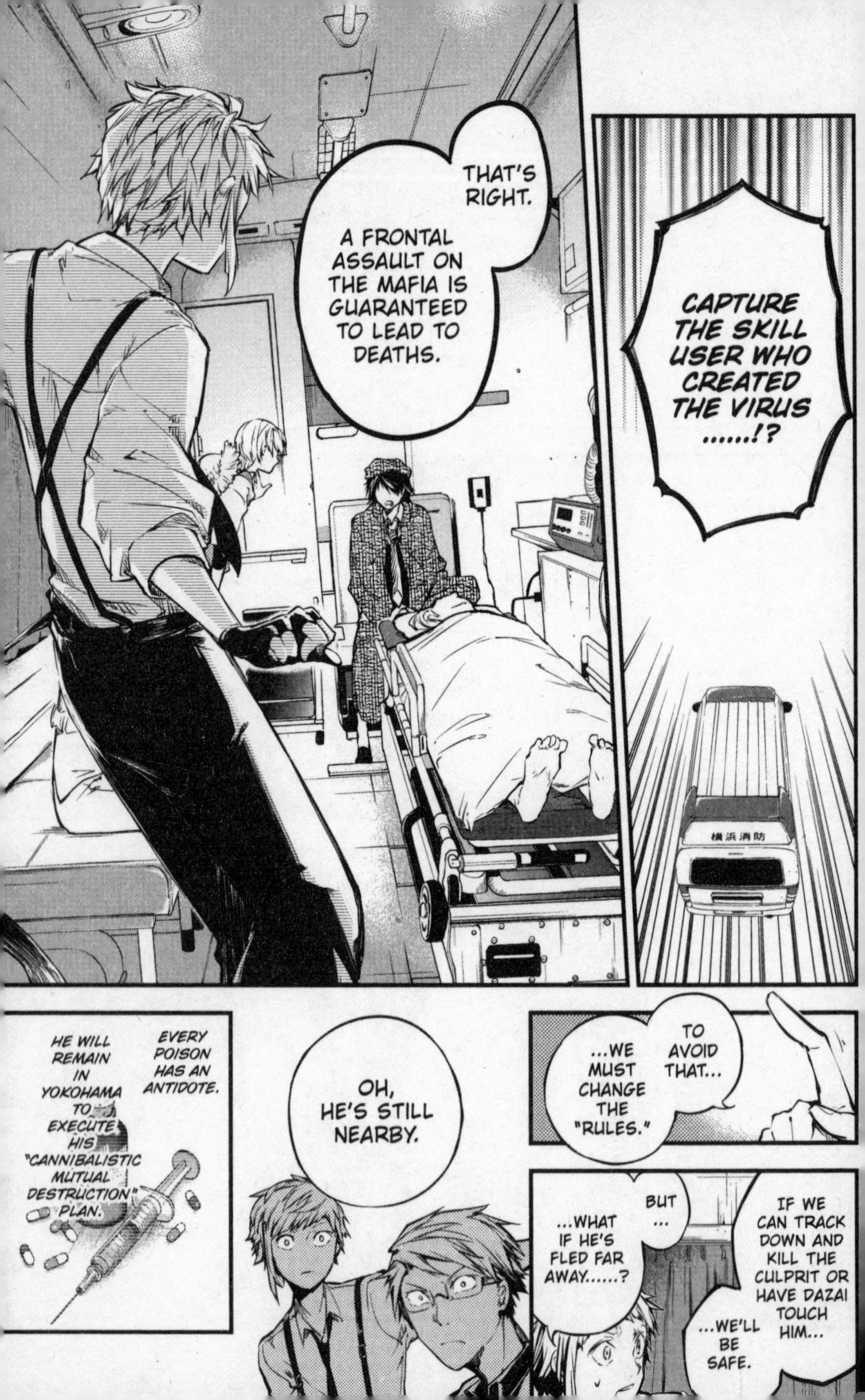
CAPTURE THE SKILL USER WHO CREATED THE VIRUS ......!?
THAT'S RIGHT.
A FRONTAL ASSAULT ON THE MAFIA IS GUARANTEED TO LEAD TO DEATHS.
TO AVOID THAT...
...WE MUST CHANGE THE "RULES."
IF WE CAN TRACK DOWN AND KILL THE CULPRIT OR HAVE DAZAI TOUCH HIM...
...WE'LL BE SAFE.
BUT ...
...WHAT IF HE'S FLED FAR AWAY......?
OH, HE'S STILL NEARBY.
EVERY POISON HAS AN ANTIDOTE.
HE WILL REMAIN IN YOKOHAMA TO EXECUTE HIS "CANNIBALISTIC MUTUAL DESTRUCTION" PLAN.

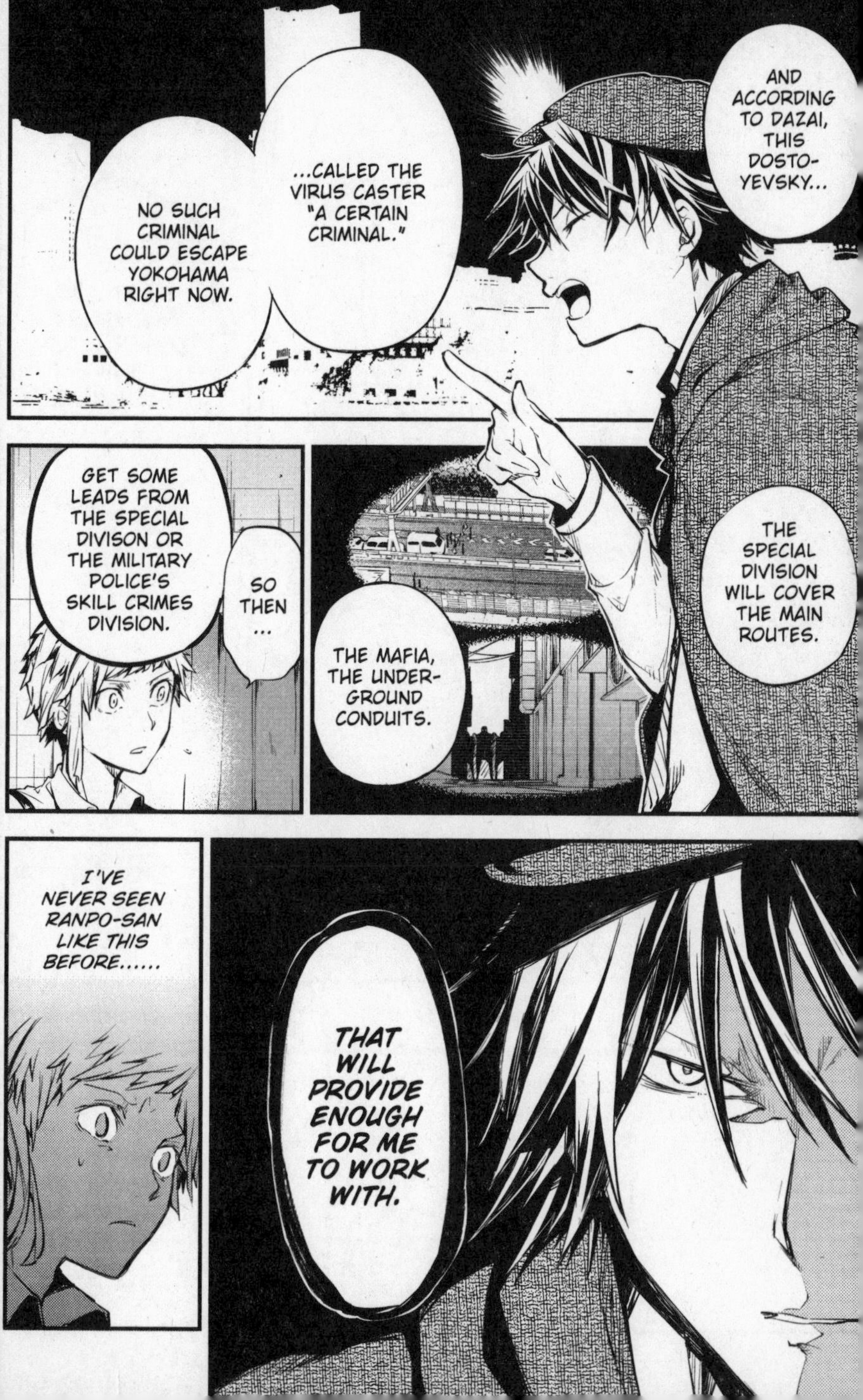
AND ACCORDING TO DAZAI, THIS DOSTO-YEVSKY...
...CALLED THE VIRUS CASTER "A CERTAIN CRIMINAL."
NO SUCH CRIMINAL COULD ESCAPE YOKOHAMA RIGHT NOW.
THE SPECIAL DIVISION WILL COVER THE MAIN ROUTES.
THE MAFIA, THE UNDER-GROUND CONDUITS.
GET SOME LEADS FROM THE SPECIAL DIVISON OR THE MILITARY POLICE'S SKILL CRIMES DIVISION.
SO THEN ...
THAT WILL PROVIDE ENOUGH FOR ME TO WORK WITH.
I'VE NEVER SEEN RANPO-SAN LIKE THIS BEFORE......

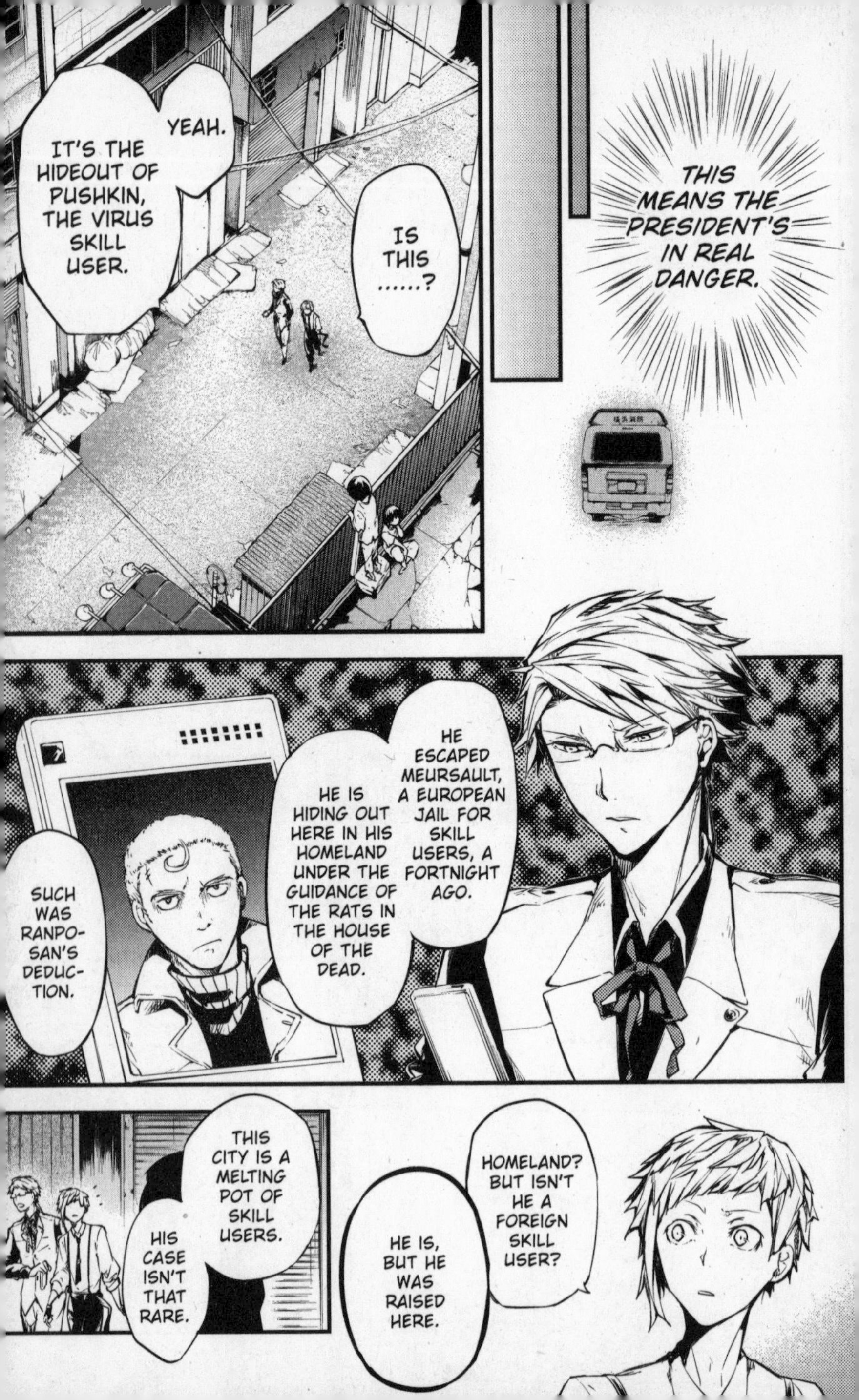
THIS MEANS THE PRESIDENT'S IN REAL DANGER.
IS THIS ......?
YEAH.
IT'S THE HIDEOUT OF PUSHKIN, THE VIRUS SKILL USER.
HE ESCAPED MEURSAULT, A EUROPEAN JAIL FOR SKILL USERS, A FORTNIGHT AGO.
HE IS HIDING OUT HERE IN HIS HOMELAND UNDER THE GUIDANCE OF THE RATS IN THE HOUSE OF THE DEAD.
SUCH WAS RANPO-SAN'S DEDUCTION.
HOMELAND? BUT ISN'T HE A FOREIGN SKILL USER?
HE IS, BUT HE WAS RAISED HERE.
THIS CITY IS A MELTING POT OF SKILL USERS.
HIS CASE ISN'T THAT RARE.

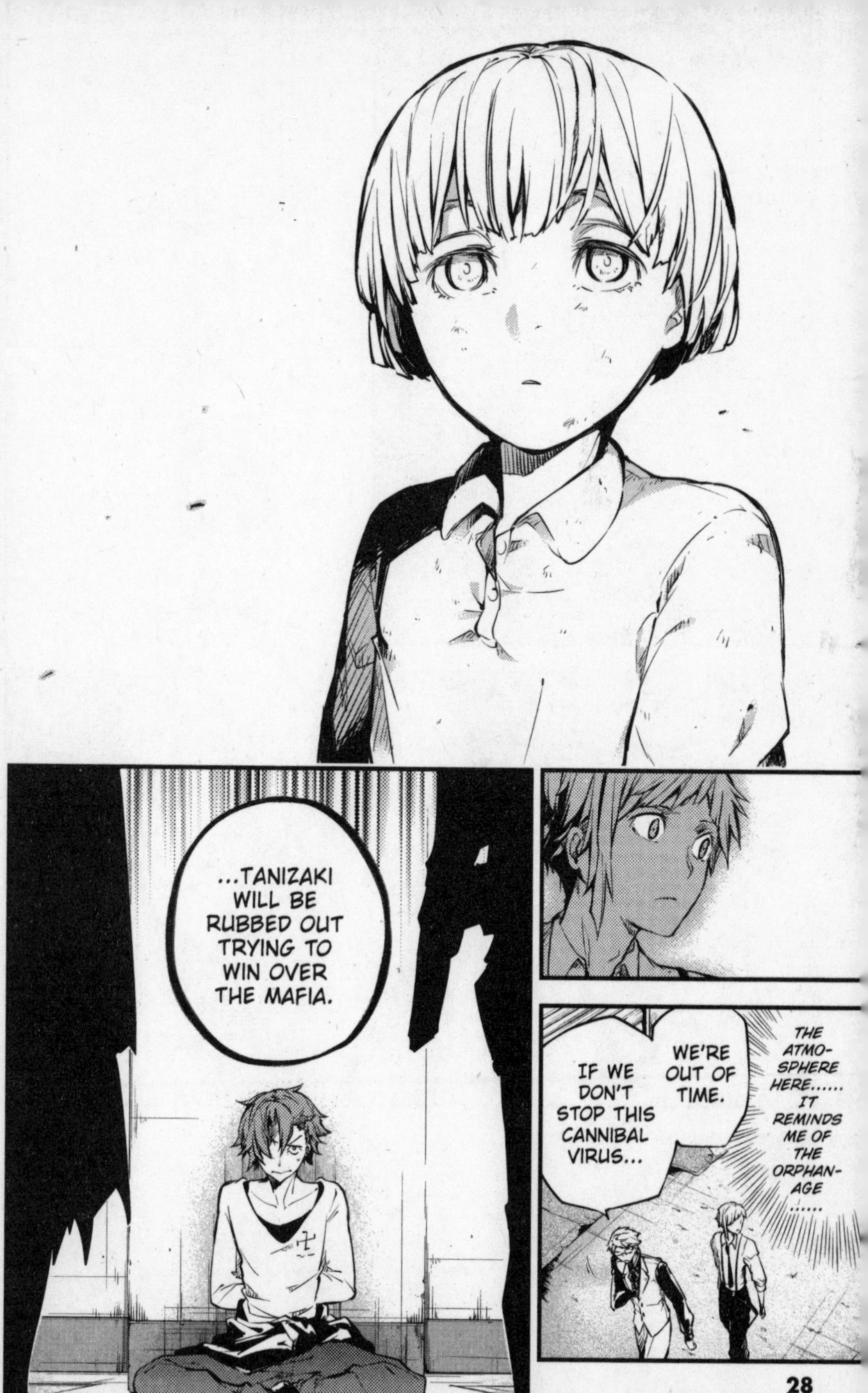
THE ATMOSPHERE HERE...... IT REMINDS ME OF THE ORPHANAGE......
WE'RE OUT OF TIME.
IF WE DON'T STOP THIS CANNIBAL VIRUS...
...TANIZAKI WILL BE RUBBED OUT TRYING TO WIN OVER THE MAFIA.

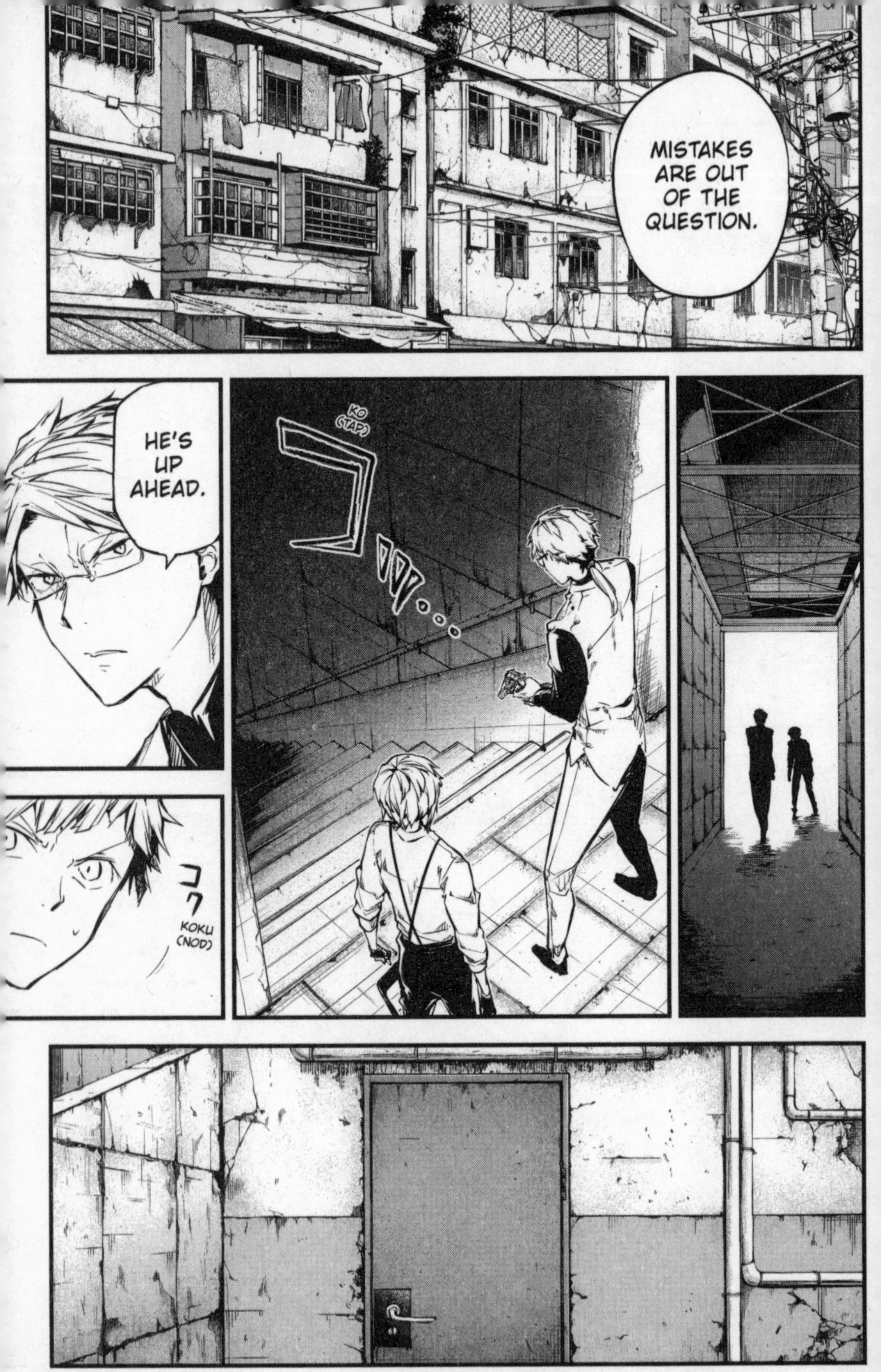
MISTAKES ARE OUT OF THE QUESTION.
KO (TAP)
HE'S UP AHEAD.
KOKU (NOD)

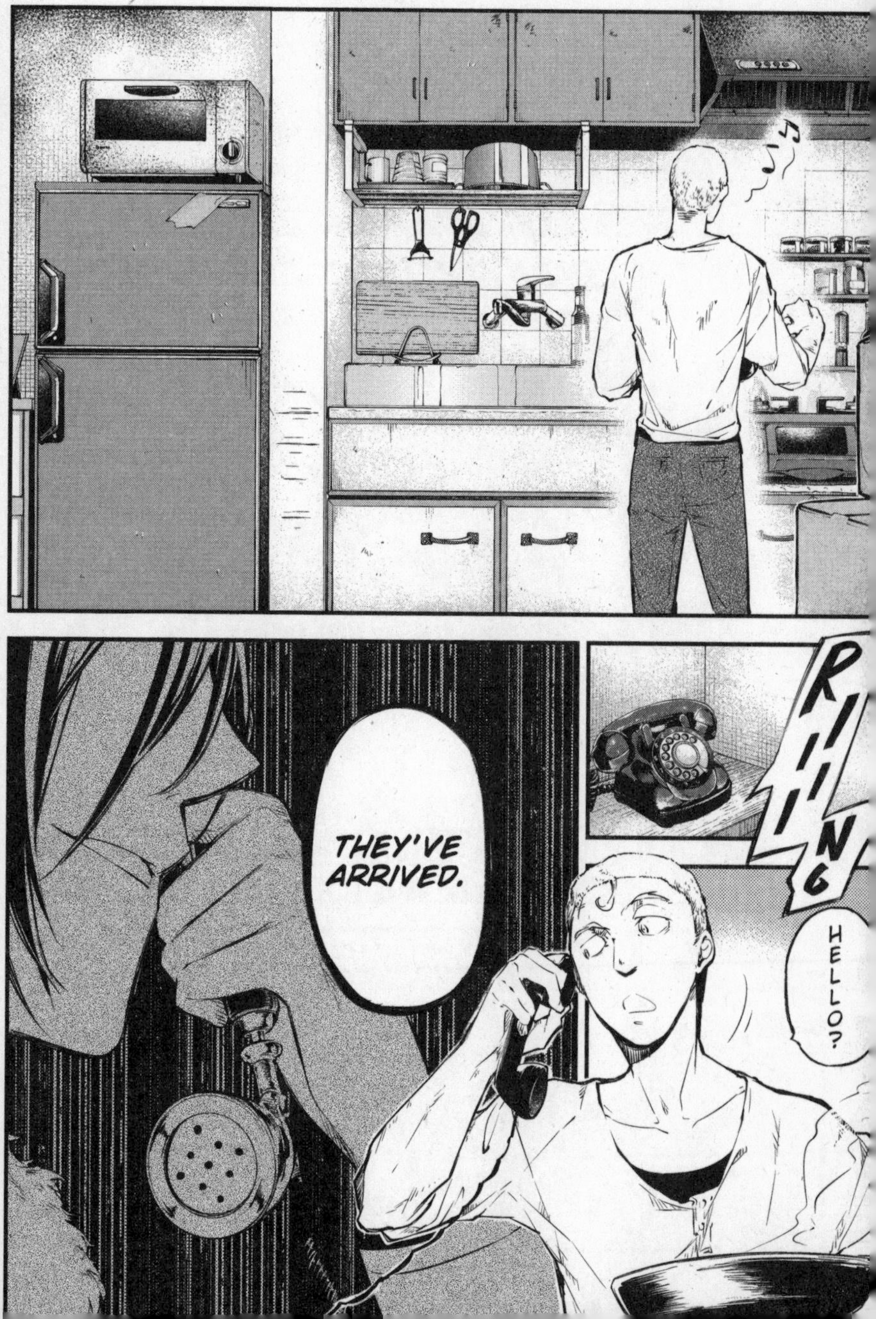
RIIIING
HELLO?
THEY'VE ARRIVED.

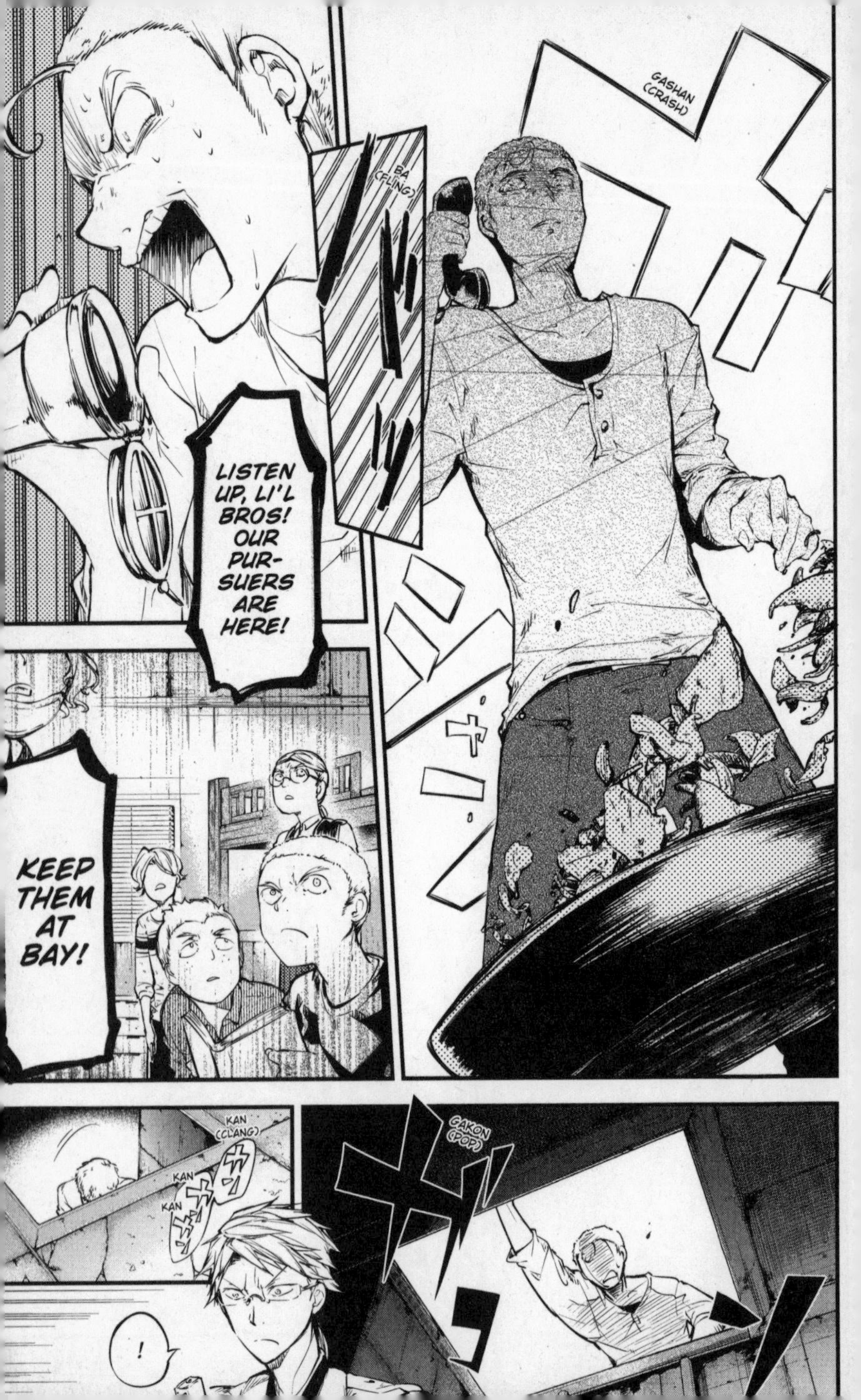
GASHAN (CRASH)
BA (FLING)
LISTEN UP, LI'L BROS! OUR PURSUERS ARE HERE!
KEEP THEM AT BAY!
GAKON (POP)
KAN (CLANG)
KAN
KAN
!

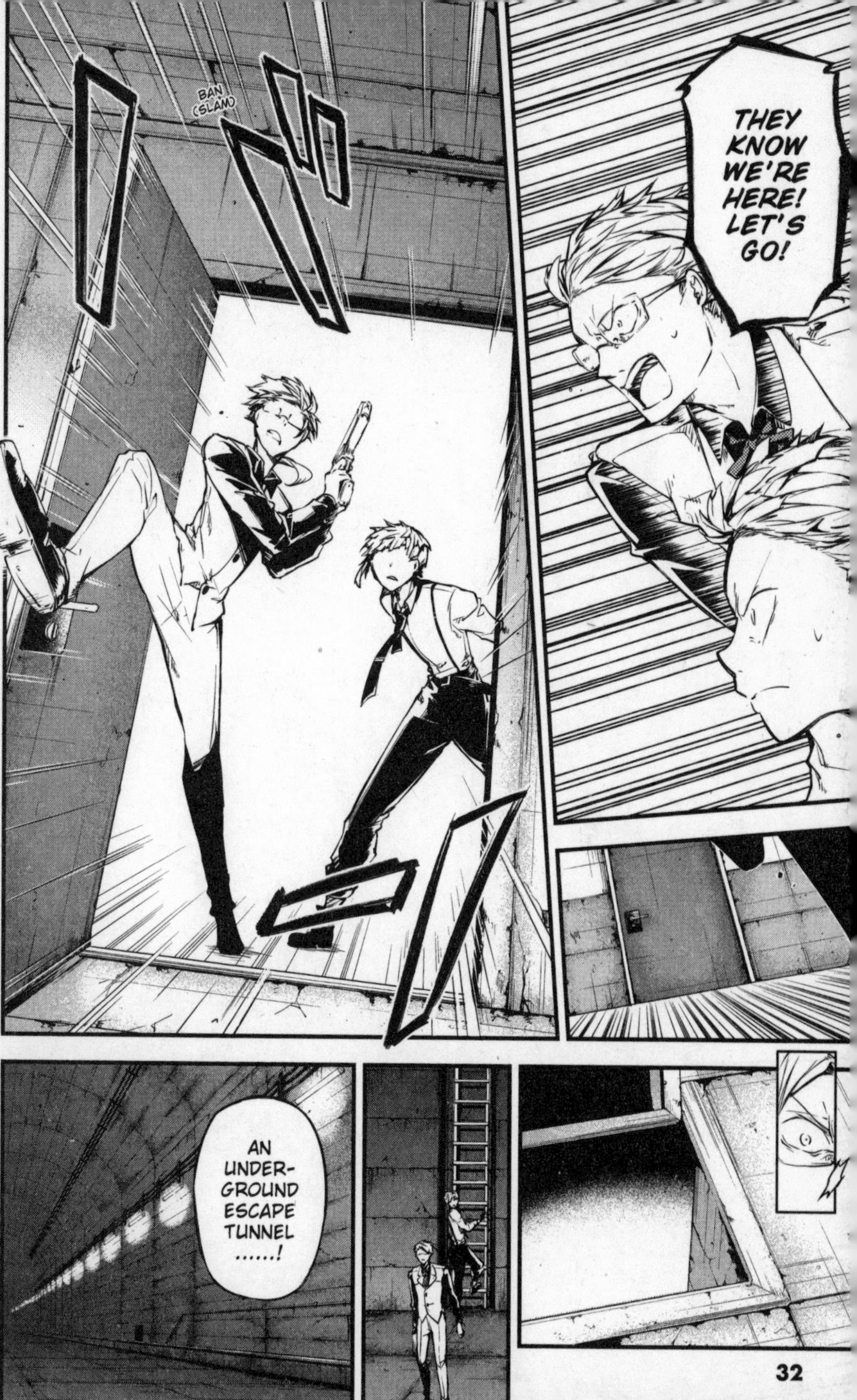
THEY KNOW WE'RE HERE! LET'S GO!
BAN (SLAM)
AN UNDER-GROUND ESCAPE TUNNEL ......!

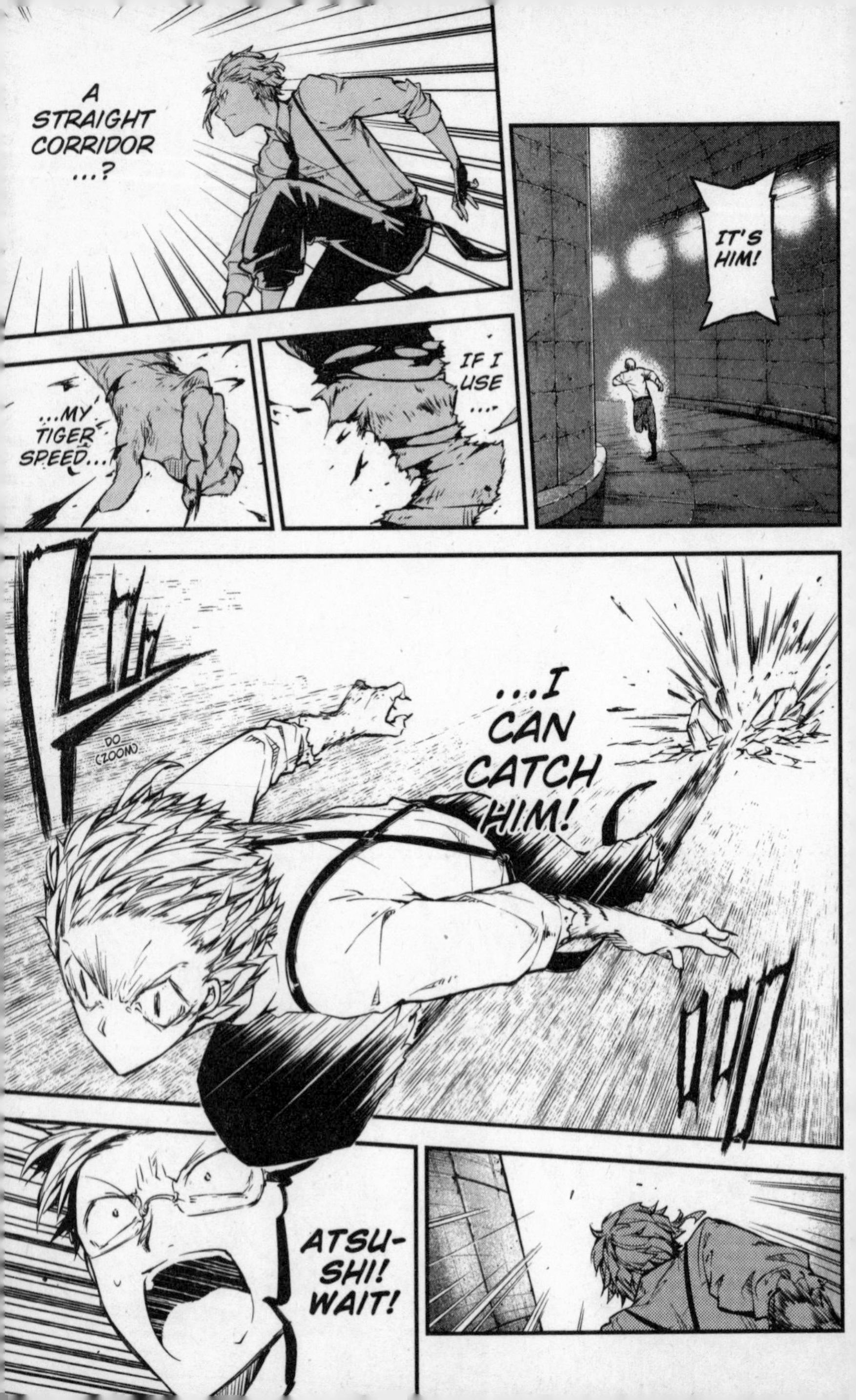
IT'S HIM!
A STRAIGHT CORRIDOR ...?
IF I USE ...
...MY TIGER SPEED...
...I CAN CATCH HIM!
DO (ZOOM)
ATSU-SHI! WAIT!

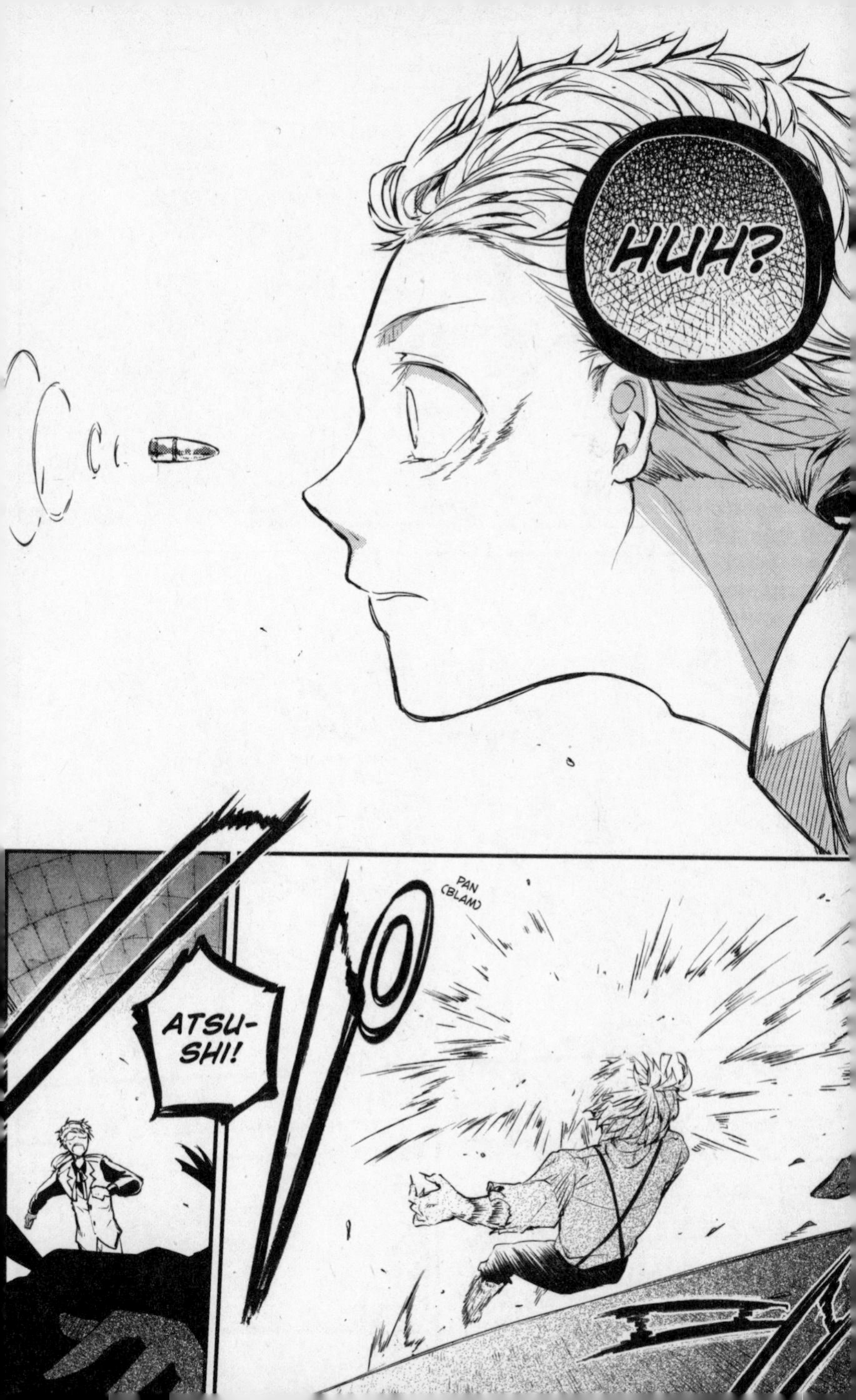
HUH?
PAN (BLAM)
ATSU-SHI!

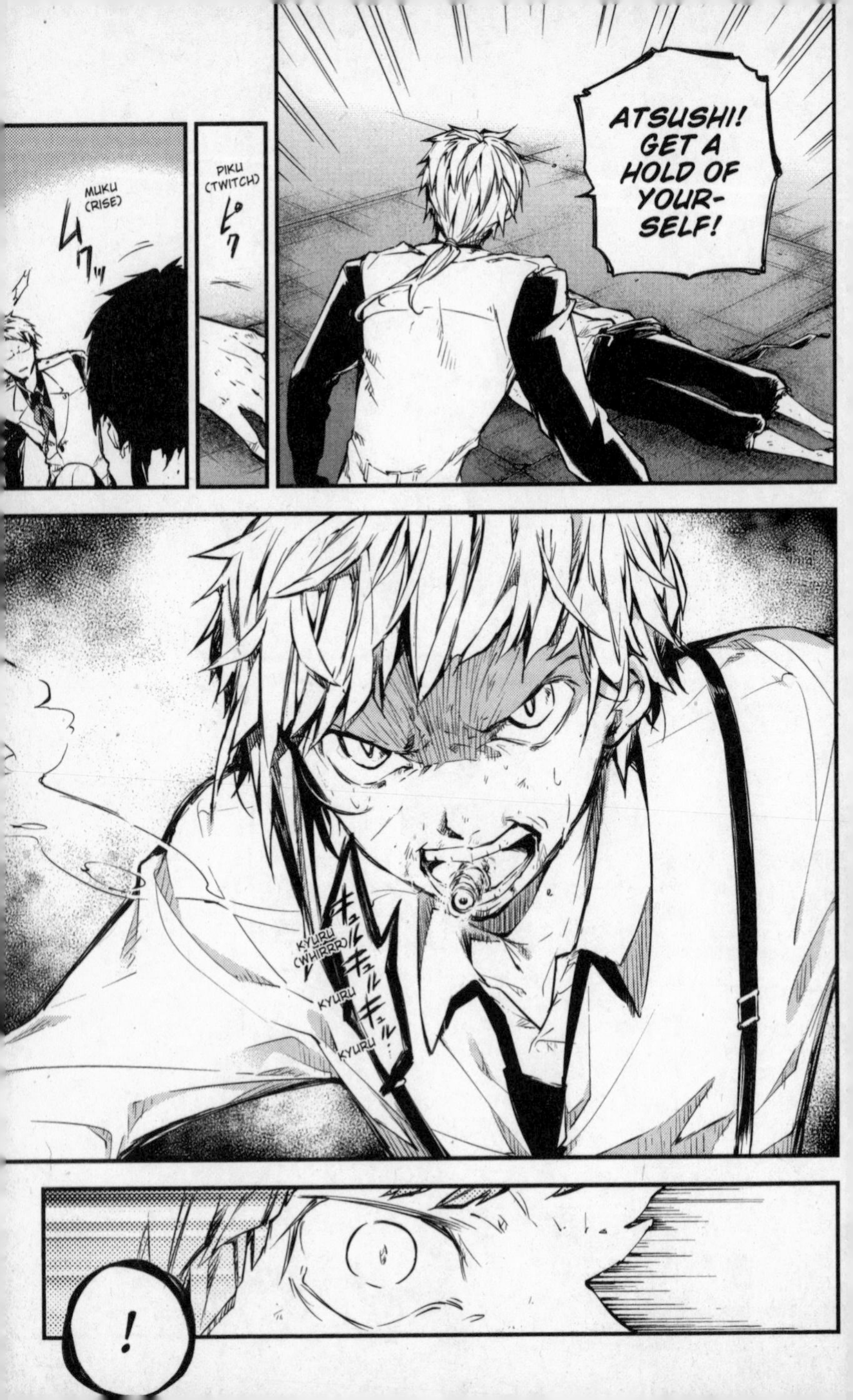
ATSUSHI! GET A HOLD OF YOURSELF!
PIKU (TWITCH)
MUKU (RISE)
KYURU (WHIRRR)
KYURU
KYURU
!

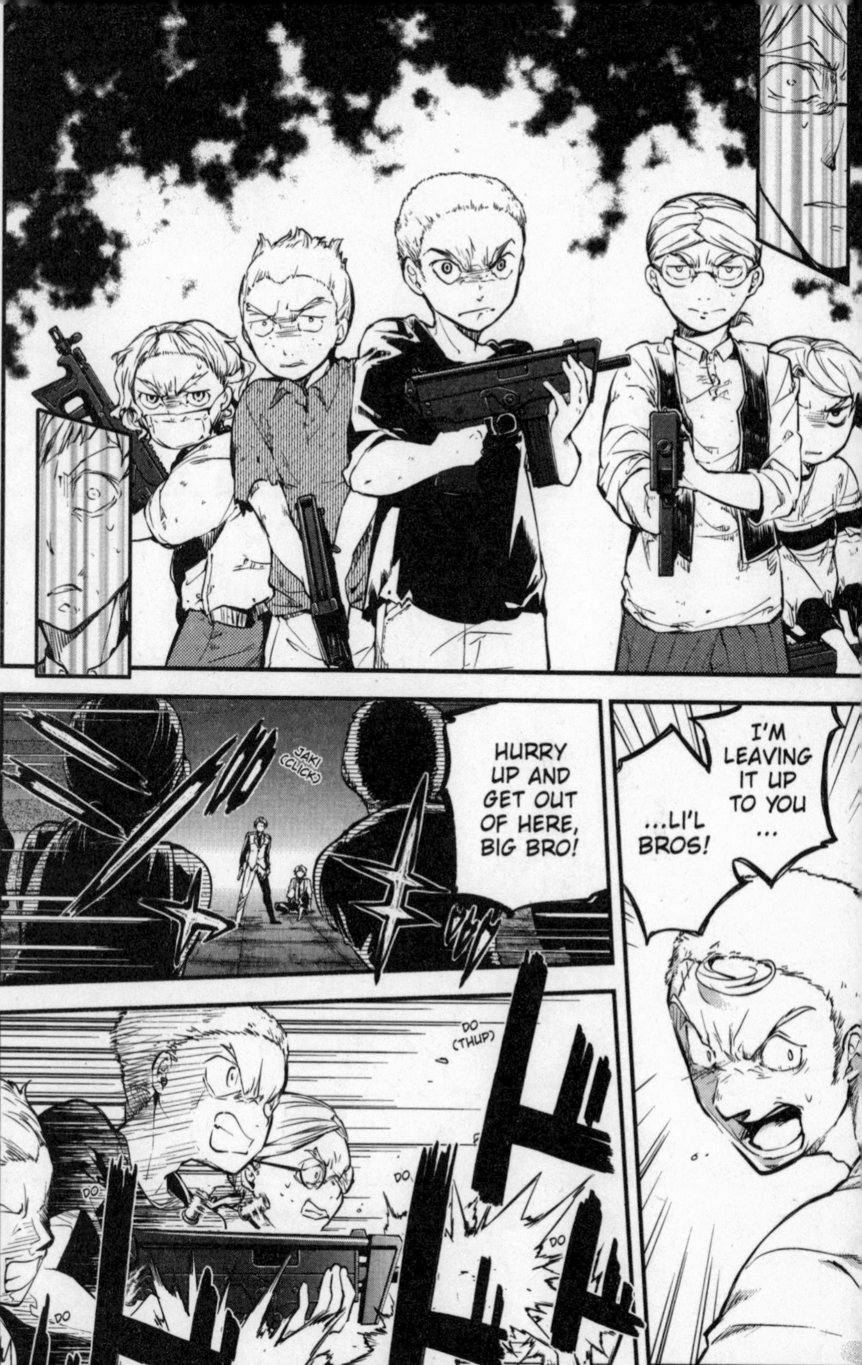
I'M LEAVING IT UP TO YOU ...
...LI'L BROS!
HURRY UP AND GET OUT OF HERE, BIG BRO!
JAKI (CLICK)
DO (THUP)
DO
DO
DO
DO

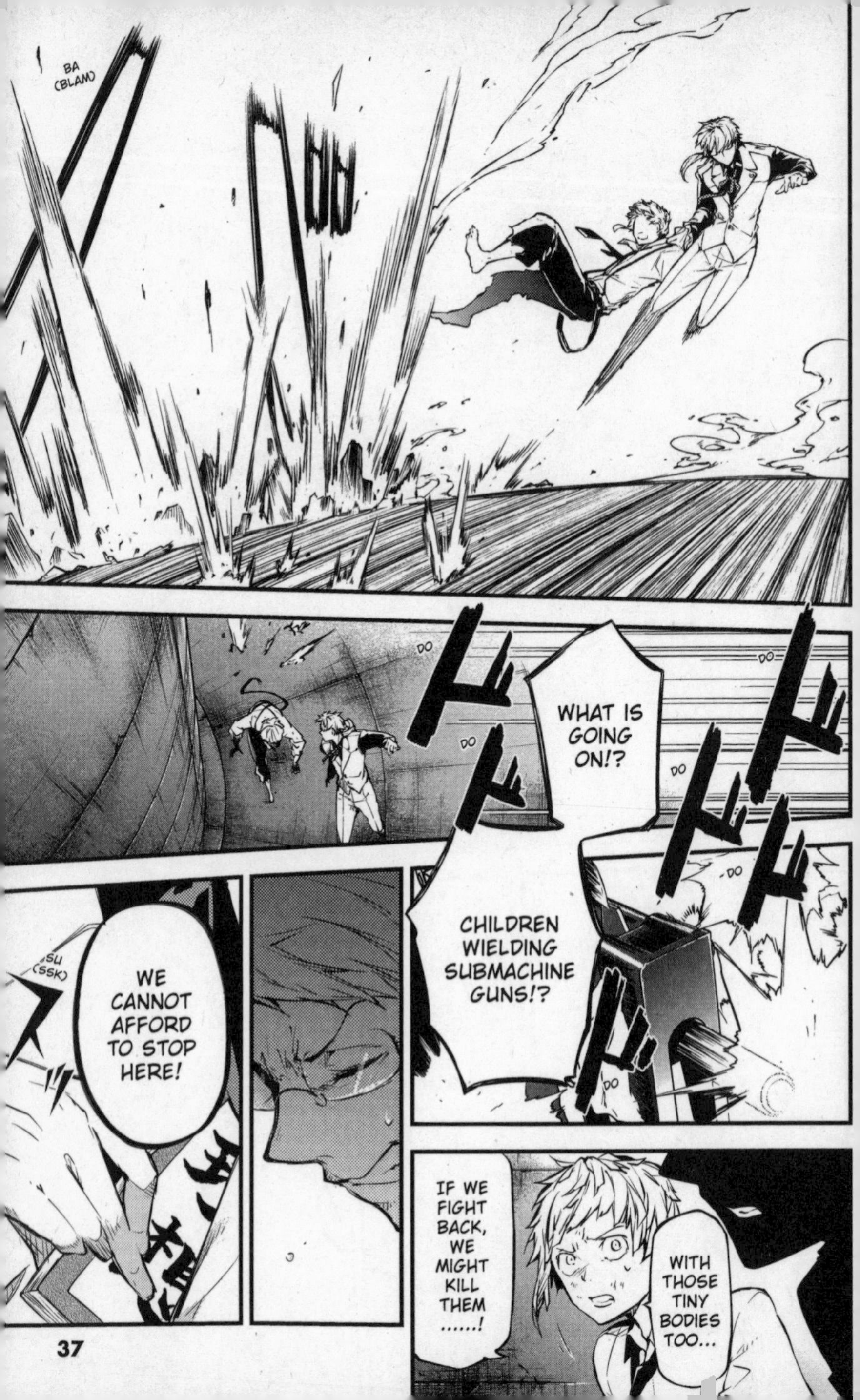
BA (BLAM)
DO
DO
DO
DO
WHAT IS GOING ON!?
CHILDREN WIELDING SUBMACHINE GUNS!?
DO
DO
IF WE FIGHT BACK, WE MIGHT KILL THEM ......!
WITH THOSE TINY BODIES TOO...
SU (SSK)
WE CANNOT AFFORD TO STOP HERE!

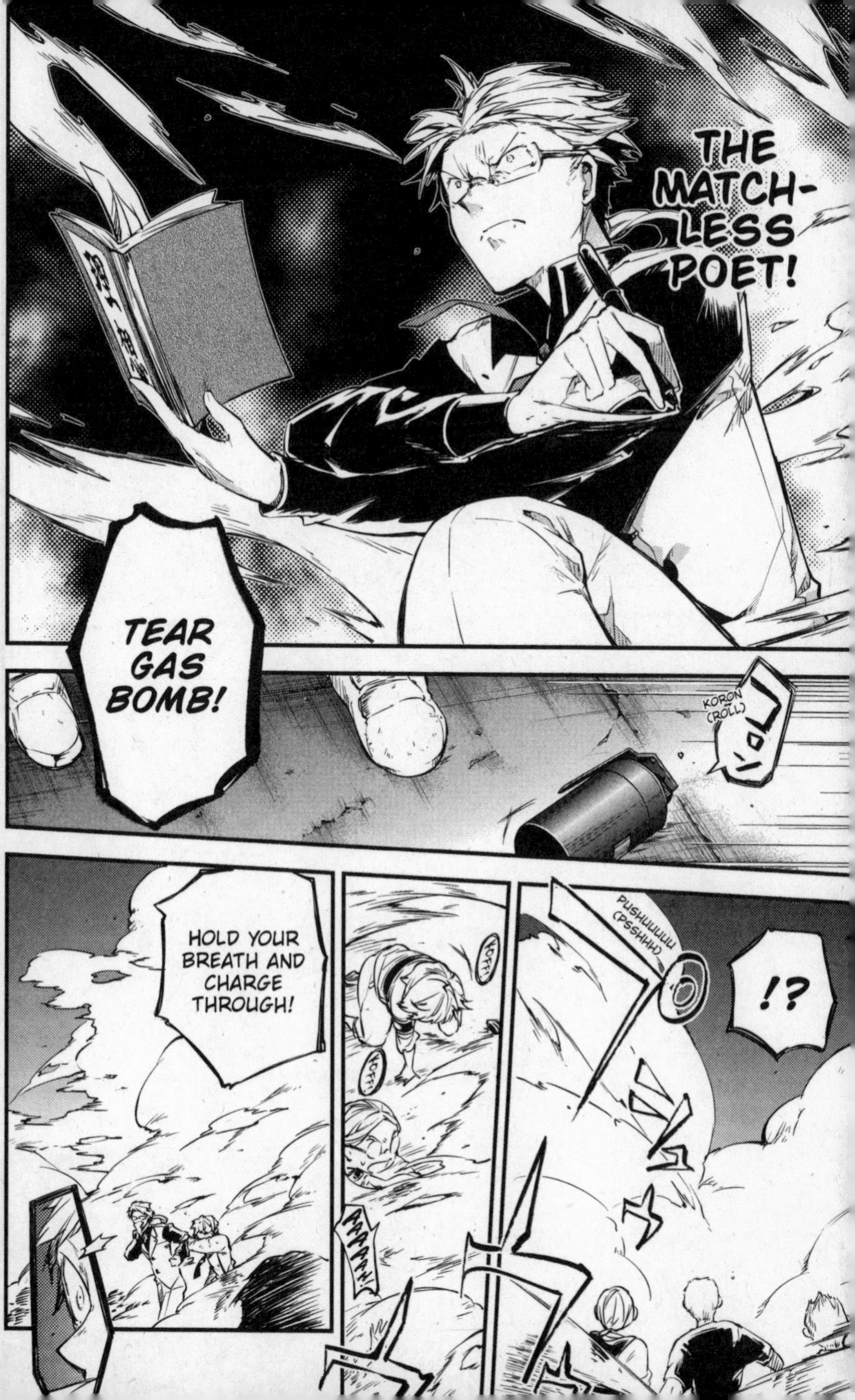
THE MATCH-LESS POET!
TEAR GAS BOMB!
KORON (ROLL)
!?
PUSHUUUUU (PSSHHH)
KOFF!
KOFF!
AAAAAAH!
HOLD YOUR BREATH AND CHARGE THROUGH!

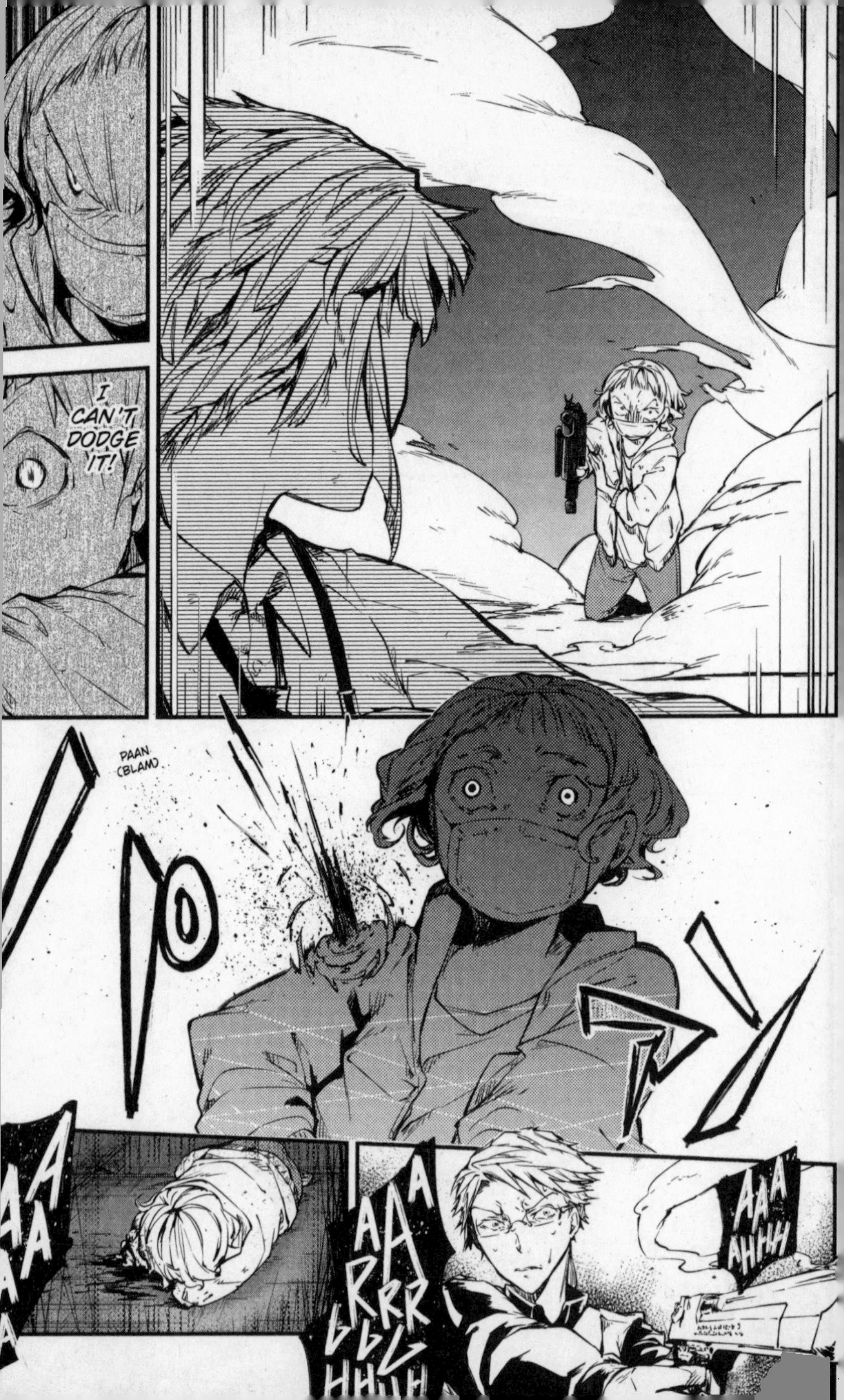
I CAN'T DODGE IT!
PAAN (BLAM)
AAAAHHHH
AAARRRGGGHHHH
AAAAAAA

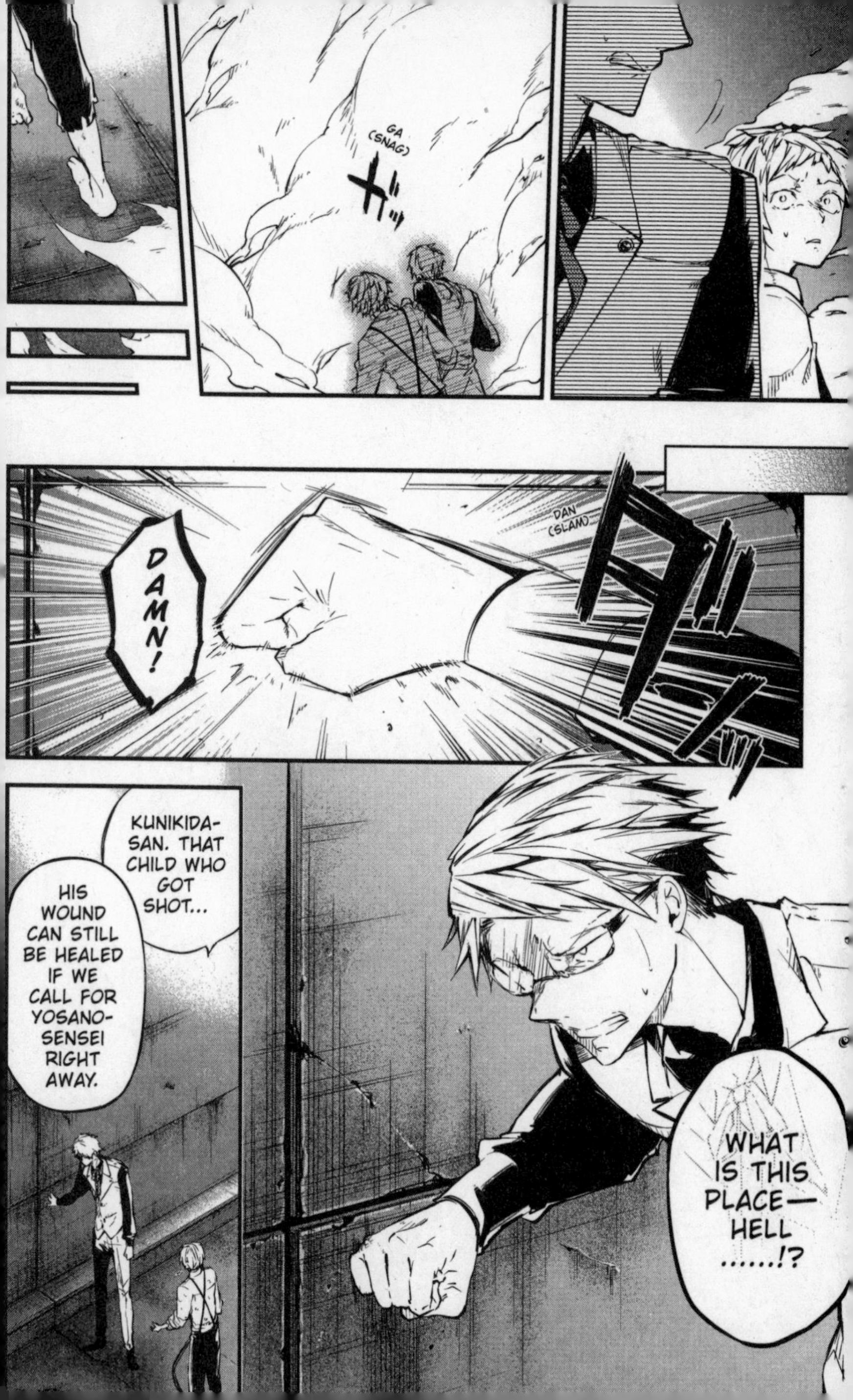
GA (SNAG)
DAN (SLAM)
DAMN!
KUNIKIDA-SAN. THAT CHILD WHO GOT SHOT...
HIS WOUND CAN STILL BE HEALED IF WE CALL FOR YOSANO-SENSEI RIGHT AWAY.
WHAT IS THIS PLACE—HELL......!?

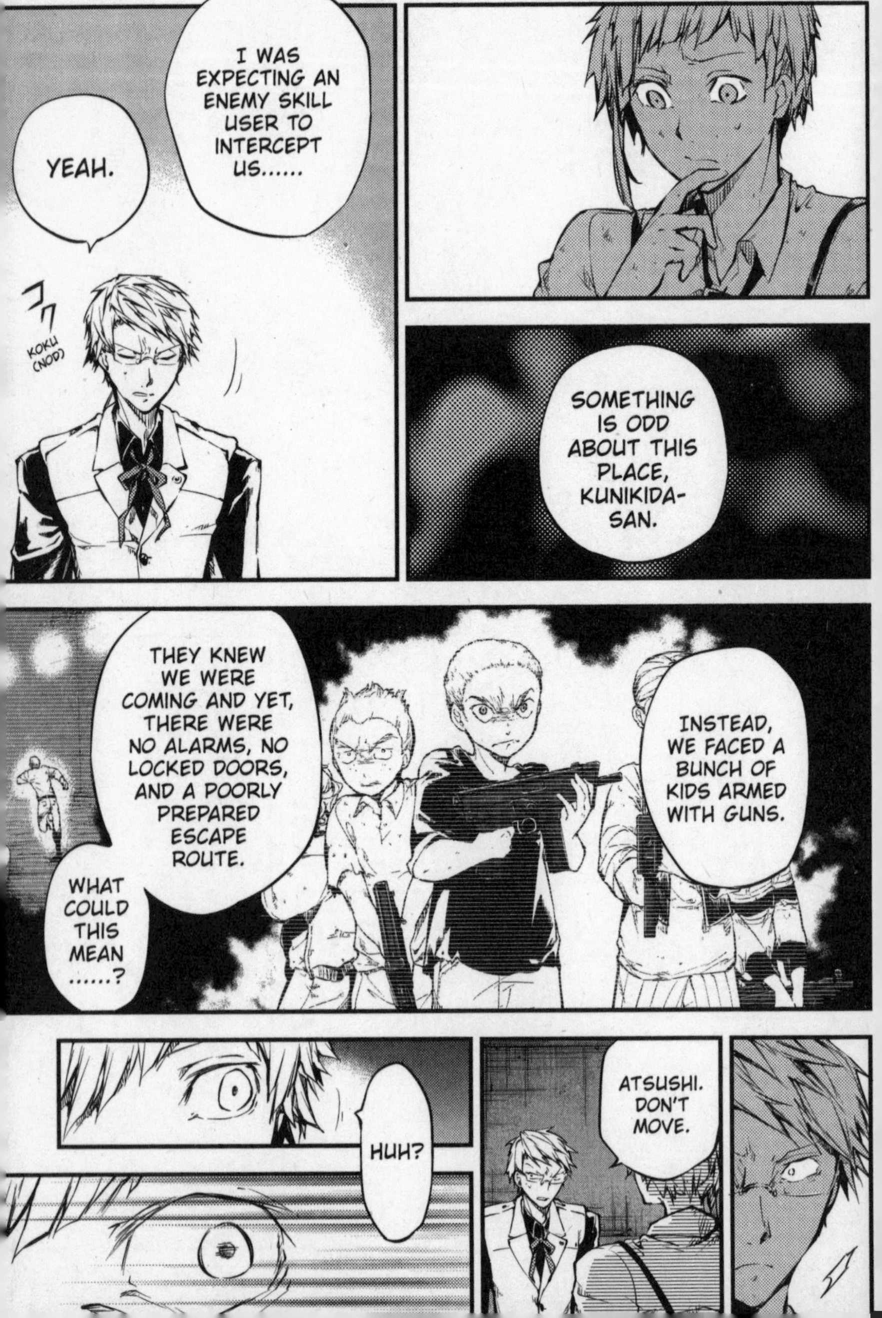
SOMETHING IS ODD ABOUT THIS PLACE, KUNIKIDA-SAN.
I WAS EXPECTING AN ENEMY SKILL USER TO INTERCEPT US......
YEAH.
コク
KOKU (NOD)
THEY KNEW WE WERE COMING AND YET, THERE WERE NO ALARMS, NO LOCKED DOORS, AND A POORLY PREPARED ESCAPE ROUTE.
INSTEAD, WE FACED A BUNCH OF KIDS ARMED WITH GUNS.
WHAT COULD THIS MEAN ......?
ATSUSHI. DON'T MOVE.
HUH?

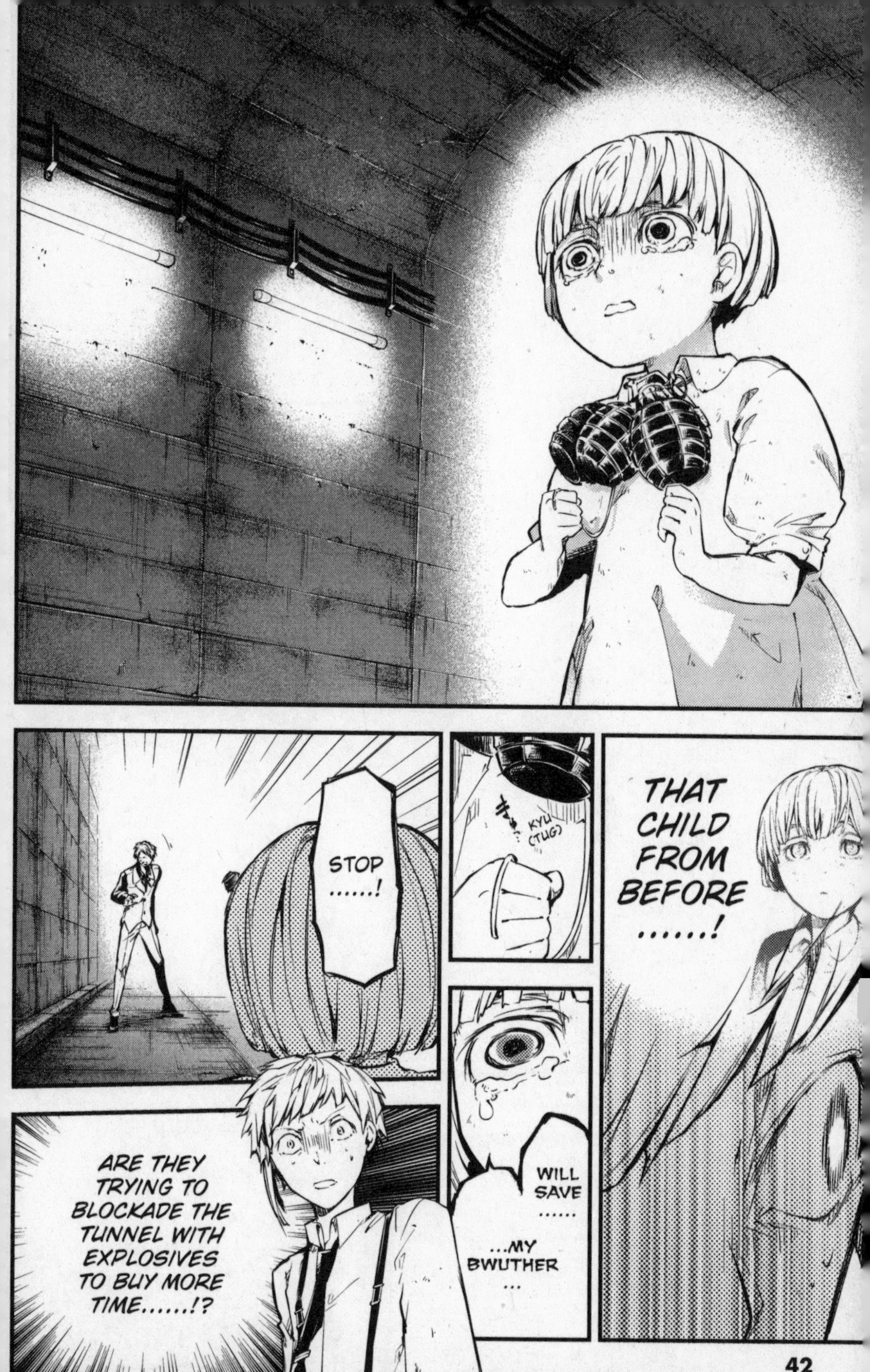
THAT CHILD FROM BEFORE ......!
KYU (TUG)
WILL SAVE ......
...MY BWUTHER ...
STOP ......!
ARE THEY TRYING TO BLOCKADE THE TUNNEL WITH EXPLOSIVES TO BUY MORE TIME......!?

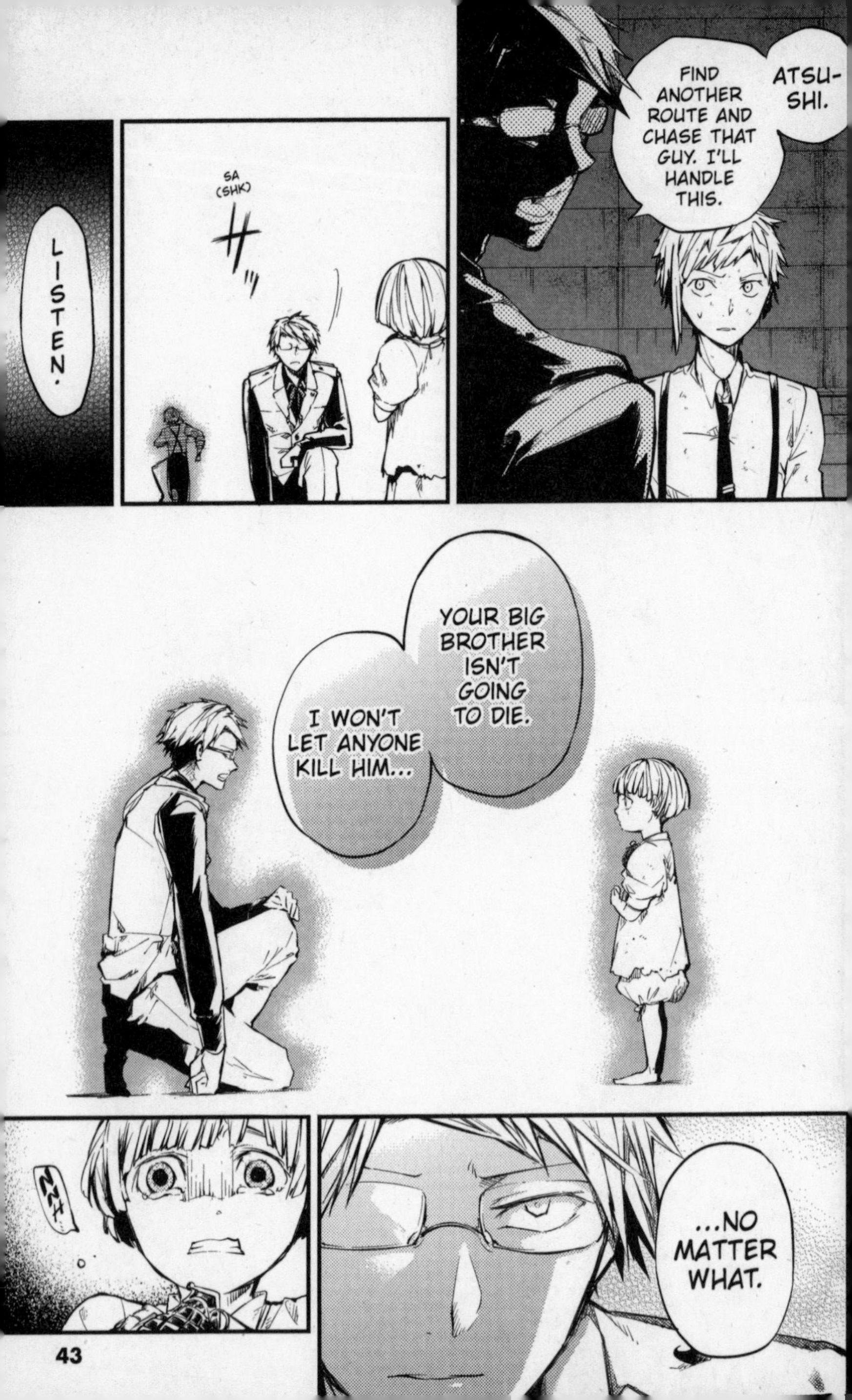
ATSU-SHI.
FIND ANOTHER ROUTE AND CHASE THAT GUY. I'LL HANDLE THIS.
SA (SHK)
LISTEN.
YOUR BIG BROTHER ISN'T GOING TO DIE.
I WON'T LET ANYONE KILL HIM...
...NO MATTER WHAT.
NNH...

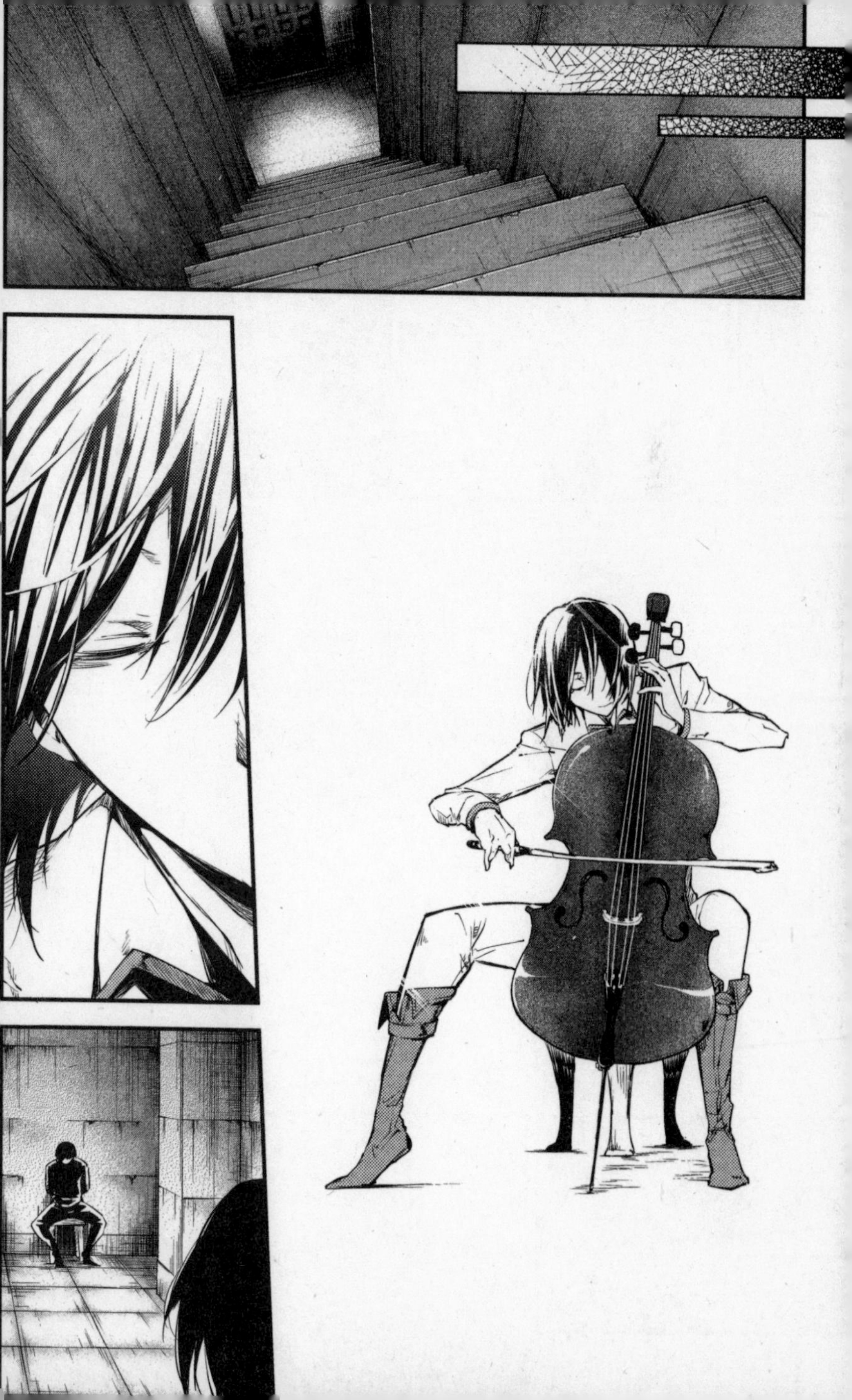

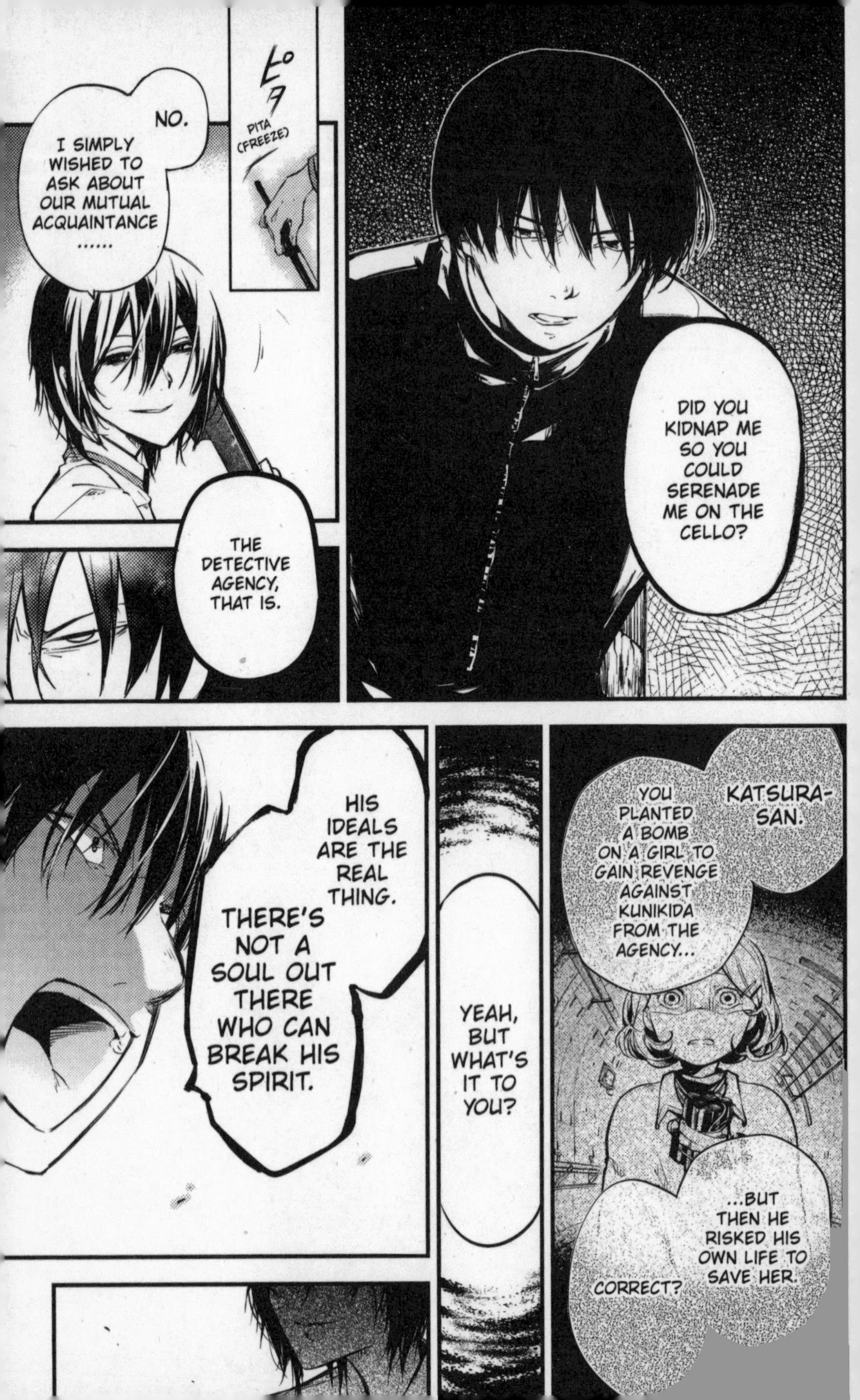
DID YOU KIDNAP ME SO YOU COULD SERENADE ME ON THE CELLO?
ピタ
PITA (FREEZE)
NO.
I SIMPLY WISHED TO ASK ABOUT OUR MUTUAL ACQUAINTANCE ......
THE DETECTIVE AGENCY, THAT IS.
KATSURA-SAN.
YOU PLANTED A BOMB ON A GIRL TO GAIN REVENGE AGAINST KUNIKIDA FROM THE AGENCY...
...BUT THEN HE RISKED HIS OWN LIFE TO SAVE HER.
CORRECT?
YEAH, BUT WHAT'S IT TO YOU?
HIS IDEALS ARE THE REAL THING.
THERE'S NOT A SOUL OUT THERE WHO CAN BREAK HIS SPIRIT.

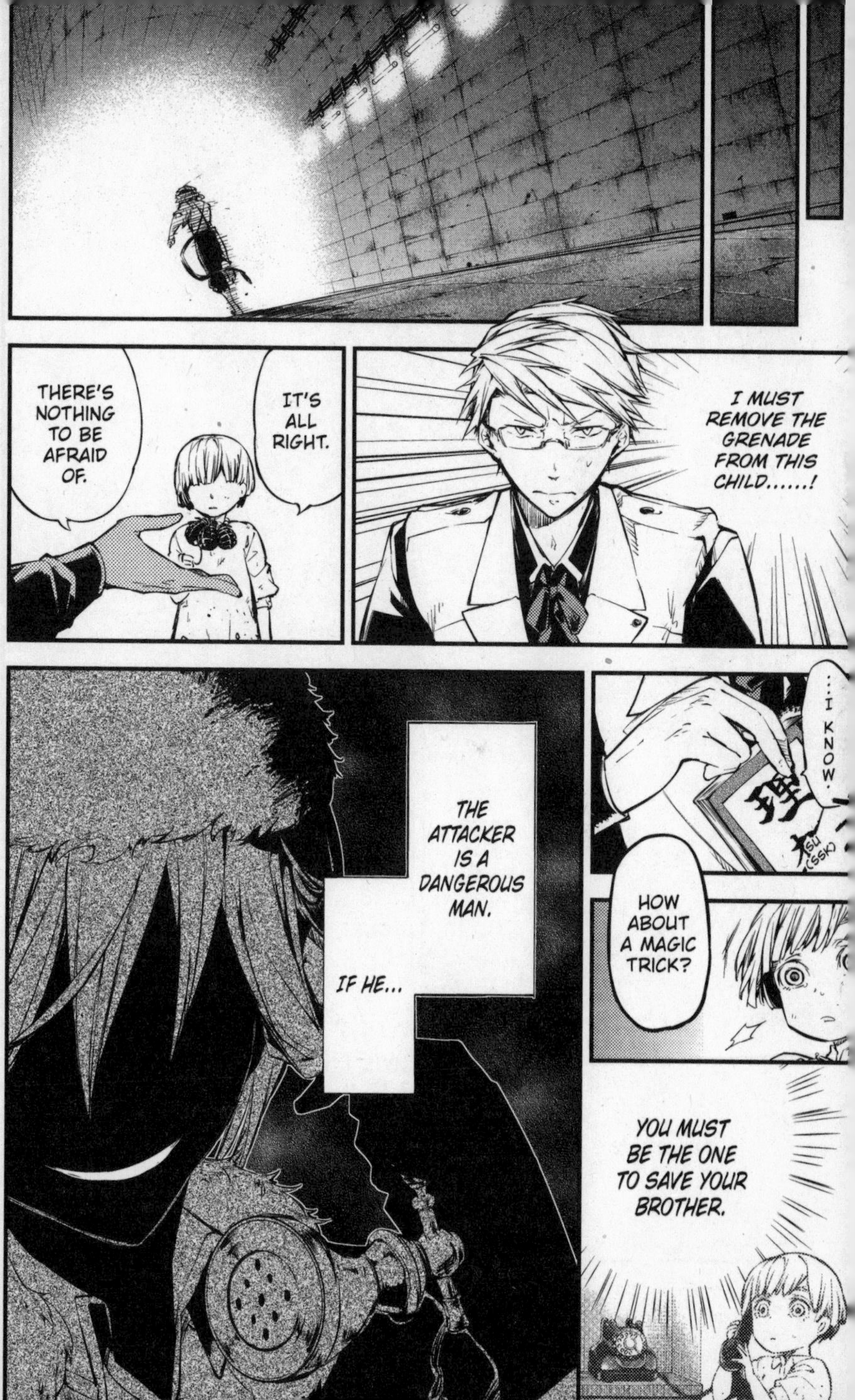
I MUST REMOVE THE GRENADE FROM THIS CHILD......!
IT'S ALL RIGHT.
THERE'S NOTHING TO BE AFRAID OF.
...I KNOW.
(SSK)
HOW ABOUT A MAGIC TRICK?
YOU MUST BE THE ONE TO SAVE YOUR BROTHER.
THE ATTACKER IS A DANGEROUS MAN.
IF HE...

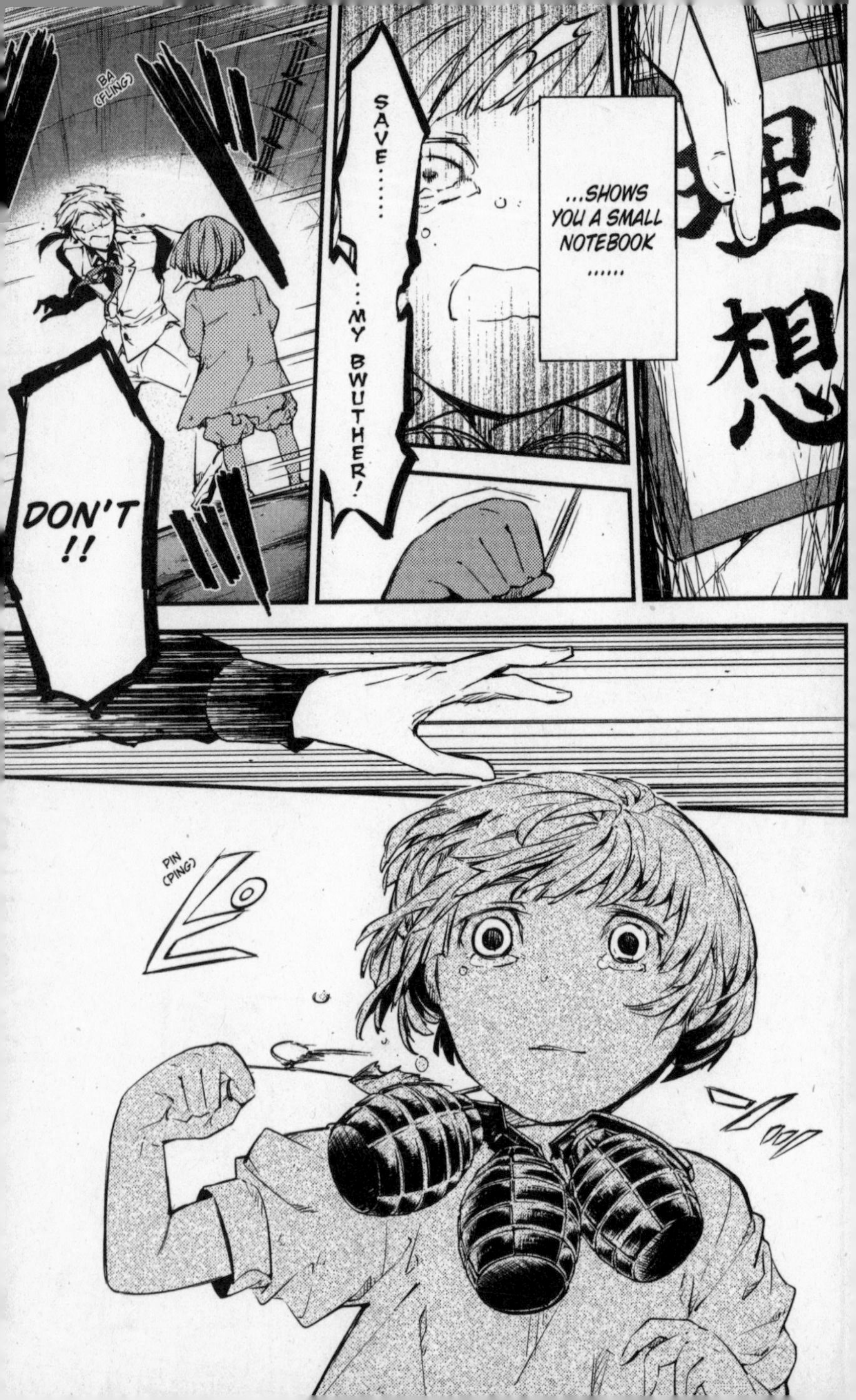
...SHOWS YOU A SMALL NOTEBOOK ......
理想
SAVE......
...MY BWUTHER!
BA (FLING)
DON'T !!
PIN (PING)

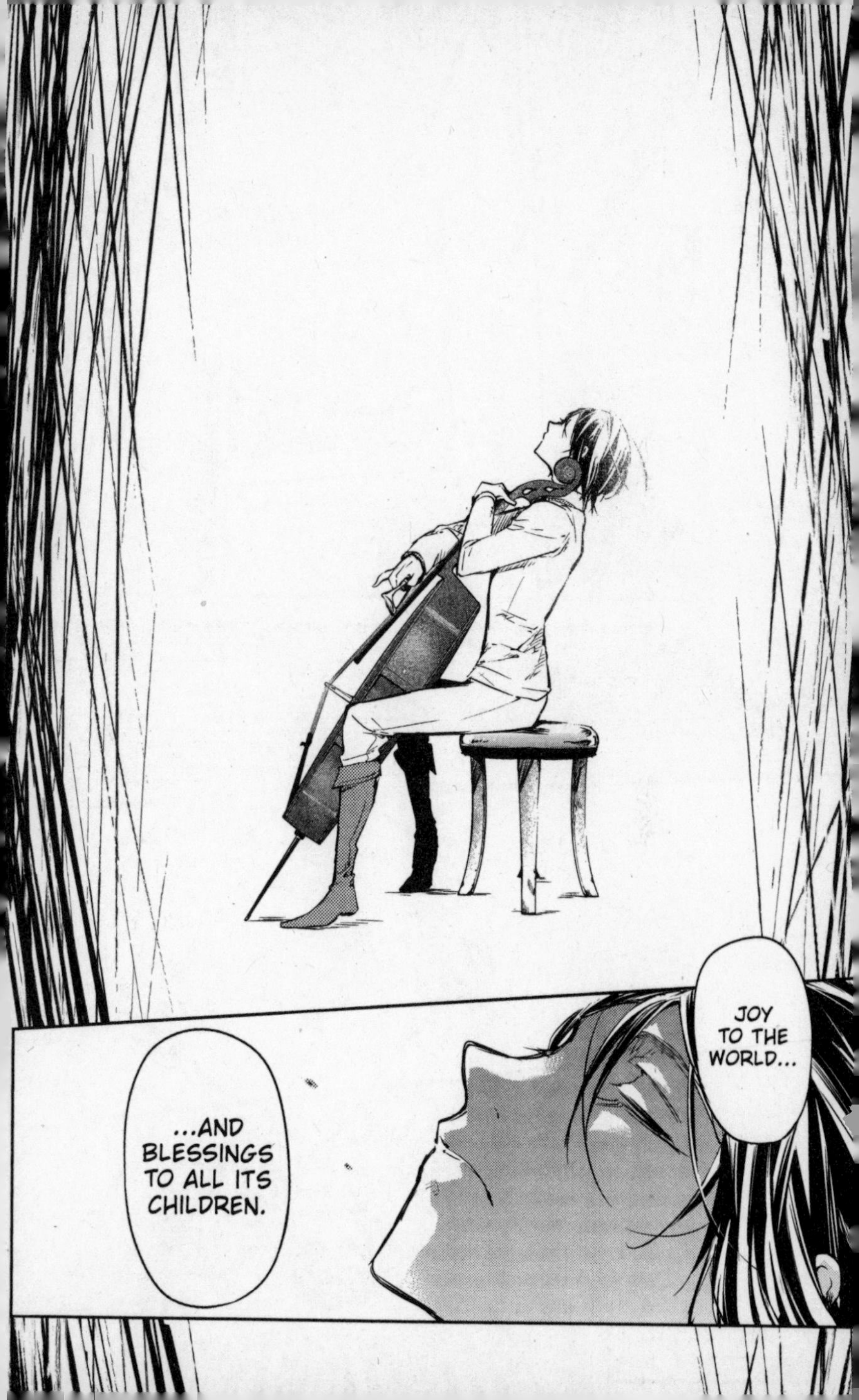
JOY TO THE WORLD...
...AND BLESSINGS TO ALL ITS CHILDREN.

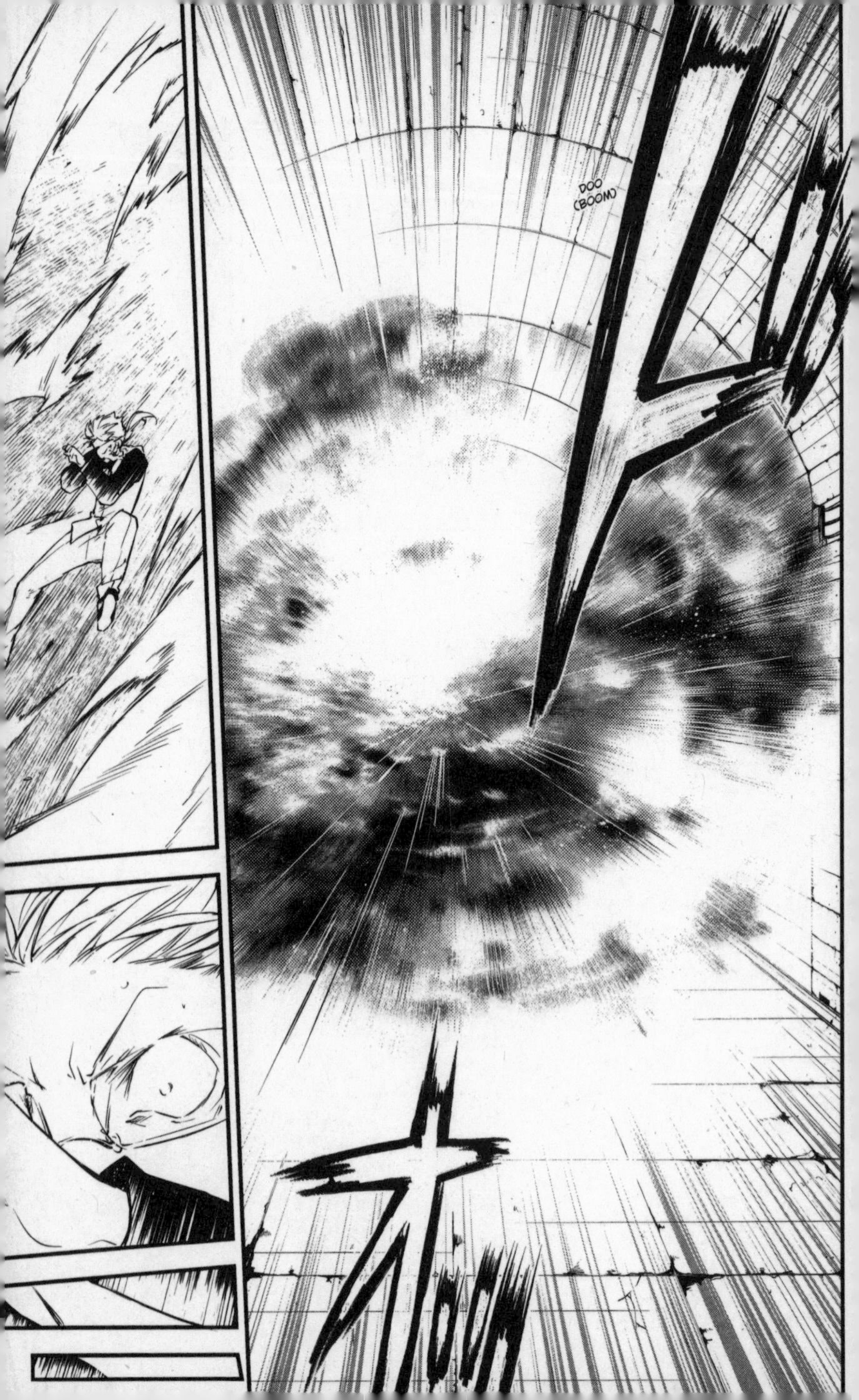
DOO
(BOOM)

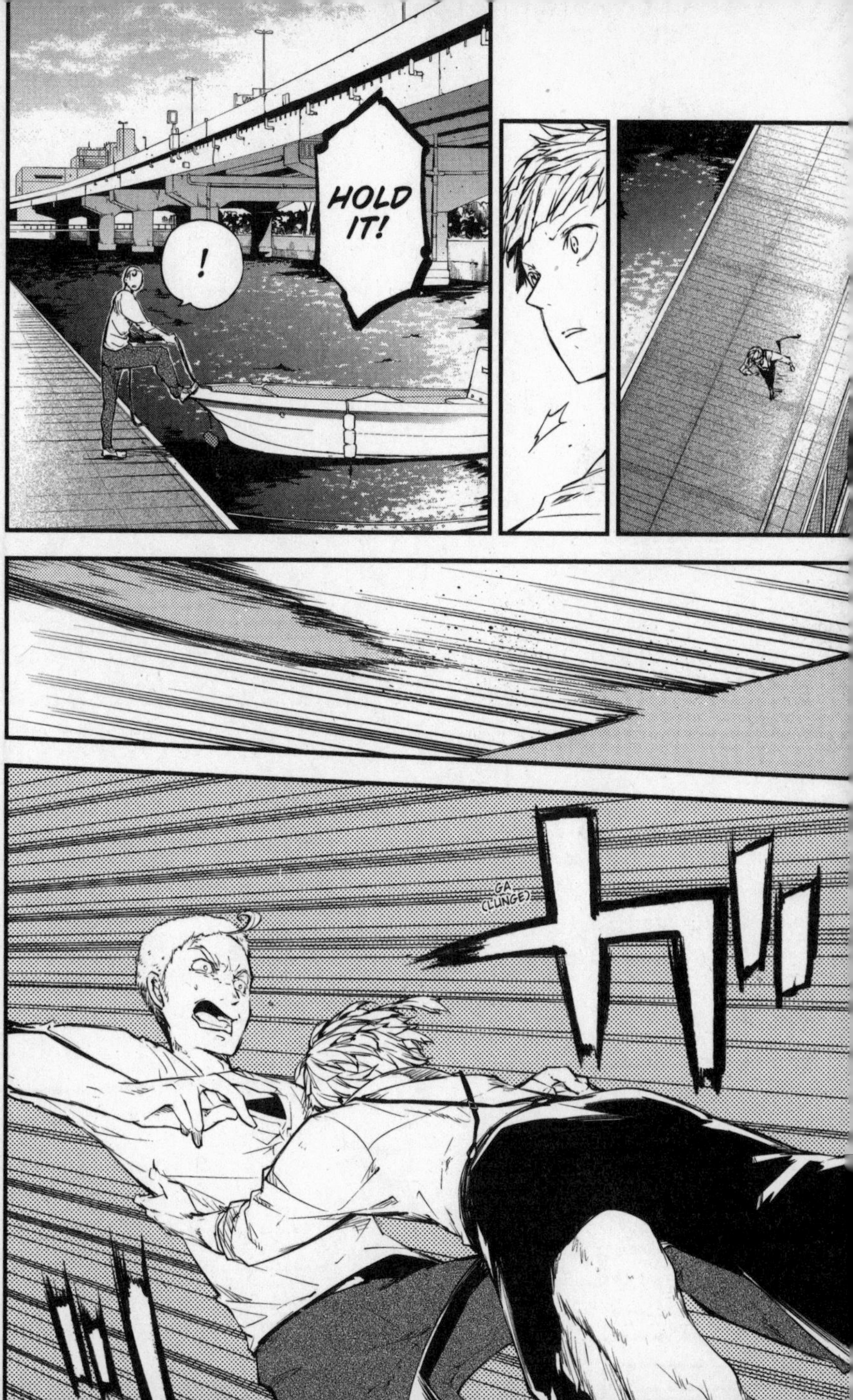
HOLD IT!
!
GA
(LUNGE)

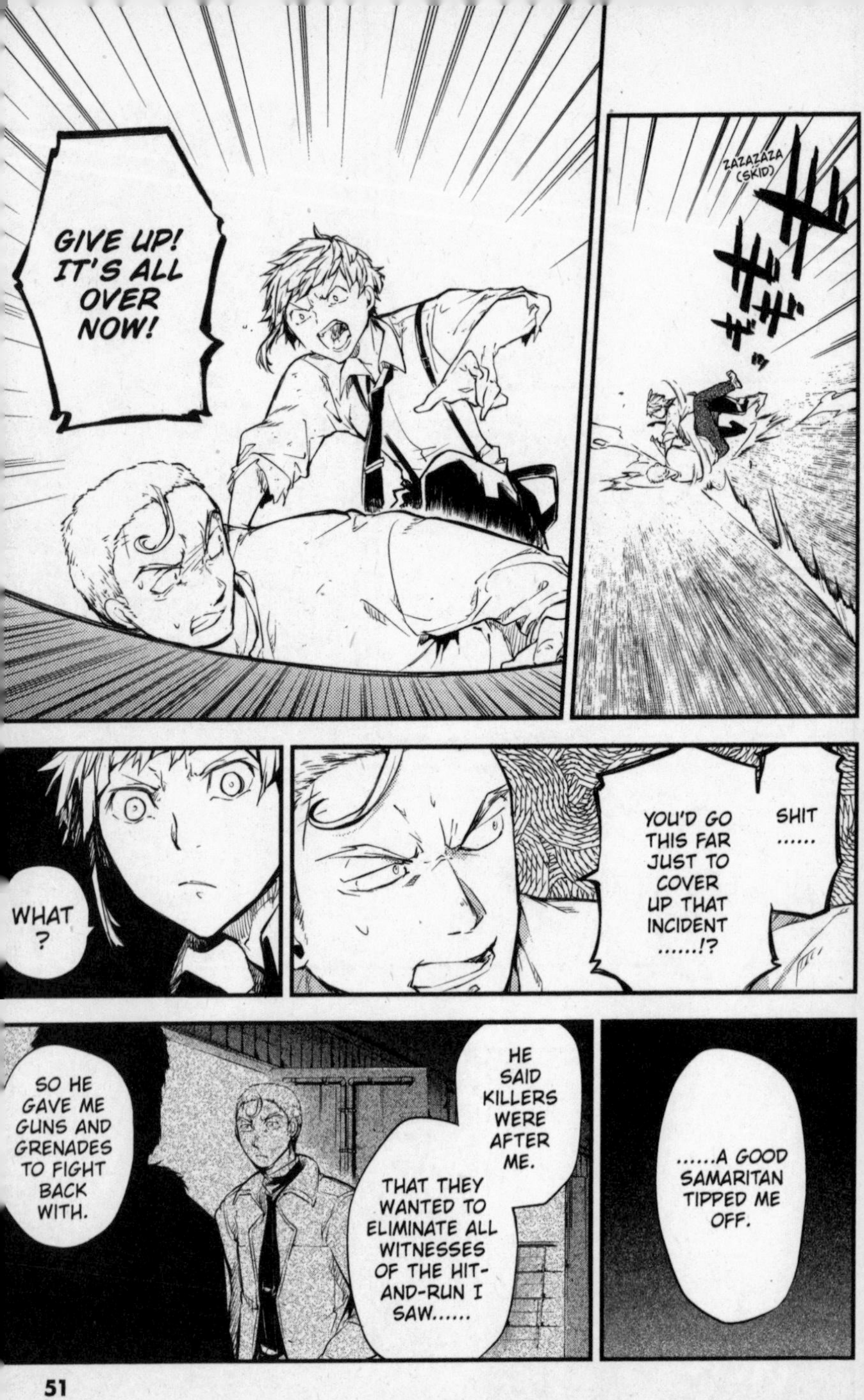
ZAZAZAZA (SKID)
GIVE UP! IT'S ALL OVER NOW!
SHIT ......
YOU'D GO THIS FAR JUST TO COVER UP THAT INCIDENT ......!?
WHAT ?
......A GOOD SAMARITAN TIPPED ME OFF.
HE SAID KILLERS WERE AFTER ME.
THAT THEY WANTED TO ELIMINATE ALL WITNESSES OF THE HIT-AND-RUN I SAW......
SO HE GAVE ME GUNS AND GRENADES TO FIGHT BACK WITH.

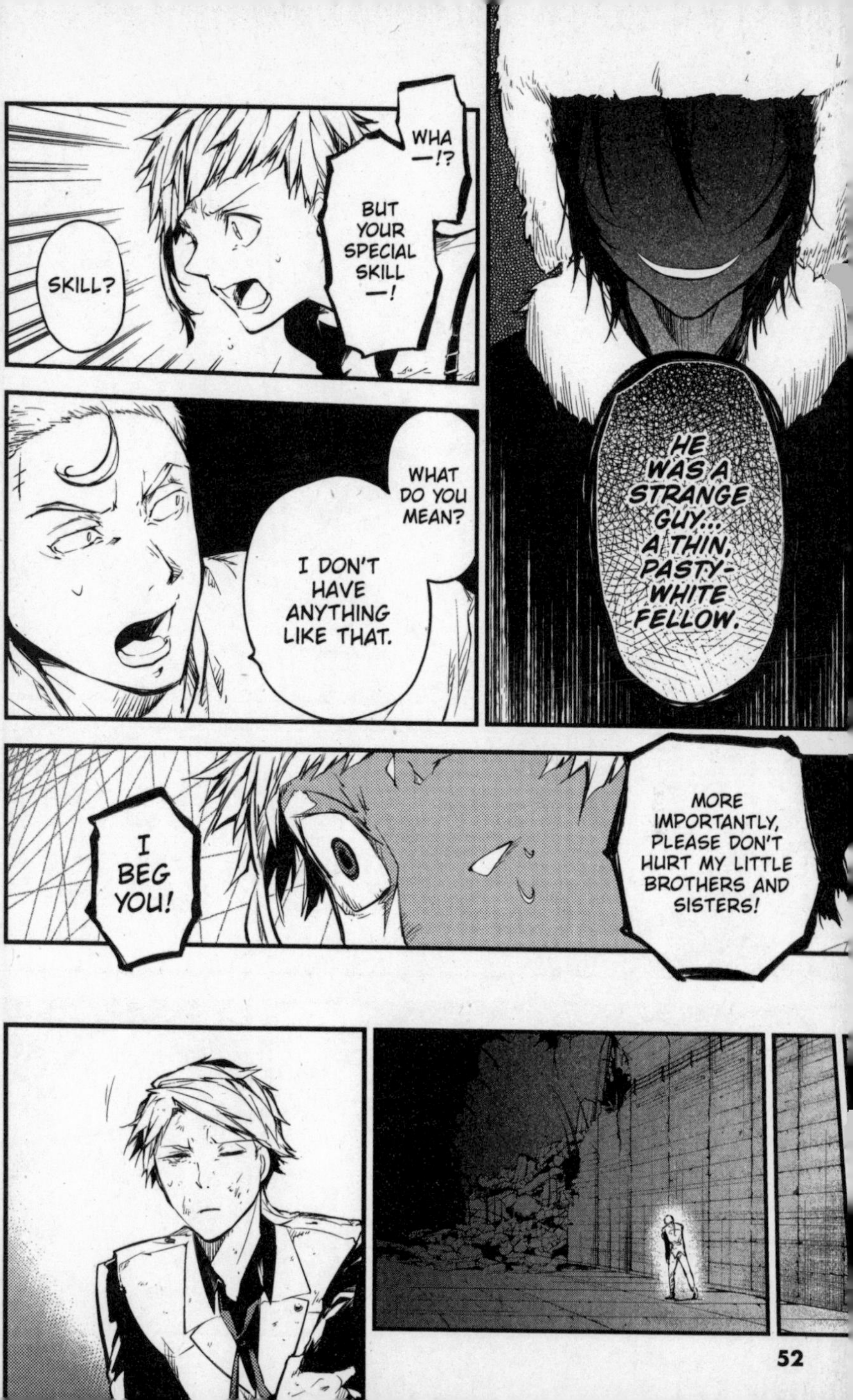
HE WAS A STRANGE GUY... A THIN, PASTY-WHITE FELLOW.
WHA—!?
BUT YOUR SPECIAL SKILL—!
SKILL?
WHAT DO YOU MEAN?
I DON'T HAVE ANYTHING LIKE THAT.
MORE IMPORTANTLY, PLEASE DON'T HURT MY LITTLE BROTHERS AND SISTERS!
I BEG YOU!

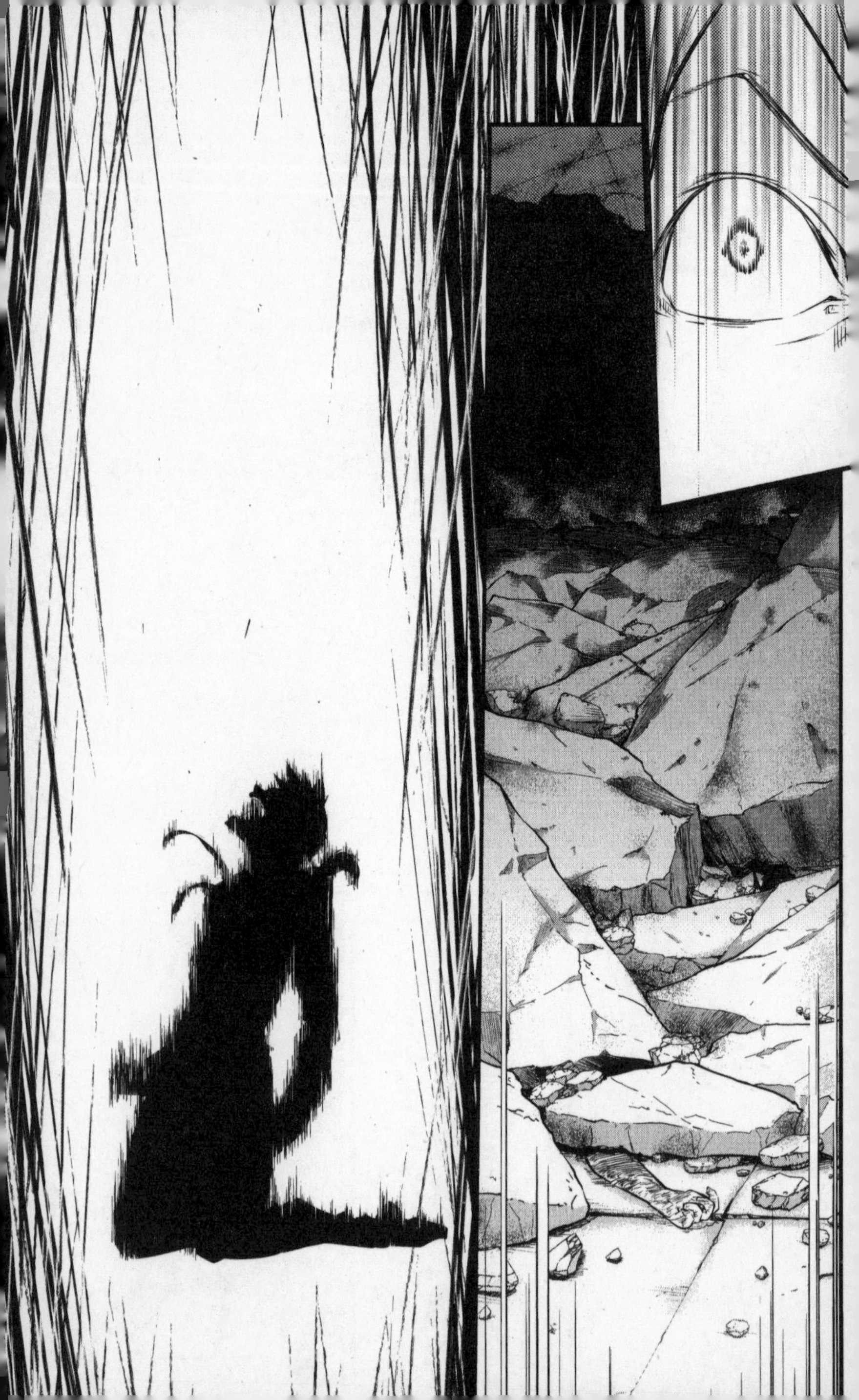

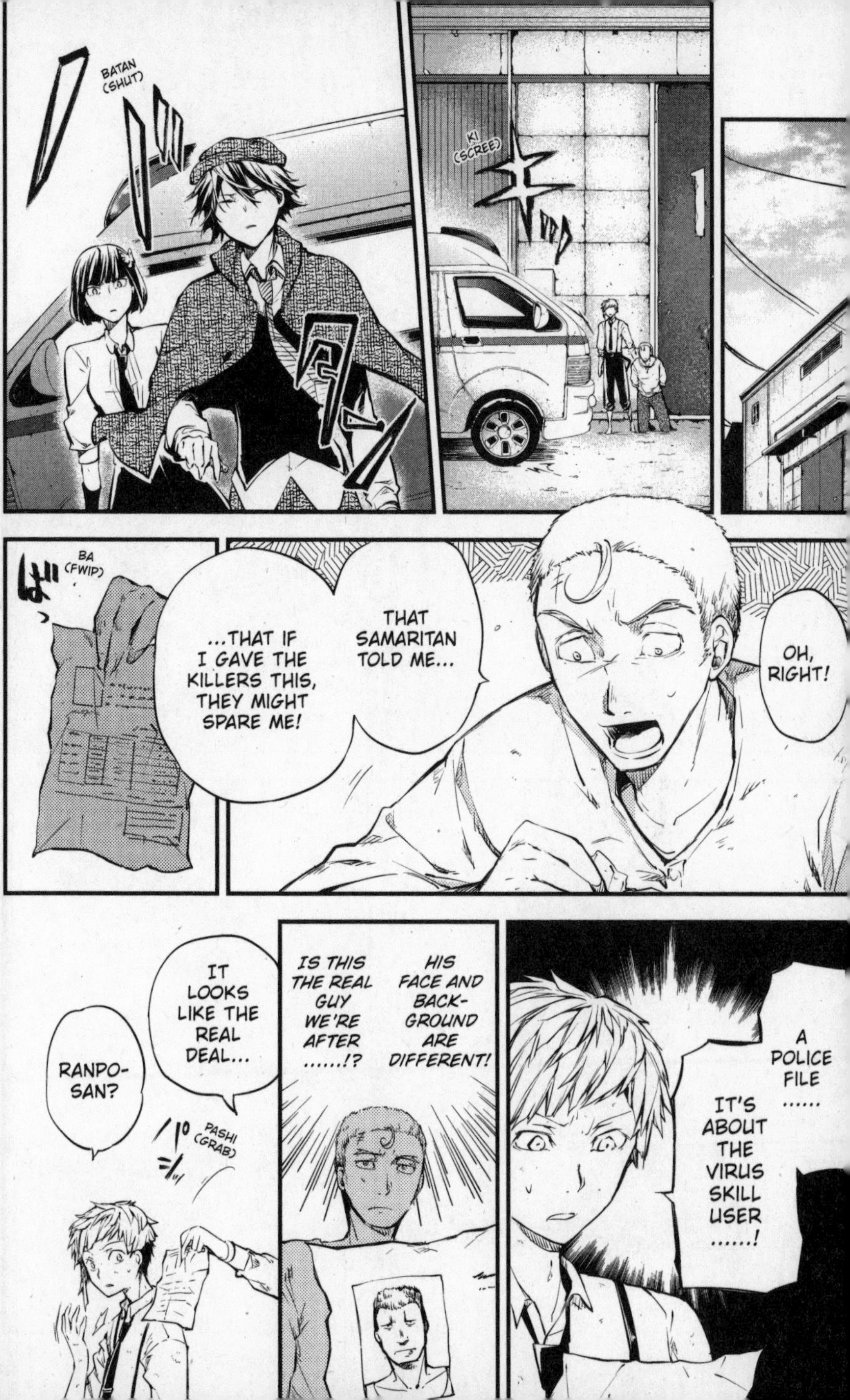
KI (SCREE)
BATAN (SHUT)
OH, RIGHT!
THAT SAMARITAN TOLD ME...
...THAT IF I GAVE THE KILLERS THIS, THEY MIGHT SPARE ME!
BA (FWIP)
A POLICE FILE ......
IT'S ABOUT THE VIRUS SKILL USER ......!
HIS FACE AND BACK-GROUND ARE DIFFERENT!
IS THIS THE REAL GUY WE'RE AFTER ......!?
IT LOOKS LIKE THE REAL DEAL...
RANPO-SAN?
PASHI (GRAB)

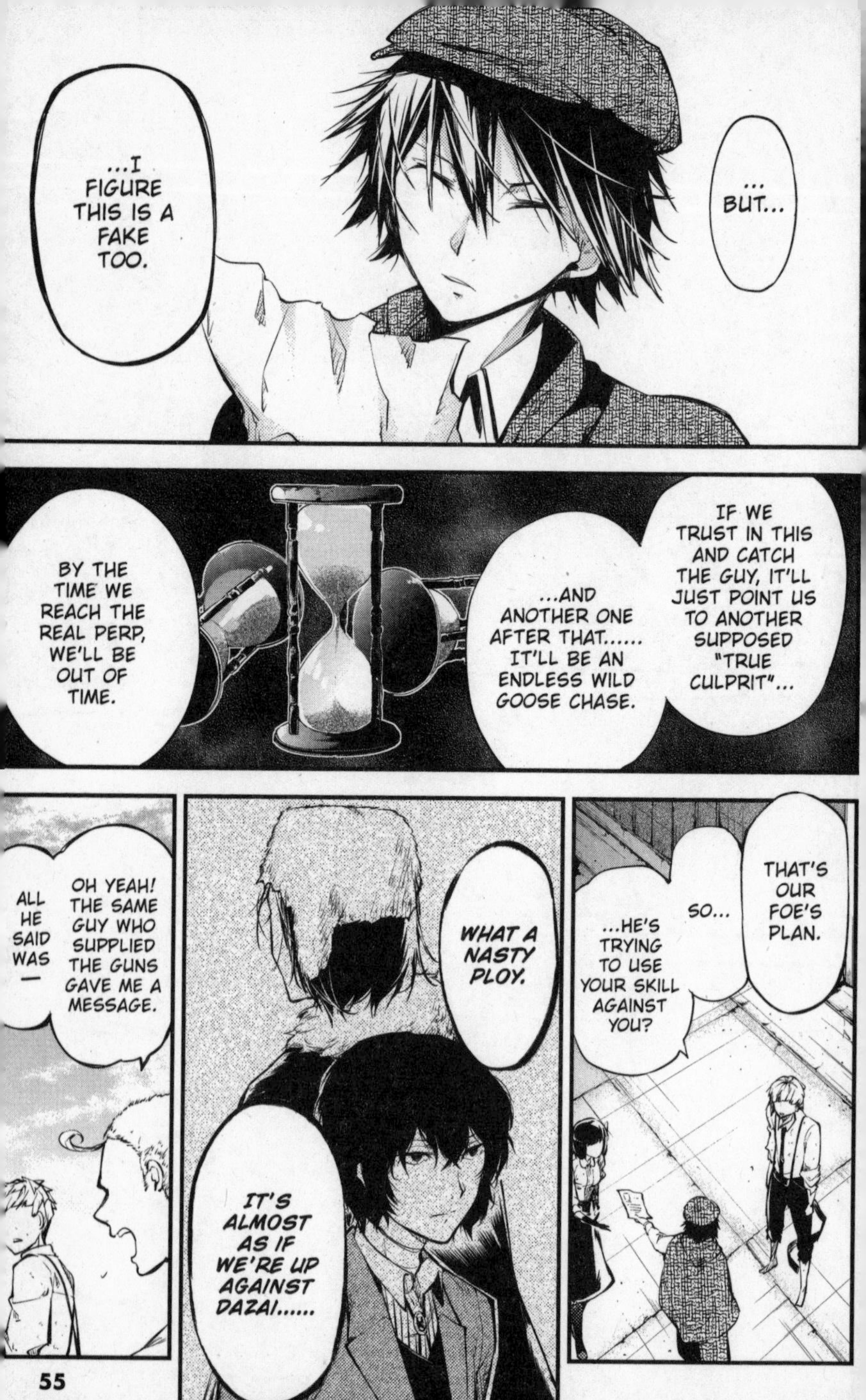

...BUT...
...I FIGURE THIS IS A FAKE TOO.
IF WE TRUST IN THIS AND CATCH THE GUY, IT'LL JUST POINT US TO ANOTHER SUPPOSED "TRUE CULPRIT"...
...AND ANOTHER ONE AFTER THAT...... IT'LL BE AN ENDLESS WILD GOOSE CHASE.
BY THE TIME WE REACH THE REAL PERP, WE'LL BE OUT OF TIME.
THAT'S OUR FOE'S PLAN.
SO...
...HE'S TRYING TO USE YOUR SKILL AGAINST YOU?
WHAT A NASTY PLOY.
IT'S ALMOST AS IF WE'RE UP AGAINST DAZAI......
OH YEAH! THE SAME GUY WHO SUPPLIED THE GUNS GAVE ME A MESSAGE.
ALL HE SAID WAS—

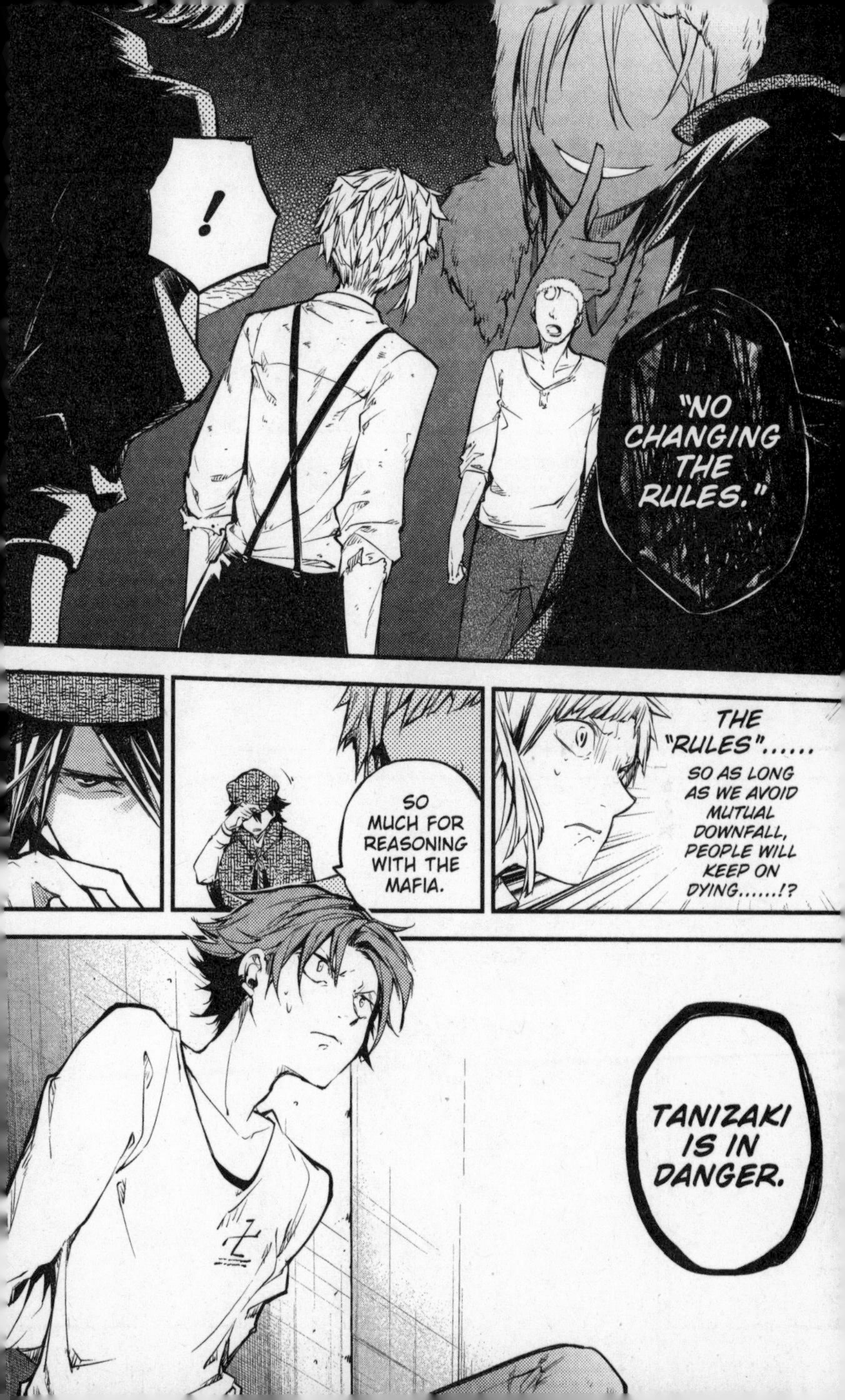
!
"NO CHANGING THE RULES."
THE "RULES"......
SO AS LONG AS WE AVOID MUTUAL DOWNFALL, PEOPLE WILL KEEP ON DYING......!?
SO MUCH FOR REASONING WITH THE MAFIA.
TANIZAKI IS IN DANGER.

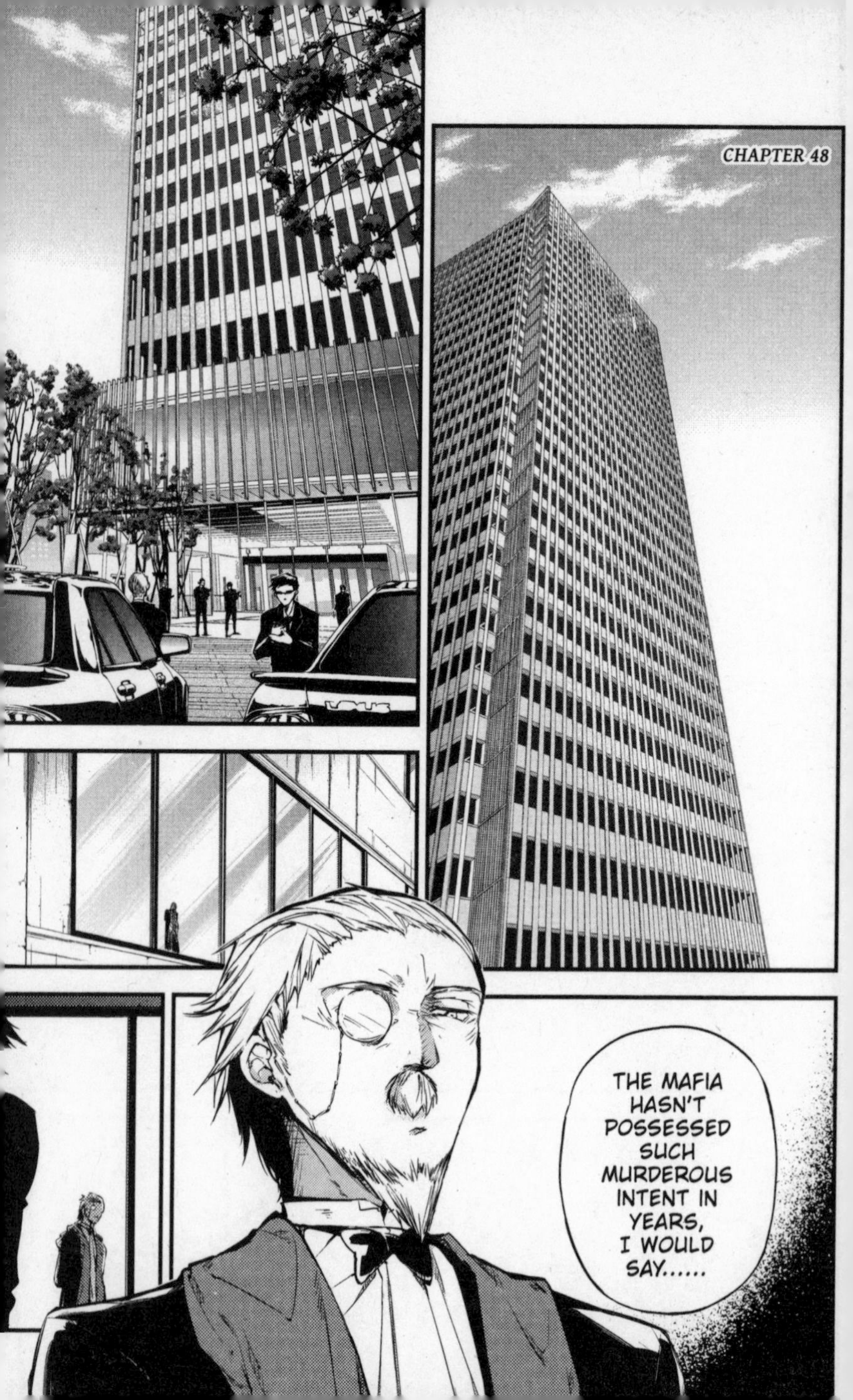
CHAPTER 48
THE MAFIA HASN'T POSSESSED SUCH MURDEROUS INTENT IN YEARS, I WOULD SAY......

CHAPTER 48
Mutual Destruction, Part 2

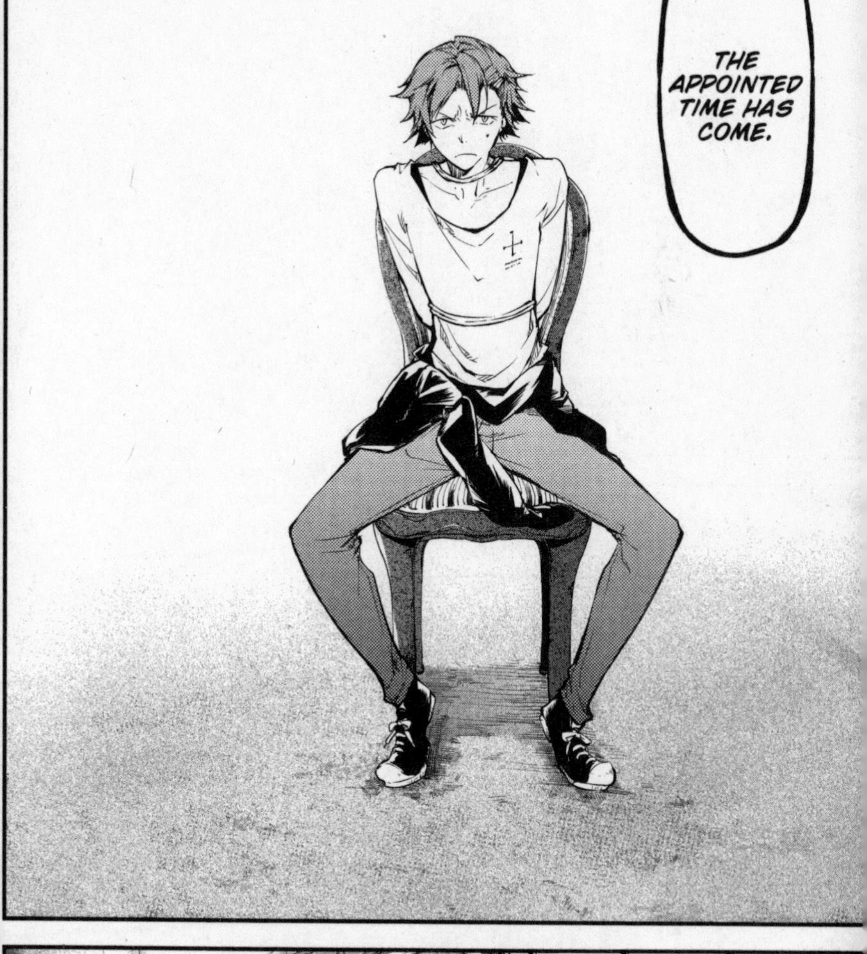
THE APPOINTED TIME HAS COME.

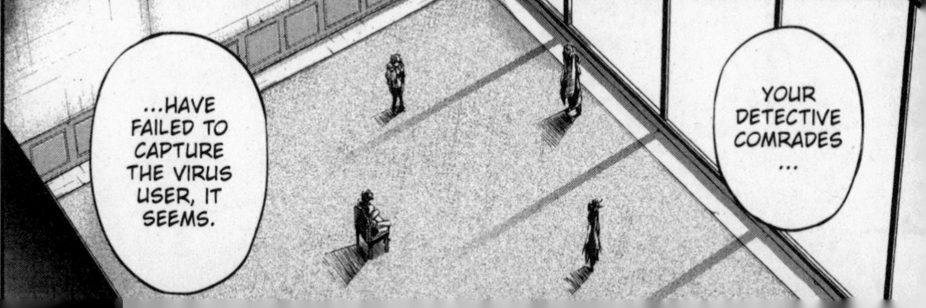
YOUR DETECTIVE COMRADES ...
...HAVE FAILED TO CAPTURE THE VIRUS USER, IT SEEMS.

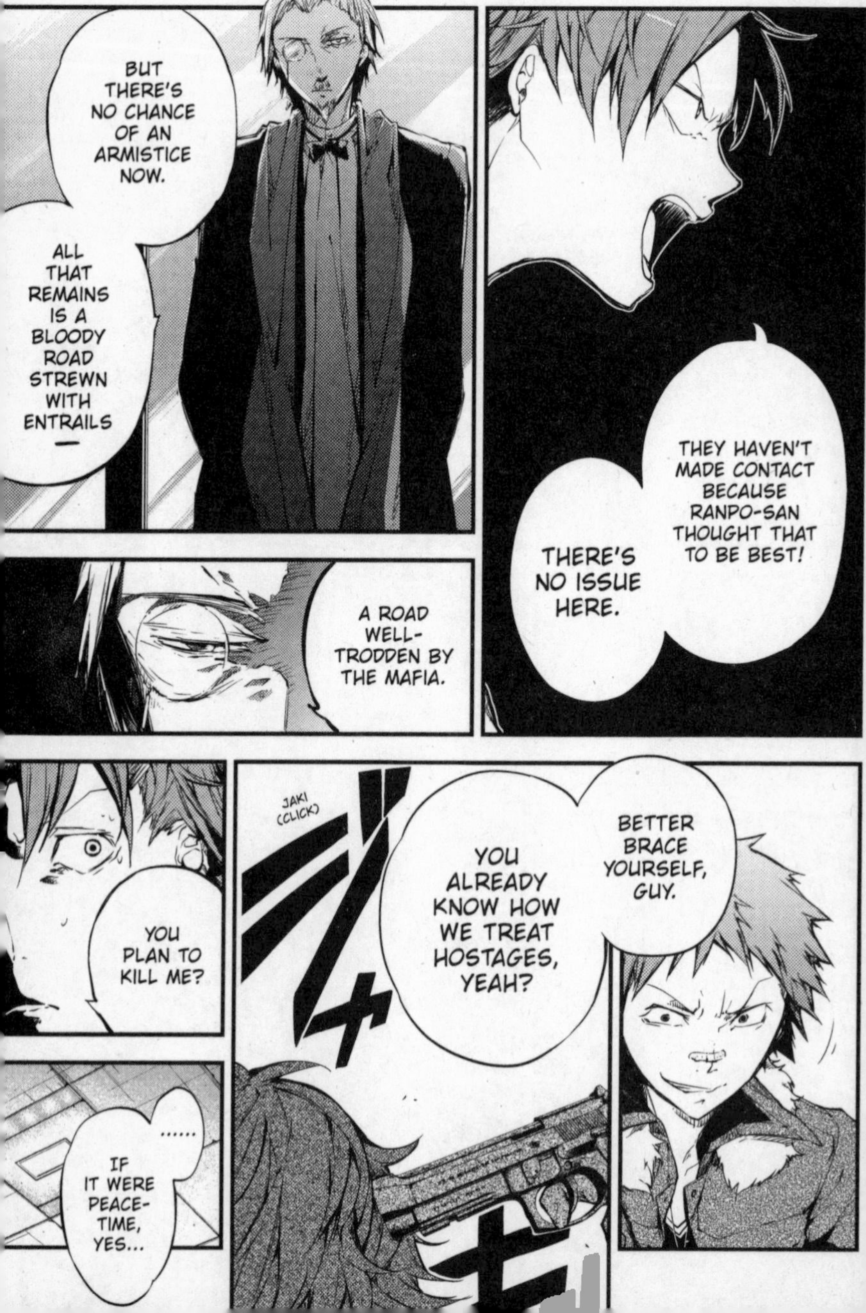
THEY HAVEN'T MADE CONTACT BECAUSE RANPO-SAN THOUGHT THAT TO BE BEST!
THERE'S NO ISSUE HERE.
BUT THERE'S NO CHANCE OF AN ARMISTICE NOW.
ALL THAT REMAINS IS A BLOODY ROAD STREWN WITH ENTRAILS—
A ROAD WELL-TRODDEN BY THE MAFIA.
BETTER BRACE YOURSELF, GUY.
YOU ALREADY KNOW HOW WE TREAT HOSTAGES, YEAH?
JAKI (CLICK)
YOU PLAN TO KILL ME?
......
IF IT WERE PEACE-TIME, YES...

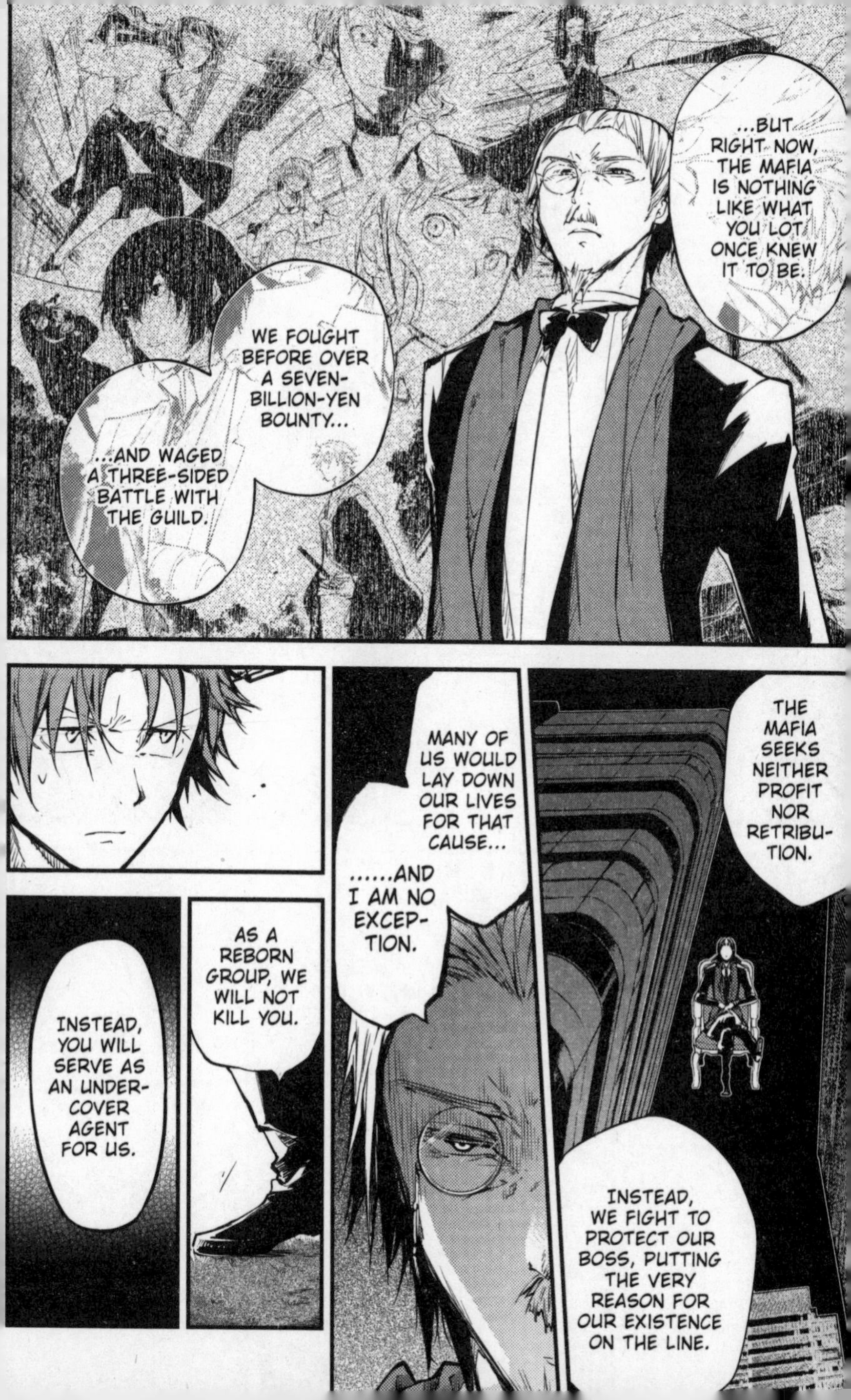
WE FOUGHT BEFORE OVER A SEVEN-BILLION-YEN BOUNTY...
...AND WAGED A THREE-SIDED BATTLE WITH THE GUILD.
...BUT RIGHT NOW, THE MAFIA IS NOTHING LIKE WHAT YOU LOT ONCE KNEW IT TO BE.
THE MAFIA SEEKS NEITHER PROFIT NOR RETRIBU-TION.
INSTEAD, WE FIGHT TO PROTECT OUR BOSS, PUTTING THE VERY REASON FOR OUR EXISTENCE ON THE LINE.
MANY OF US WOULD LAY DOWN OUR LIVES FOR THAT CAUSE...
......AND I AM NO EXCEP-TION.
AS A REBORN GROUP, WE WILL NOT KILL YOU.
INSTEAD, YOU WILL SERVE AS AN UNDER-COVER AGENT FOR US.

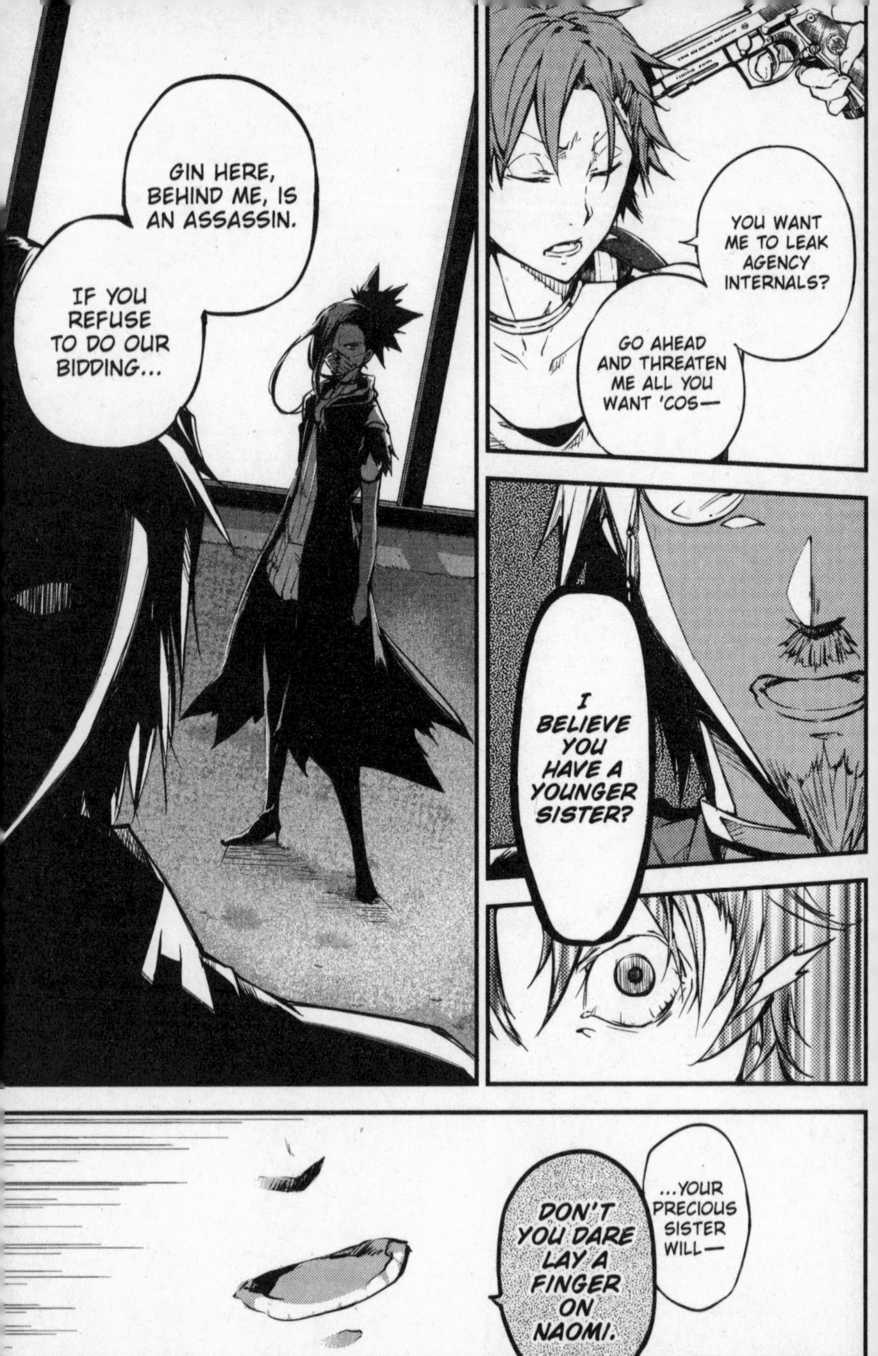
YOU WANT ME TO LEAK AGENCY INTERNALS?
GO AHEAD AND THREATEN ME ALL YOU WANT 'COS—
I BELIEVE YOU HAVE A YOUNGER SISTER?
GIN HERE, BEHIND ME, IS AN ASSASSIN.
IF YOU REFUSE TO DO OUR BIDDING...
...YOUR PRECIOUS SISTER WILL—
DON'T YOU DARE LAY A FINGER ON NAOMI.

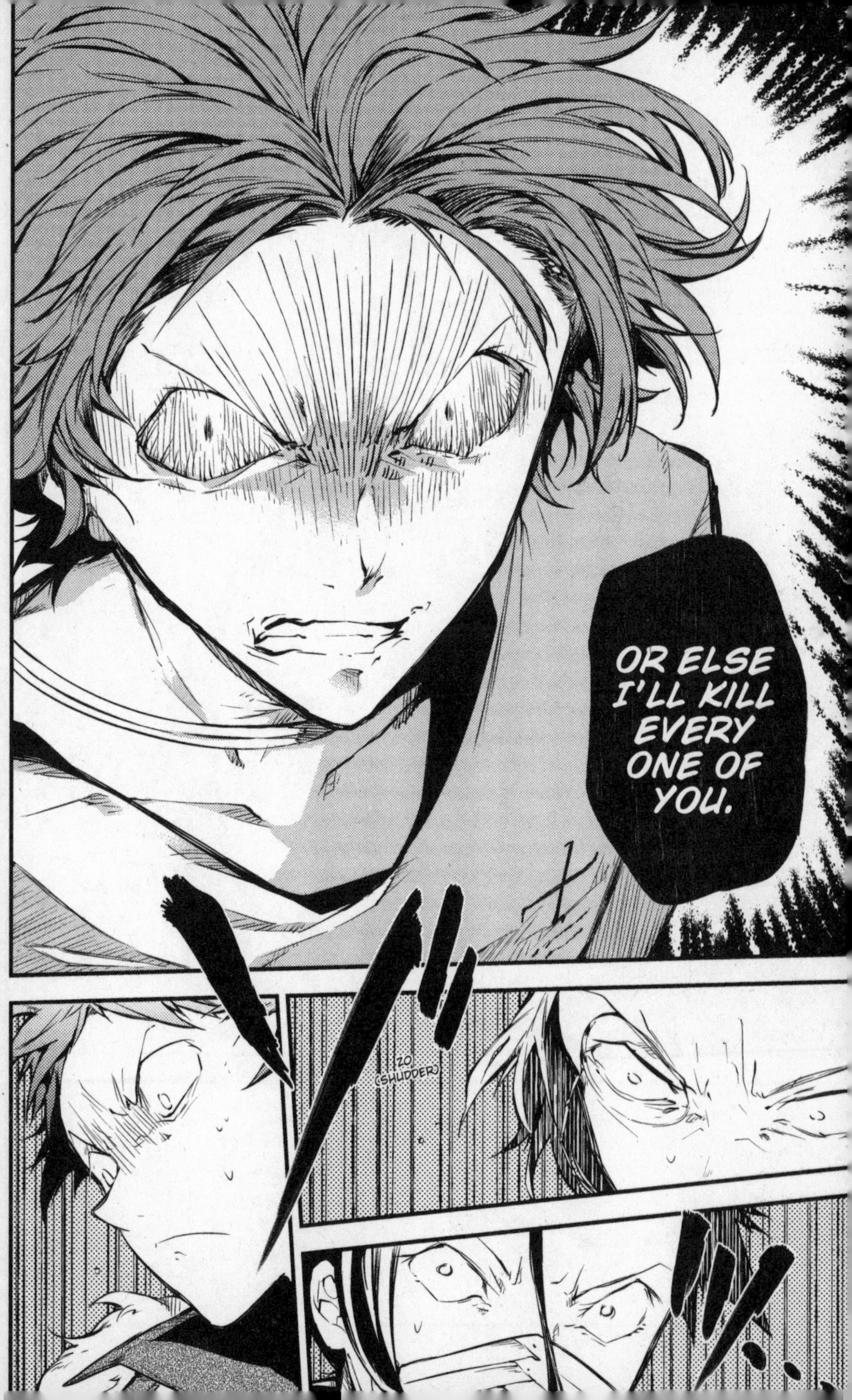
OR ELSE I'LL KILL EVERY ONE OF YOU.
ZO (SHUDDER)

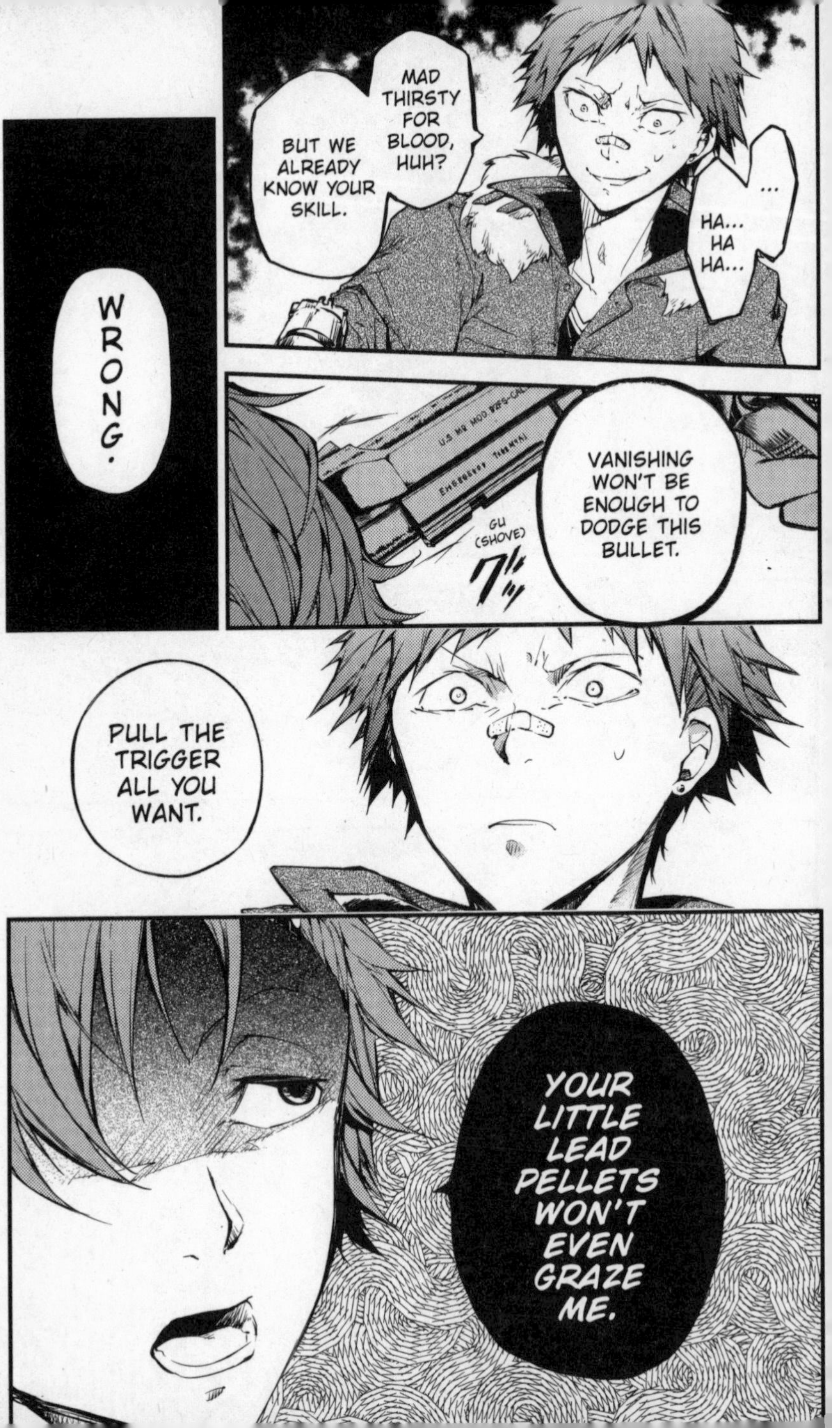
... HA... HA HA...
MAD THIRSTY FOR BLOOD, HUH?
BUT WE ALREADY KNOW YOUR SKILL.
VANISHING WON'T BE ENOUGH TO DODGE THIS BULLET.
GU (SHOVE)
WRONG.
PULL THE TRIGGER ALL YOU WANT.
YOUR LITTLE LEAD PELLETS WON'T EVEN GRAZE ME.

YOU TOOK THAT AS AN EMPTY THREAT?

FIRE AWAY.

KACHI (CLICK)

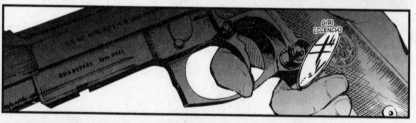

GIRI (CLENCH)

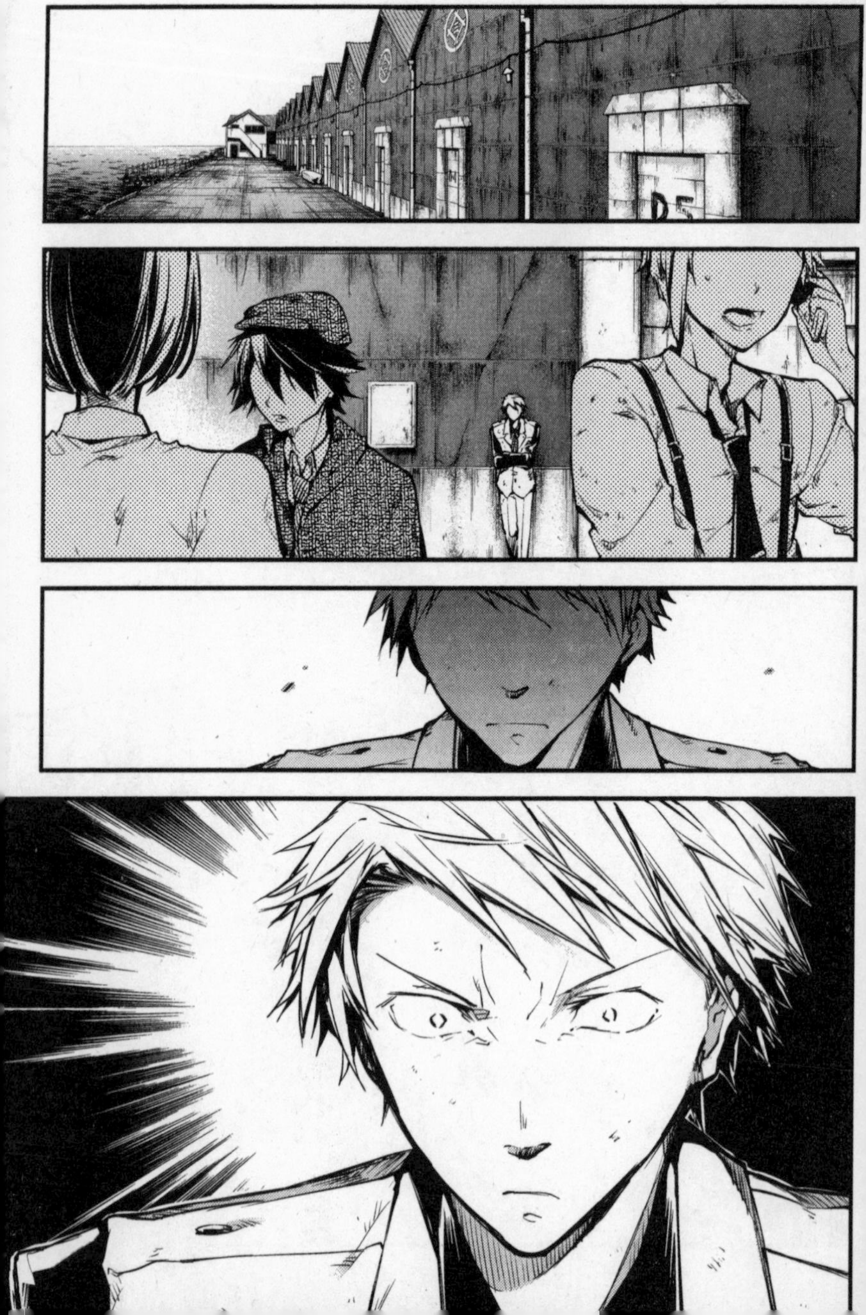

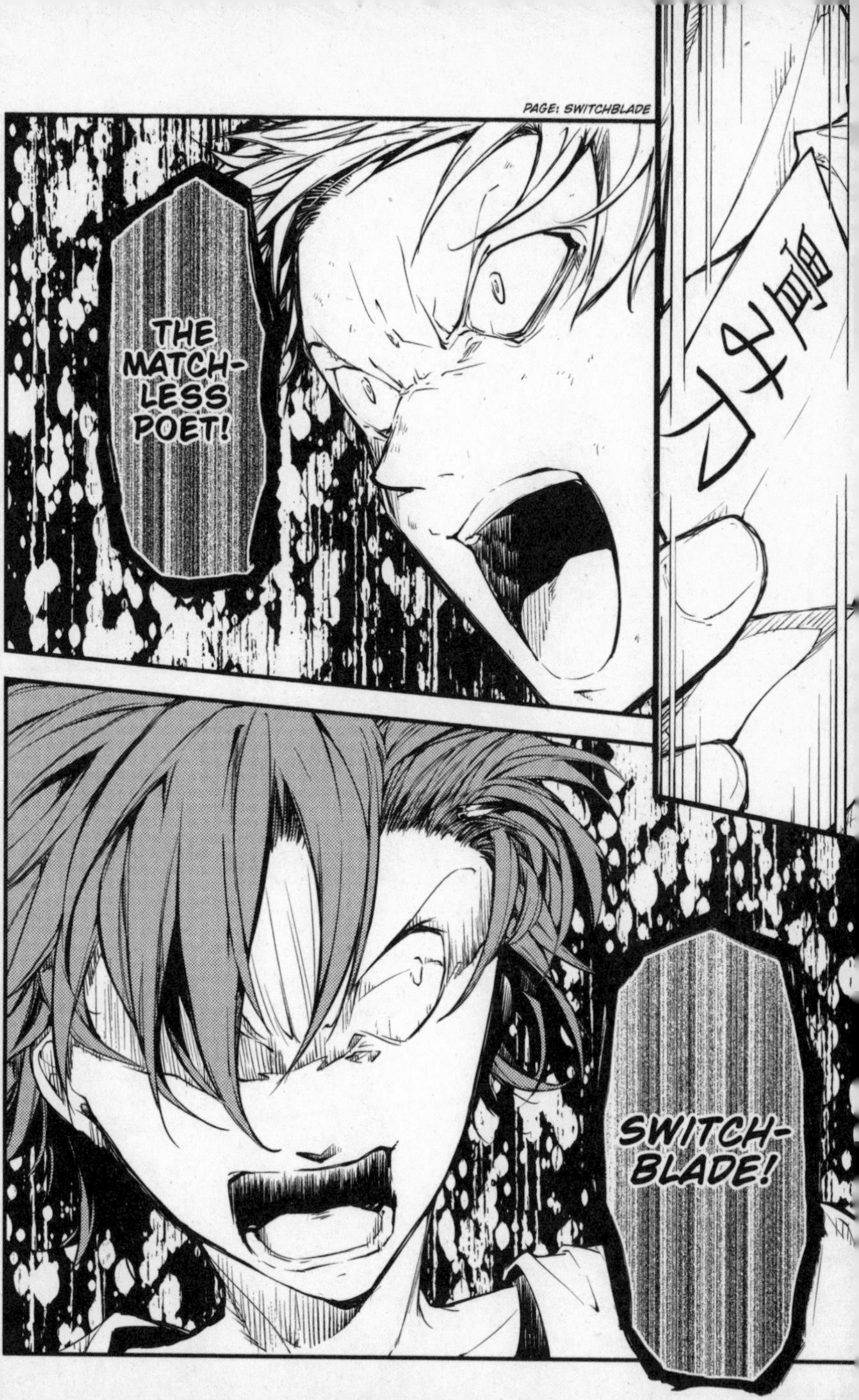
PAGE: SWITCHBLADE
THE MATCH-LESS POET!
SWITCH-BLADE!

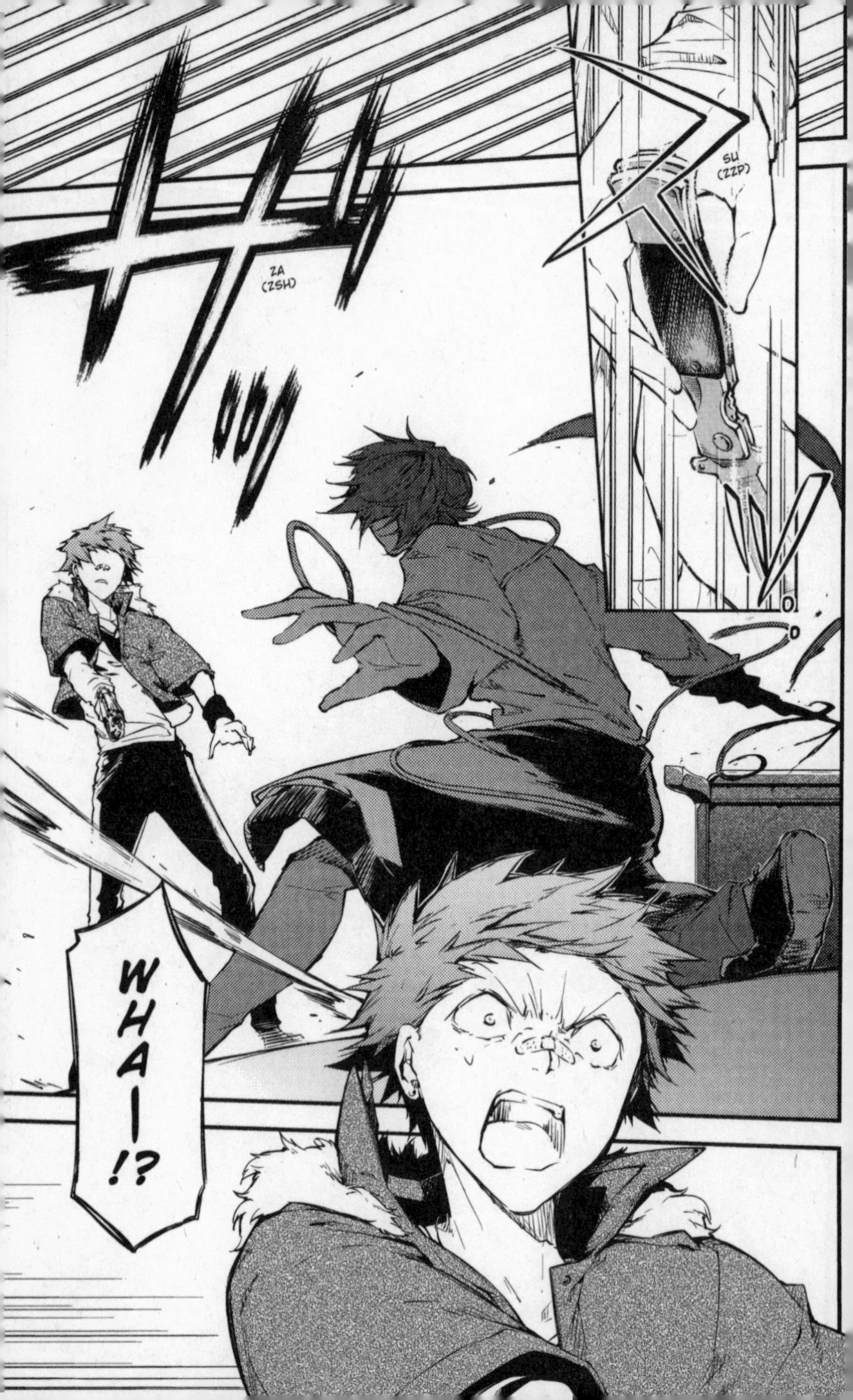
SU
(ZZP)
ZA
(ZSH)
WHA-!?

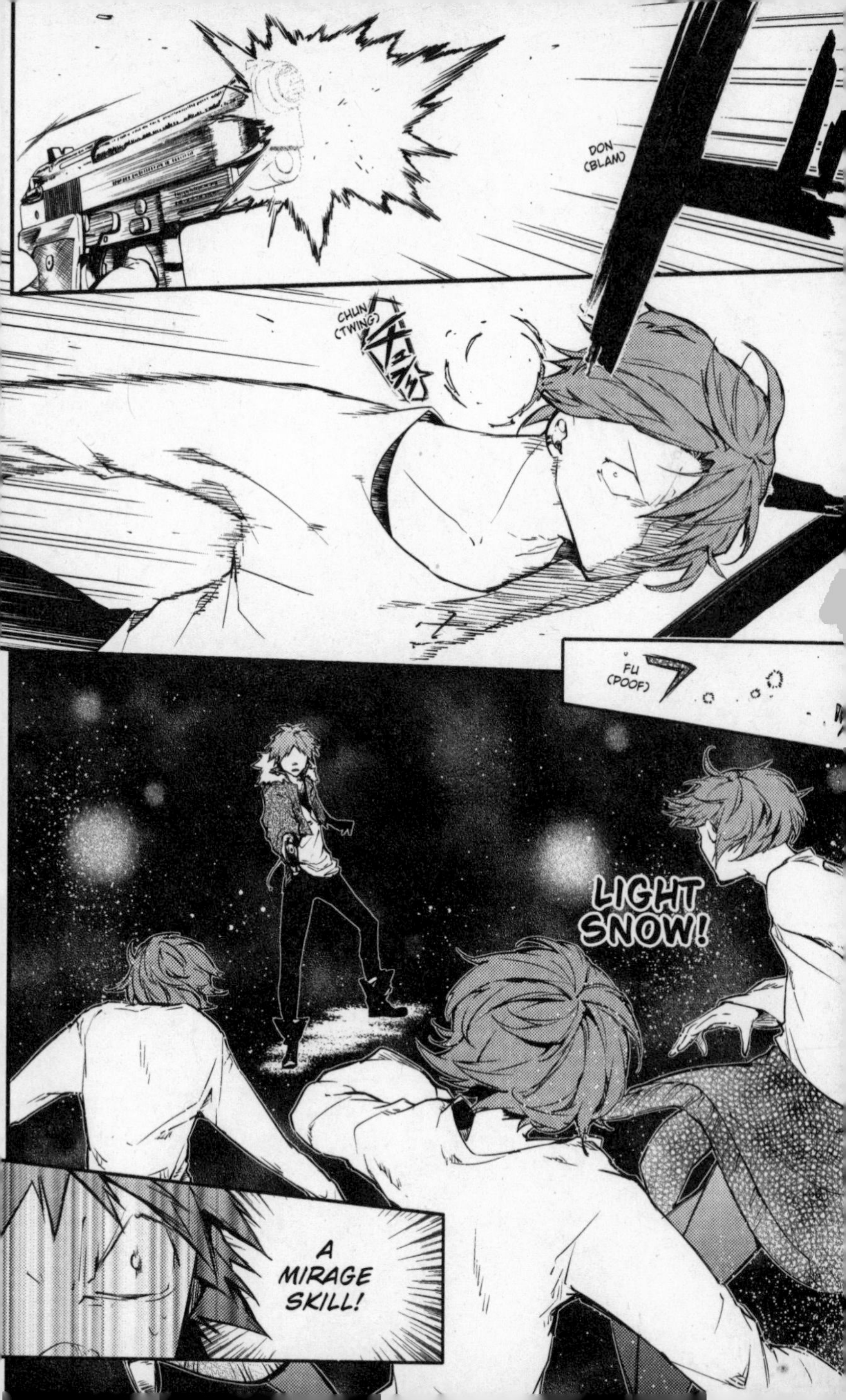
DON (BLAM)
CHUN (TWING)
FU (POOF)
LIGHT SNOW!
A MIRAGE SKILL!

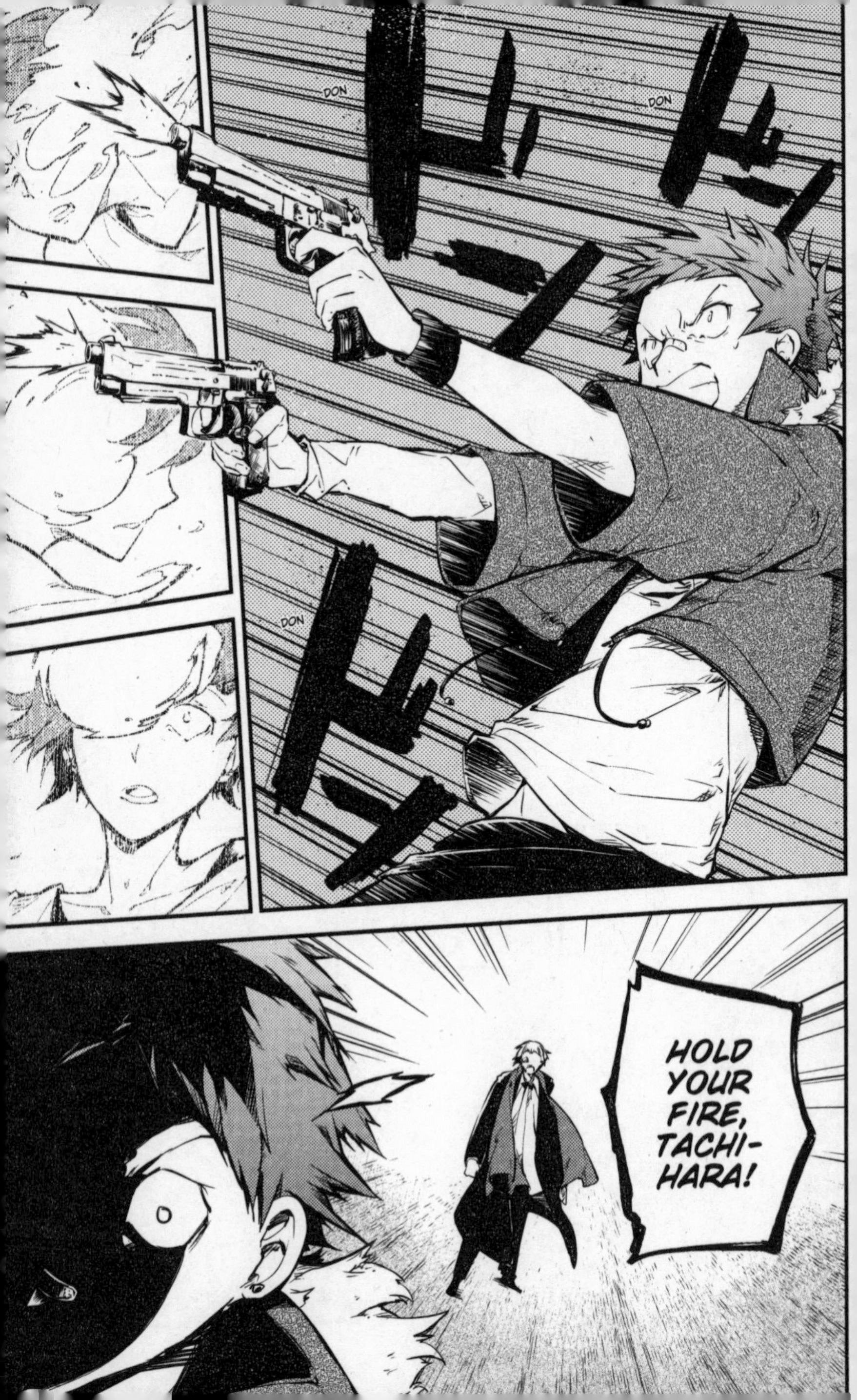
DON
DON
DON
HOLD YOUR FIRE, TACHI-HARA!

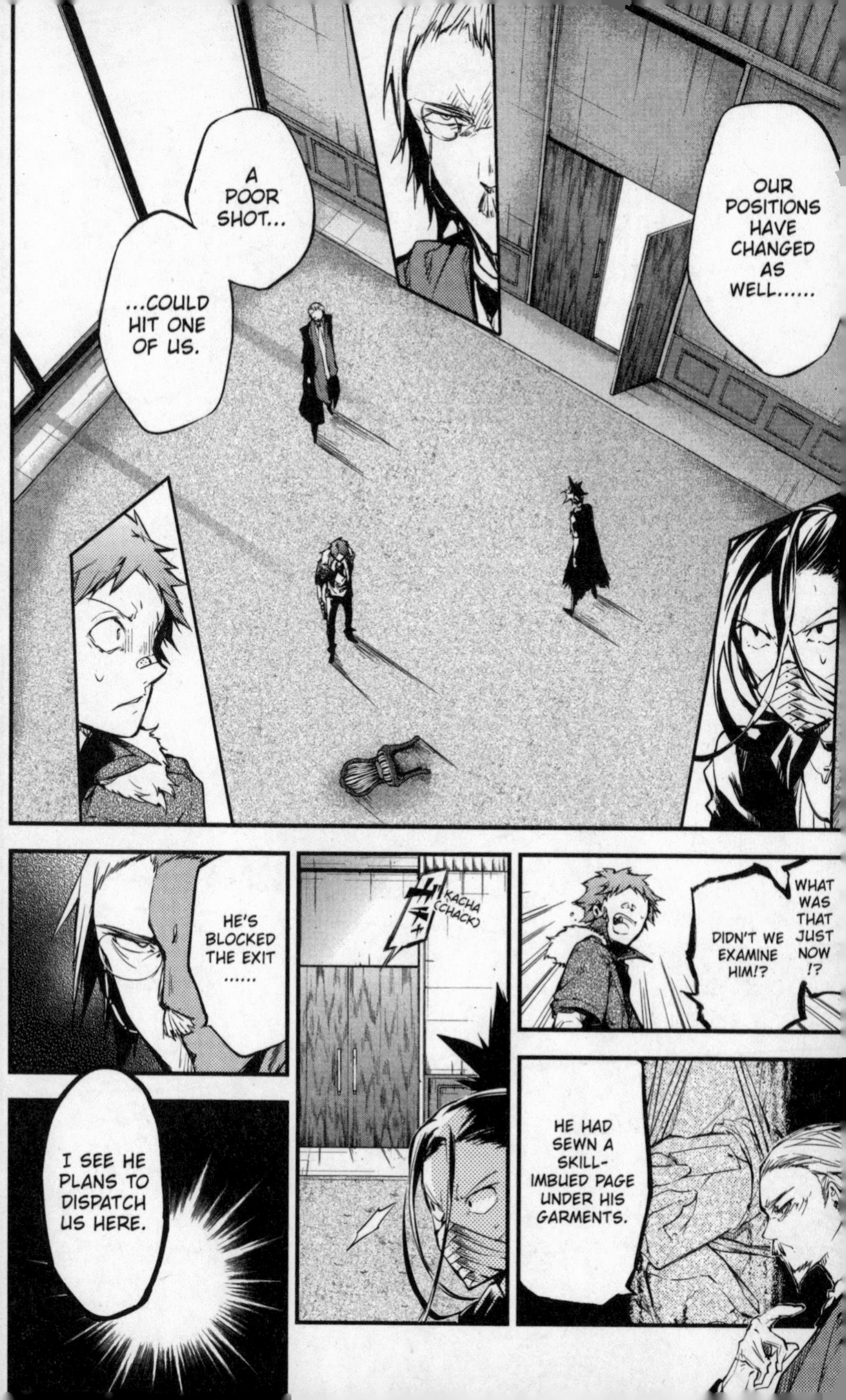
OUR POSITIONS HAVE CHANGED AS WELL......
A POOR SHOT...
...COULD HIT ONE OF US.
WHAT WAS THAT JUST NOW!?
DIDN'T WE EXAMINE HIM!?
HE HAD SEWN A SKILL-IMBUED PAGE UNDER HIS GARMENTS.
KACHA (CHACK)
HE'S BLOCKED THE EXIT ......
I SEE HE PLANS TO DISPATCH US HERE.

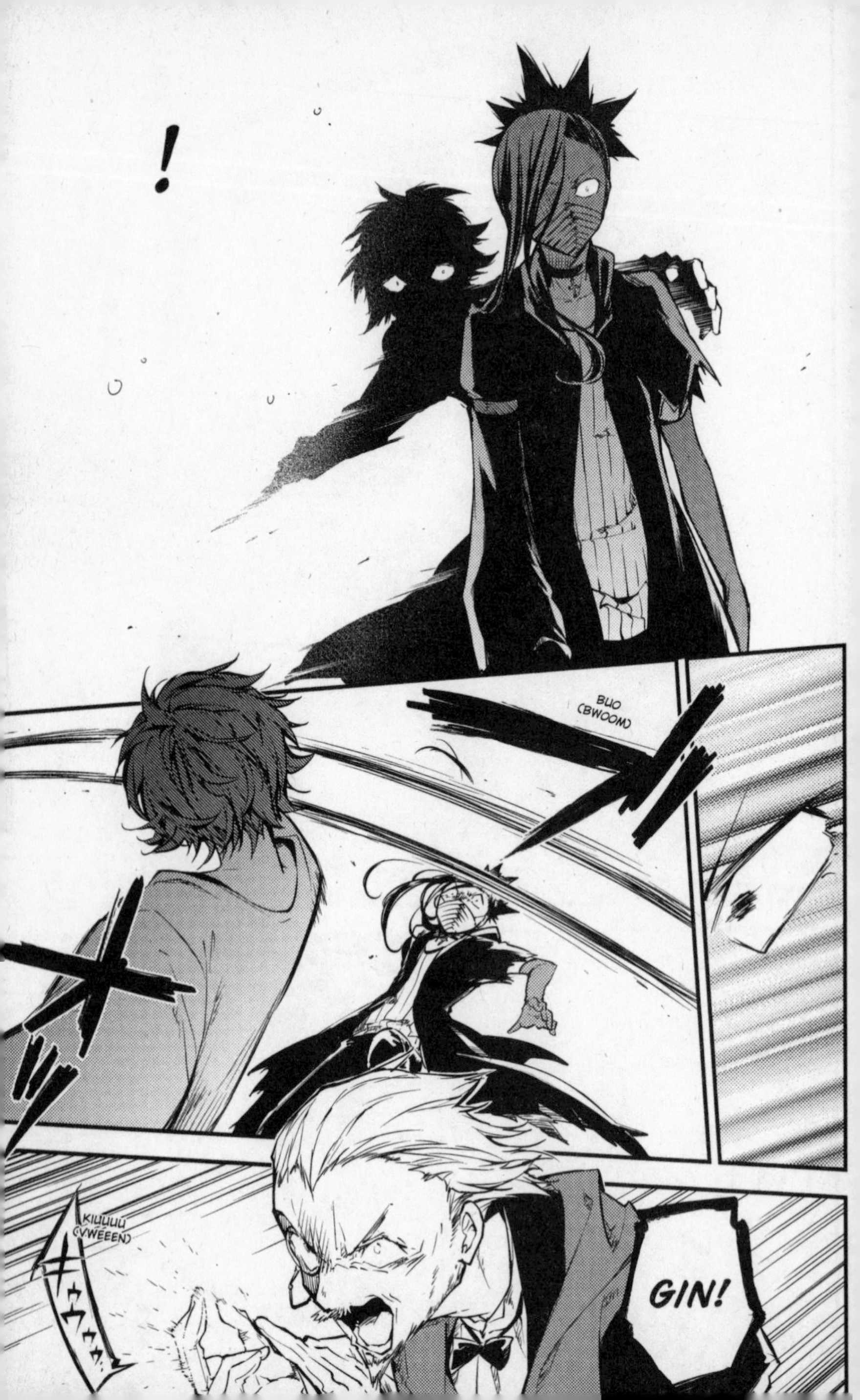
!
BUO
(BWOOM)
GIN!
KIUUUU
(VWEEEN)

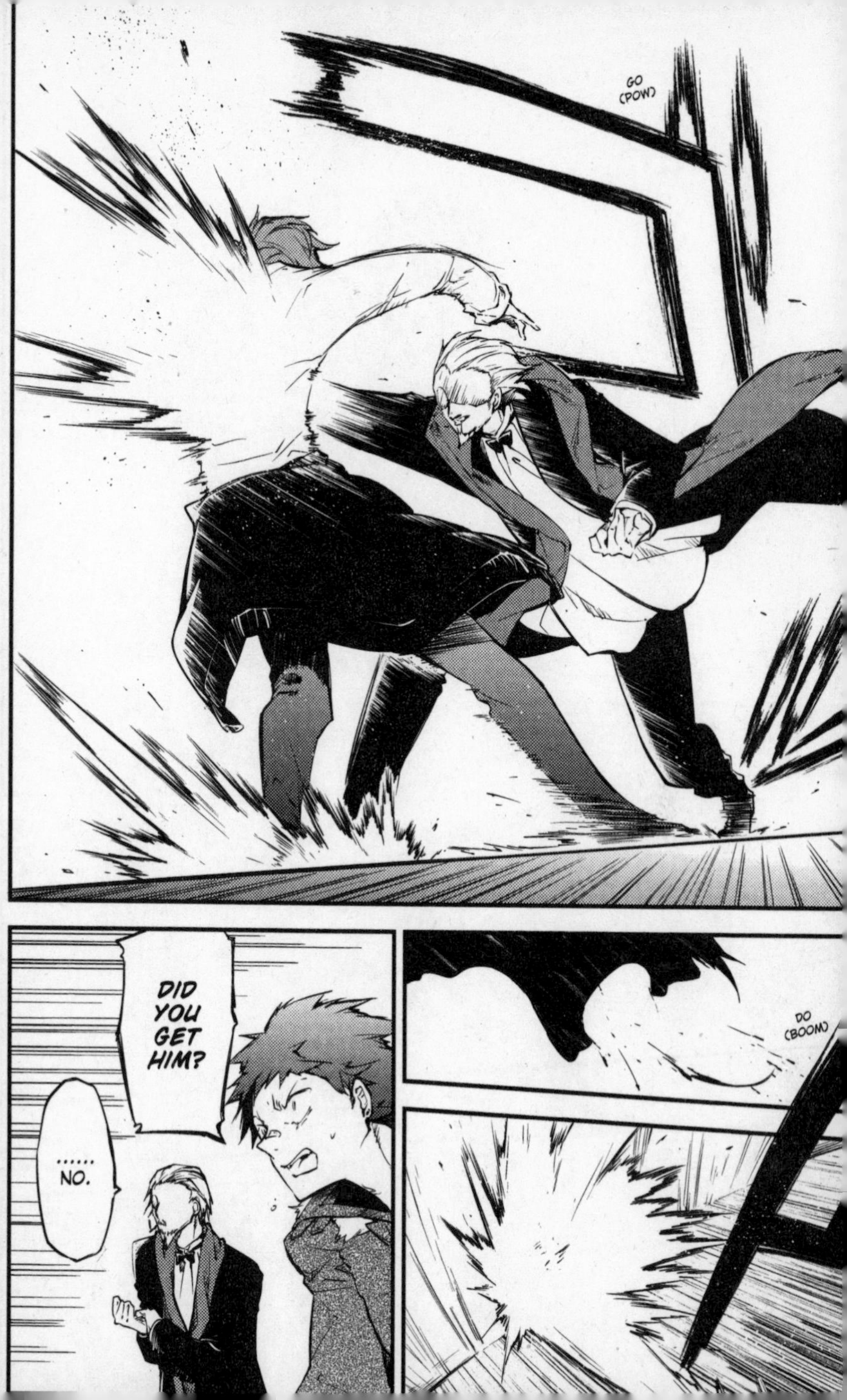
GO (POW)
DO (BOOM)
DID YOU GET HIM?
...... NO.

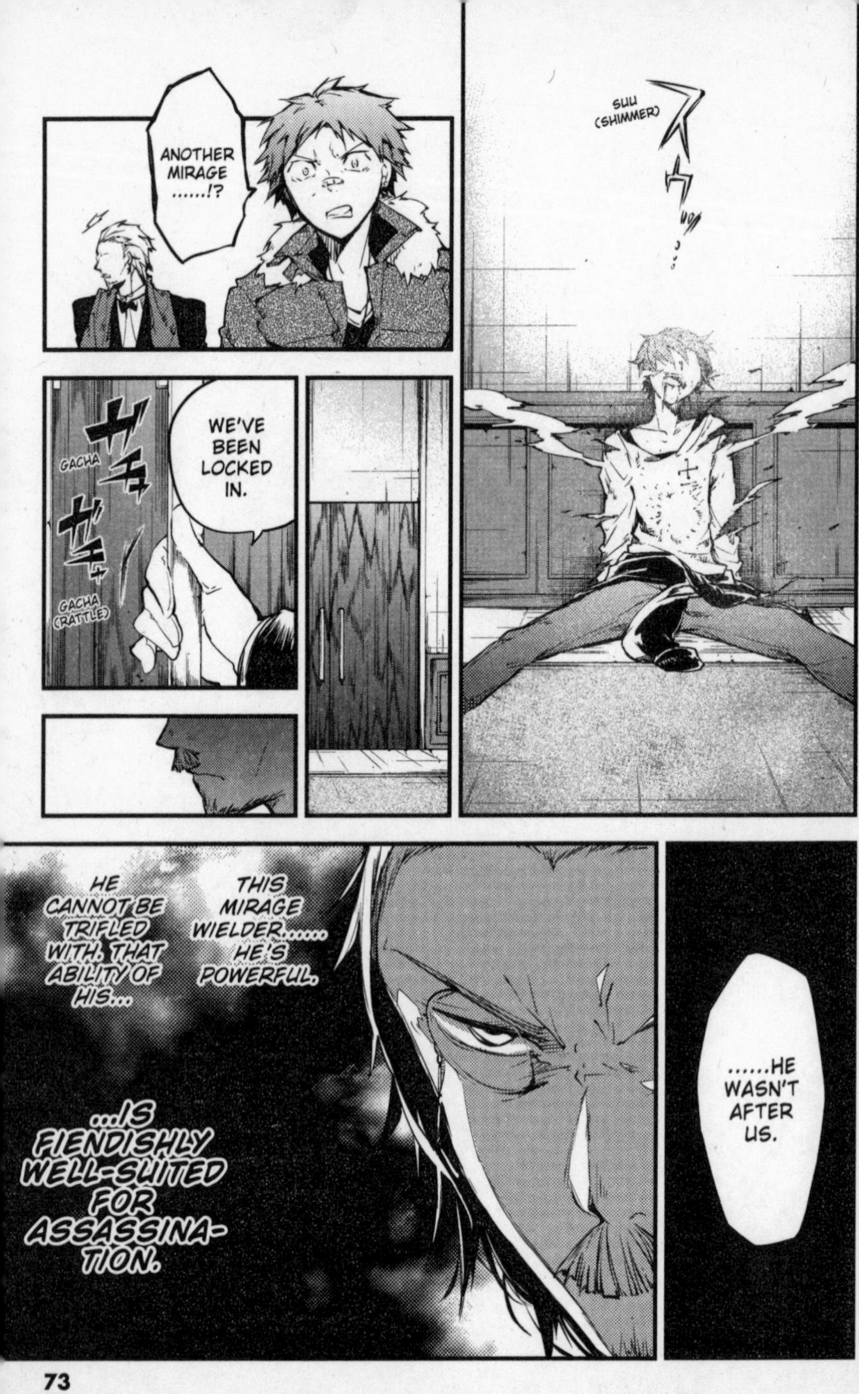
SUU (SHIMMER)
ANOTHER MIRAGE ......!?
GACHA
GACHA (RATTLE)
WE'VE BEEN LOCKED IN.
......HE WASN'T AFTER US.
THIS MIRAGE WIELDER...... HE'S POWERFUL.
HE CANNOT BE TRIFLED WITH. THAT ABILITY OF HIS...
...IS FIENDISHLY WELL-SUITED FOR ASSASSINATION.

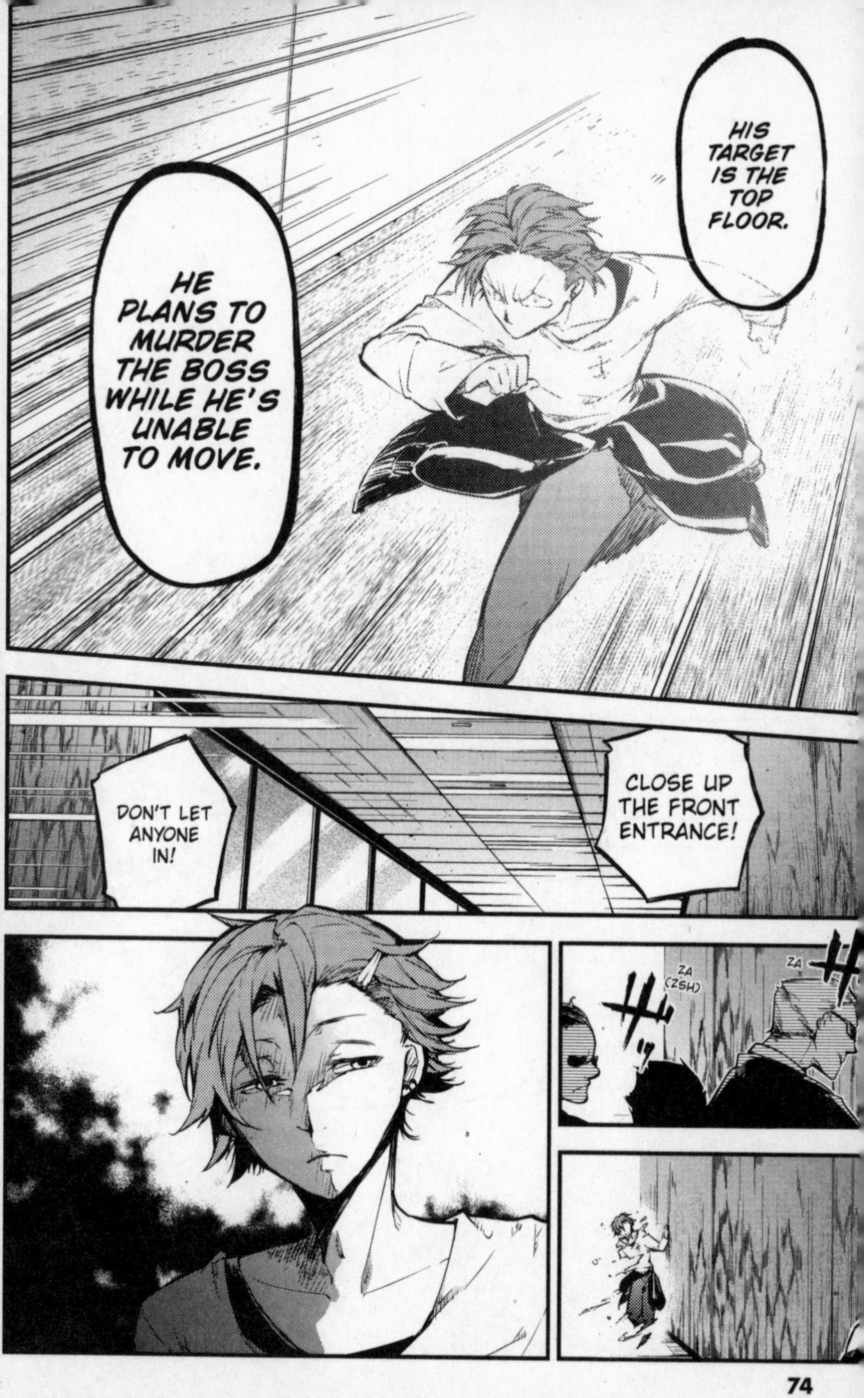
HIS TARGET IS THE TOP FLOOR.
HE PLANS TO MURDER THE BOSS WHILE HE'S UNABLE TO MOVE.
CLOSE UP THE FRONT ENTRANCE!
DON'T LET ANYONE IN!
ZA
ZA (ZSH)

FOR THE BATTLE TO END...

...THIS IS OUR ONLY OPTION.

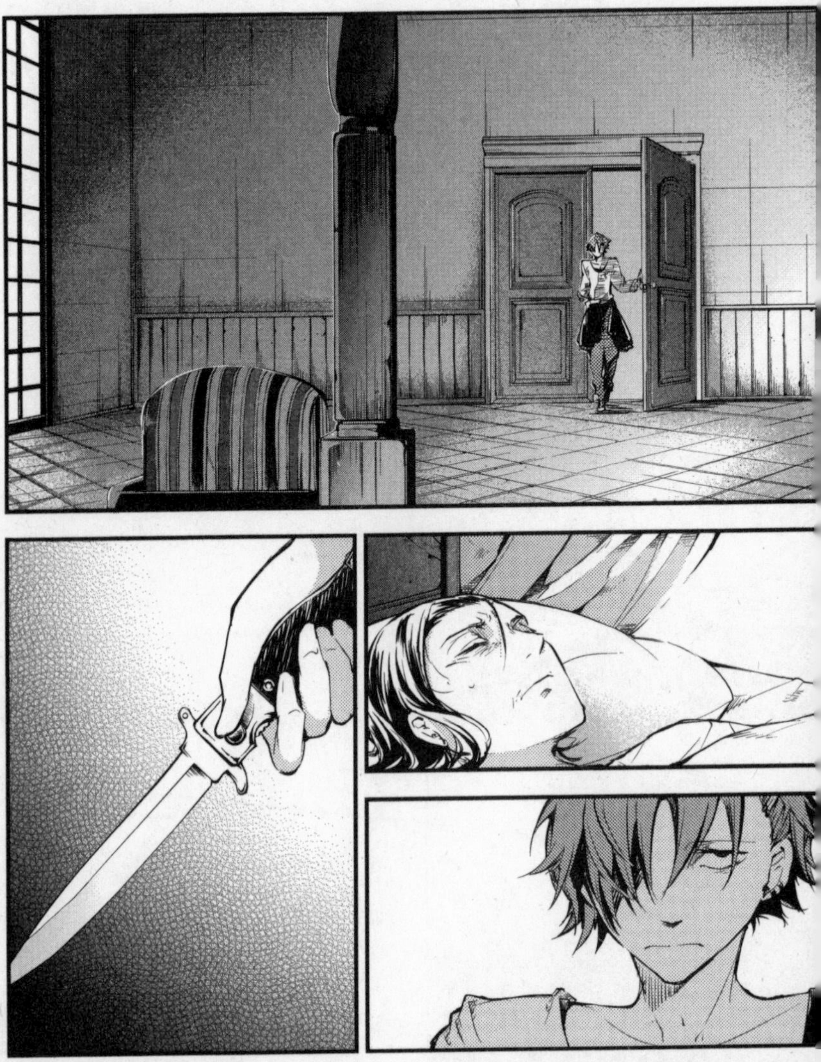

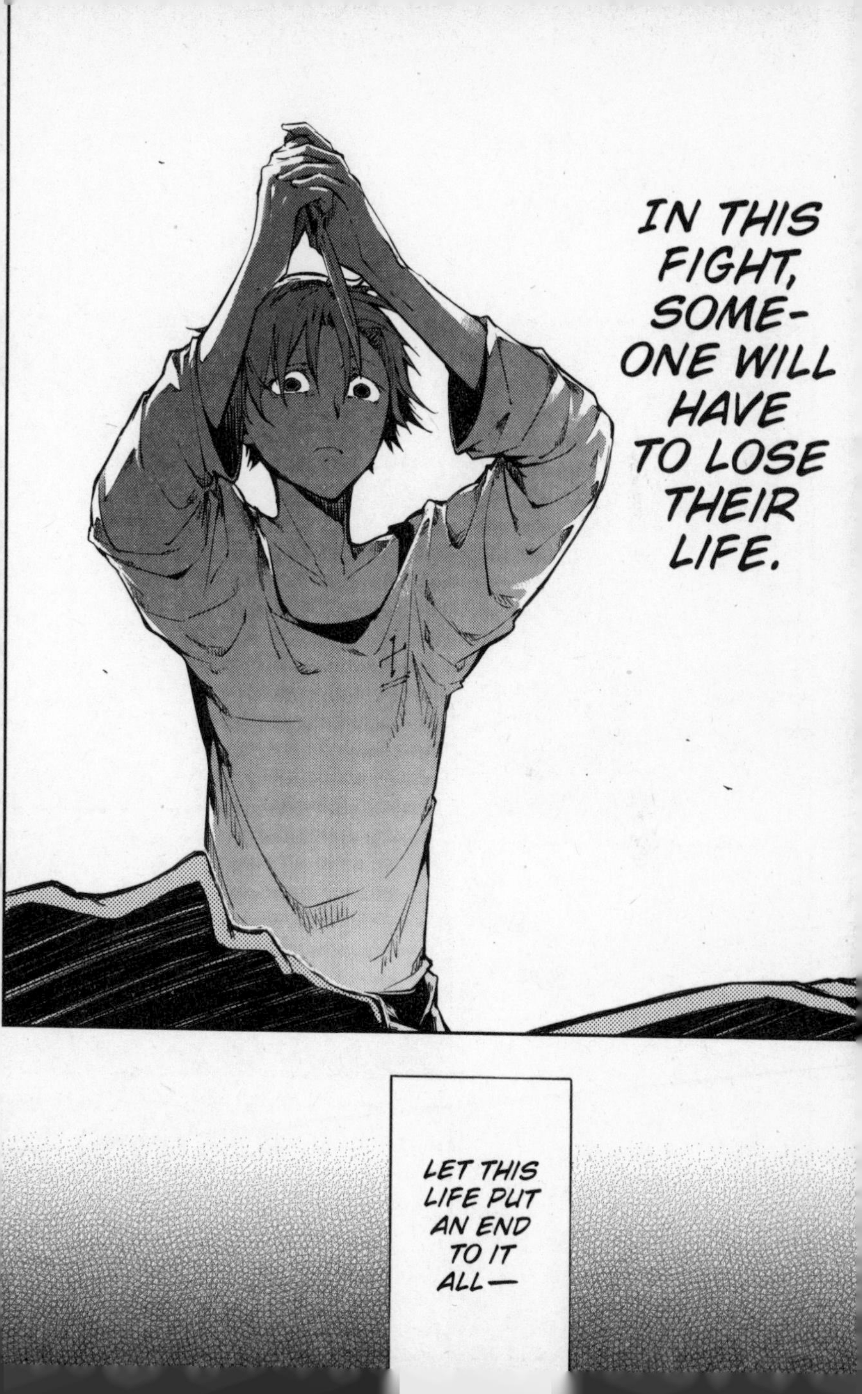
IN THIS FIGHT, SOME-ONE WILL HAVE TO LOSE THEIR LIFE.
LET THIS LIFE PUT AN END TO IT ALL—

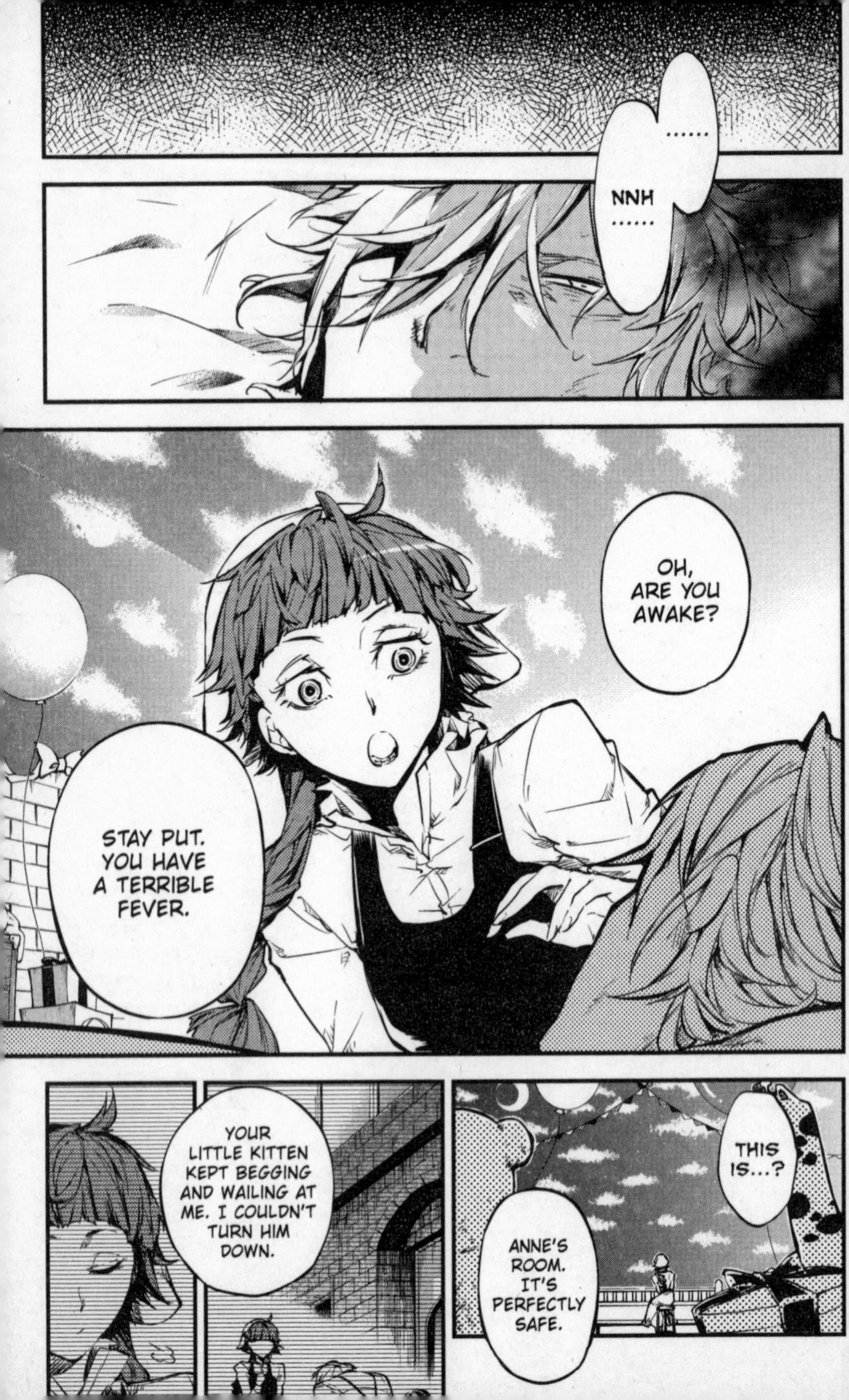
......
NNH ......
OH, ARE YOU AWAKE?
STAY PUT. YOU HAVE A TERRIBLE FEVER.
THIS IS...?
ANNE'S ROOM. IT'S PERFECTLY SAFE.
YOUR LITTLE KITTEN KEPT BEGGING AND WAILING AT ME. I COULDN'T TURN HIM DOWN.

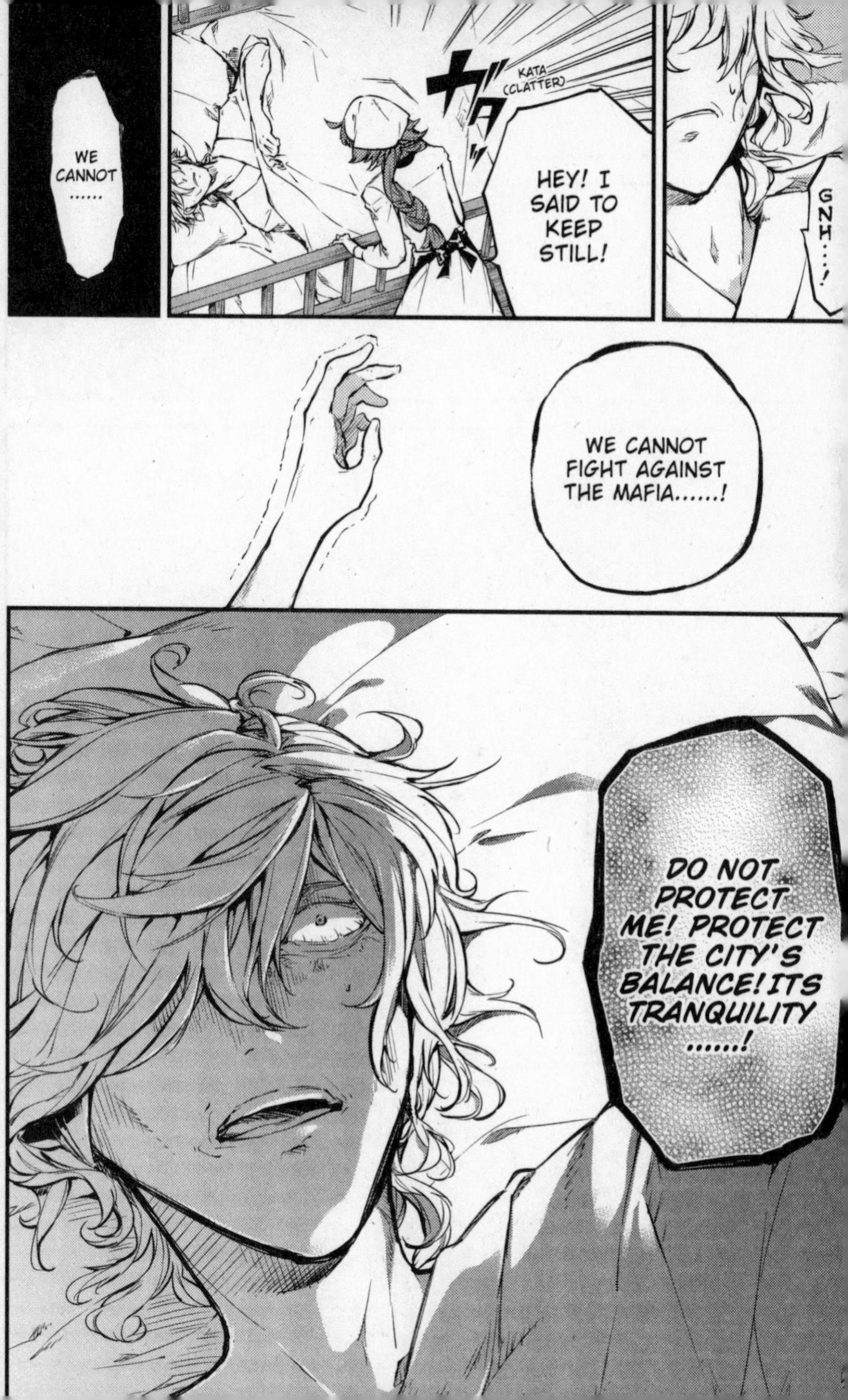
GNH...!
KATA (CLATTER)
HEY! I SAID TO KEEP STILL!
WE CANNOT ......
WE CANNOT FIGHT AGAINST THE MAFIA......!
DO NOT PROTECT ME! PROTECT THE CITY'S BALANCE! ITS TRANQUILITY ......!

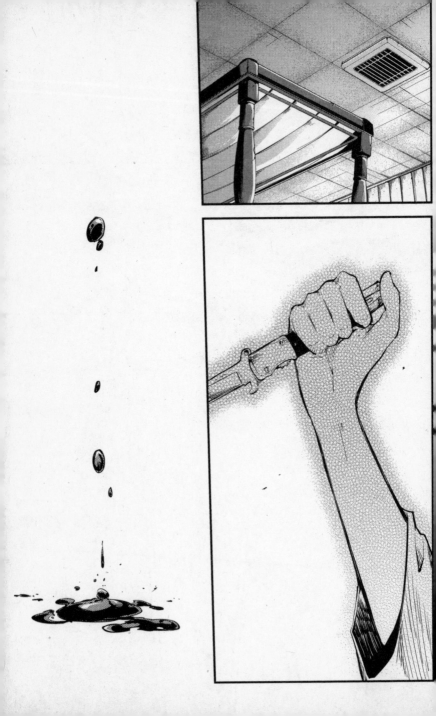

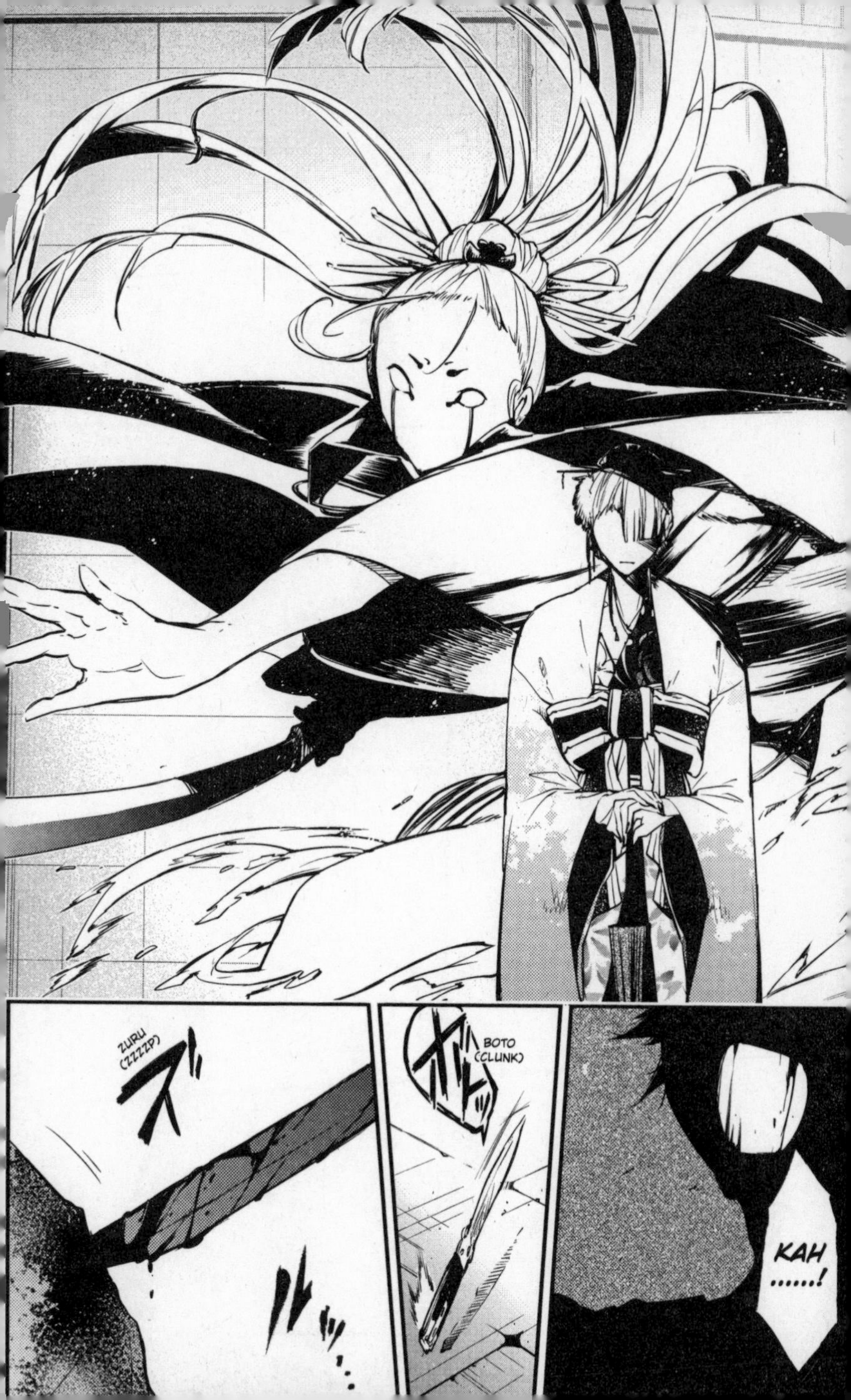
KAH ......!
BOTO (CLUNK)
ZURU (ZZZZP)

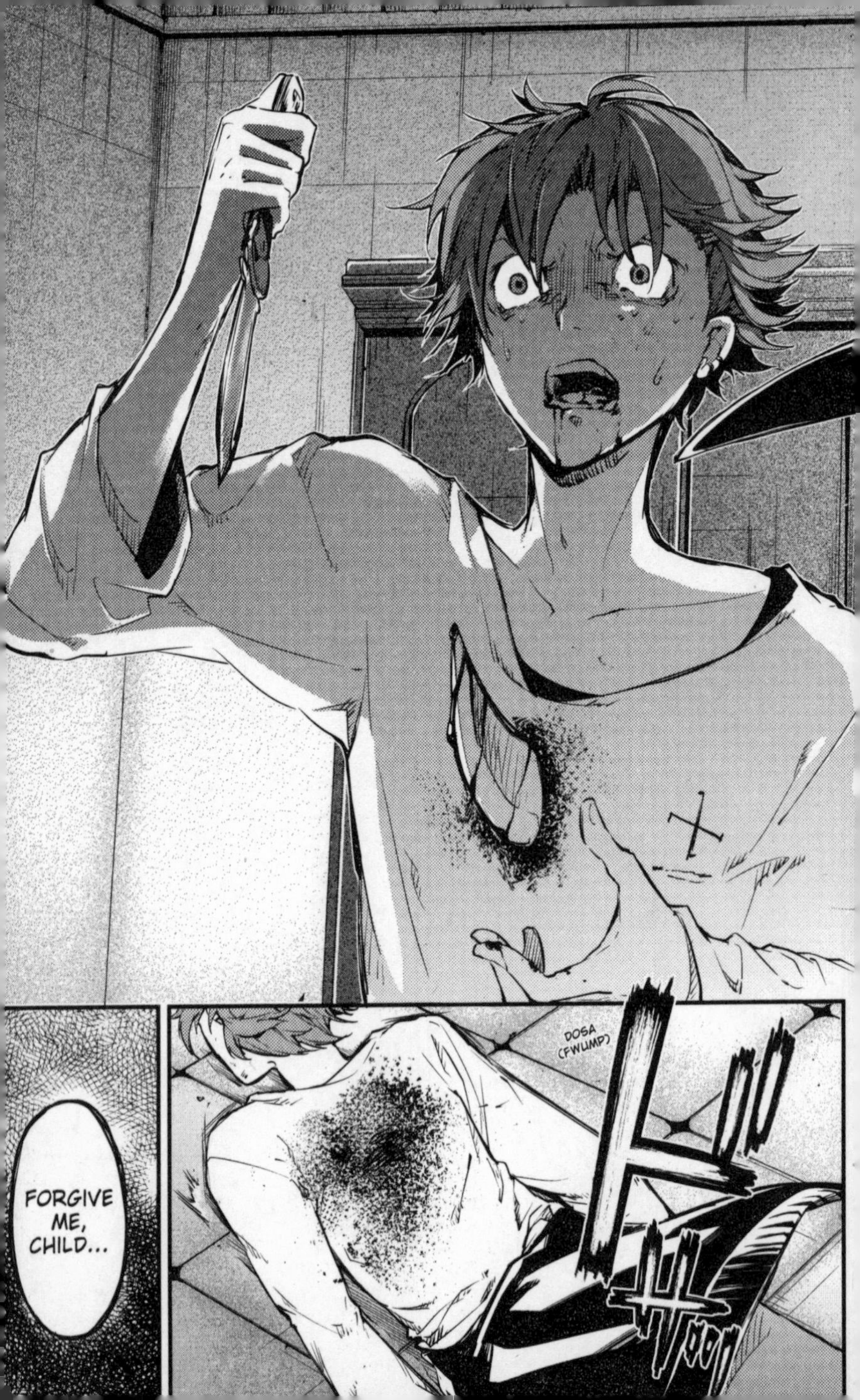
DOSA
(FWUMP)
FORGIVE ME, CHILD...

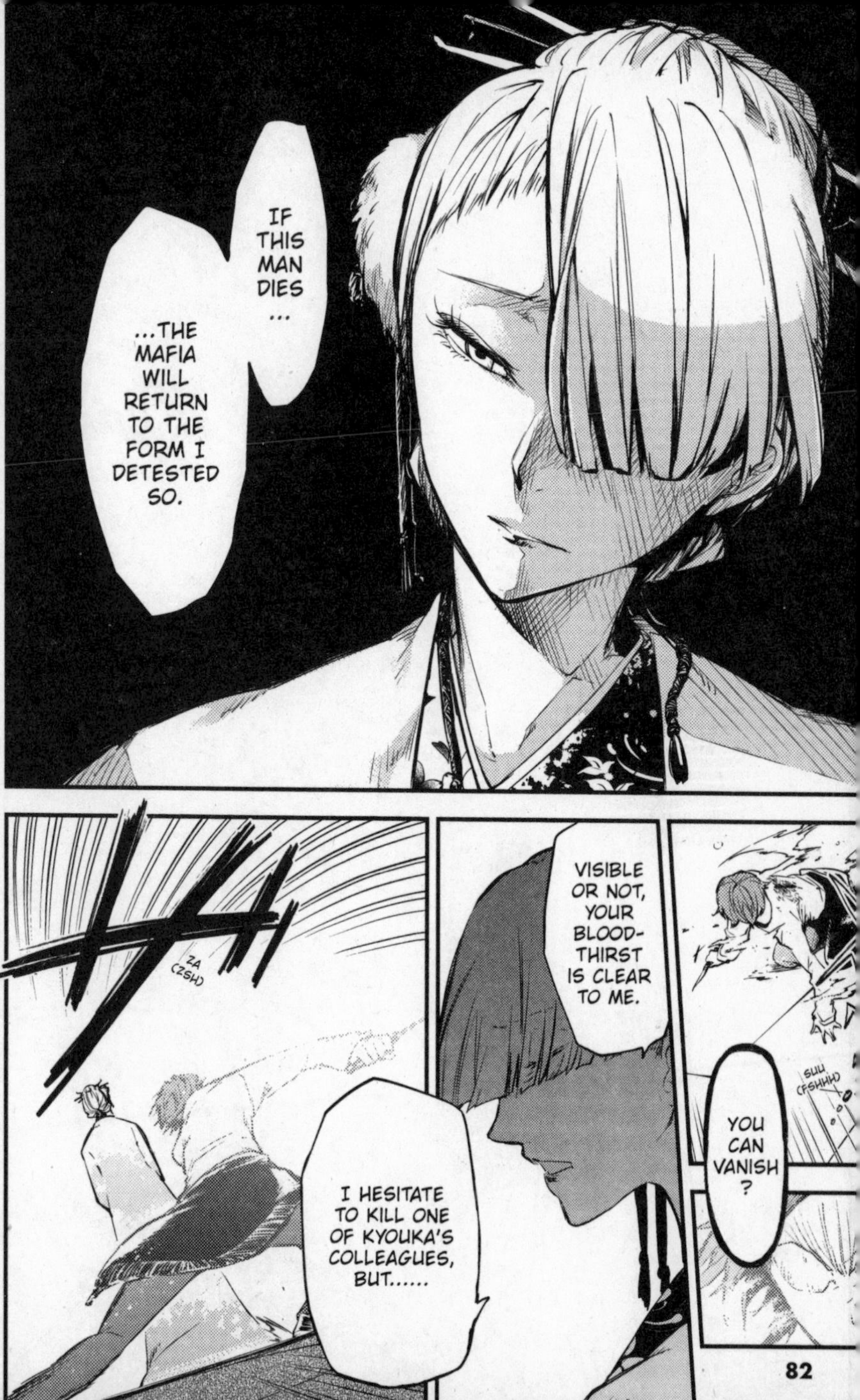
IF THIS MAN DIES...
...THE MAFIA WILL RETURN TO THE FORM I DETESTED SO.
SUU (FSHHH)
YOU CAN VANISH?
VISIBLE OR NOT, YOUR BLOOD-THIRST IS CLEAR TO ME.
I HESITATE TO KILL ONE OF KYOUKA'S COLLEAGUES, BUT......
ZA (ZSH)

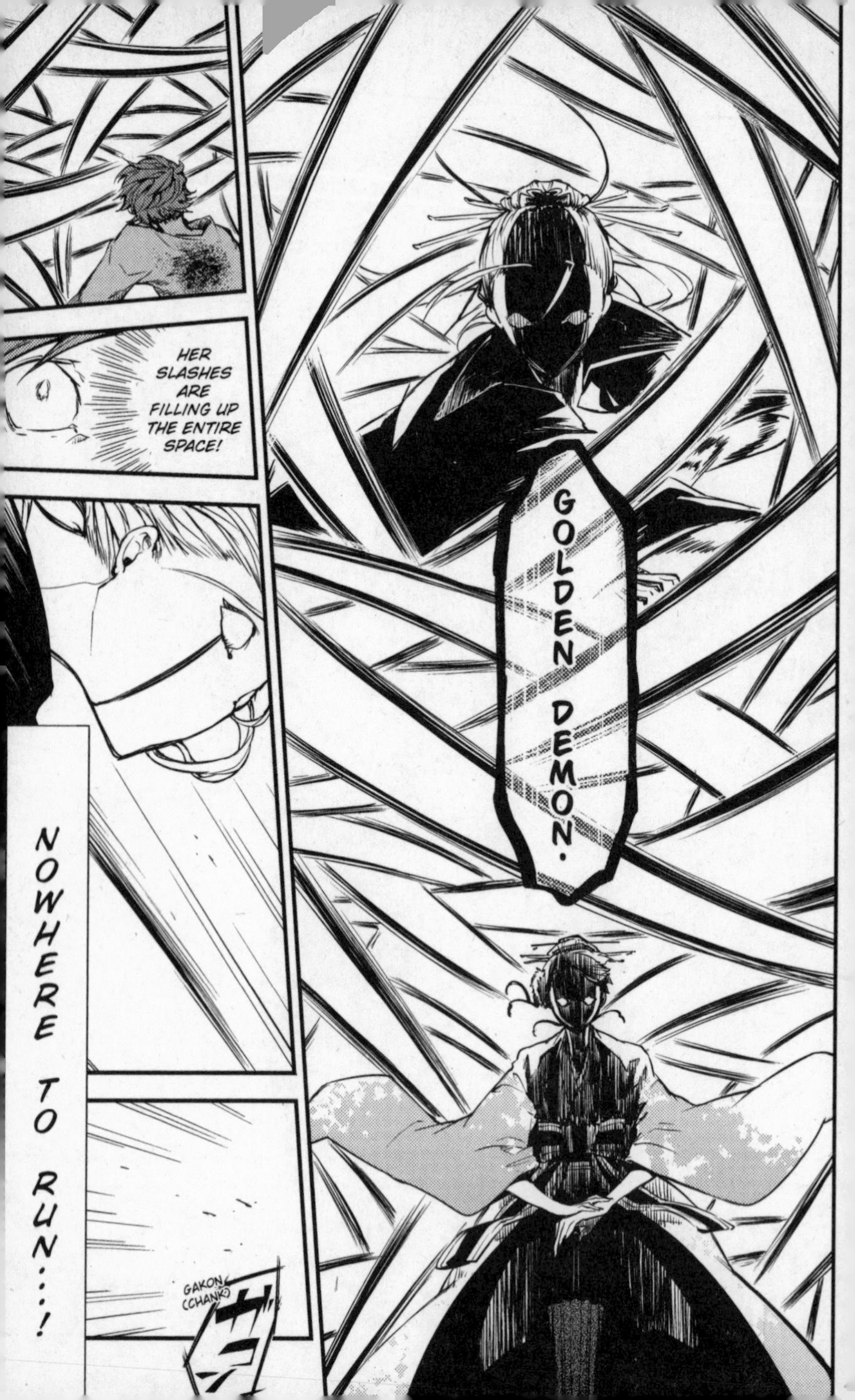
GOLDEN DEMON.
HER SLASHES ARE FILLING UP THE ENTIRE SPACE!
NOWHERE TO RUN...!
GAKON (CHANK)

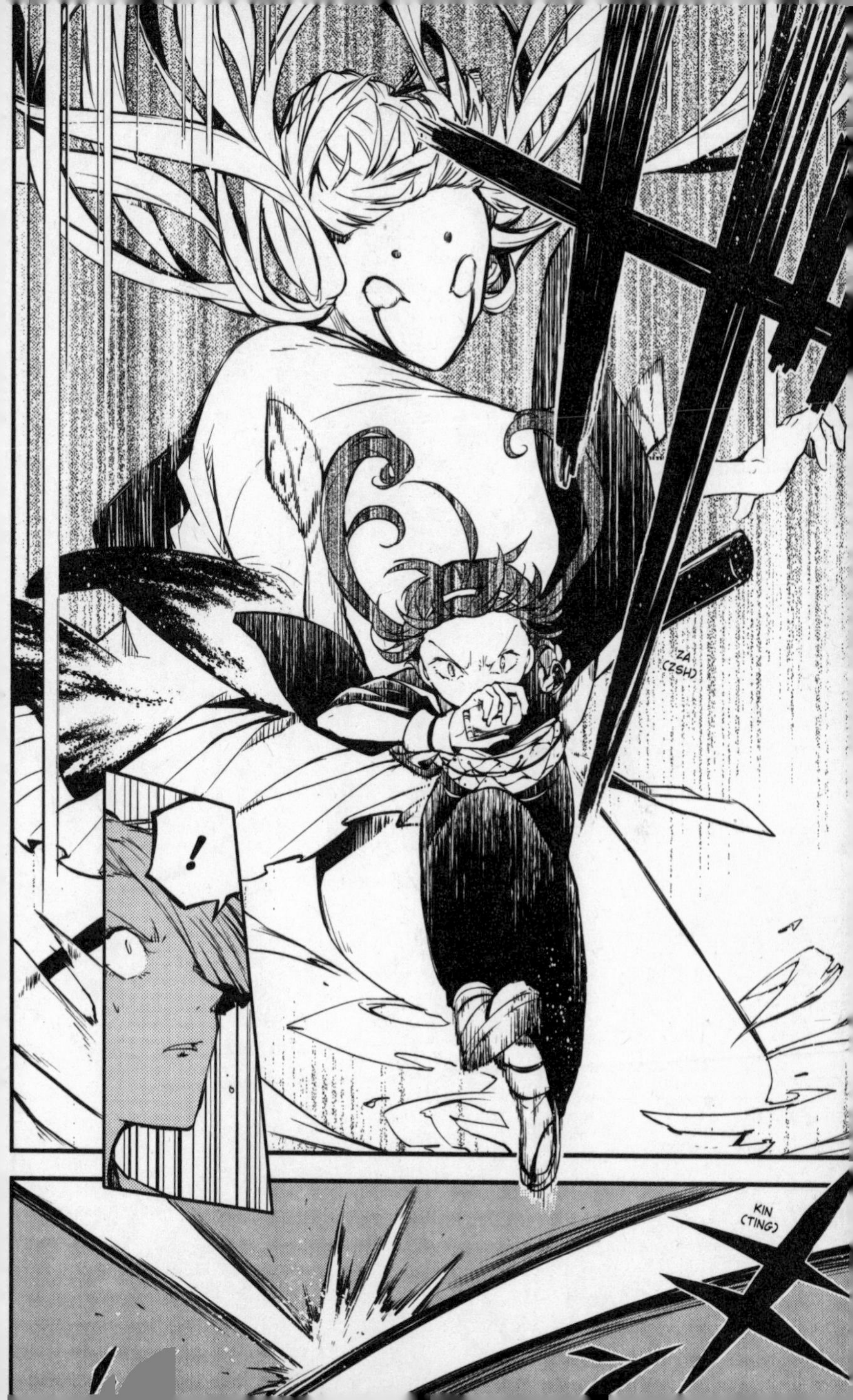
ZA
(ZSH)
!
KIN
(TING)

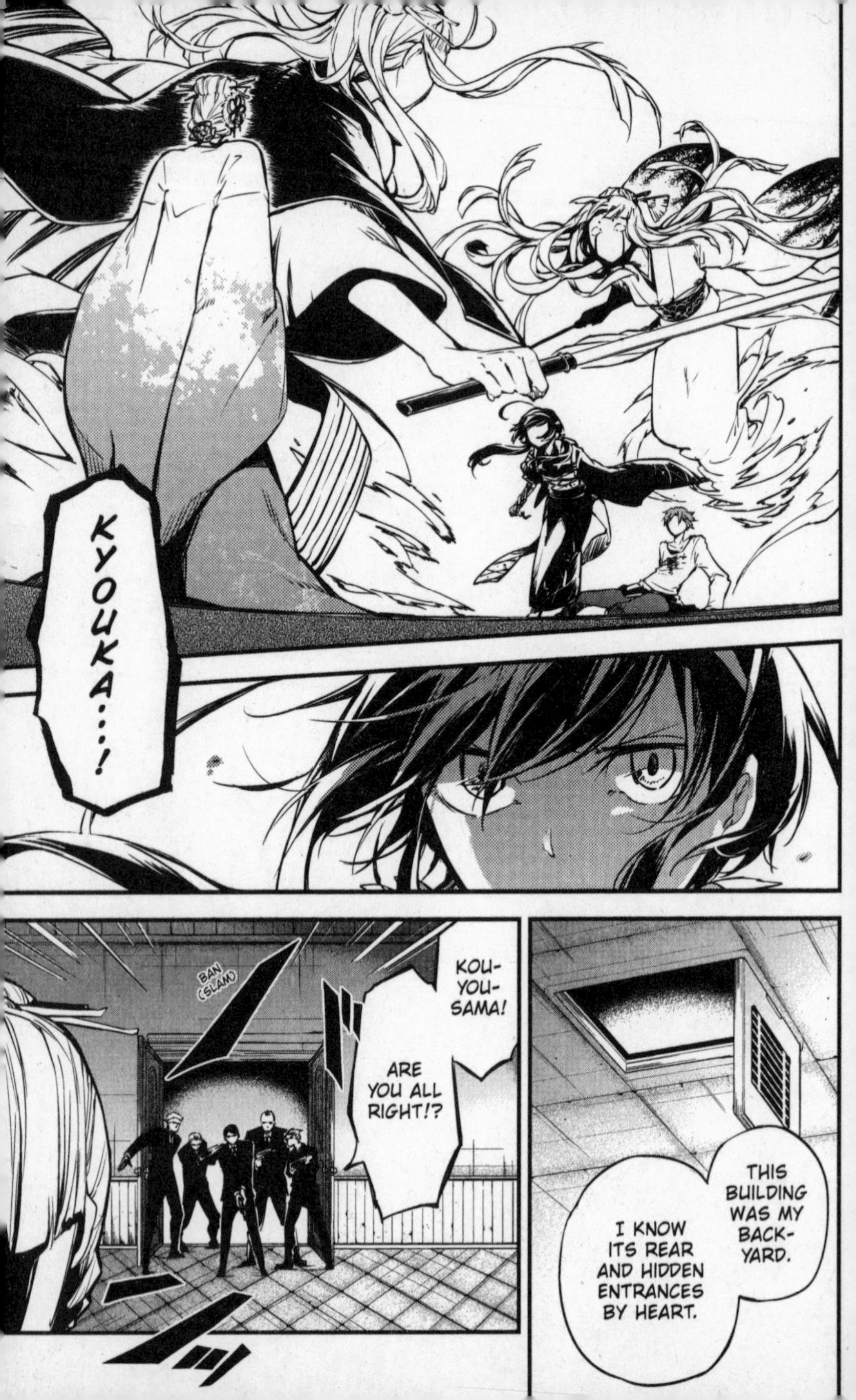
KYOUKA...!
THIS BUILDING WAS MY BACK-YARD.
I KNOW ITS REAR AND HIDDEN ENTRANCES BY HEART.
BAN (SLAM)
KOU-YOU-SAMA!
ARE YOU ALL RIGHT!?

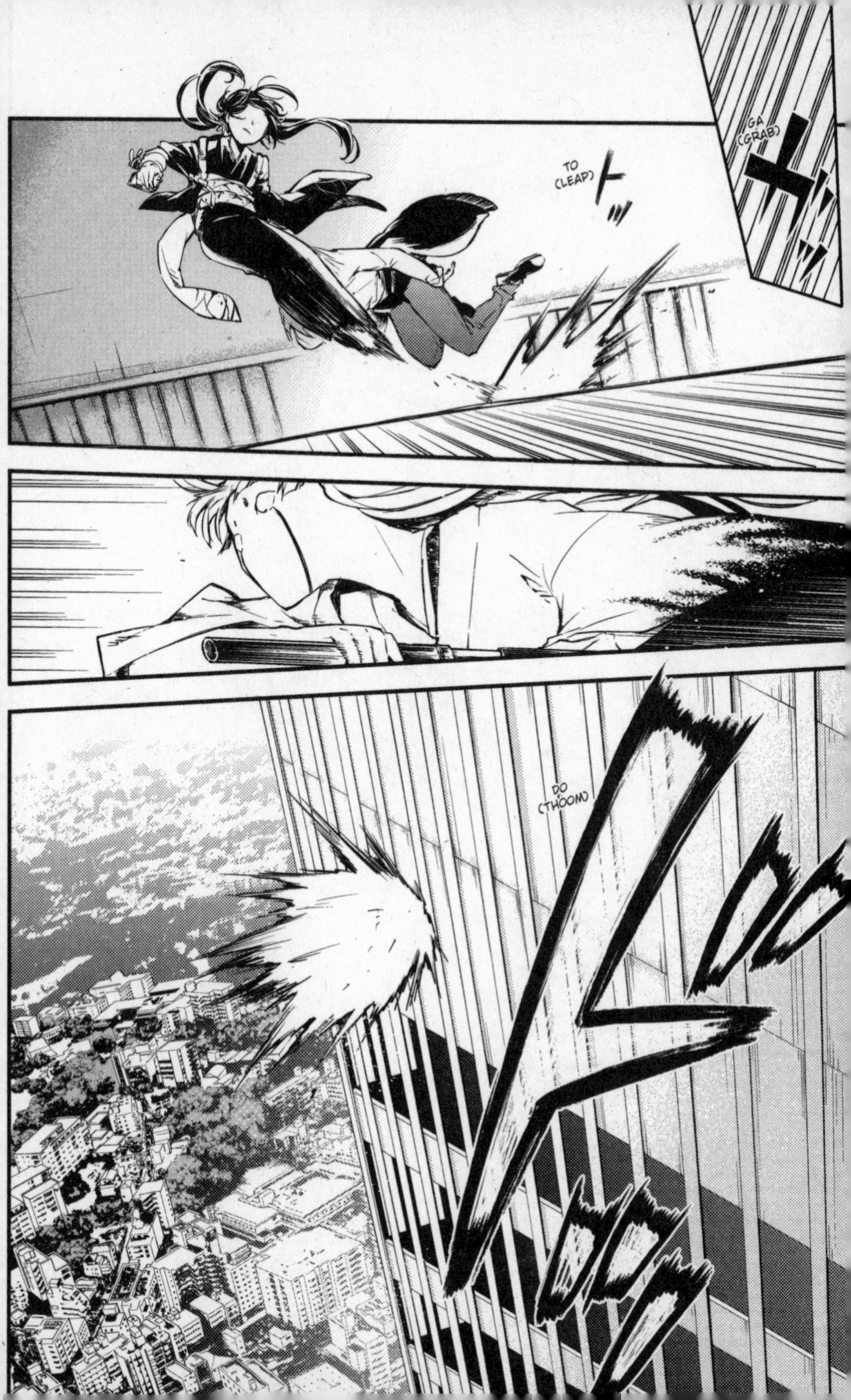
GA (GRAB)
TO (LEAP)
DO (THOOM)

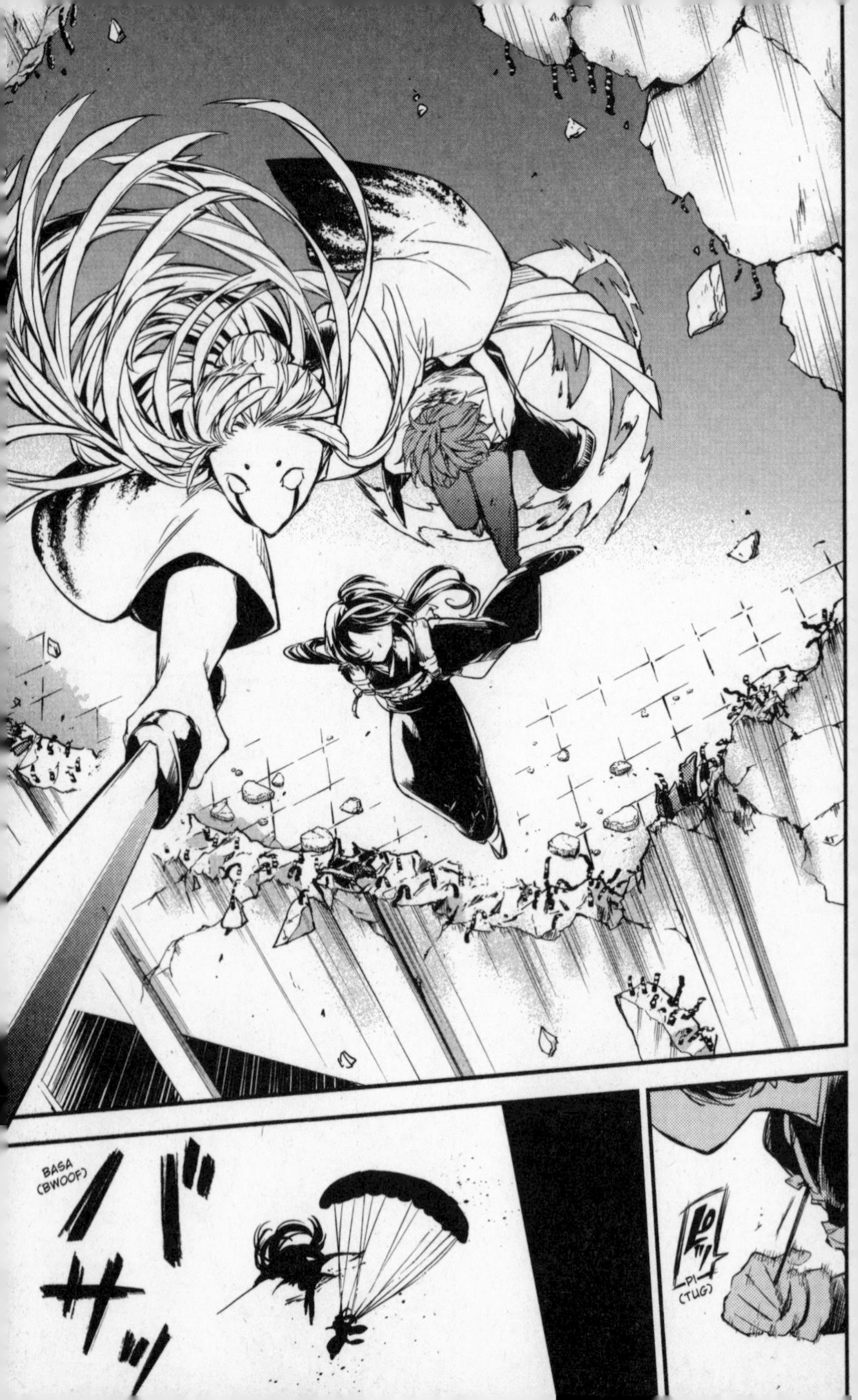
PI
(TUG)
BASA
(BWOOF)

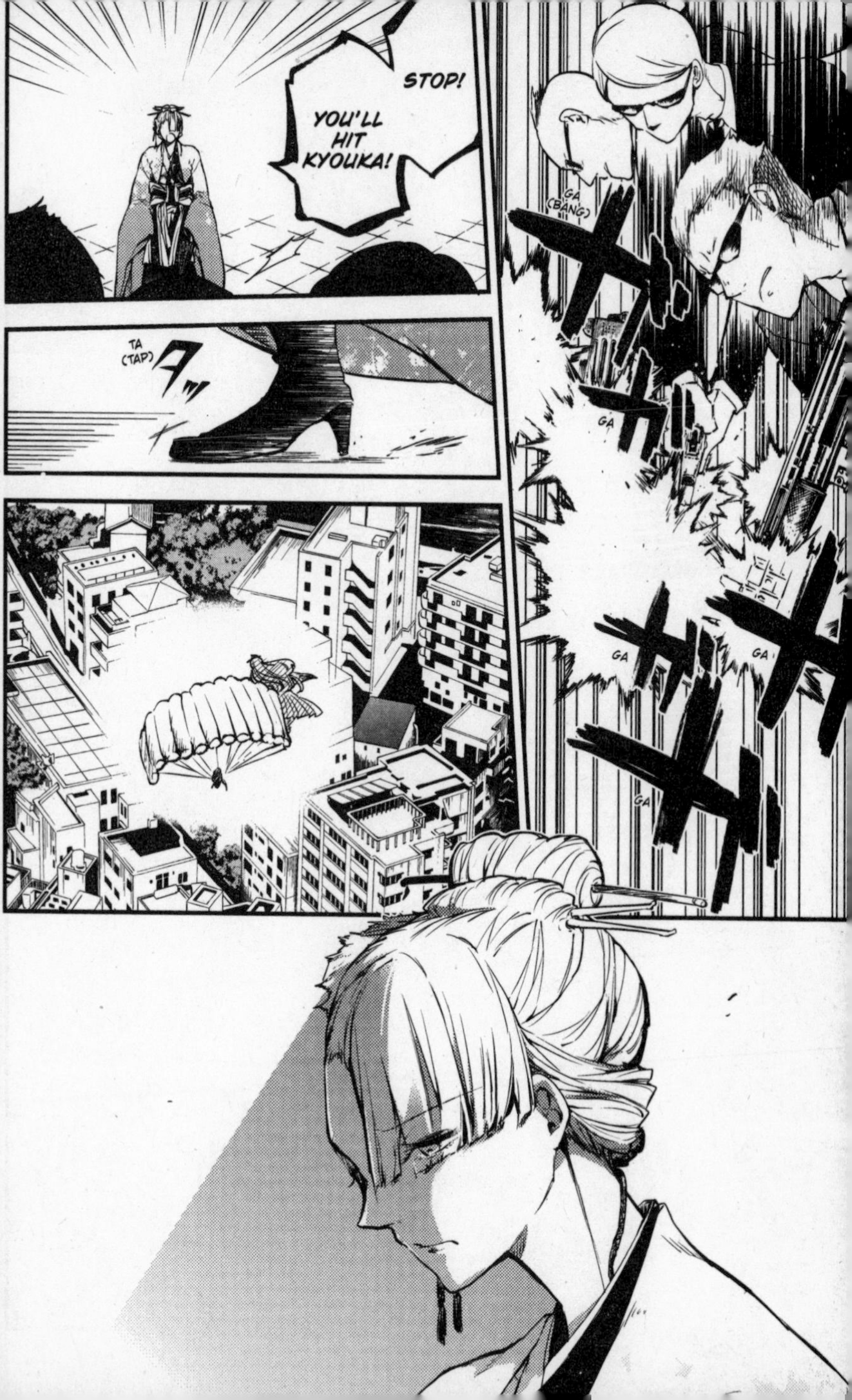
GA (BANG)
GA
GA
GA
GA
STOP!
YOU'LL HIT KYOUKA!
TA (TAP)

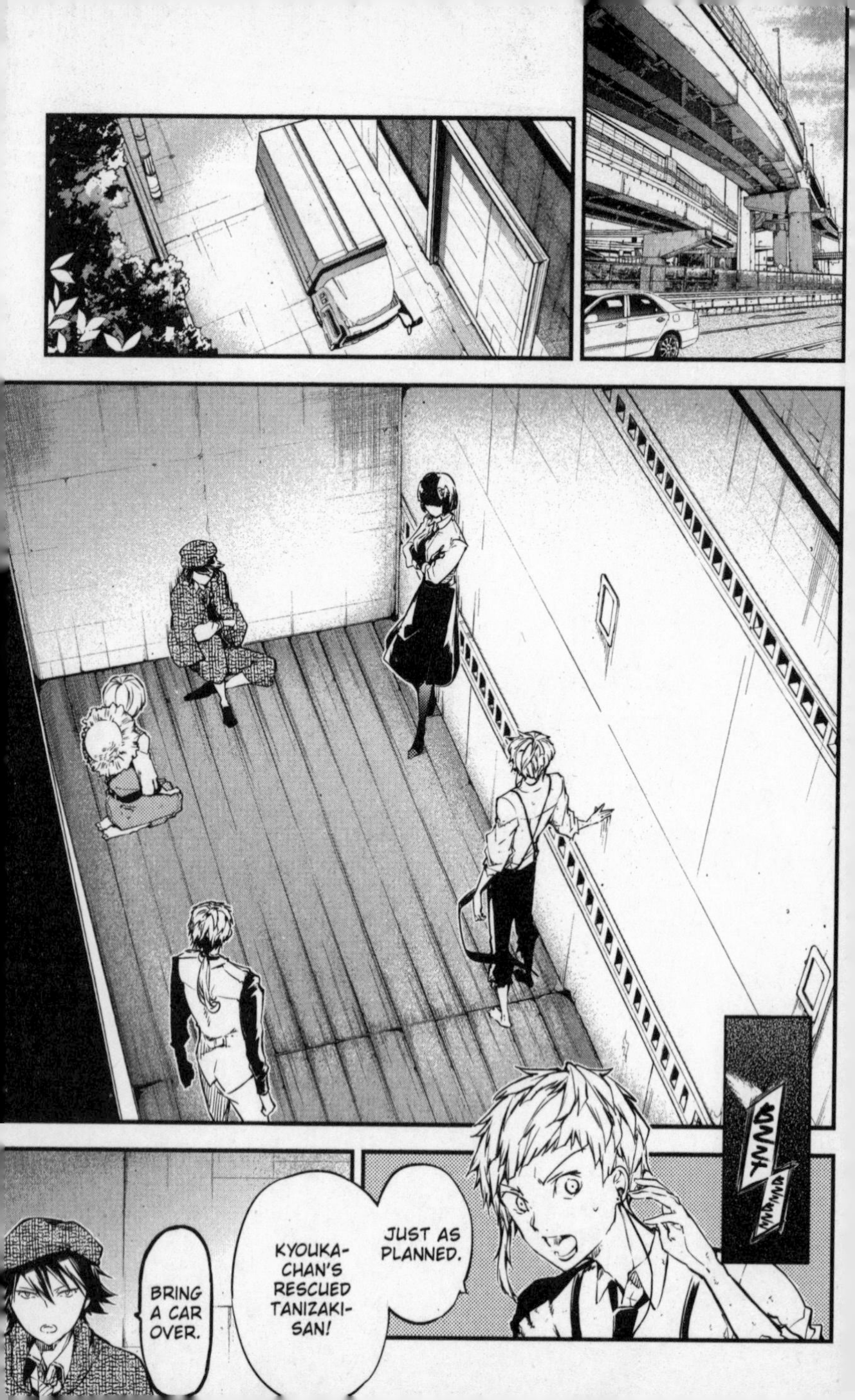
KYOUKA-CHAN'S RESCUED TANIZAKI-SAN!
JUST AS PLANNED.
BRING A CAR OVER.

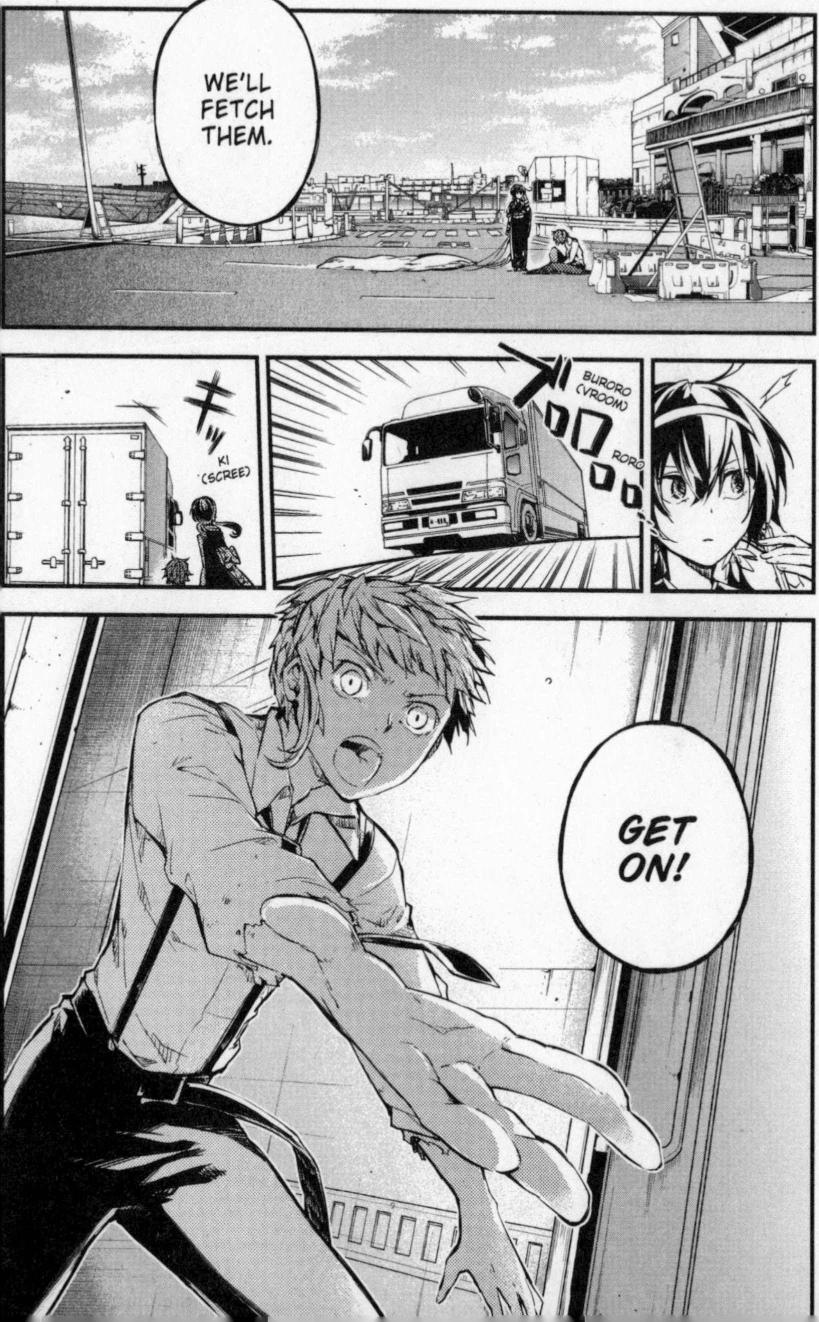
WE'LL FETCH THEM.
BURORO (VROOM)
RORO
KI (SCREE)
GET ON!

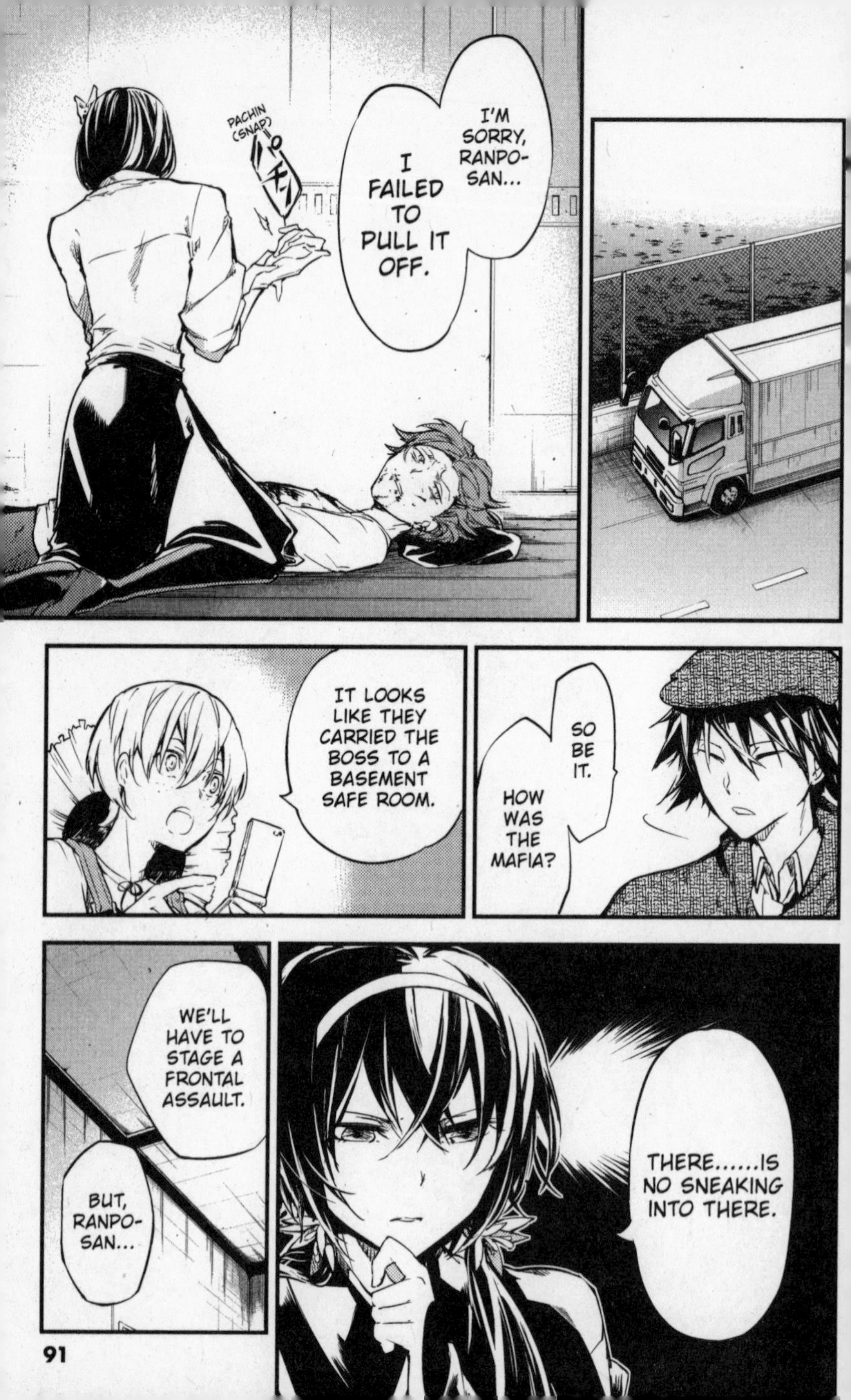
I'M SORRY, RANPO-SAN...
I FAILED TO PULL IT OFF.
PACHIN (SNAP)
SO BE IT.
HOW WAS THE MAFIA?
IT LOOKS LIKE THEY CARRIED THE BOSS TO A BASEMENT SAFE ROOM.
THERE......IS NO SNEAKING INTO THERE.
WE'LL HAVE TO STAGE A FRONTAL ASSAULT.
BUT, RANPO-SAN...

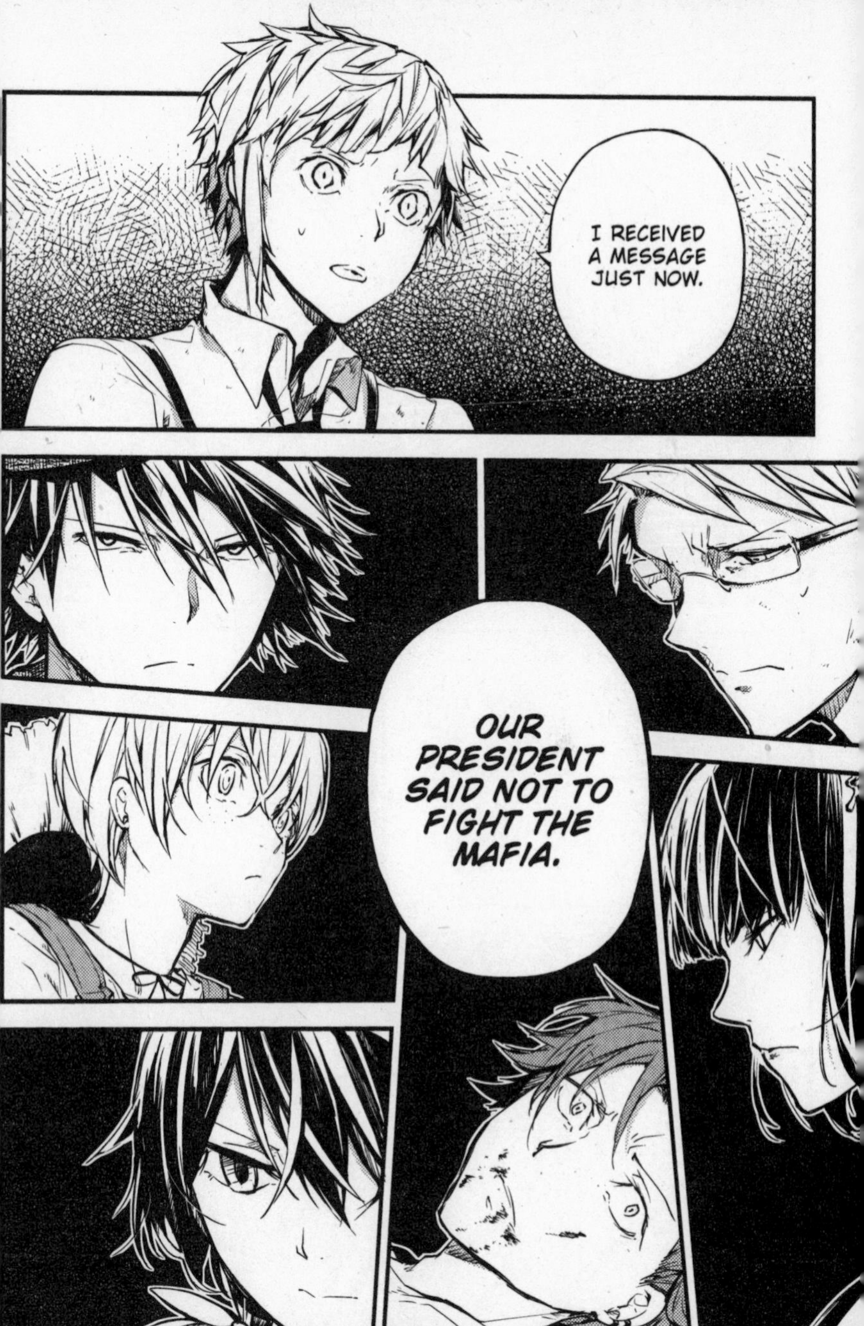
I RECEIVED A MESSAGE JUST NOW.
OUR PRESIDENT SAID NOT TO FIGHT THE MAFIA.

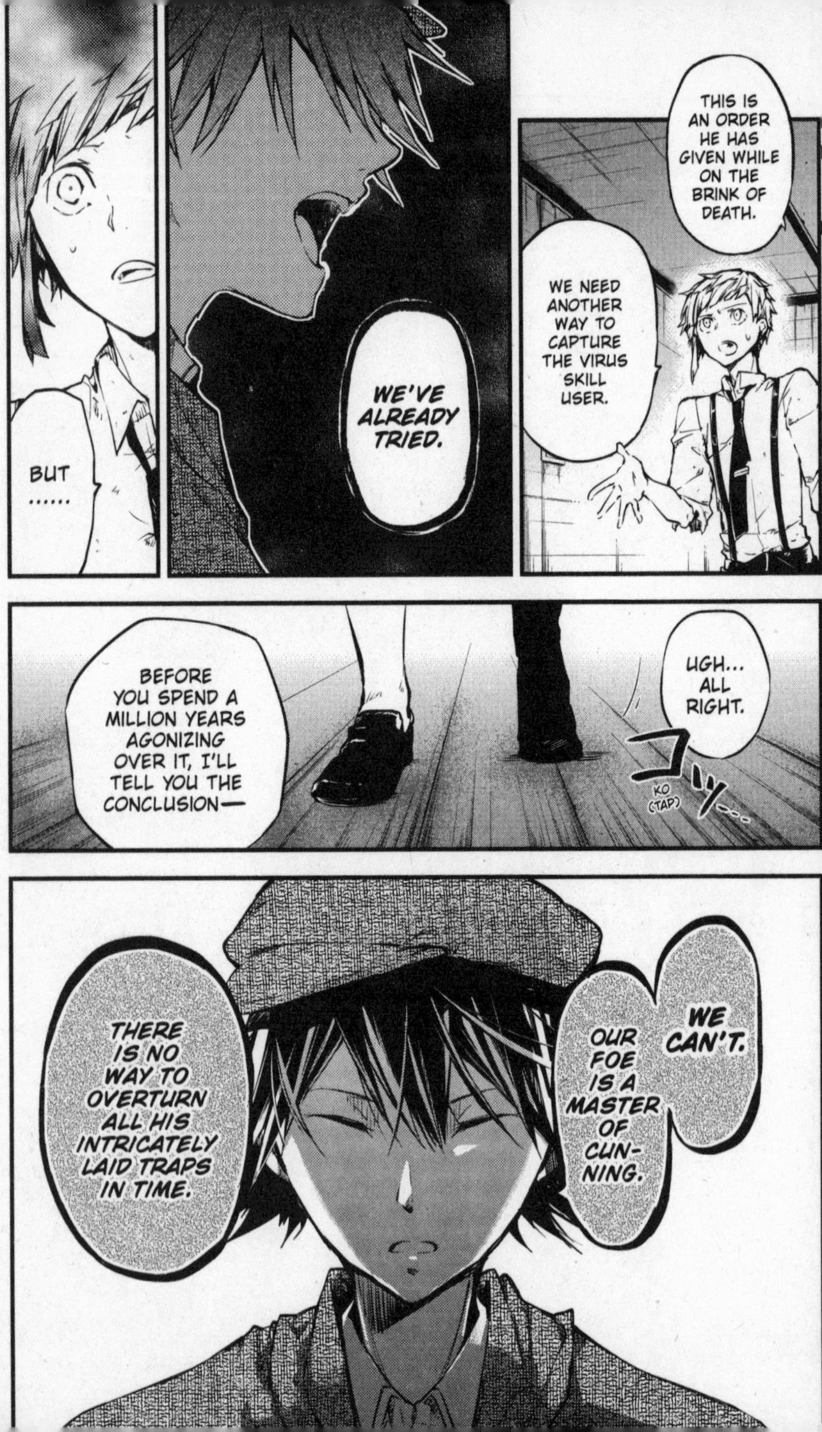
THIS IS AN ORDER HE HAS GIVEN WHILE ON THE BRINK OF DEATH.
WE NEED ANOTHER WAY TO CAPTURE THE VIRUS SKILL USER.
WE'VE ALREADY TRIED.
BUT ......
UGH... ALL RIGHT.
KO (TAP)
BEFORE YOU SPEND A MILLION YEARS AGONIZING OVER IT, I'LL TELL YOU THE CONCLUSION—
WE CAN'T.
OUR FOE IS A MASTER OF CUN-NING.
THERE IS NO WAY TO OVERTURN ALL HIS INTRICATELY LAID TRAPS IN TIME.

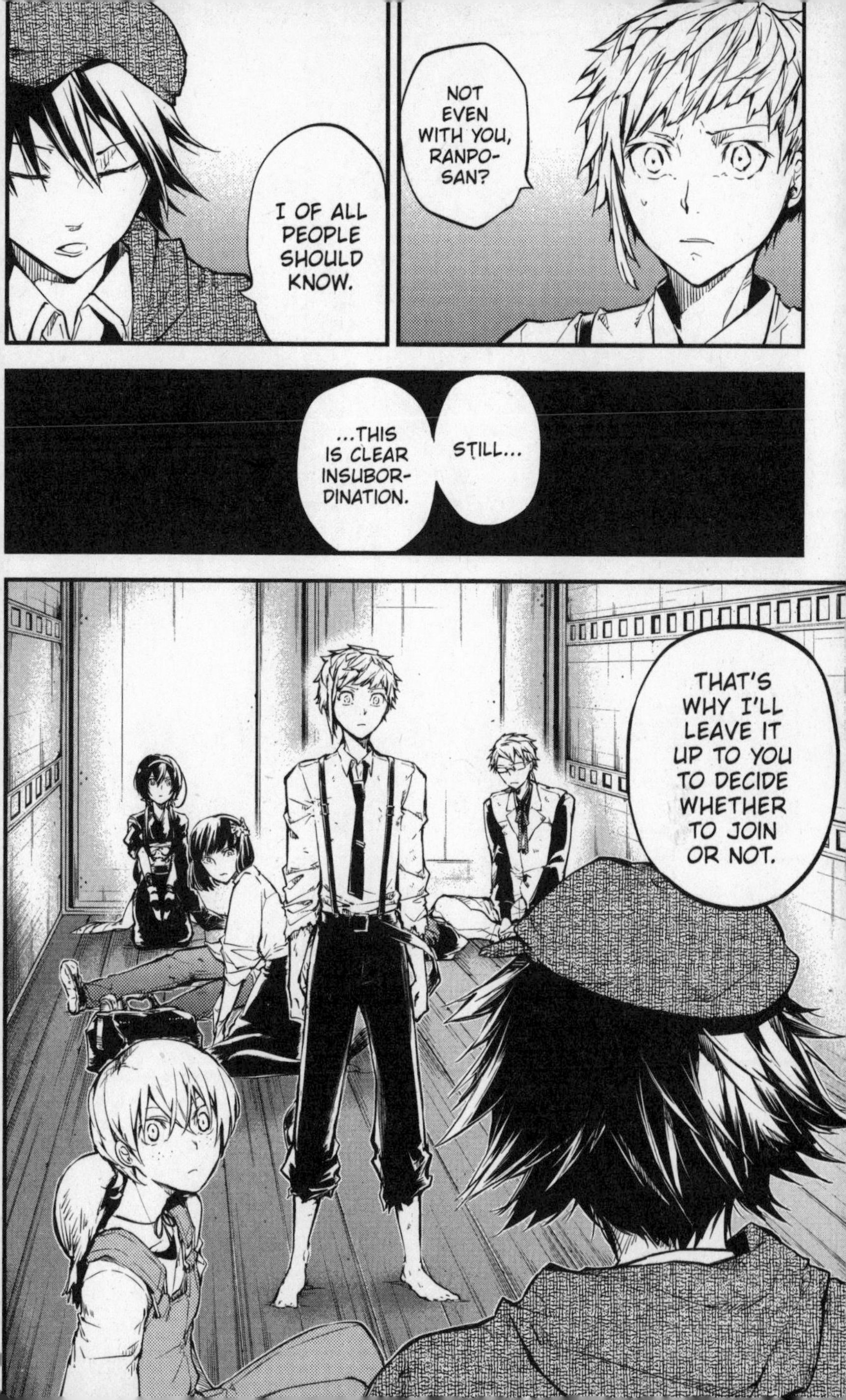
NOT EVEN WITH YOU, RANPO-SAN?
I OF ALL PEOPLE SHOULD KNOW.
STILL...
...THIS IS CLEAR INSUBOR-DINATION.
THAT'S WHY I'LL LEAVE IT UP TO YOU TO DECIDE WHETHER TO JOIN OR NOT.

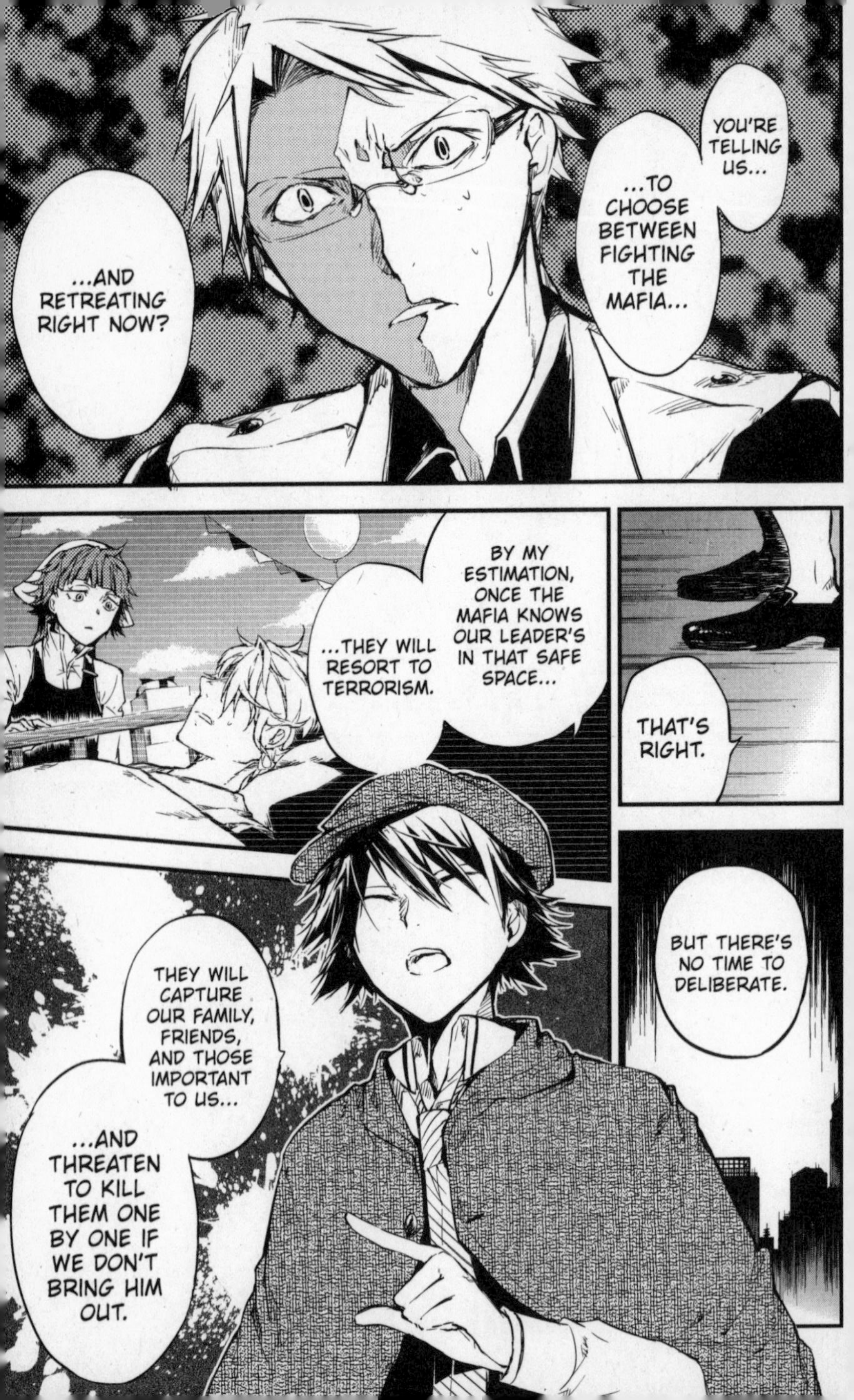
YOU'RE TELLING US...
...TO CHOOSE BETWEEN FIGHTING THE MAFIA...
...AND RETREATING RIGHT NOW?
THAT'S RIGHT.
BY MY ESTIMATION, ONCE THE MAFIA KNOWS OUR LEADER'S IN THAT SAFE SPACE...
...THEY WILL RESORT TO TERRORISM.
BUT THERE'S NO TIME TO DELIBERATE.
THEY WILL CAPTURE OUR FAMILY, FRIENDS, AND THOSE IMPORTANT TO US...
...AND THREATEN TO KILL THEM ONE BY ONE IF WE DON'T BRING HIM OUT.

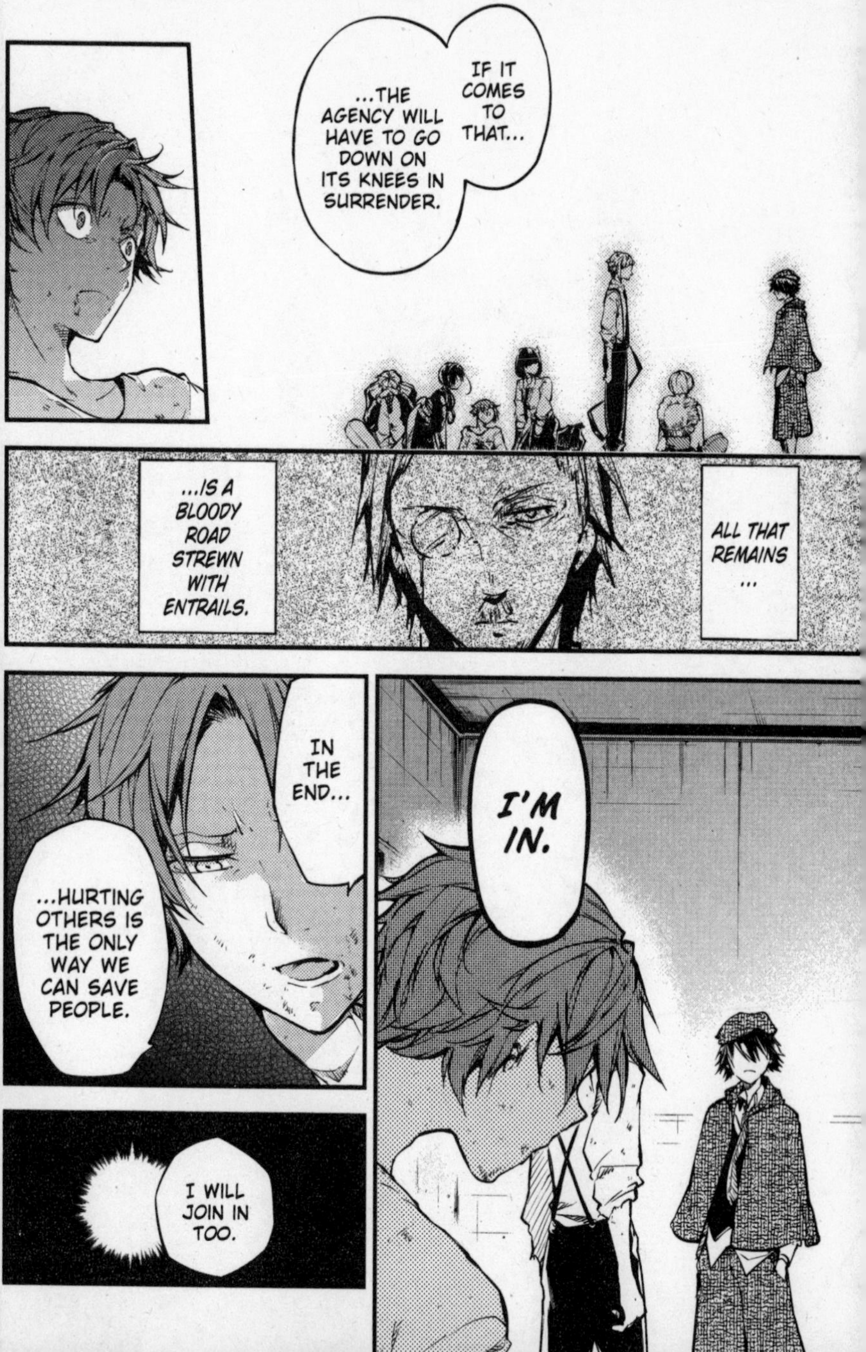
IF IT COMES TO THAT...
...THE AGENCY WILL HAVE TO GO DOWN ON ITS KNEES IN SURRENDER.
ALL THAT REMAINS ...
...IS A BLOODY ROAD STREWN WITH ENTRAILS.
I'M IN.
IN THE END...
...HURTING OTHERS IS THE ONLY WAY WE CAN SAVE PEOPLE.
I WILL JOIN IN TOO.

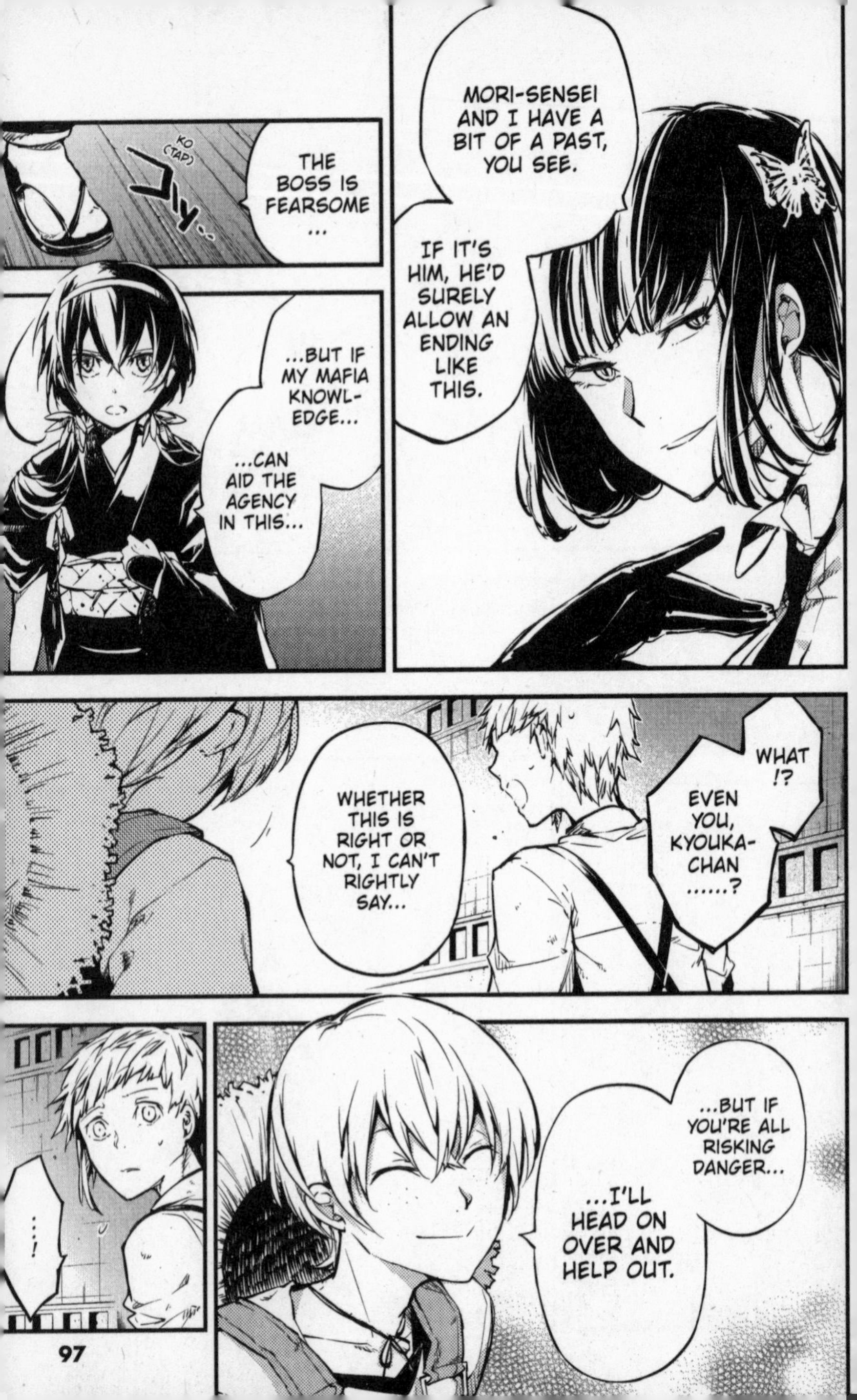
MORI-SENSEI AND I HAVE A BIT OF A PAST, YOU SEE.
IF IT'S HIM, HE'D SURELY ALLOW AN ENDING LIKE THIS.
KO (TAP)
THE BOSS IS FEARSOME ...
...BUT IF MY MAFIA KNOWL-EDGE...
...CAN AID THE AGENCY IN THIS...
WHAT !?
EVEN YOU, KYOUKA-CHAN ......?
WHETHER THIS IS RIGHT OR NOT, I CAN'T RIGHTLY SAY...
...BUT IF YOU'RE ALL RISKING DANGER...
...I'LL HEAD ON OVER AND HELP OUT.
...!

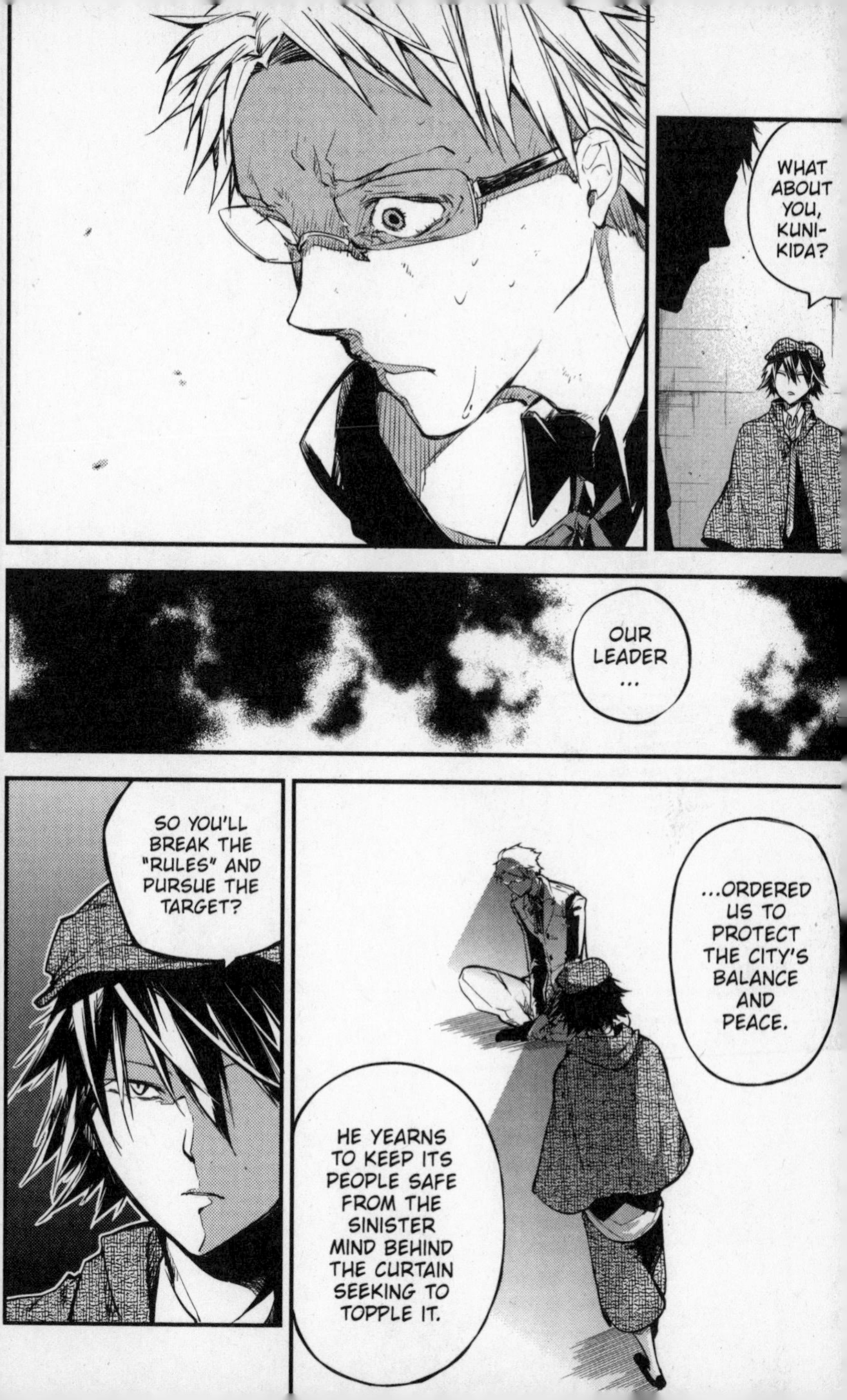
WHAT ABOUT YOU, KUNI-KIDA?
OUR LEADER ...
...ORDERED US TO PROTECT THE CITY'S BALANCE AND PEACE.
HE YEARNS TO KEEP ITS PEOPLE SAFE FROM THE SINISTER MIND BEHIND THE CURTAIN SEEKING TO TOPPLE IT.
SO YOU'LL BREAK THE "RULES" AND PURSUE THE TARGET?

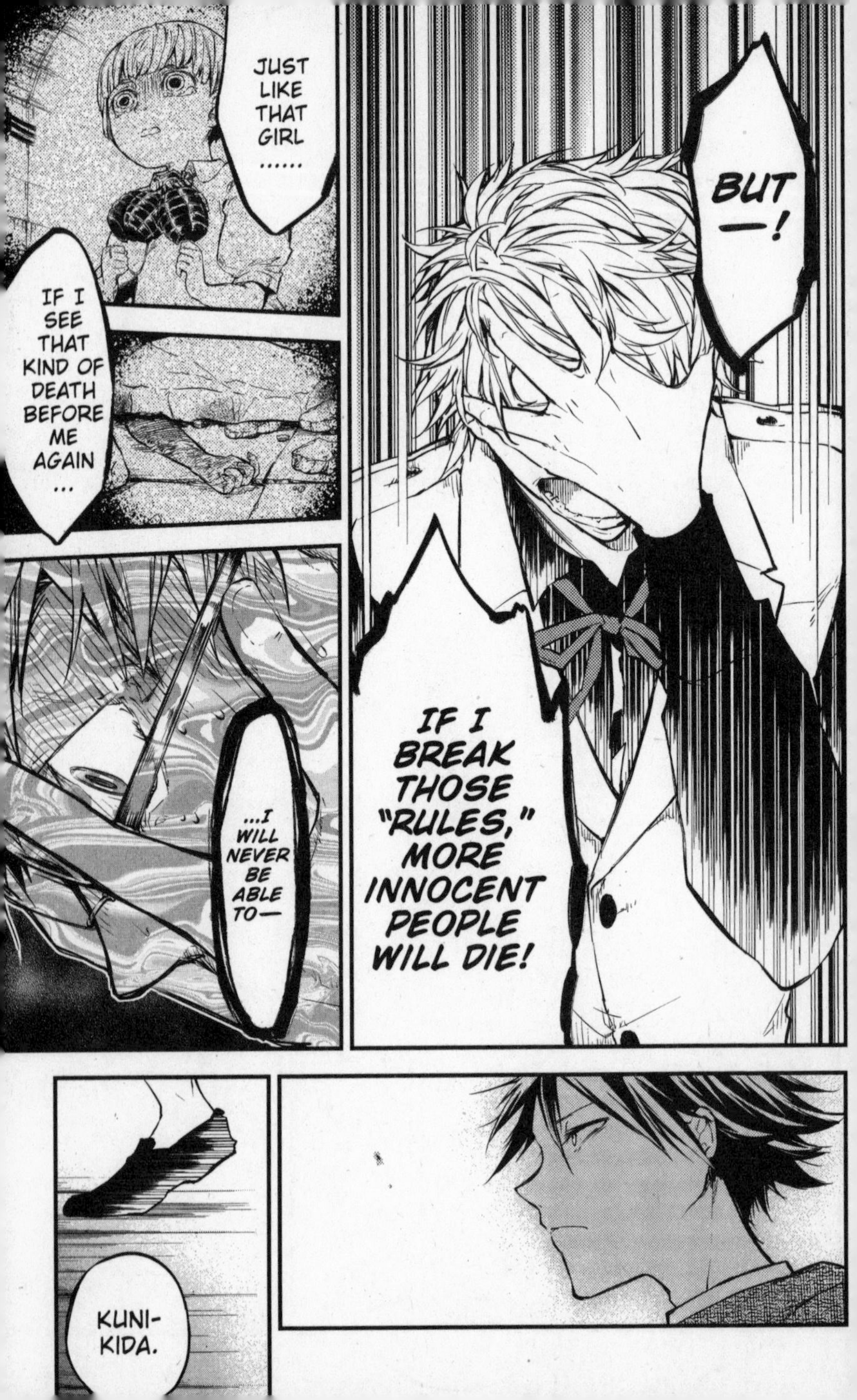
BUT—!
IF I BREAK THOSE "RULES," MORE INNOCENT PEOPLE WILL DIE!
JUST LIKE THAT GIRL......
IF I SEE THAT KIND OF DEATH BEFORE ME AGAIN...
...I WILL NEVER BE ABLE TO—
KUNI-KIDA.

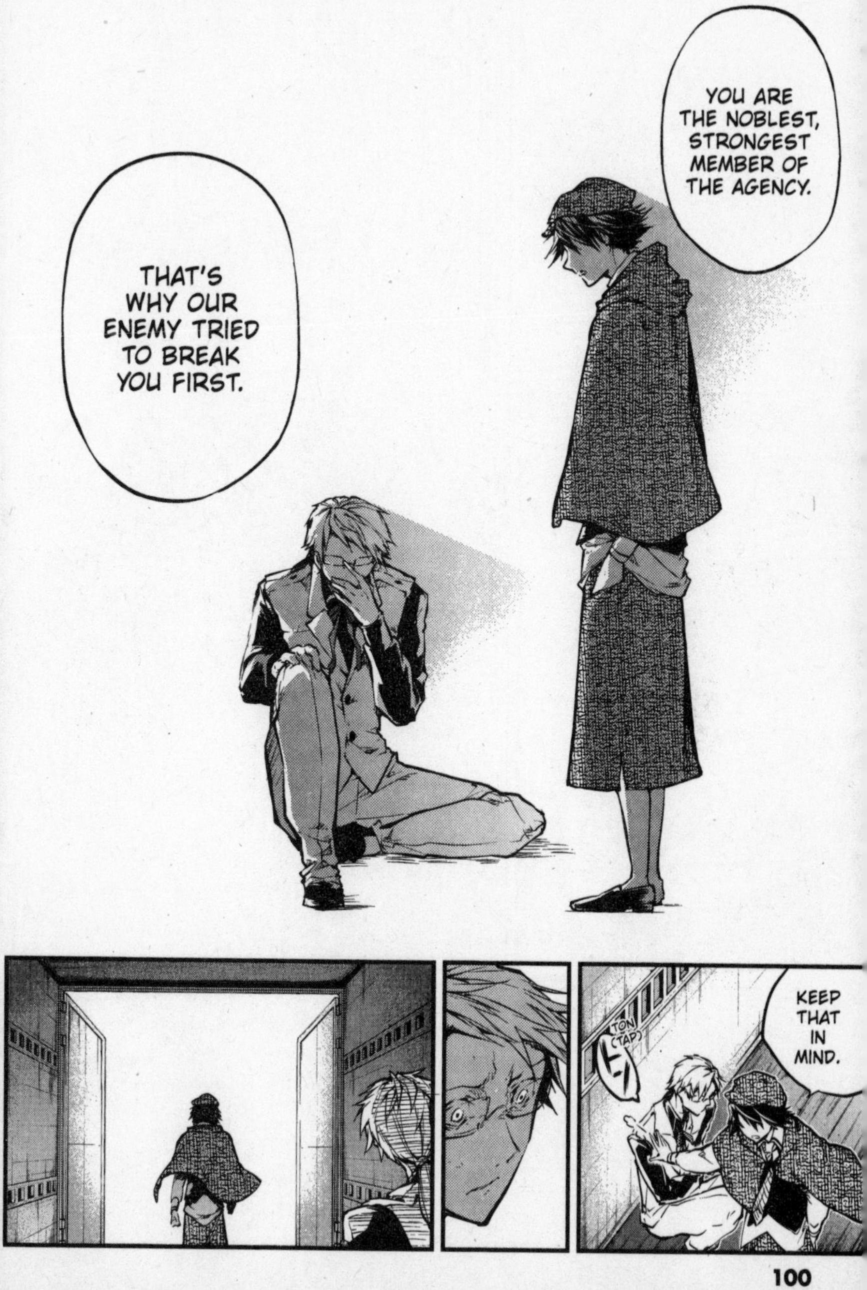
YOU ARE THE NOBLEST, STRONGEST MEMBER OF THE AGENCY.
THAT'S WHY OUR ENEMY TRIED TO BREAK YOU FIRST.
KEEP THAT IN MIND.
TON (TAP)

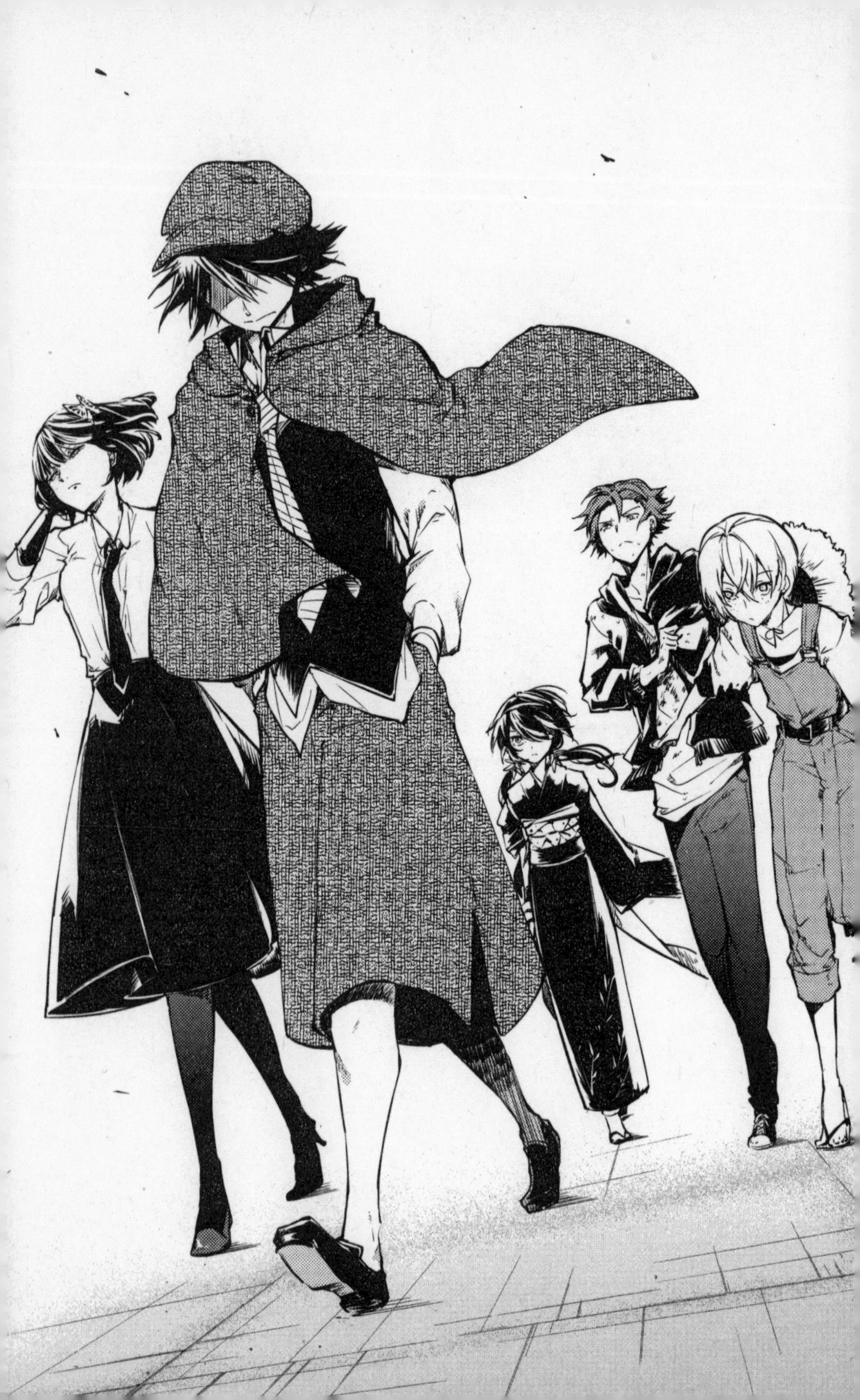

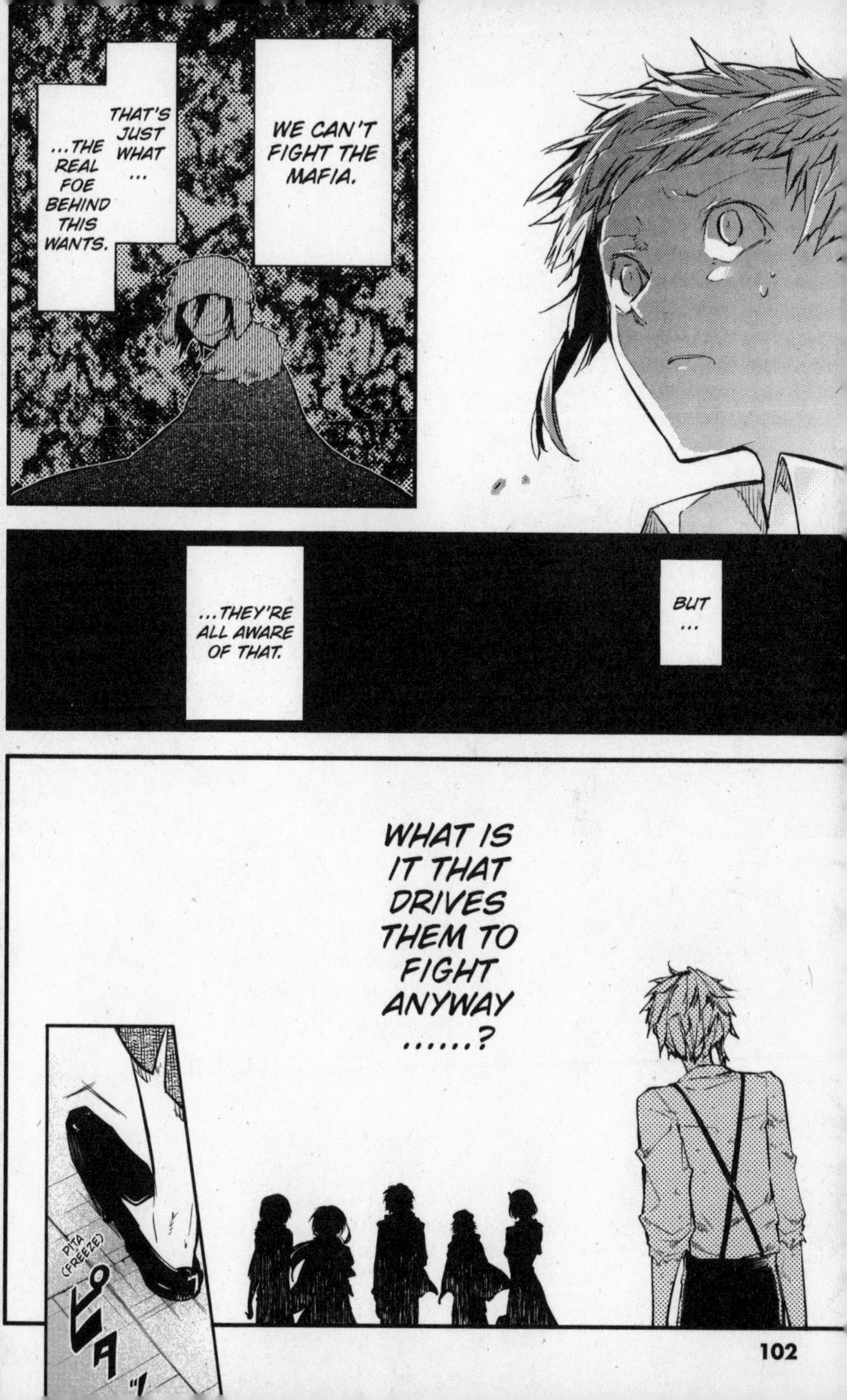
WE CAN'T FIGHT THE MAFIA.
THAT'S JUST WHAT...
...THE REAL FOE BEHIND THIS WANTS.
BUT...
...THEY'RE ALL AWARE OF THAT.
WHAT IS IT THAT DRIVES THEM TO FIGHT ANYWAY......?
PITA (FREEZE)

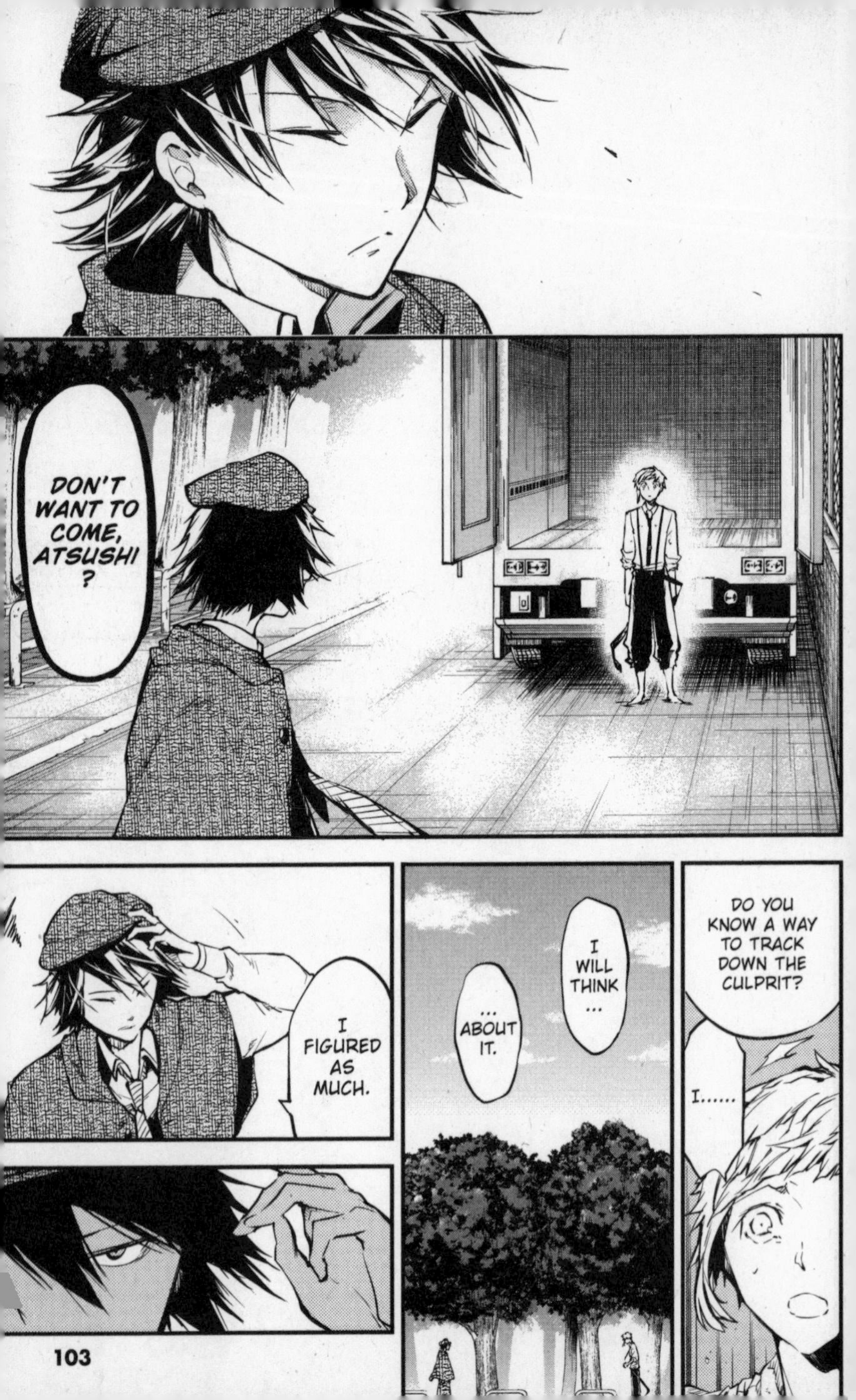
DON'T WANT TO COME, ATSUSHI?
DO YOU KNOW A WAY TO TRACK DOWN THE CULPRIT?
I......
I WILL THINK...
...ABOUT IT.
I FIGURED AS MUCH.

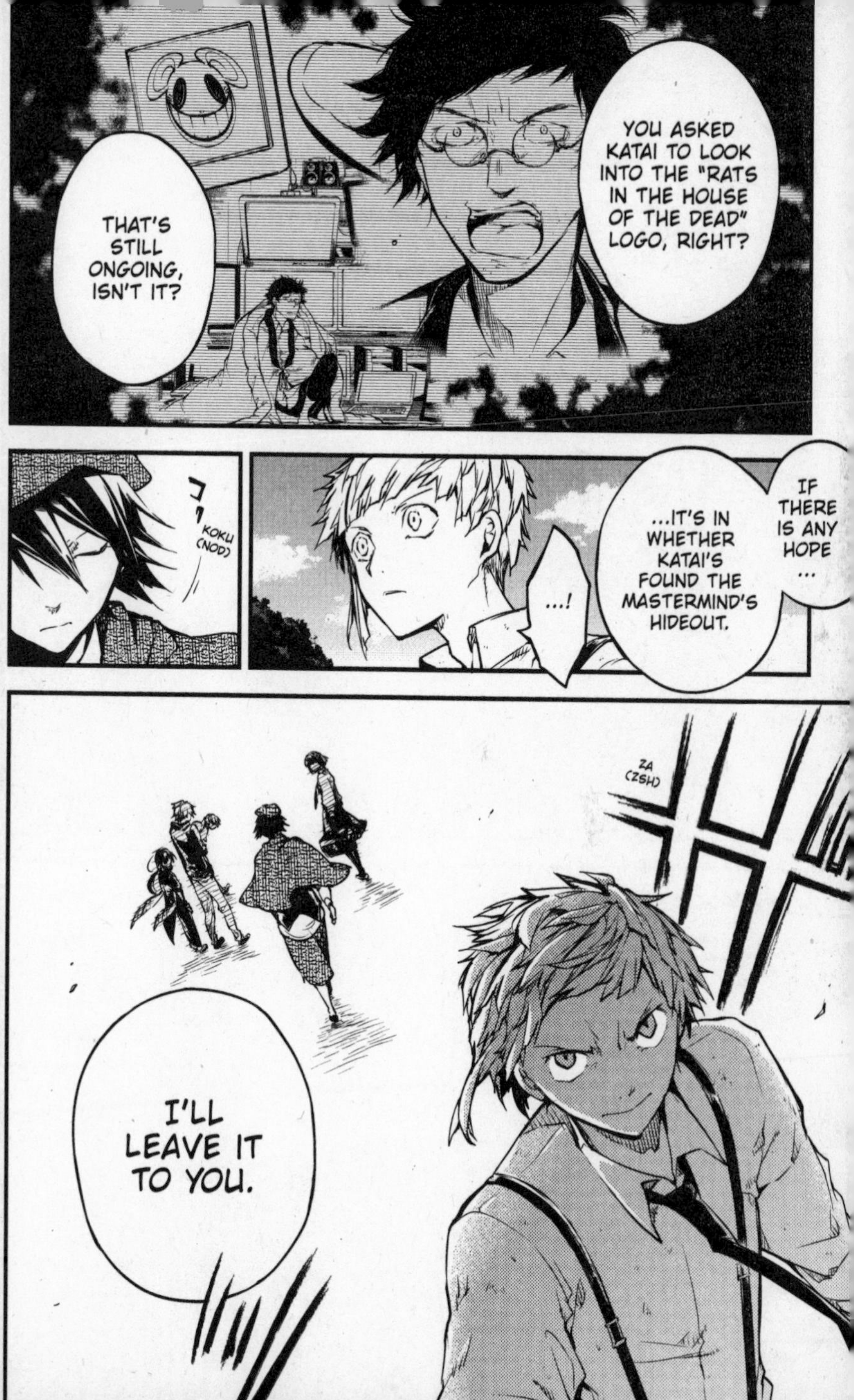
YOU ASKED KATAI TO LOOK INTO THE "RATS IN THE HOUSE OF THE DEAD" LOGO, RIGHT?
THAT'S STILL ONGOING, ISN'T IT?
IF THERE IS ANY HOPE...
...IT'S IN WHETHER KATAI'S FOUND THE MASTERMIND'S HIDEOUT.
...!
KOKU (NOD)
ZA (ZSH)
I'LL LEAVE IT TO YOU.

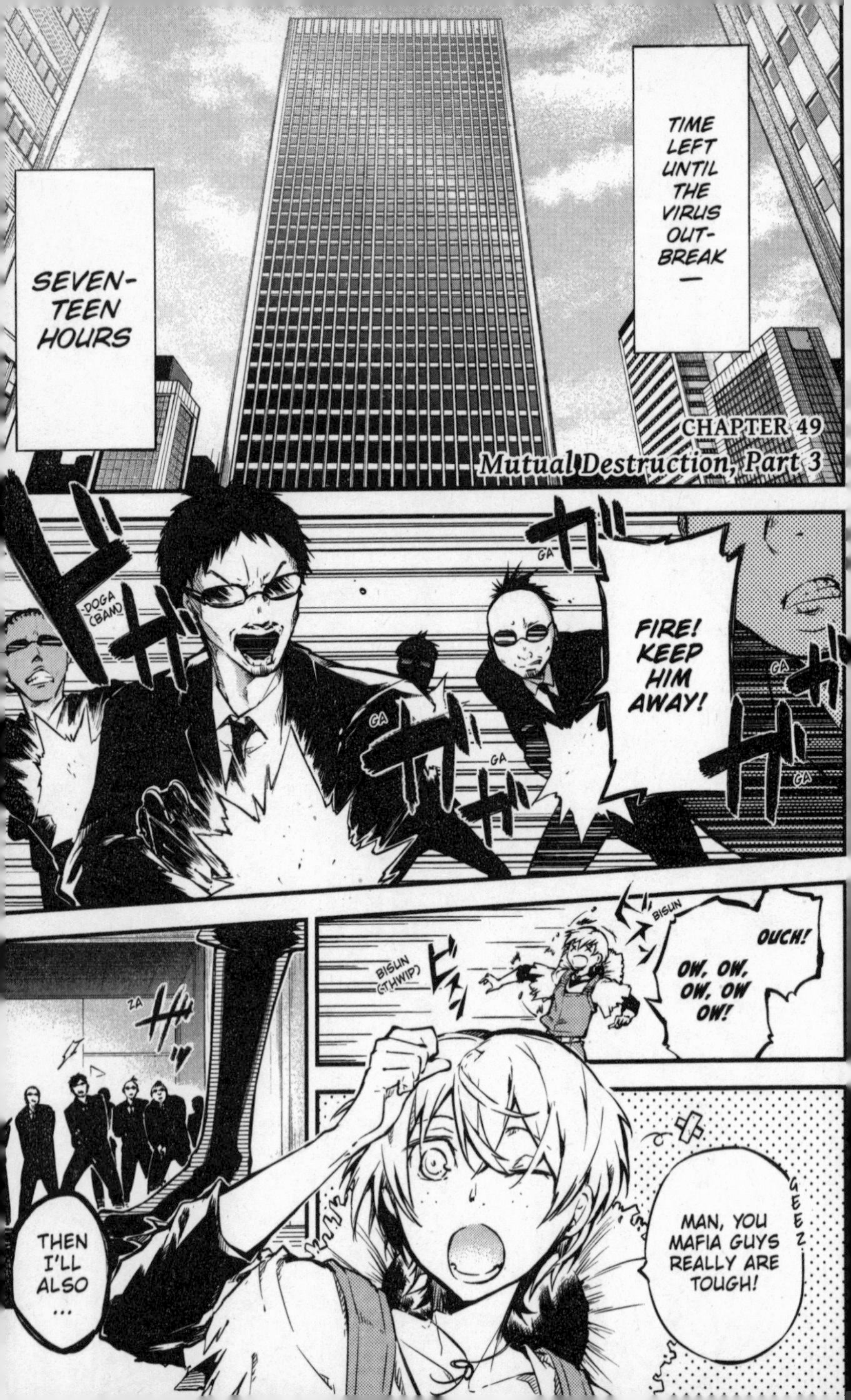
TIME LEFT UNTIL THE VIRUS OUT-BREAK —
SEVEN-TEEN HOURS
CHAPTER 49
Mutual Destruction, Part 3
GA
FIRE! KEEP HIM AWAY!
GA
GA
GA
GA
DOGA (BAM)
BISUN
OUCH!
OW, OW, OW, OW OW!
BISUN (THWIP)
GEEZ
MAN, YOU MAFIA GUYS REALLY ARE TOUGH!
THEN I'LL ALSO ...
ZA

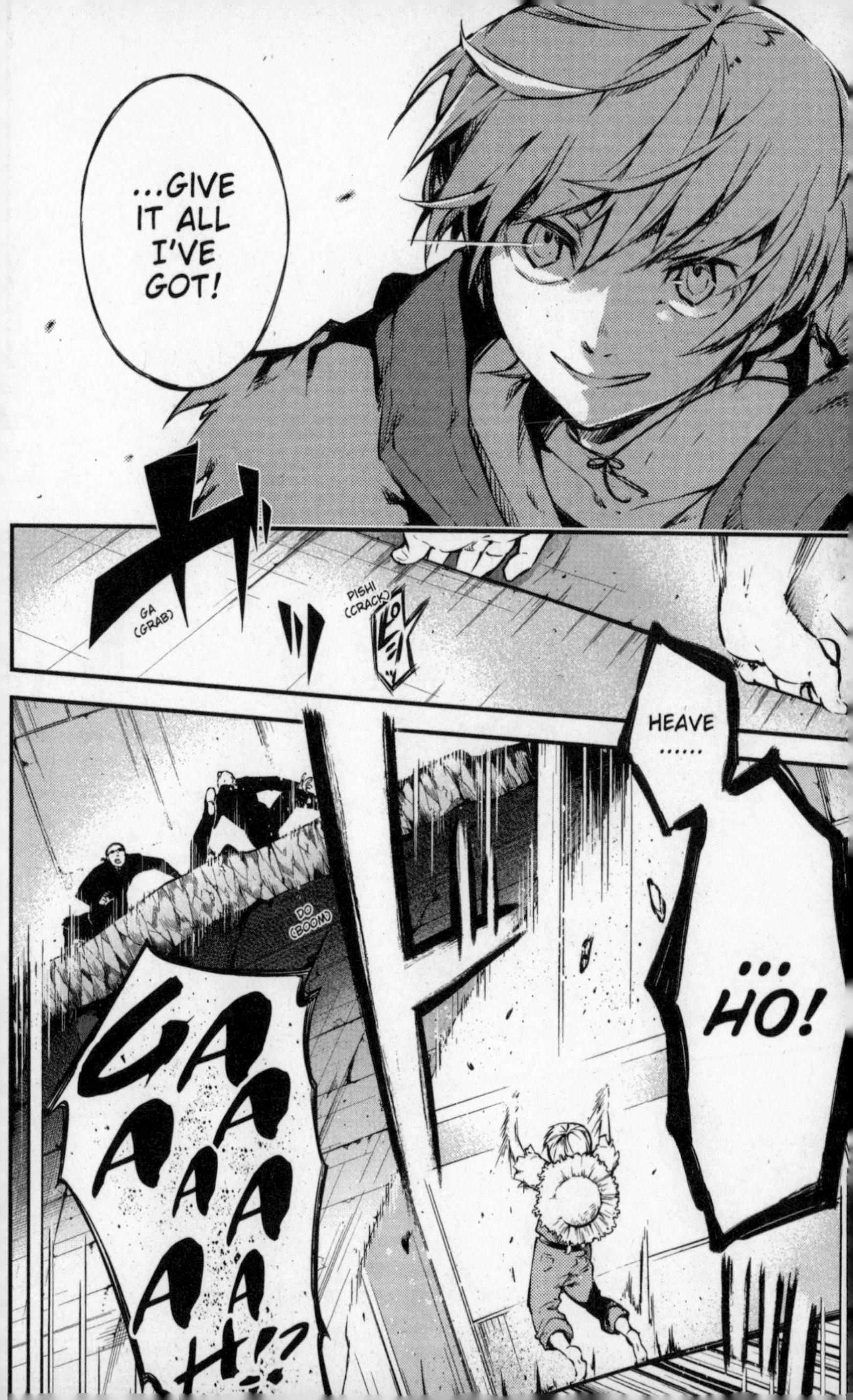
...GIVE IT ALL I'VE GOT!
PISHI (CRACK)
GA (GRAB)
HEAVE ......
...HÖ!
DO (BOOM)
GAAAAAAAAAH!?

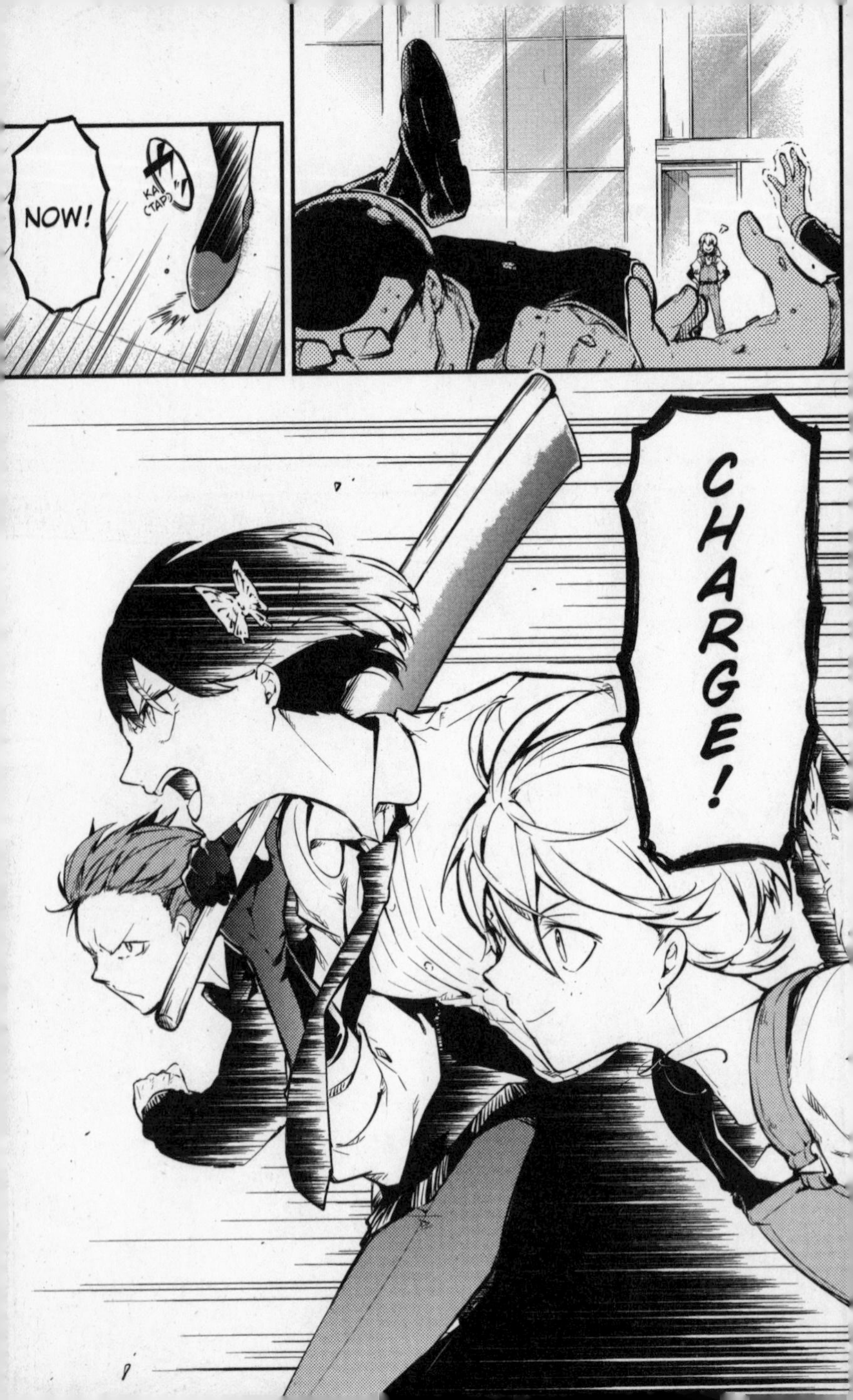
KA (TAP)
NOW!
CHARGE!

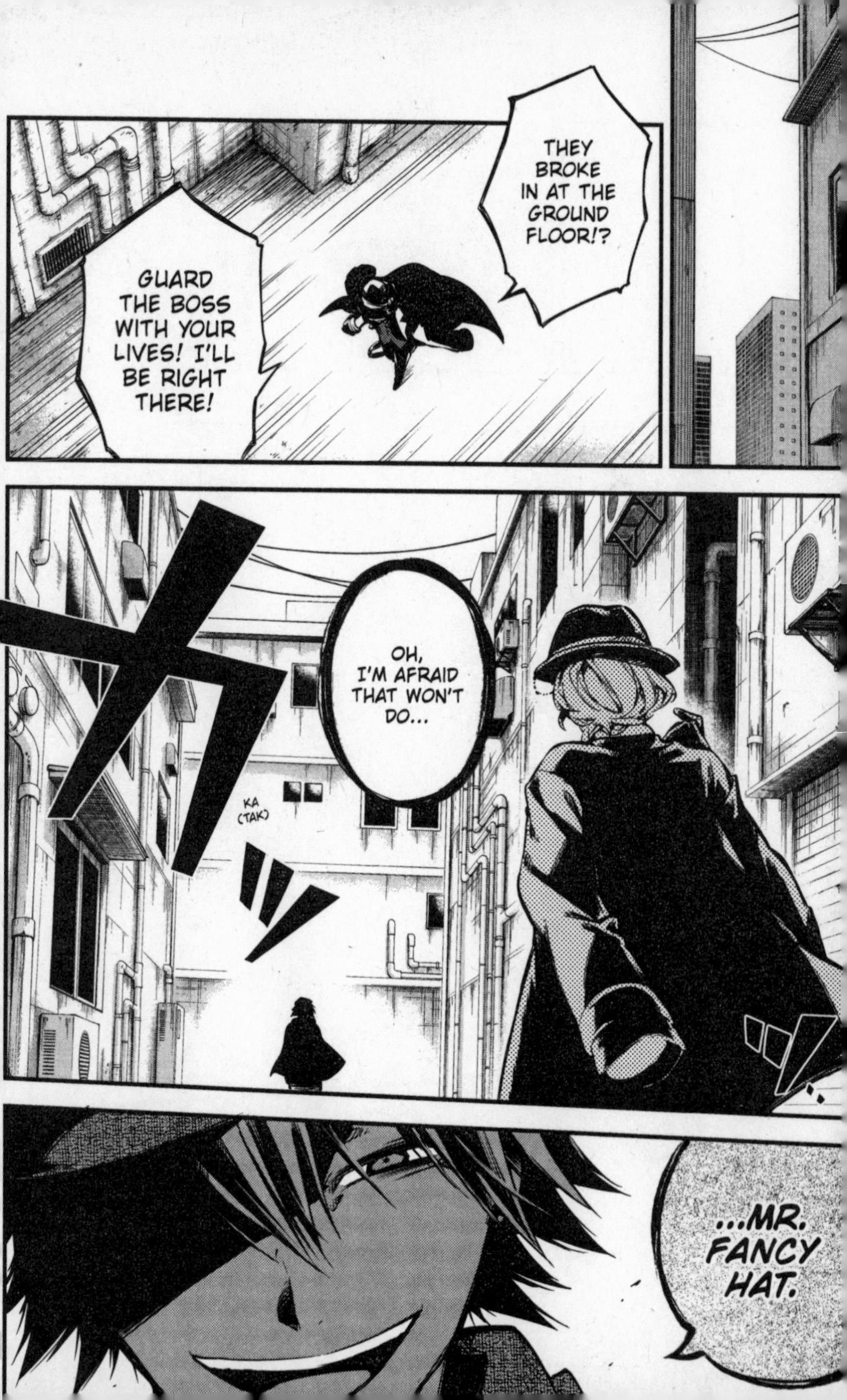
THEY BROKE IN AT THE GROUND FLOOR!?
GUARD THE BOSS WITH YOUR LIVES! I'LL BE RIGHT THERE!
OH, I'M AFRAID THAT WON'T DO...
KA (TAK)
...MR. FANCY HAT.

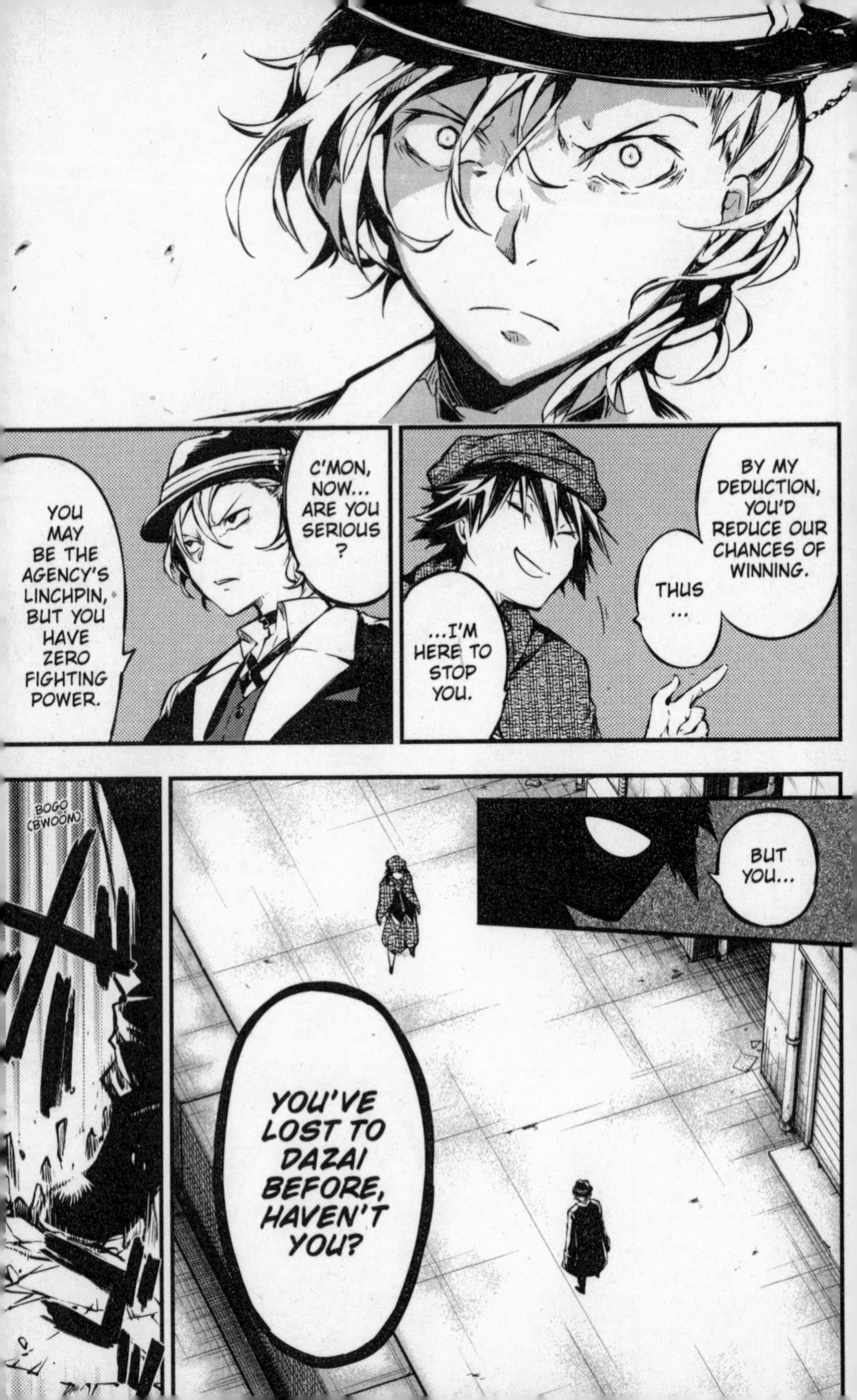
BY MY DEDUCTION, YOU'D REDUCE OUR CHANCES OF WINNING.
THUS...
...I'M HERE TO STOP YOU.
C'MON, NOW... ARE YOU SERIOUS?
YOU MAY BE THE AGENCY'S LINCHPIN, BUT YOU HAVE ZERO FIGHTING POWER.
BUT YOU...
YOU'VE LOST TO DAZAI BEFORE, HAVEN'T YOU?
BOGO (BWOOM)

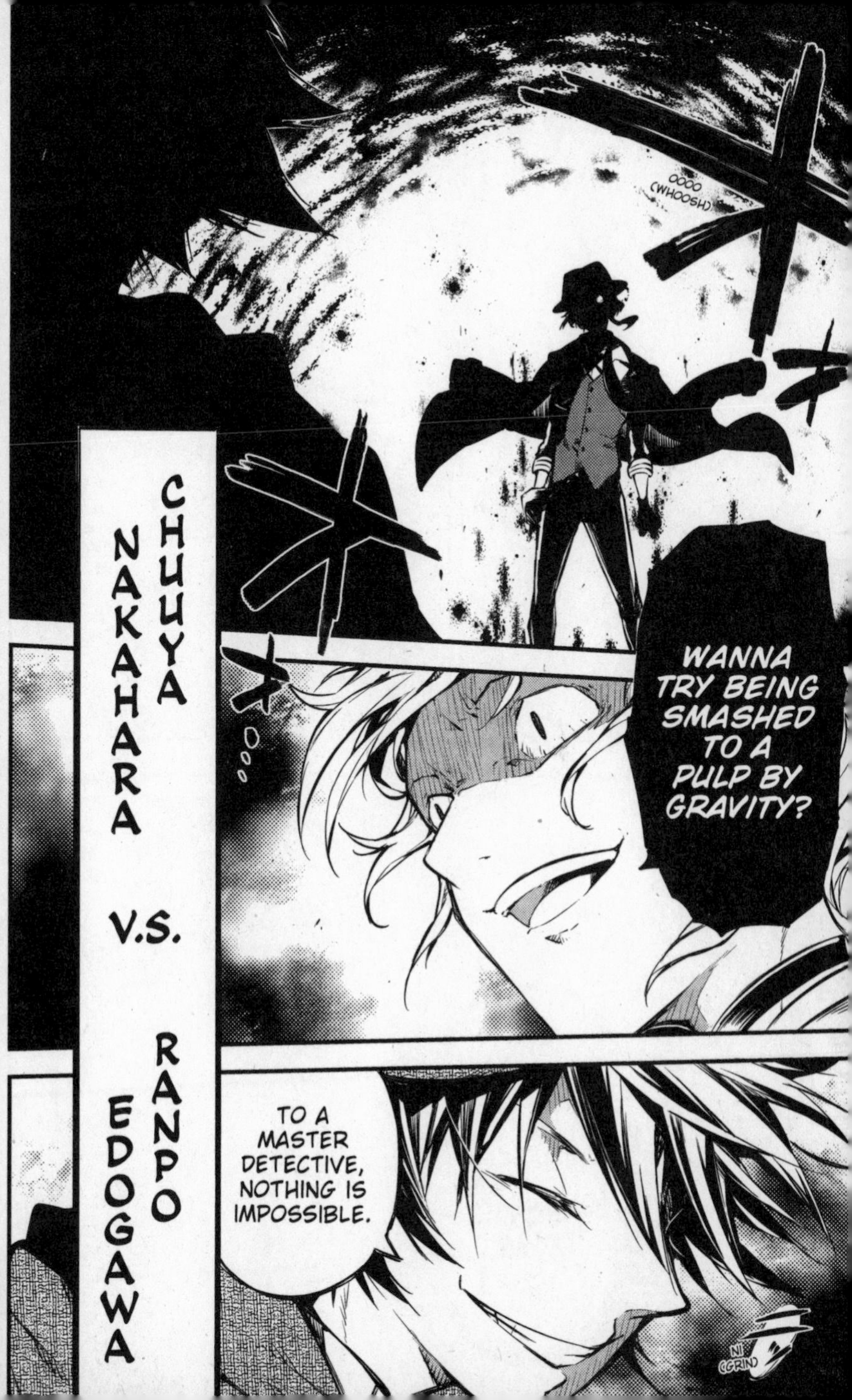
OOOO (WHOOSH)
WANNA TRY BEING SMASHED TO A PULP BY GRAVITY?
TO A MASTER DETECTIVE, NOTHING IS IMPOSSIBLE.
NI (GRIN)
CHUUYA NAKAHARA V.S. RANPO EDOGAWA

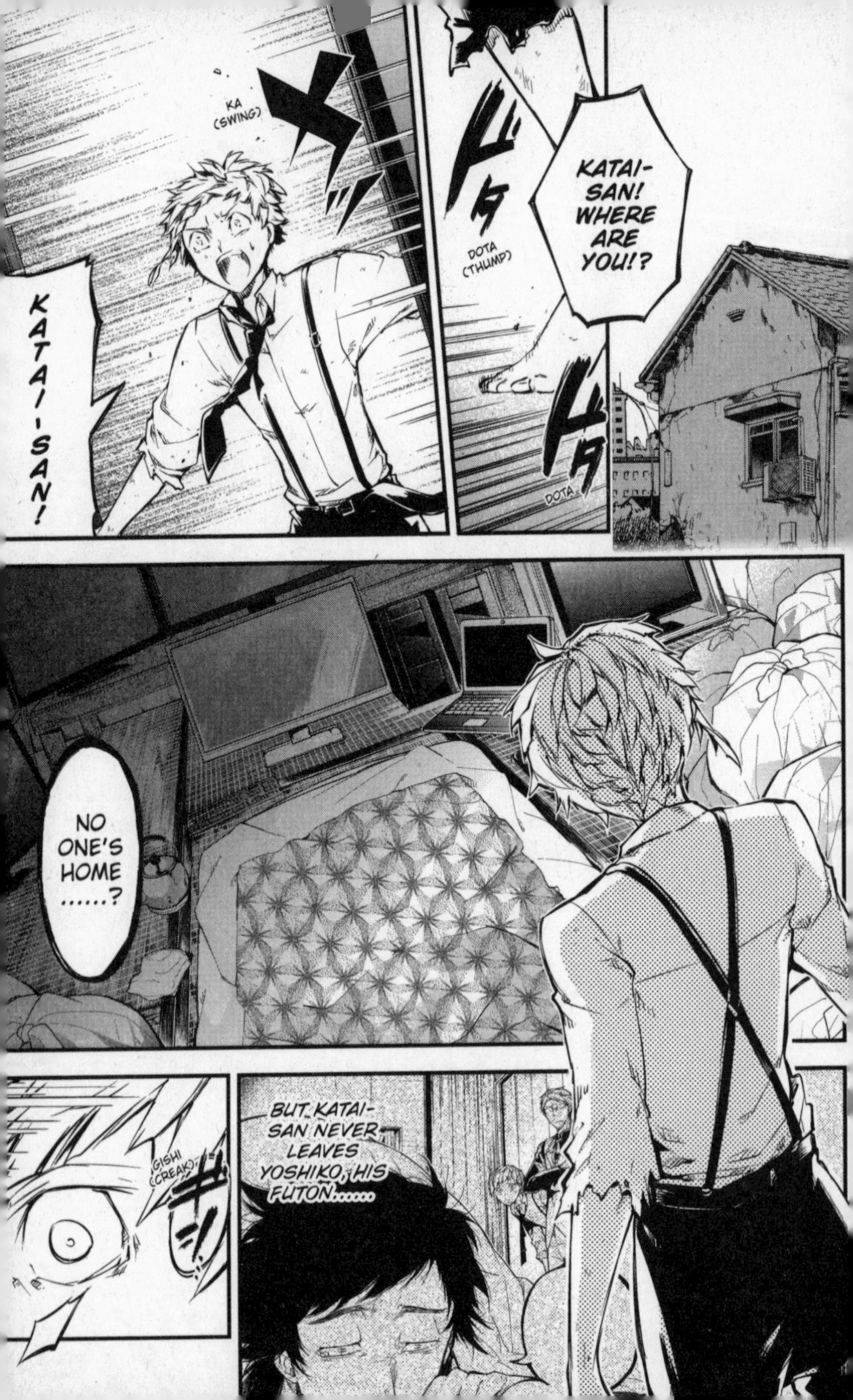
KATAI-SAN! WHERE ARE YOU!?
DOTA (THUMP)
DOTA
KA (SWING)
KATAI-SAN!
NO ONE'S HOME ......?
BUT KATAI-SAN NEVER LEAVES YOSHIKO, HIS FUTON......
GISHI (CREAK)

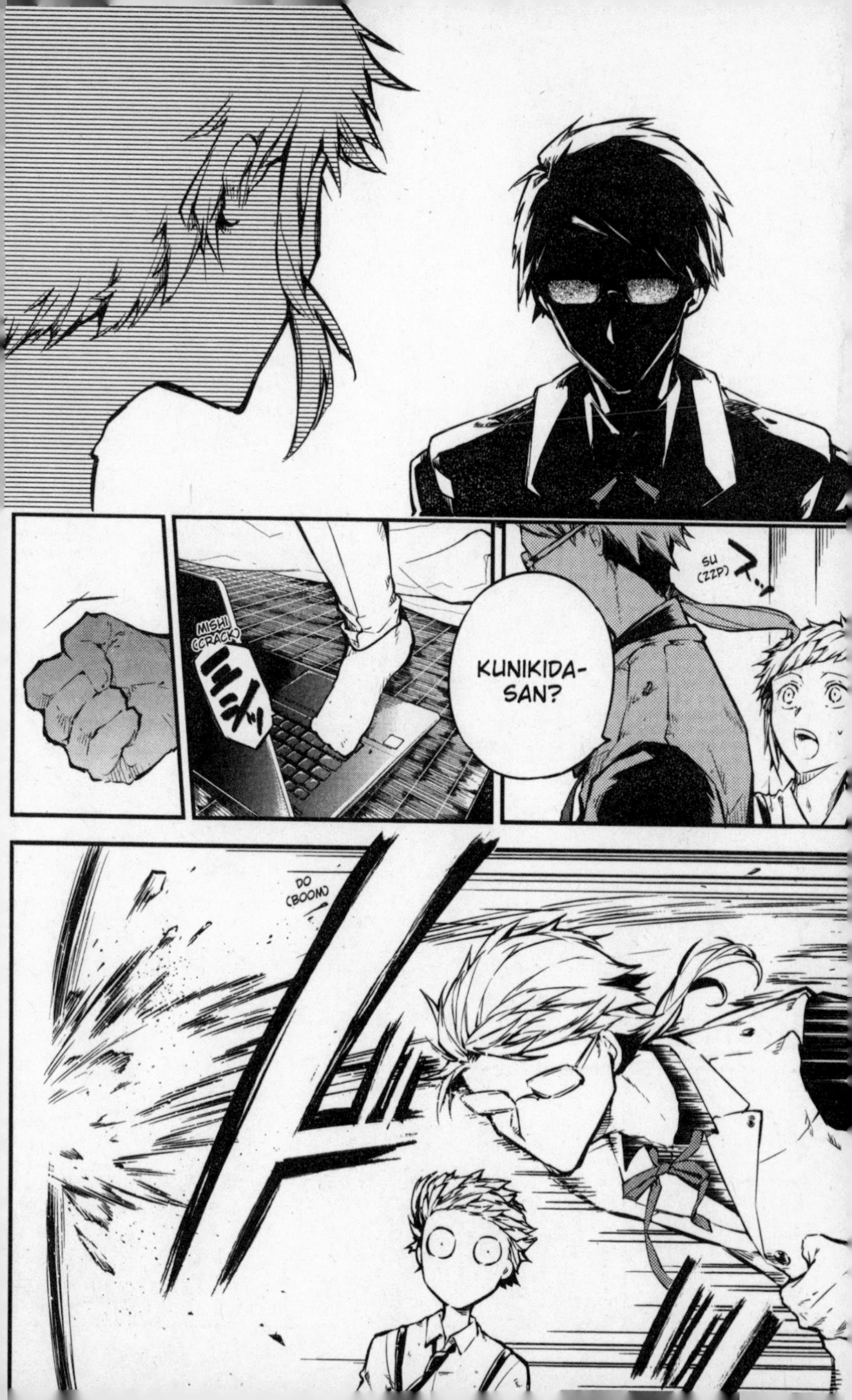
SU (ZZP)
KUNIKIDA-SAN?
MISHI (CRACK)
DO (BOOM)

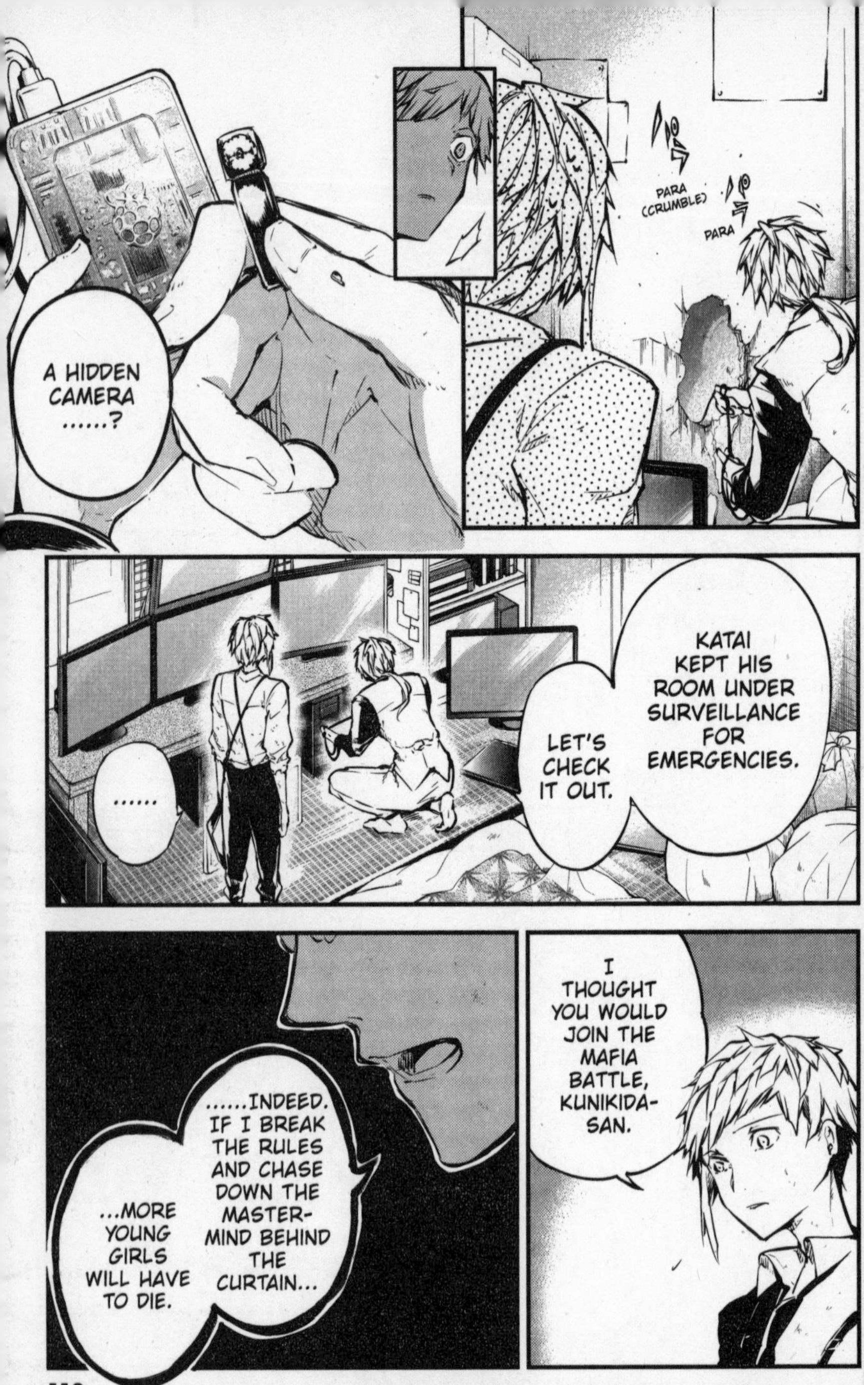
PARA (CRUMBLE)
PARA
A HIDDEN CAMERA ......?
KATAI KEPT HIS ROOM UNDER SURVEILLANCE FOR EMERGENCIES.
LET'S CHECK IT OUT.
......
I THOUGHT YOU WOULD JOIN THE MAFIA BATTLE, KUNIKIDA-SAN.
......INDEED. IF I BREAK THE RULES AND CHASE DOWN THE MASTER-MIND BEHIND THE CURTAIN...
...MORE YOUNG GIRLS WILL HAVE TO DIE.

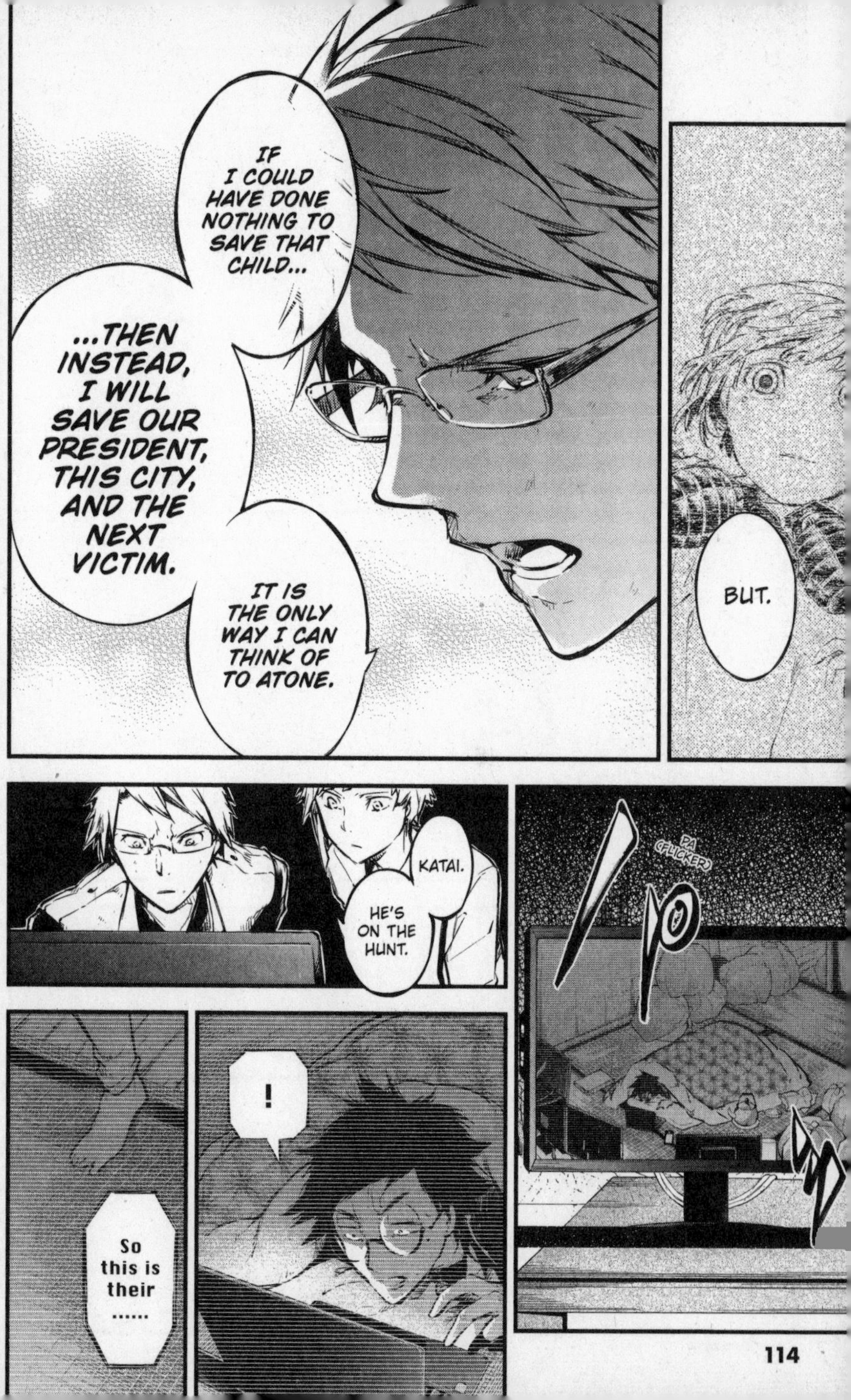
BUT.
IF I COULD HAVE DONE NOTHING TO SAVE THAT CHILD...
...THEN INSTEAD, I WILL SAVE OUR PRESIDENT, THIS CITY, AND THE NEXT VICTIM.
IT IS THE ONLY WAY I CAN THINK OF TO ATONE.
PA (FLICKER)
KATAI.
HE'S ON THE HUNT.
!
So this is their ......

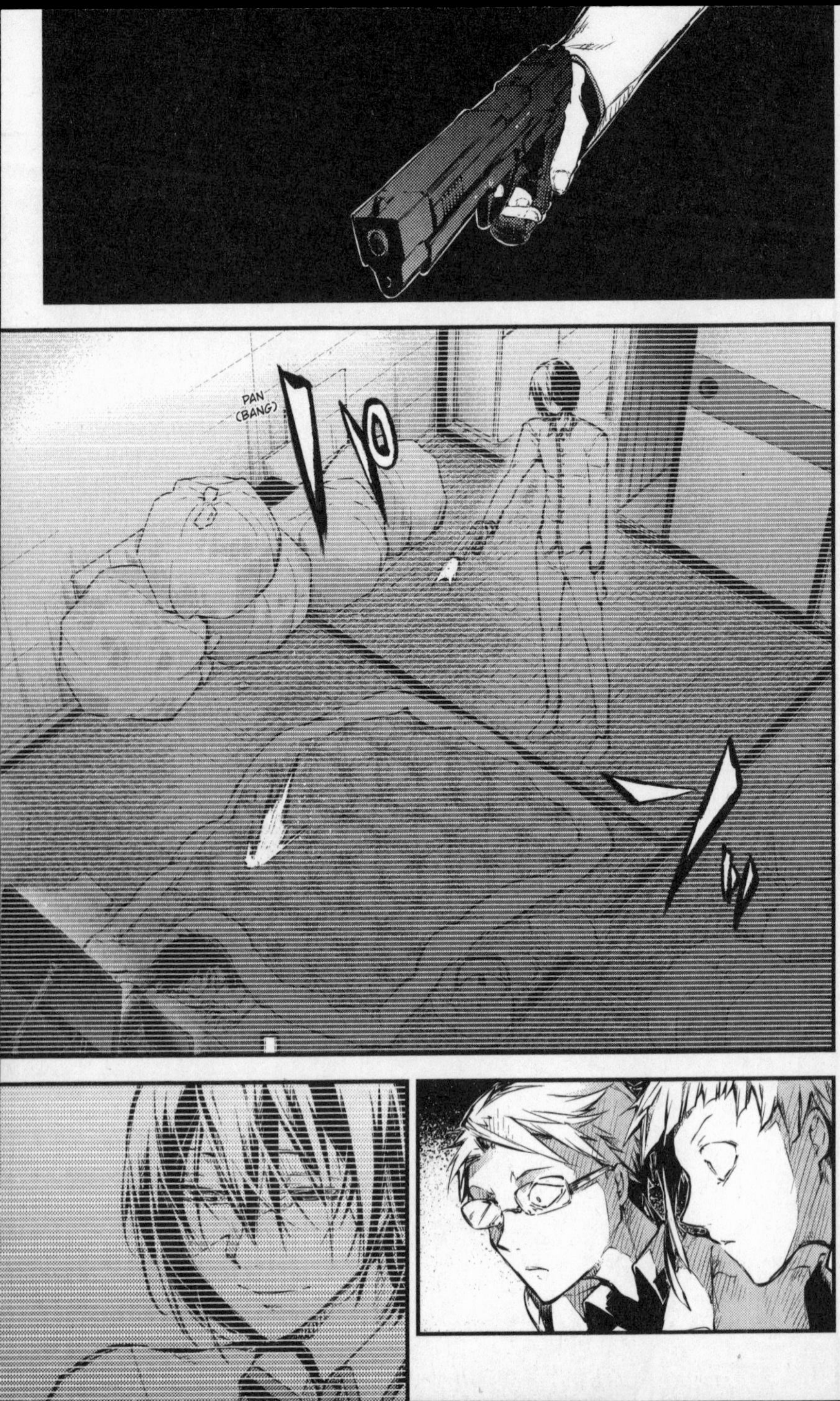
PAN
(BANG)

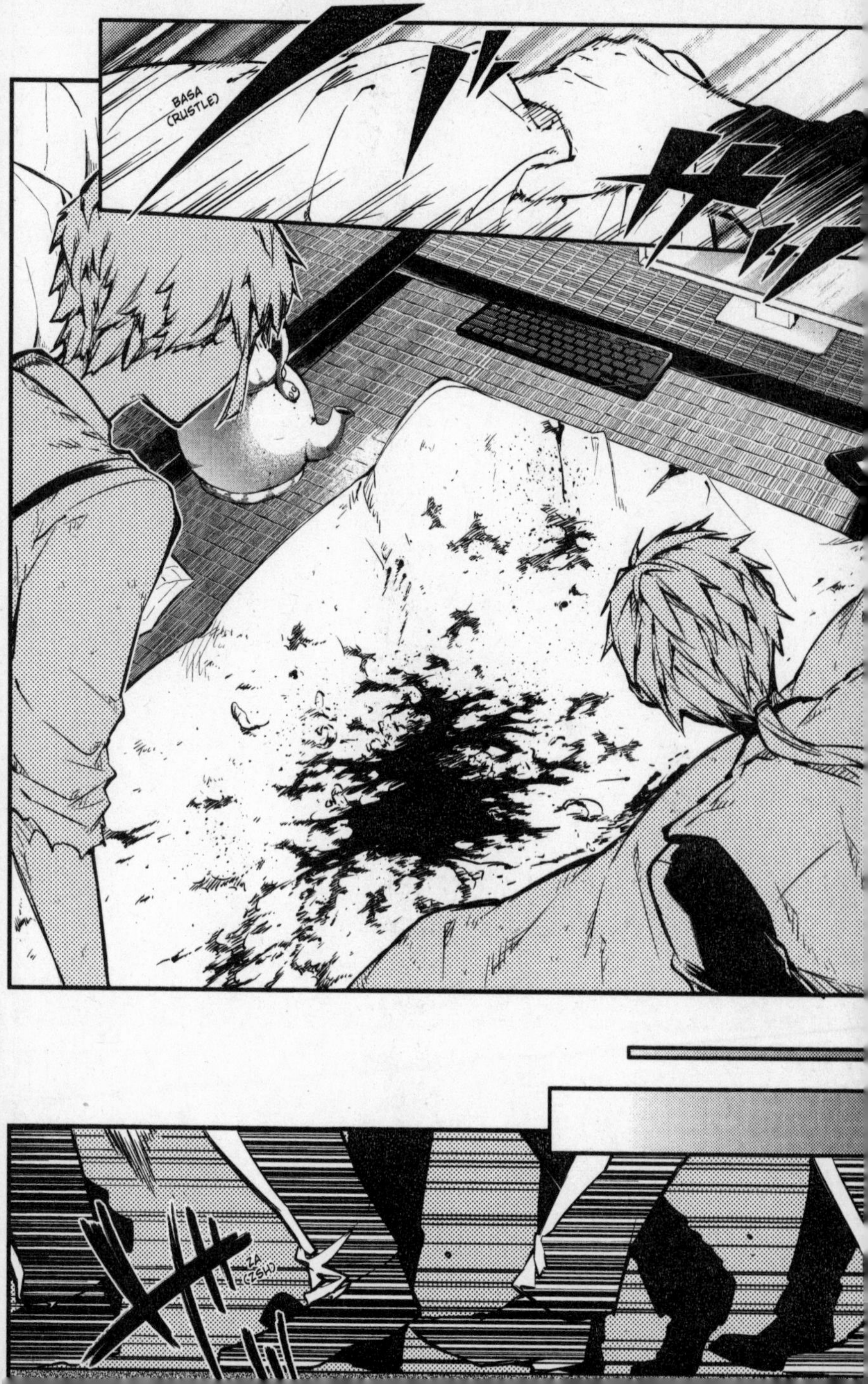
BASA
(RUSTLE)
ZA
(ZSH)

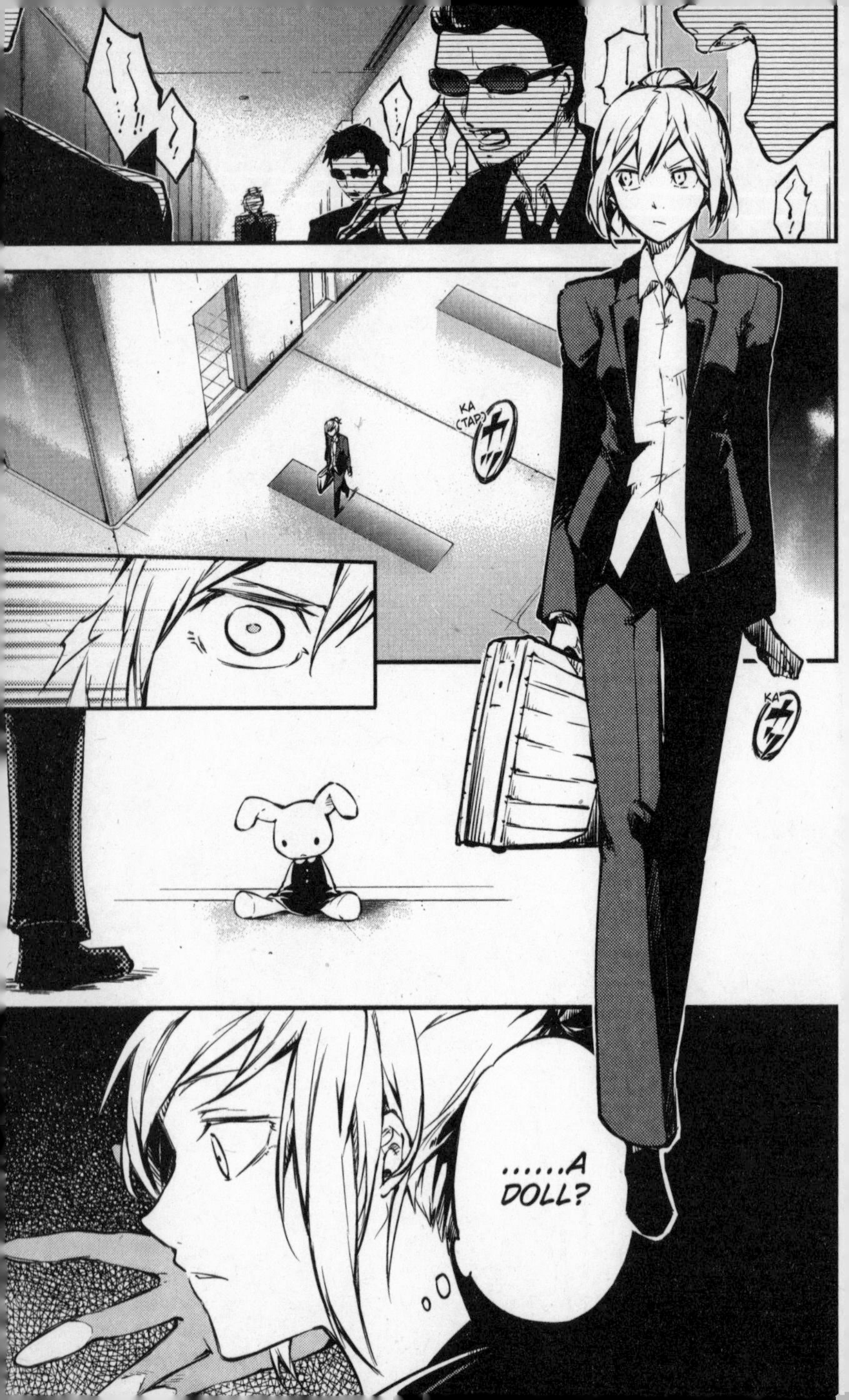

KA (TAP)
KA
......A DOLL?

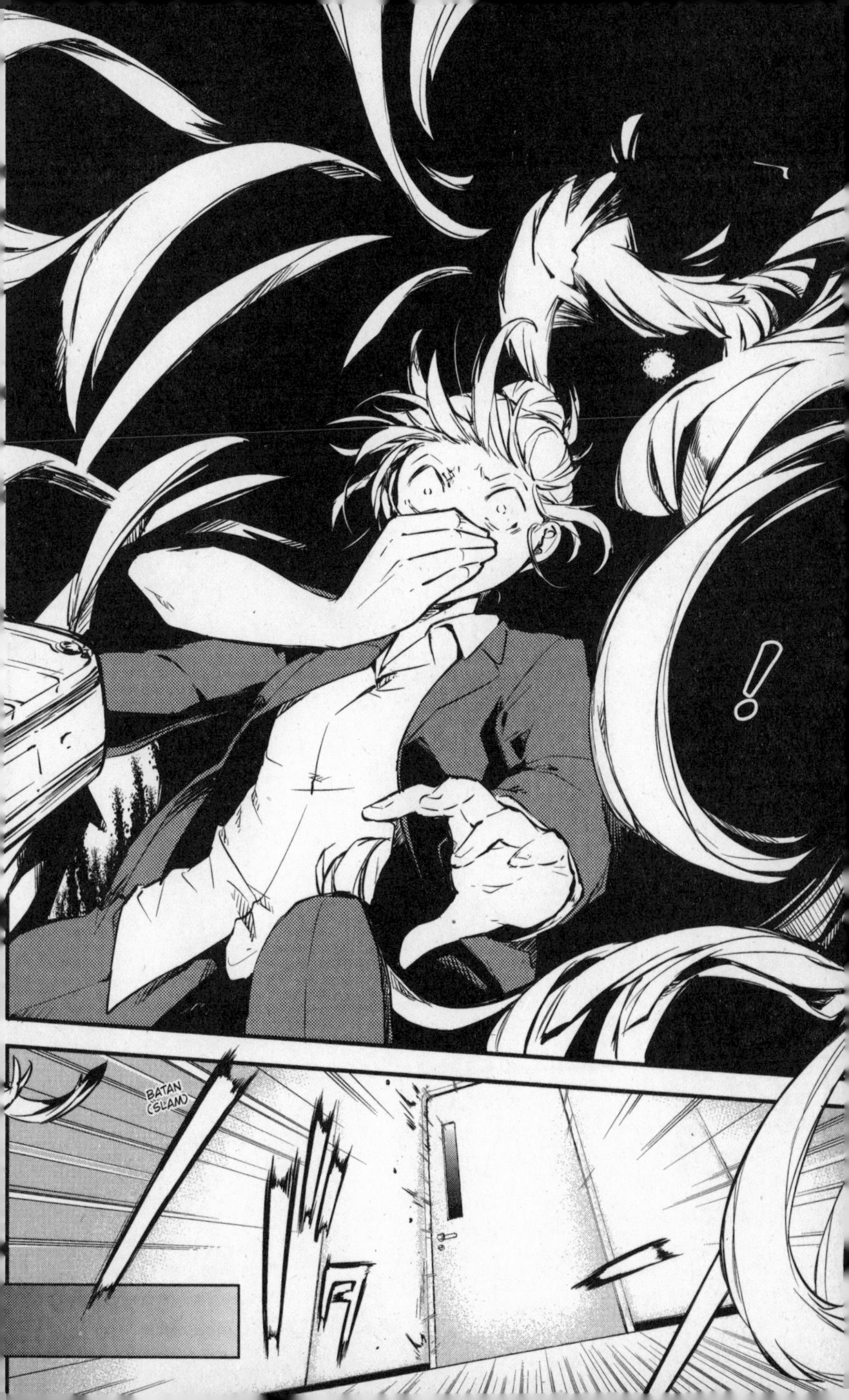
!
BATAN (SLAM)

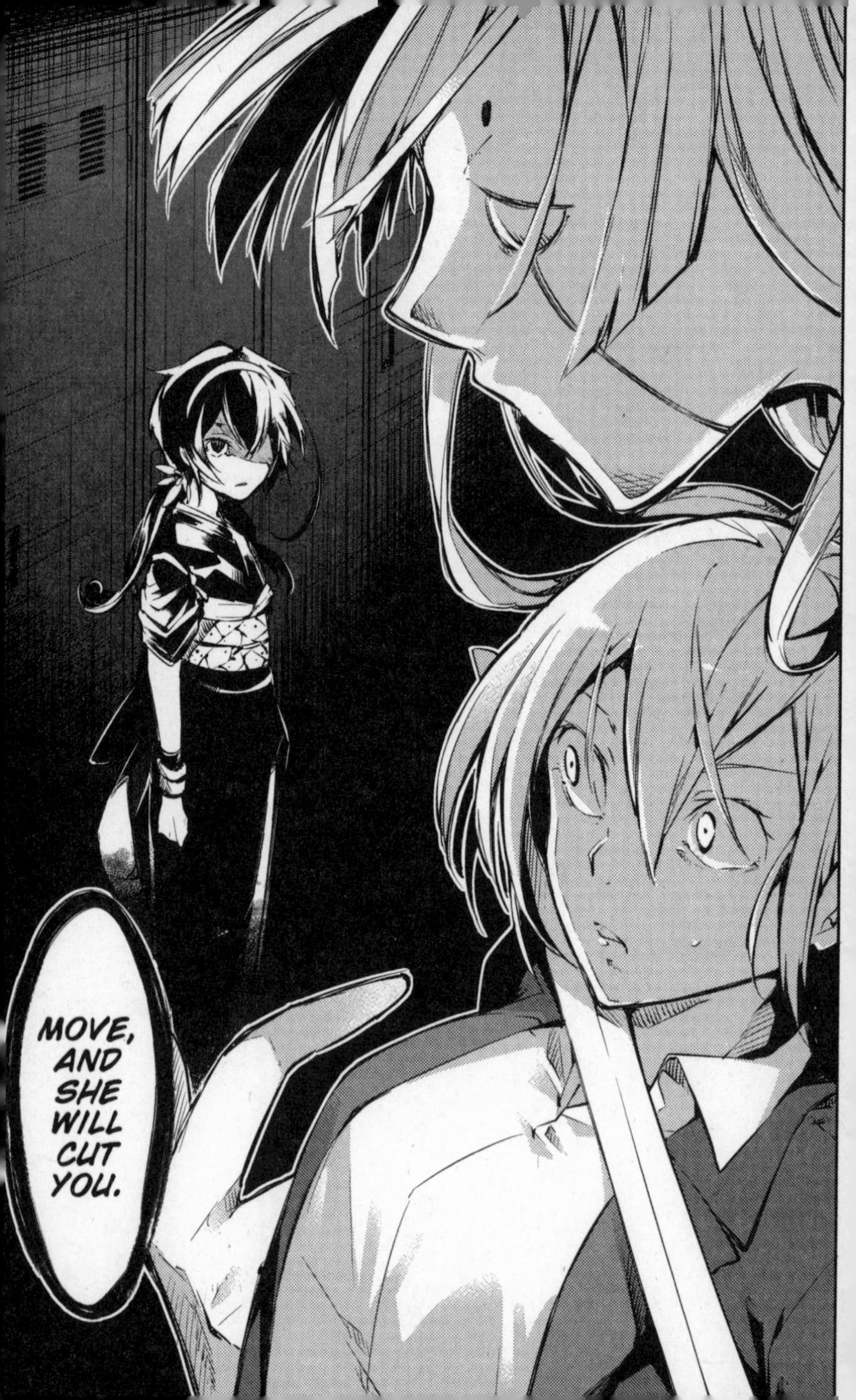
MOVE, AND SHE WILL CUT YOU.

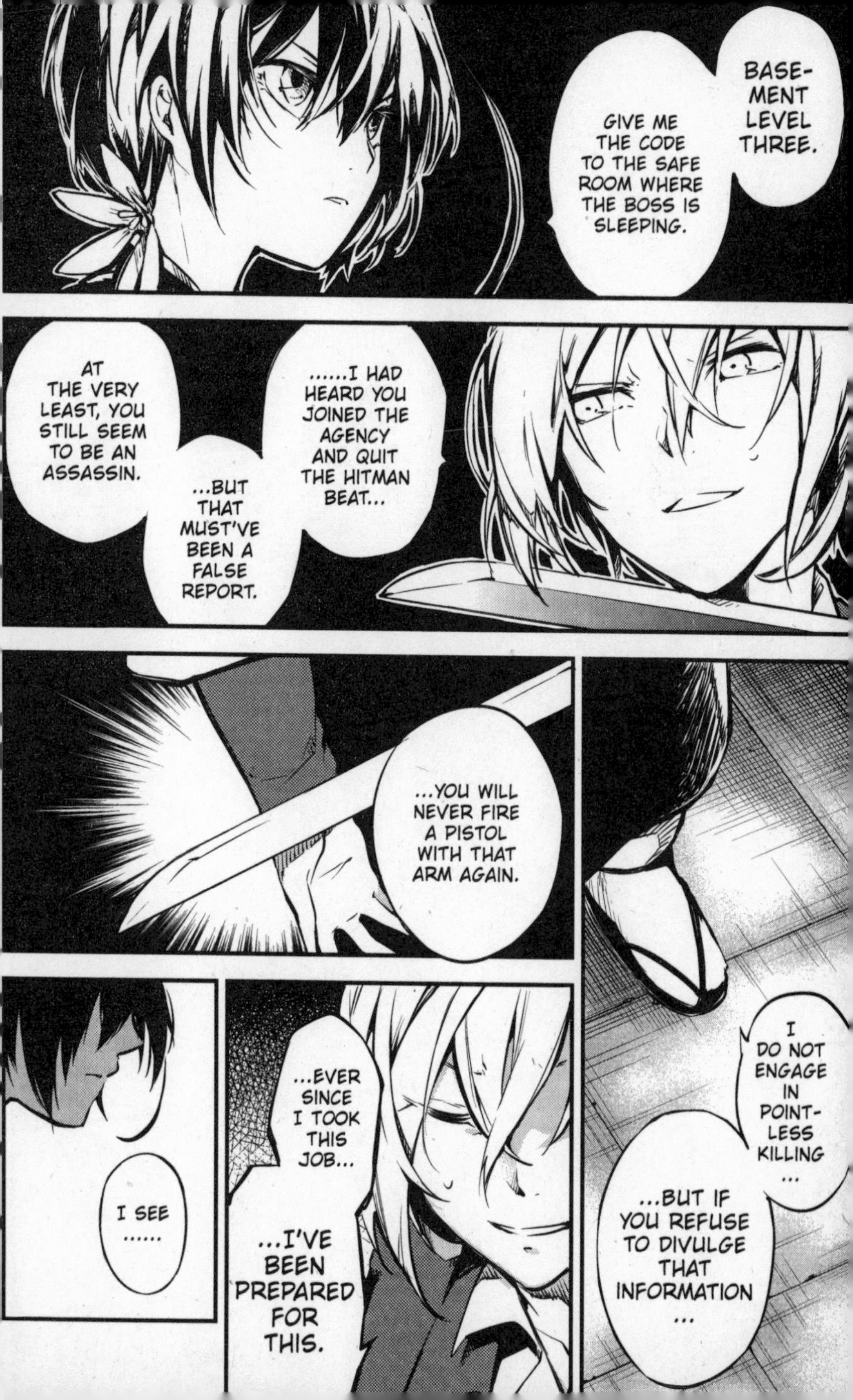
BASE-MENT LEVEL THREE.
GIVE ME THE CODE TO THE SAFE ROOM WHERE THE BOSS IS SLEEPING.
......I HAD HEARD YOU JOINED THE AGENCY AND QUIT THE HITMAN BEAT...
...BUT THAT MUST'VE BEEN A FALSE REPORT.
AT THE VERY LEAST, YOU STILL SEEM TO BE AN ASSASSIN.
I DO NOT ENGAGE IN POINT-LESS KILLING...
...BUT IF YOU REFUSE TO DIVULGE THAT INFORMATION...
...YOU WILL NEVER FIRE A PISTOL WITH THAT ARM AGAIN.
...EVER SINCE I TOOK THIS JOB...
...I'VE BEEN PREPARED FOR THIS.
I SEE ......

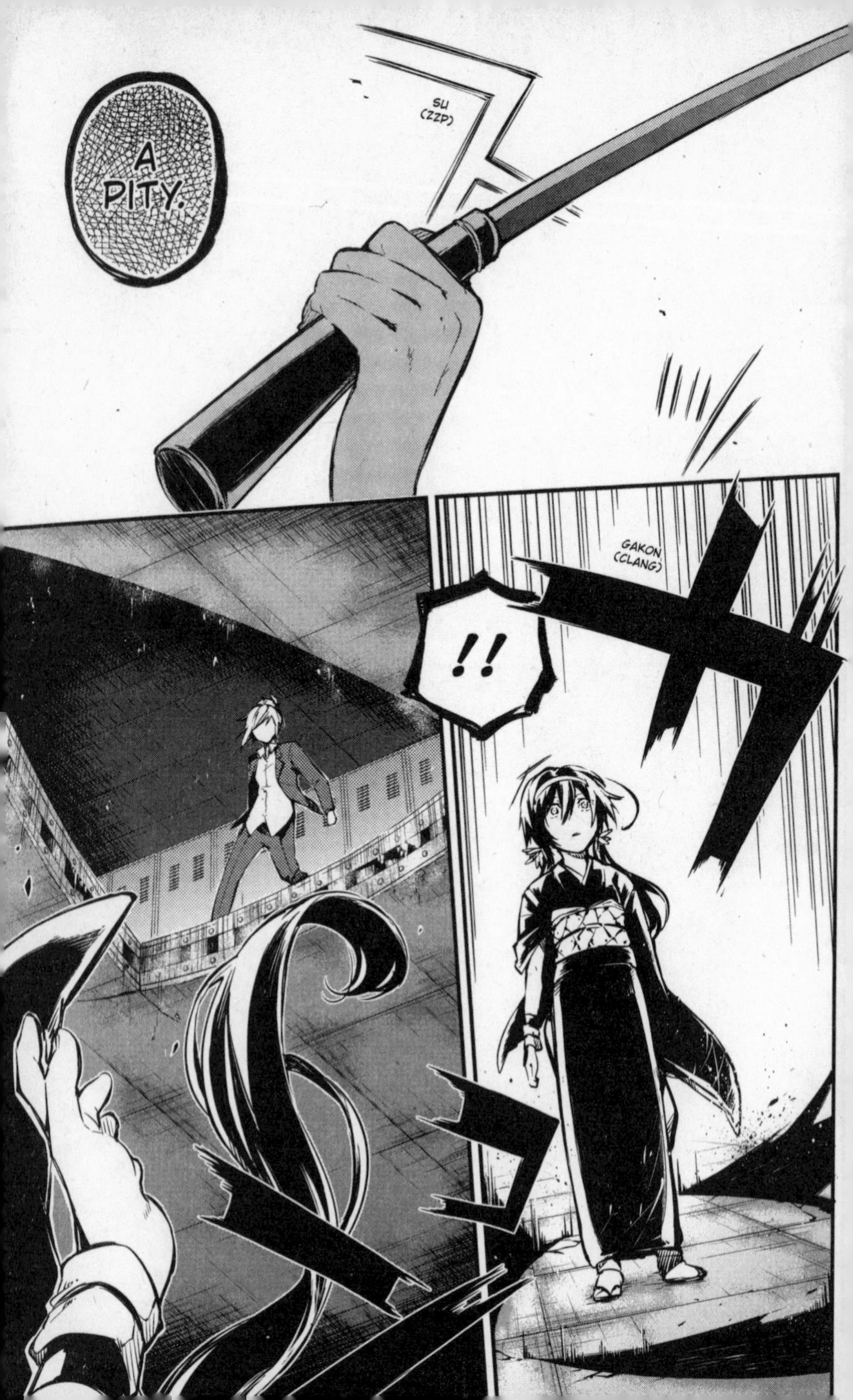
SU
(ZZP)
A PITY.
GAKON
(CLANG)
!!

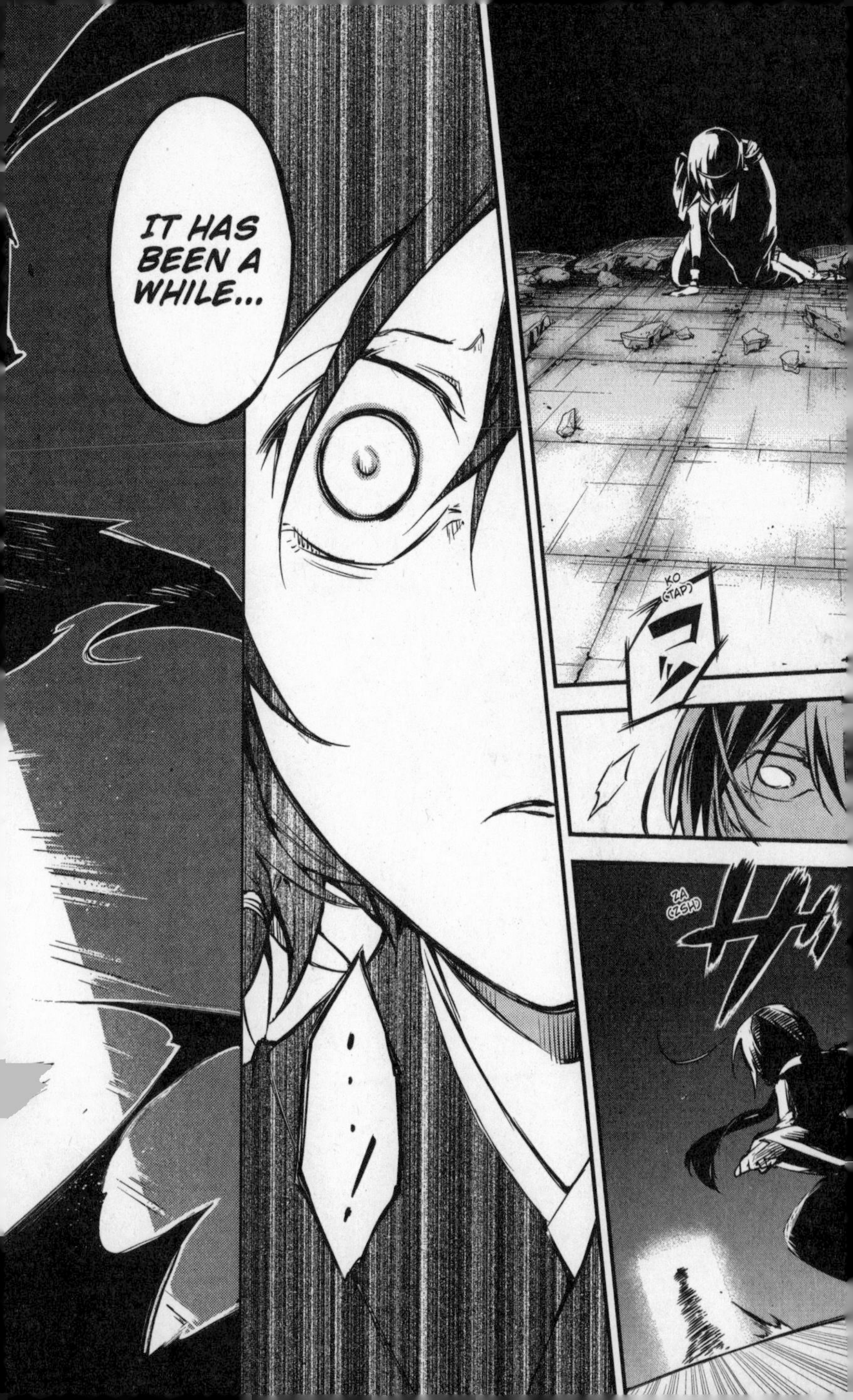
KO (TAP)
ZA (ZSH)
...!
IT HAS BEEN A WHILE...

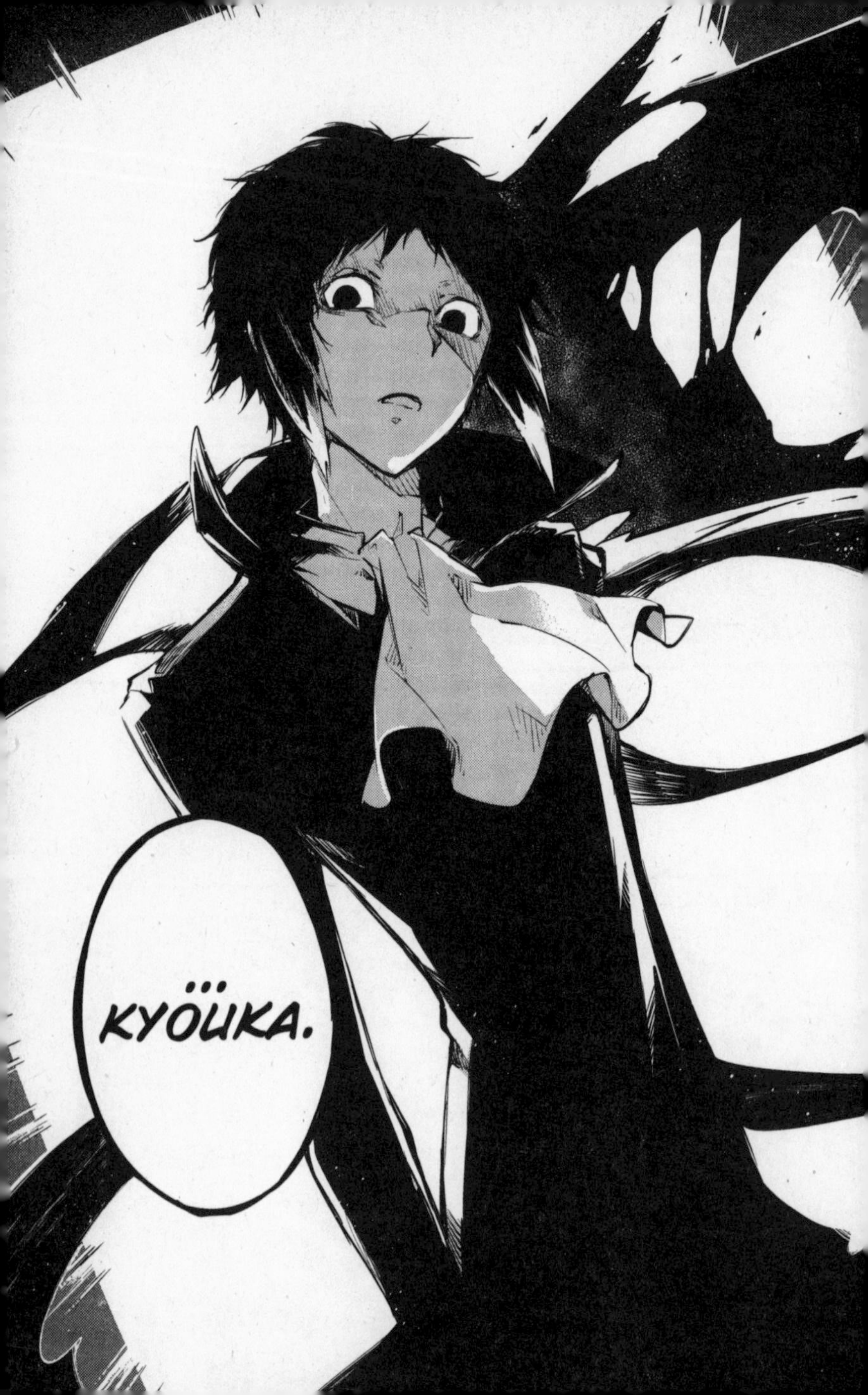
...KYÖUKA.

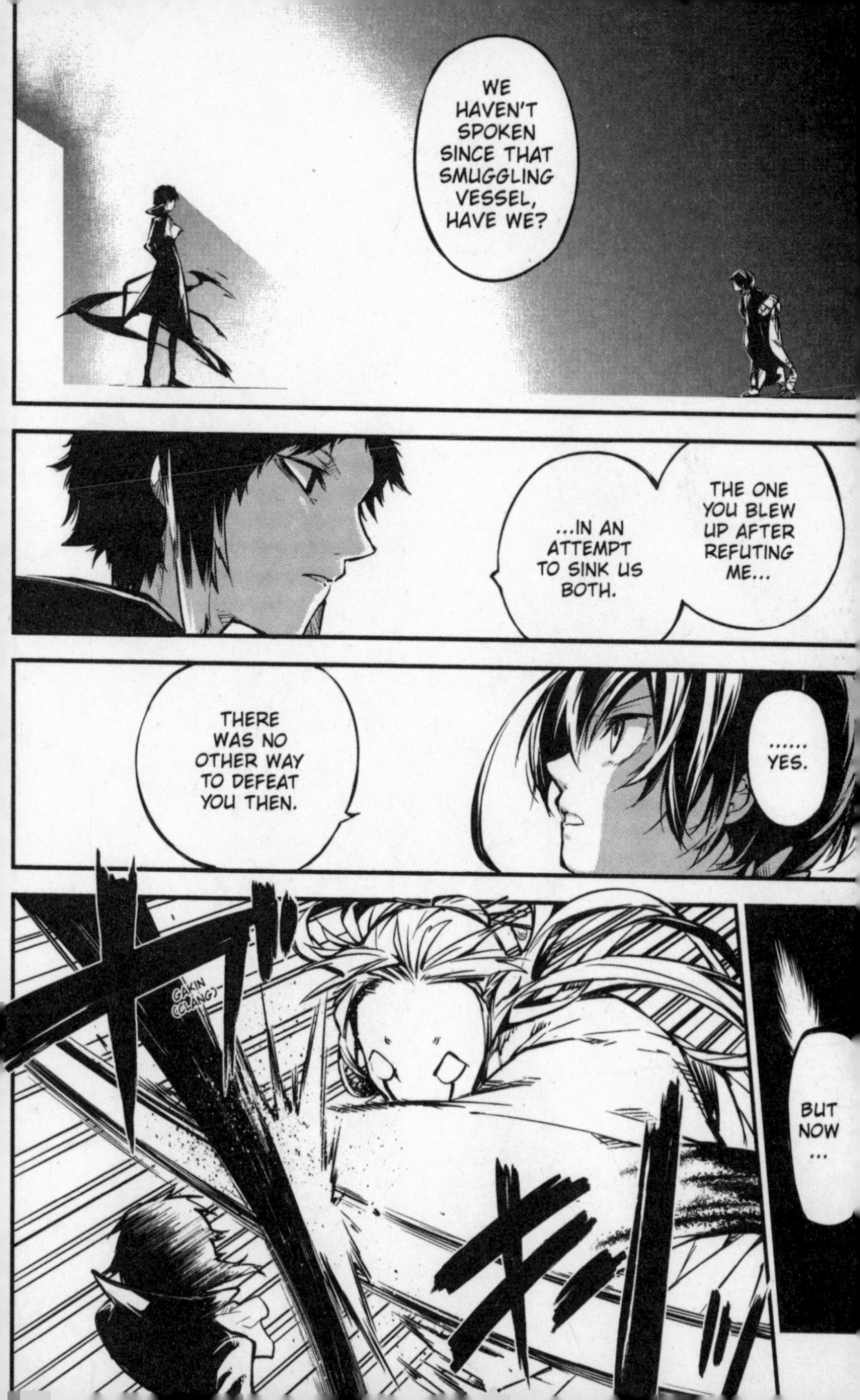
WE HAVEN'T SPOKEN SINCE THAT SMUGGLING VESSEL, HAVE WE?
THE ONE YOU BLEW UP AFTER REFUTING ME...
...IN AN ATTEMPT TO SINK US BOTH.
......YES.
THERE WAS NO OTHER WAY TO DEFEAT YOU THEN.
BUT NOW...
GAKIN (CLANG)

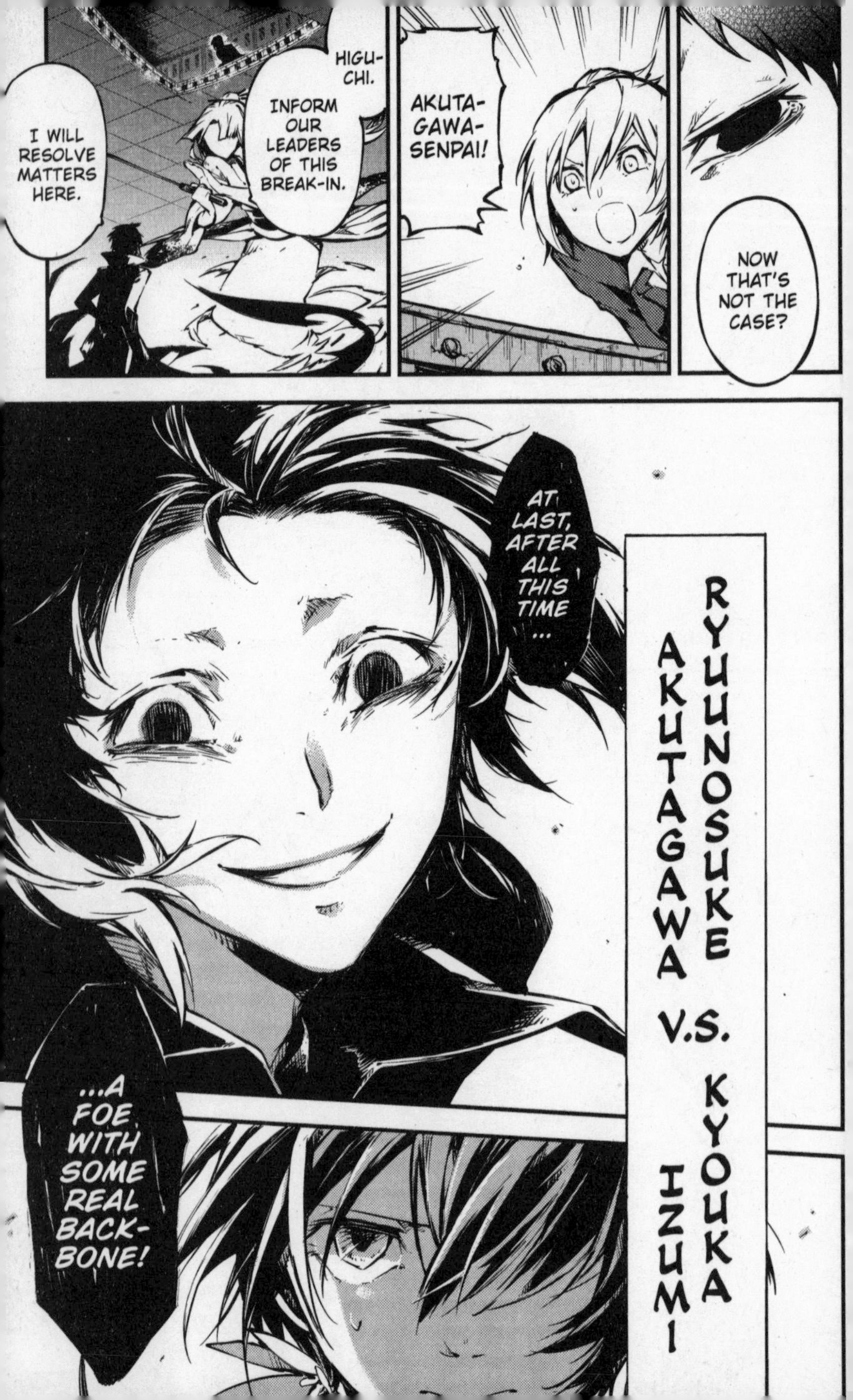

NOW THAT'S NOT THE CASE?
AKUTA-GAWA-SENPAI!
HIGU-CHI.
INFORM OUR LEADERS OF THIS BREAK-IN.
I WILL RESOLVE MATTERS HERE.
AT LAST, AFTER ALL THIS TIME...
RYUUNOSUKE AKUTAGAWA V.S. KYOUKA IZUMI
...A FOE WITH SOME REAL BACK-BONE!

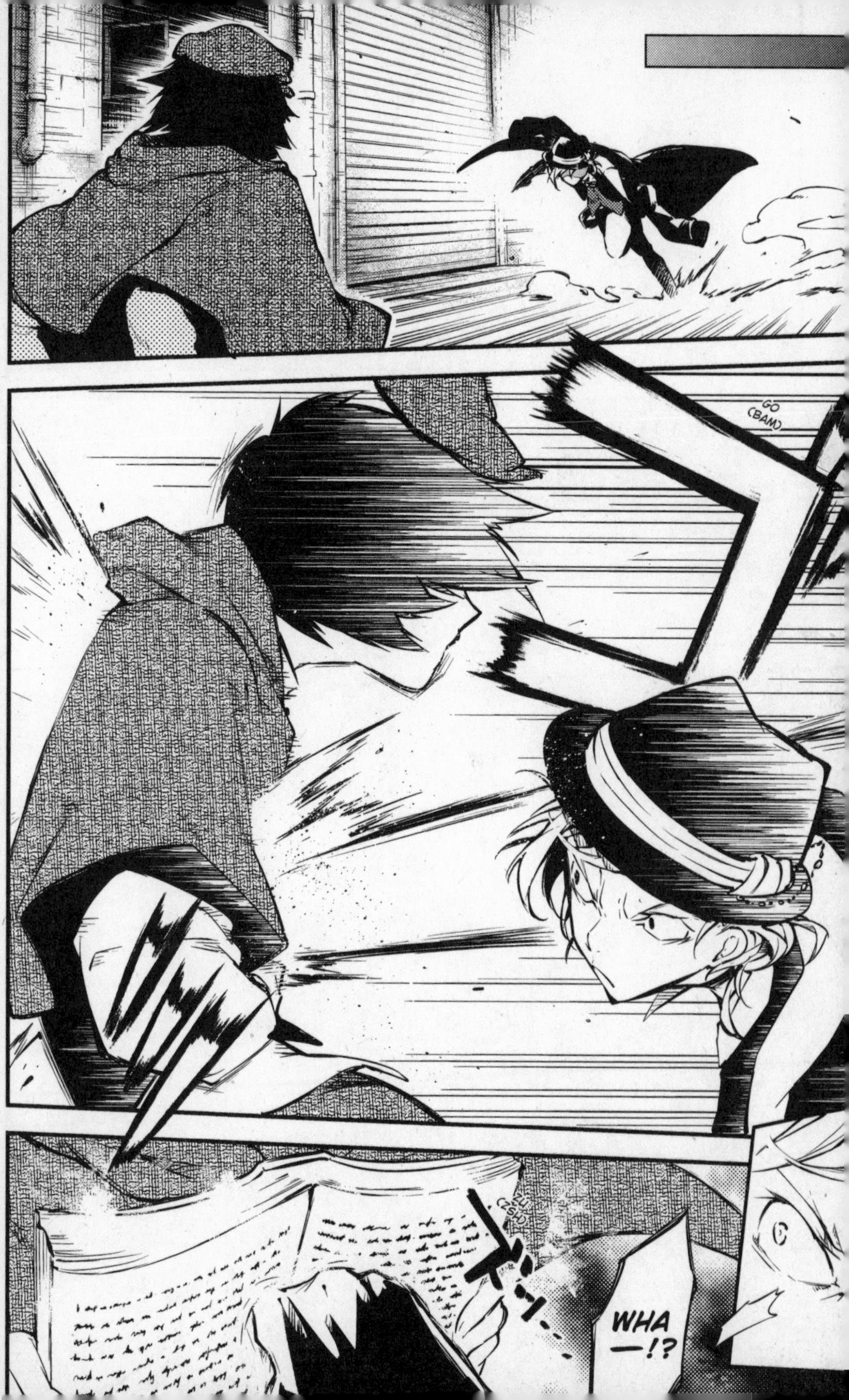
GO
(BAM)
ZU
(ZSH)
WHA—!?

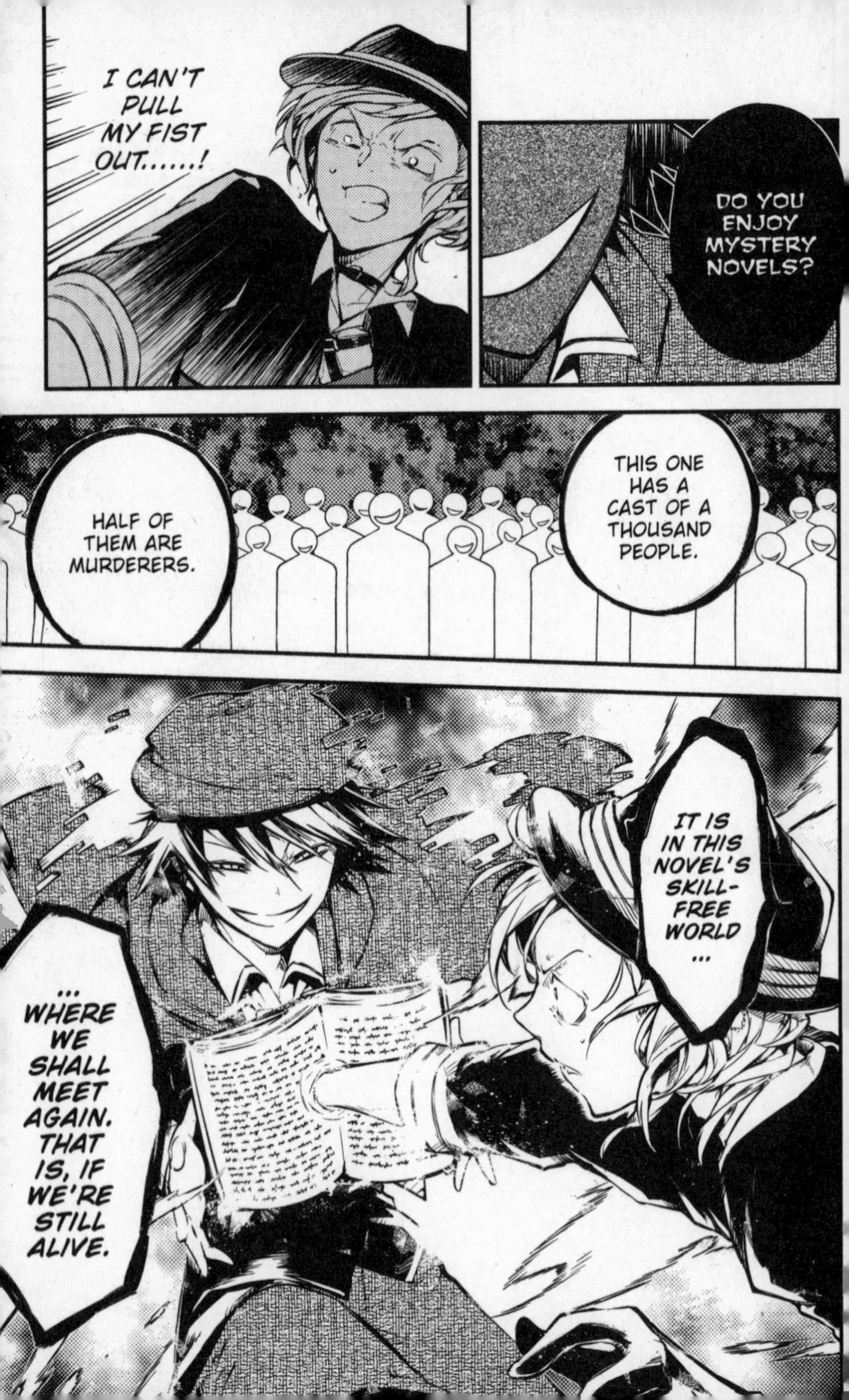
DO YOU ENJOY MYSTERY NOVELS?
I CAN'T PULL MY FIST OUT......!
THIS ONE HAS A CAST OF A THOUSAND PEOPLE.
HALF OF THEM ARE MURDERERS.
IT IS IN THIS NOVEL'S SKILL-FREE WORLD ...
... WHERE WE SHALL MEET AGAIN. THAT IS, IF WE'RE STILL ALIVE.

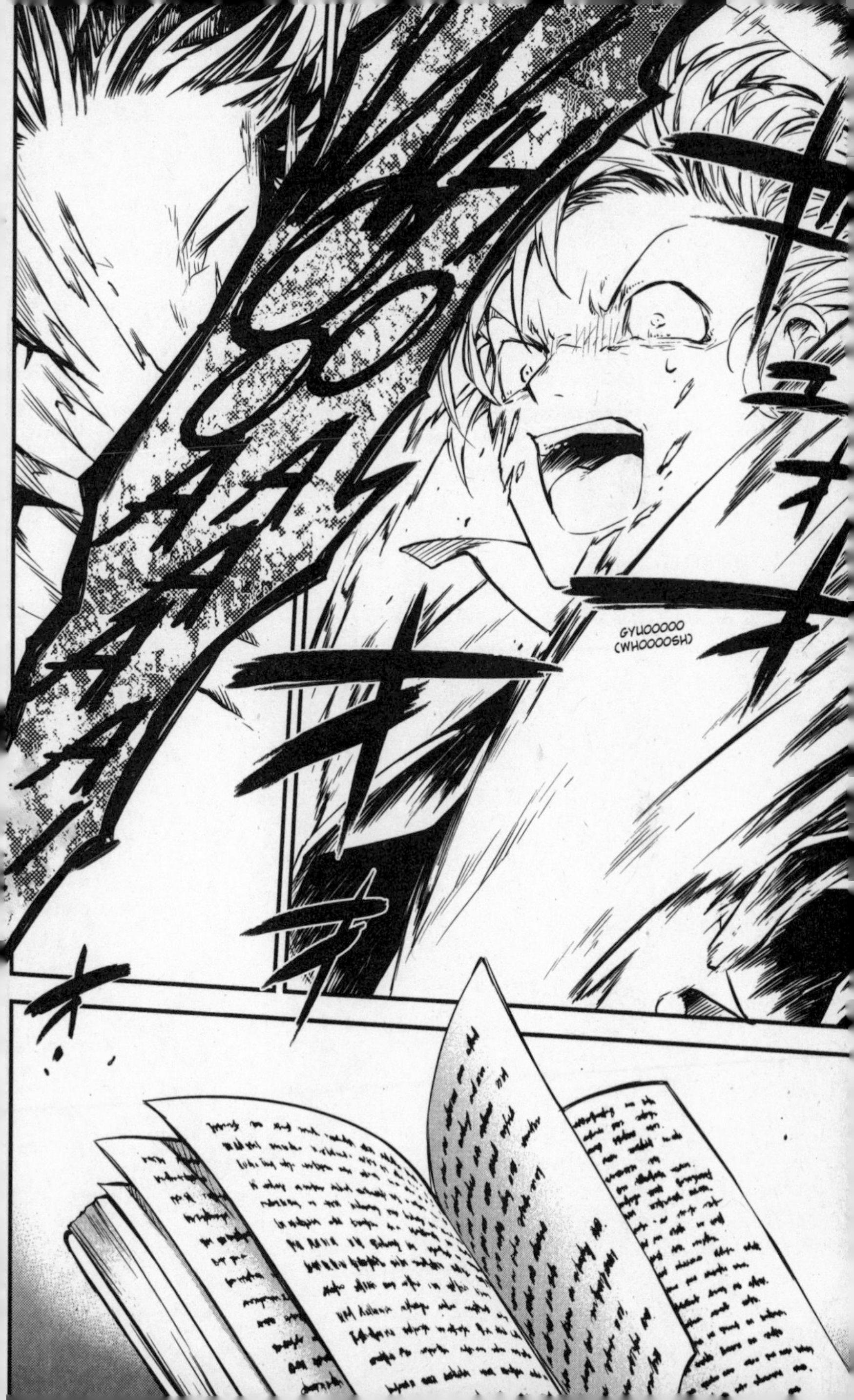
GYUOOOOO
(WHOOOOSH)

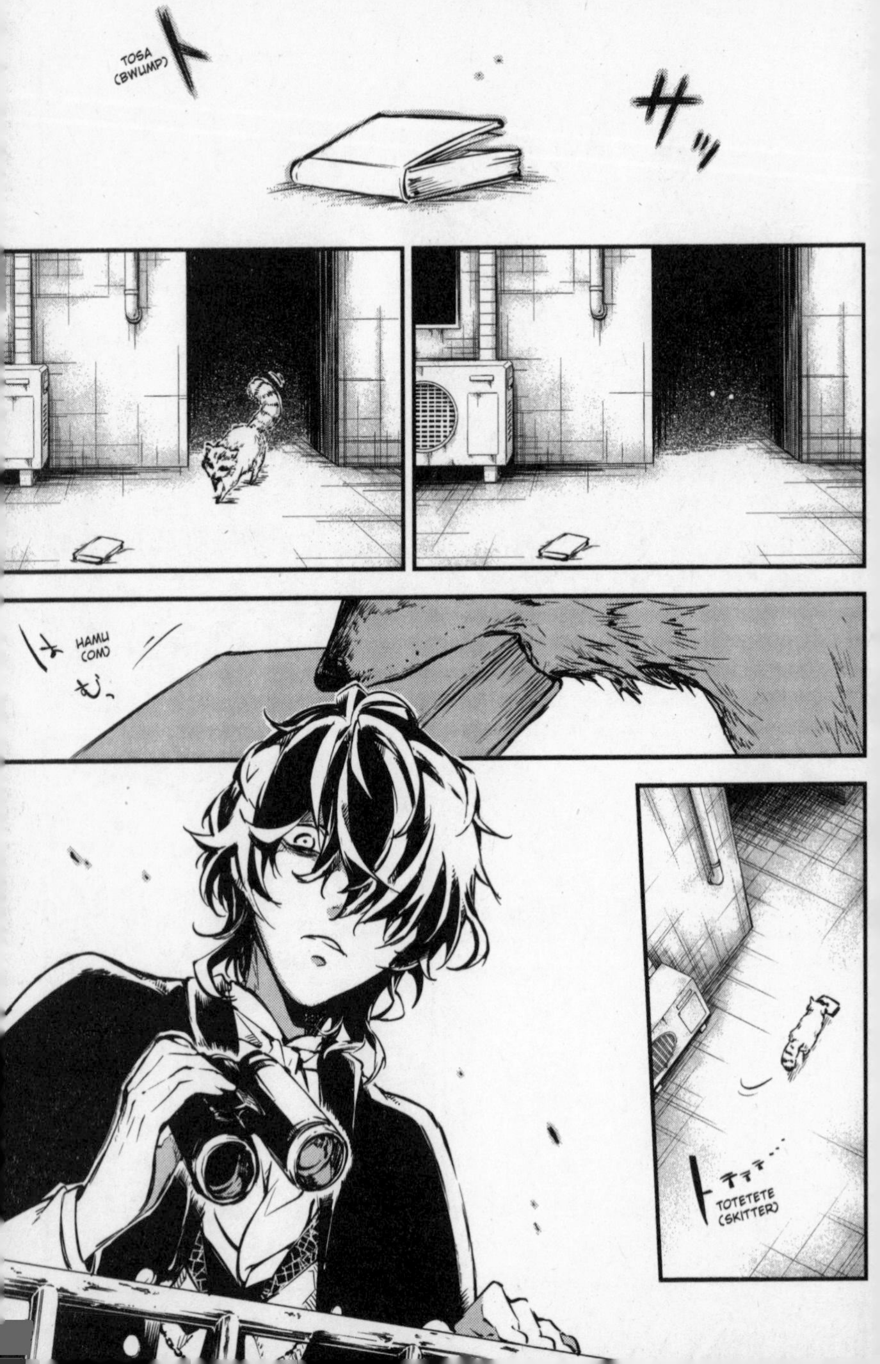

TOSA
(BWUMP)
HAMU
(OM)
TOTETETE
(SKITTER)

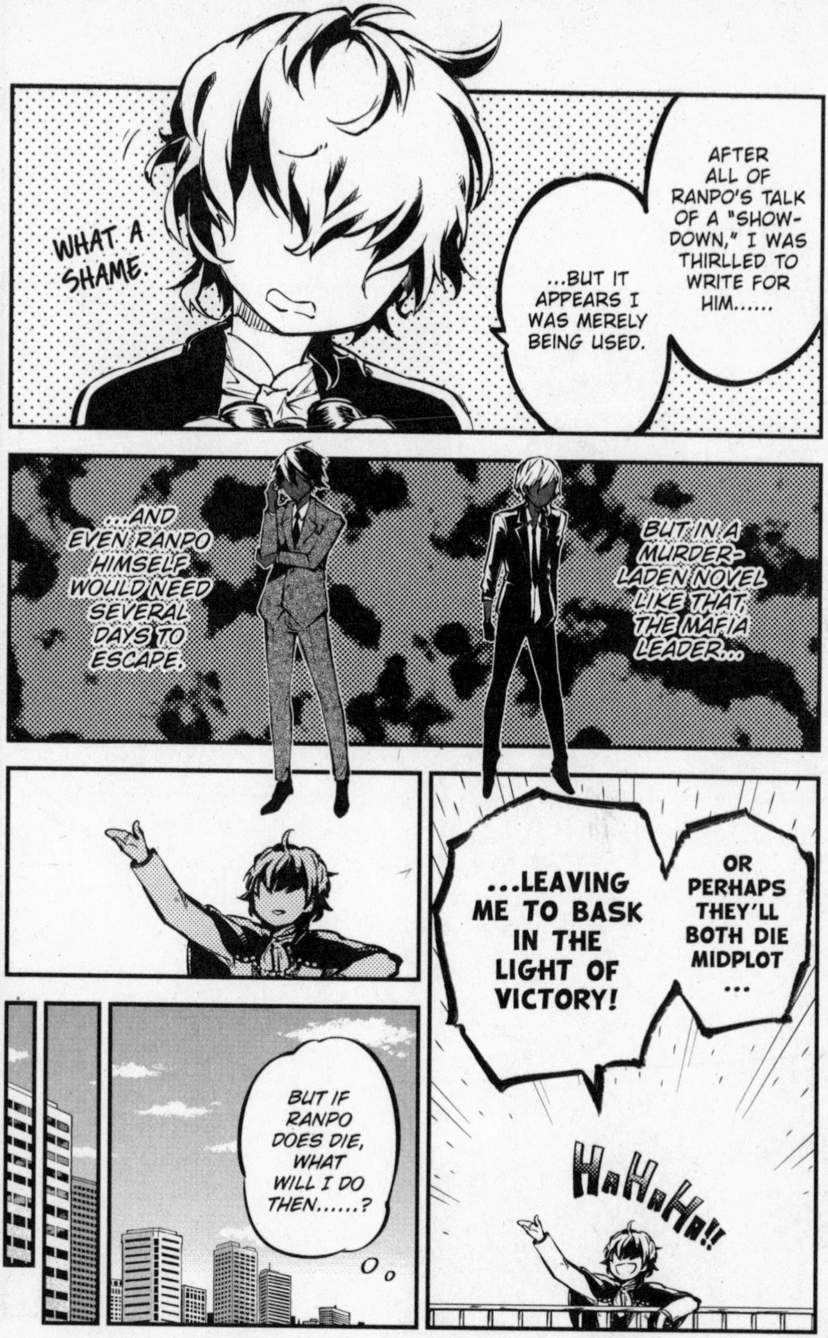
AFTER ALL OF RANPO'S TALK OF A "SHOW-DOWN," I WAS THIRLLED TO WRITE FOR HIM......
...BUT IT APPEARS I WAS MERELY BEING USED.
WHAT A SHAME.
BUT IN A MURDER-LADEN NOVEL LIKE THAT, THE MAFIA LEADER...
...AND EVEN RANPO HIMSELF WOULD NEED SEVERAL DAYS TO ESCAPE.
OR PERHAPS THEY'LL BOTH DIE MIDPLOT ...
...LEAVING ME TO BASK IN THE LIGHT OF VICTORY!
HaHaHa!!
BUT IF RANPO DOES DIE, WHAT WILL I DO THEN......?

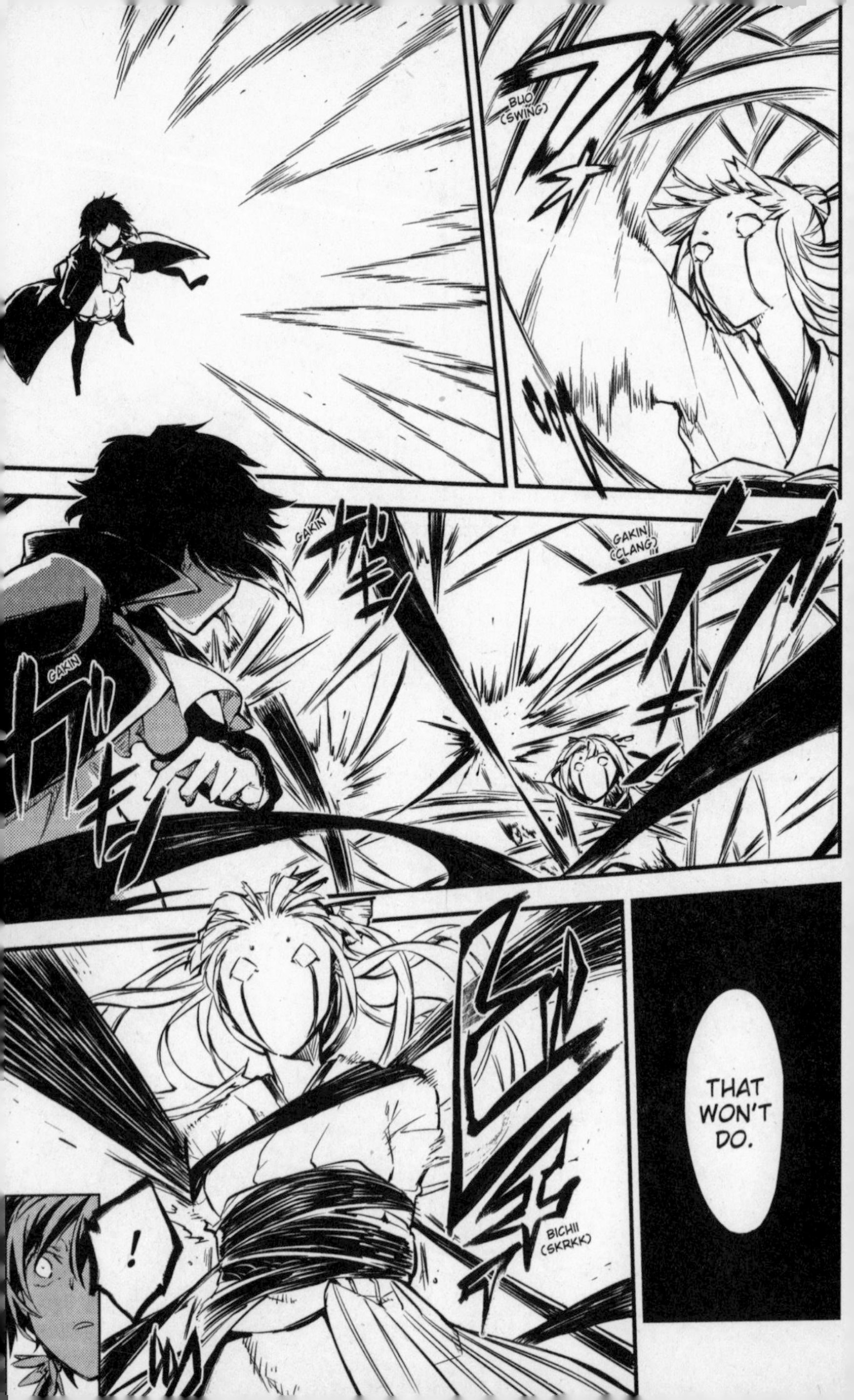
BUO (SWING)
GAKIN (CLANG)
GAKIN
GAKIN
THAT WON'T DO.
BICHII (SKRKK)
!

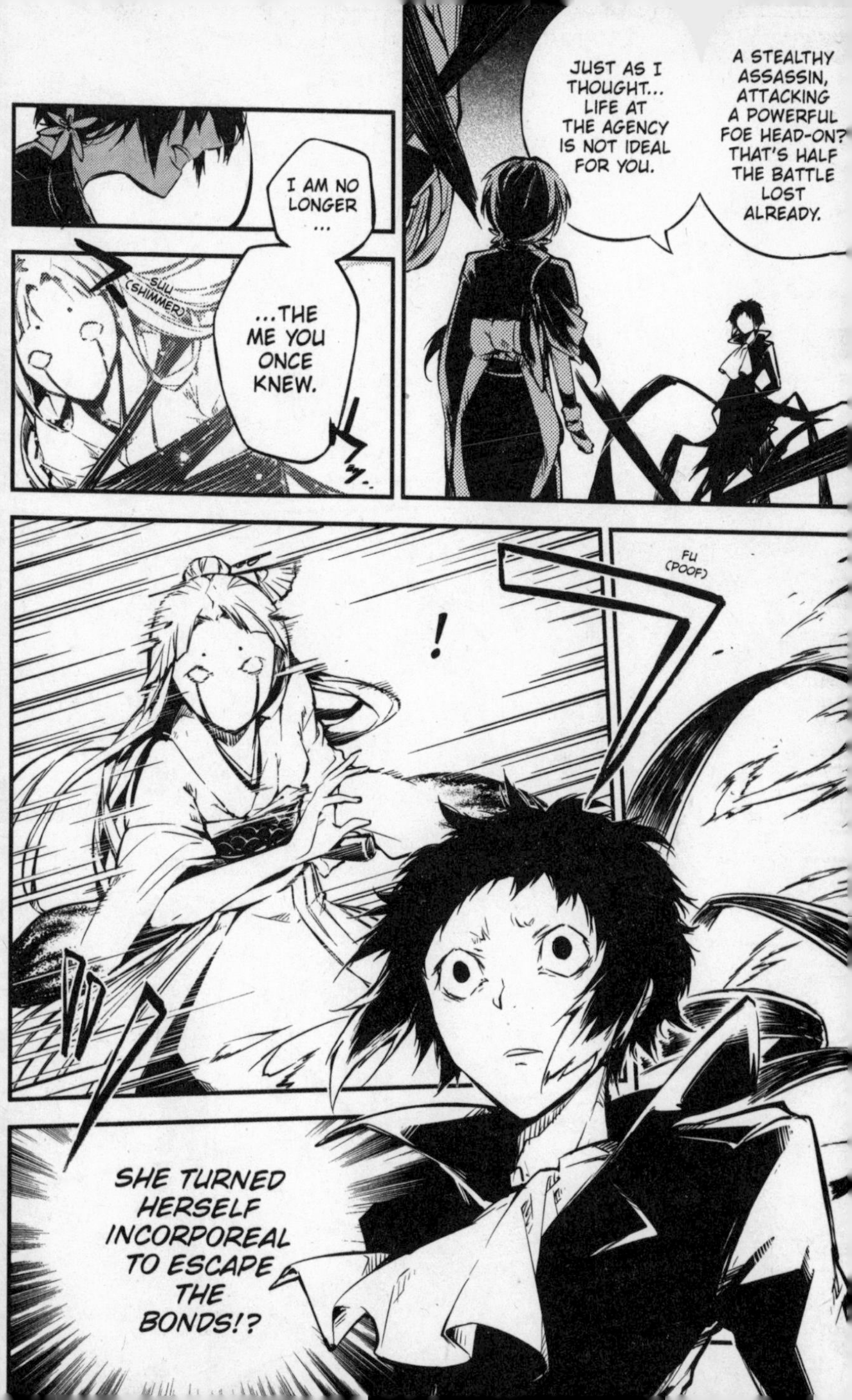
JUST AS I THOUGHT... LIFE AT THE AGENCY IS NOT IDEAL FOR YOU.
A STEALTHY ASSASSIN, ATTACKING A POWERFUL FOE HEAD-ON? THAT'S HALF THE BATTLE LOST ALREADY.
I AM NO LONGER ...
...THE ME YOU ONCE KNEW.
SUU (SHIMMER)
FU (POOF)
!
SHE TURNED HERSELF INCORPOREAL TO ESCAPE THE BONDS!?

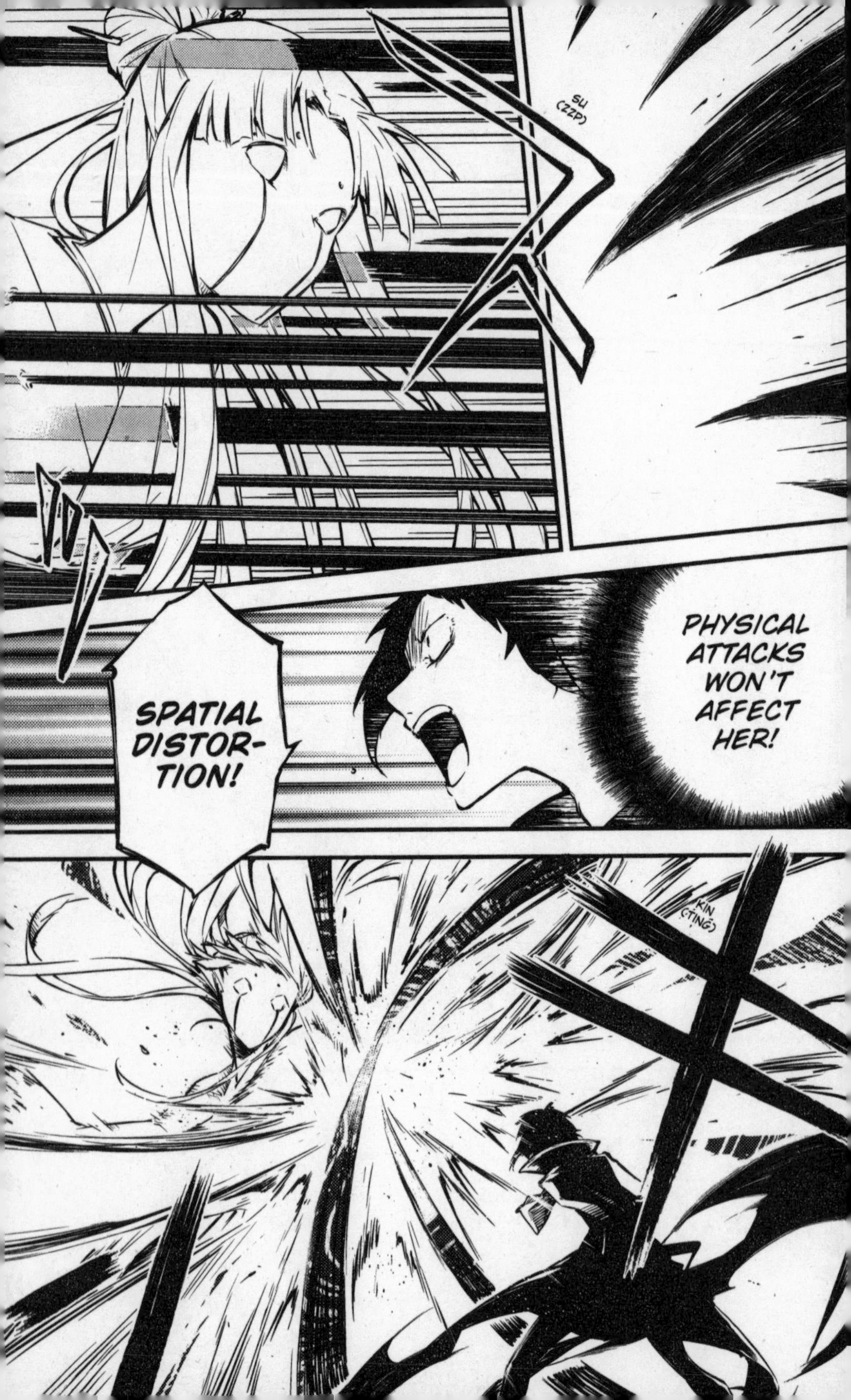
SU (ZZP)
PHYSICAL ATTACKS WON'T AFFECT HER!
SPATIAL DISTOR-TION!
KIN (TING)

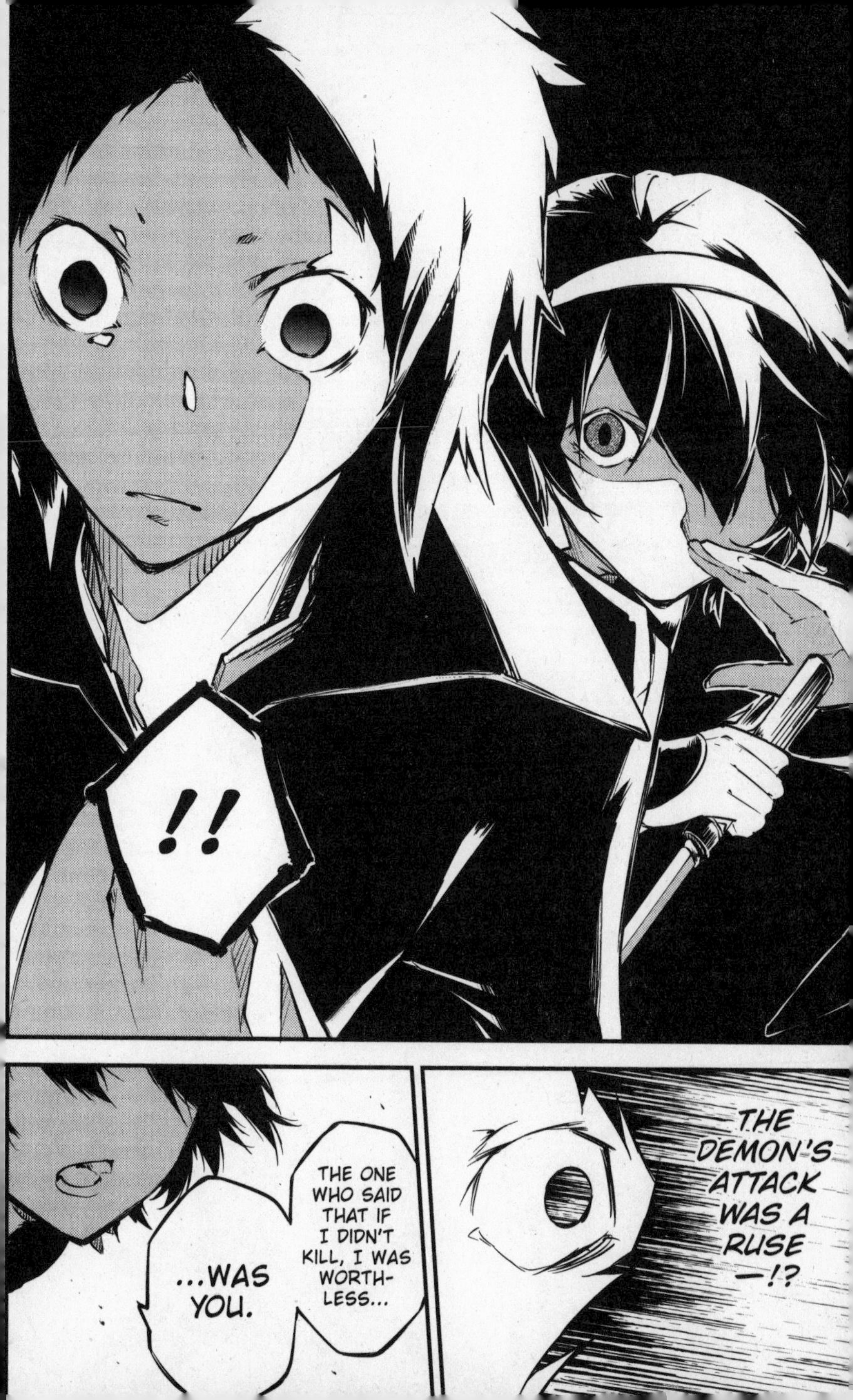
!!
THE DEMON'S ATTACK WAS A RUSE —!?
THE ONE WHO SAID THAT IF I DIDN'T KILL, I WAS WORTHLESS...
...WAS YOU.

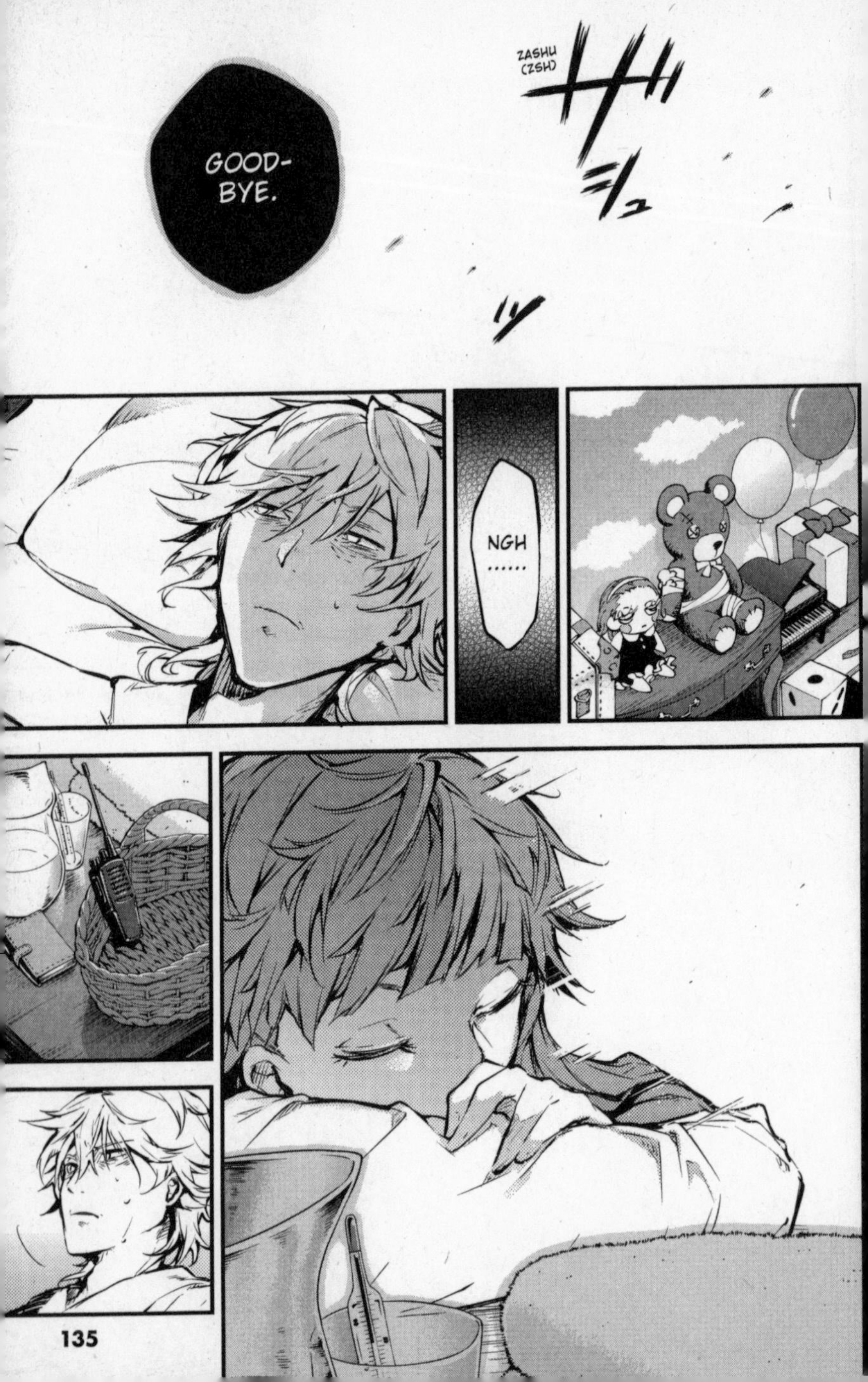
ZASHU (ZSH)
GOOD-BYE.
NGH ......

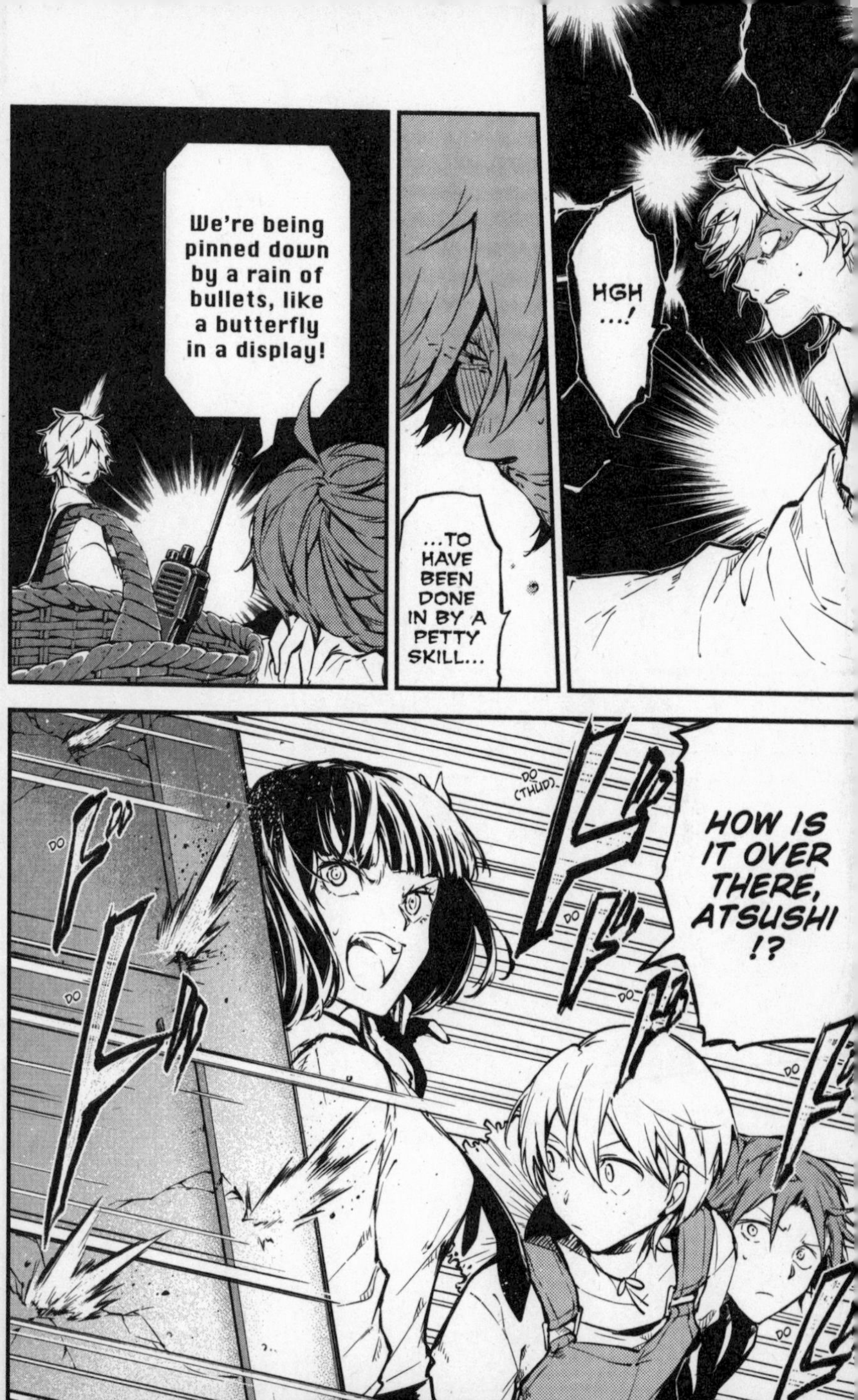
HGH ...!
...TO HAVE BEEN DONE IN BY A PETTY SKILL...
We're being pinned down by a rain of bullets, like a butterfly in a display!
HOW IS IT OVER THERE, ATSUSHI!?
DO (THUD)
DO
DO
DO
DO
DO
DO

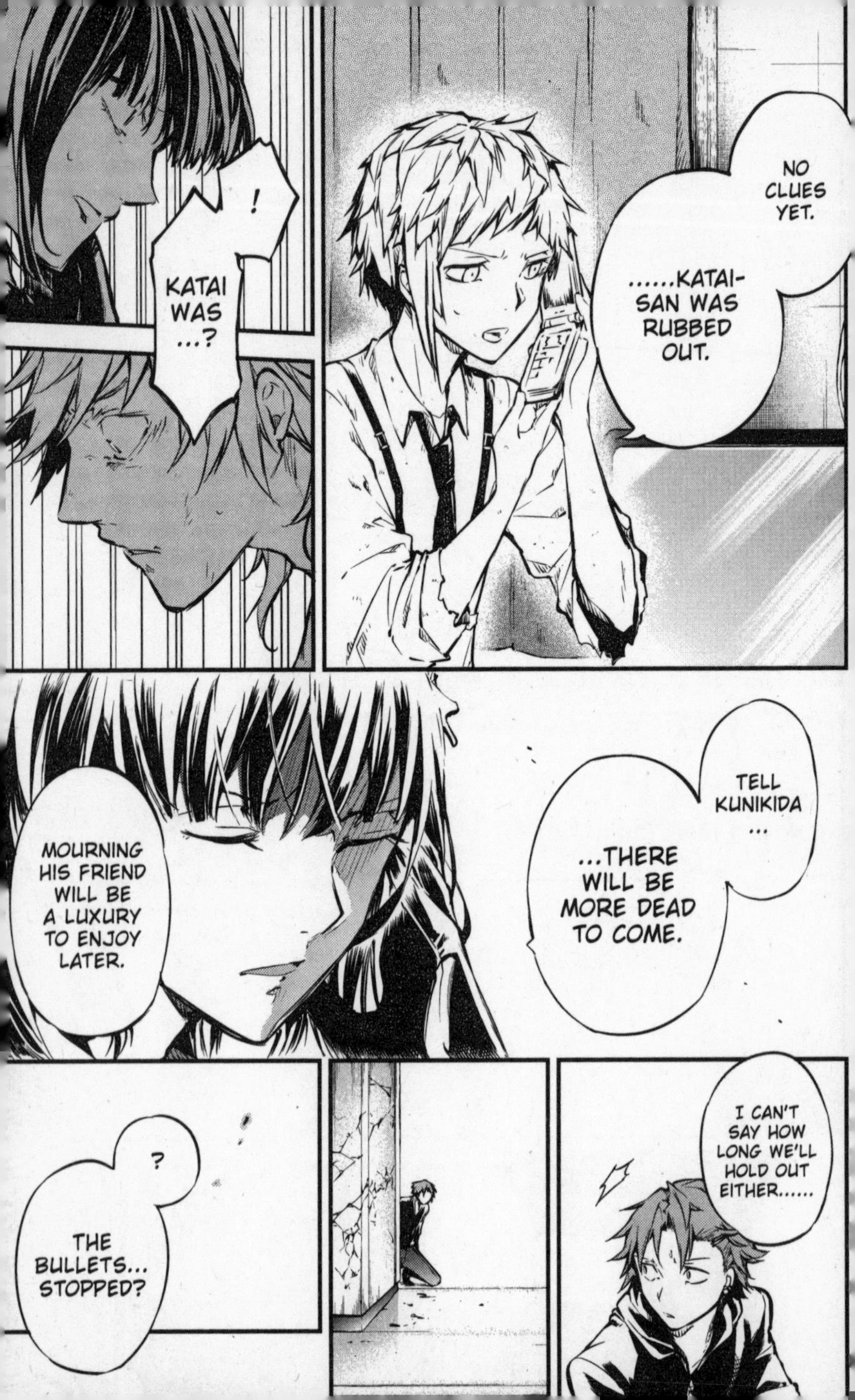
NO CLUES YET.
......KATAI-SAN WAS RUBBED OUT.
!
KATAI WAS ...?
TELL KUNIKIDA ...
...THERE WILL BE MORE DEAD TO COME.
MOURNING HIS FRIEND WILL BE A LUXURY TO ENJOY LATER.
I CAN'T SAY HOW LONG WE'LL HOLD OUT EITHER......
?
THE BULLETS... STOPPED?

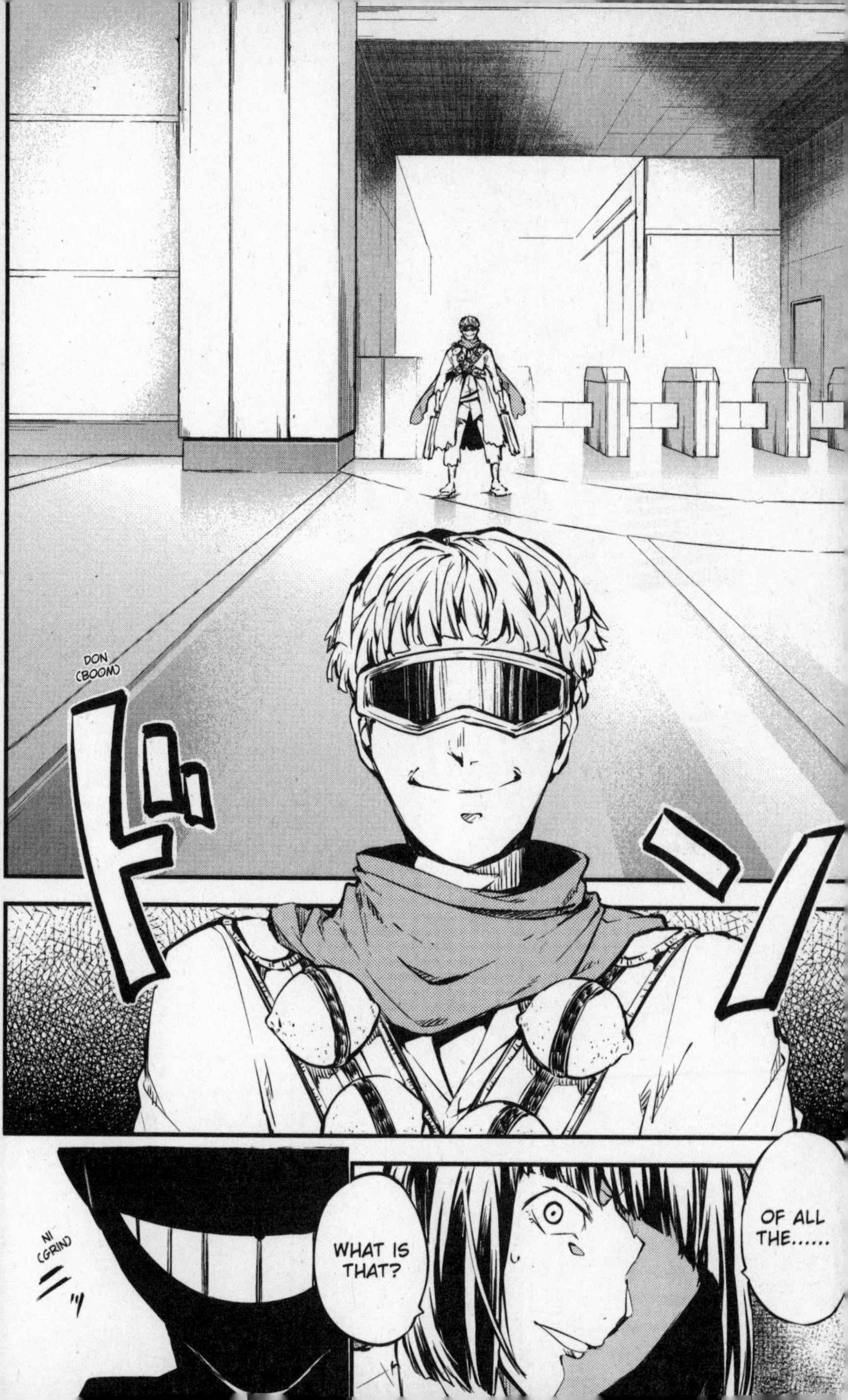
DON (BOOM)
OF ALL THE......
WHAT IS THAT?
NI (GRIND)

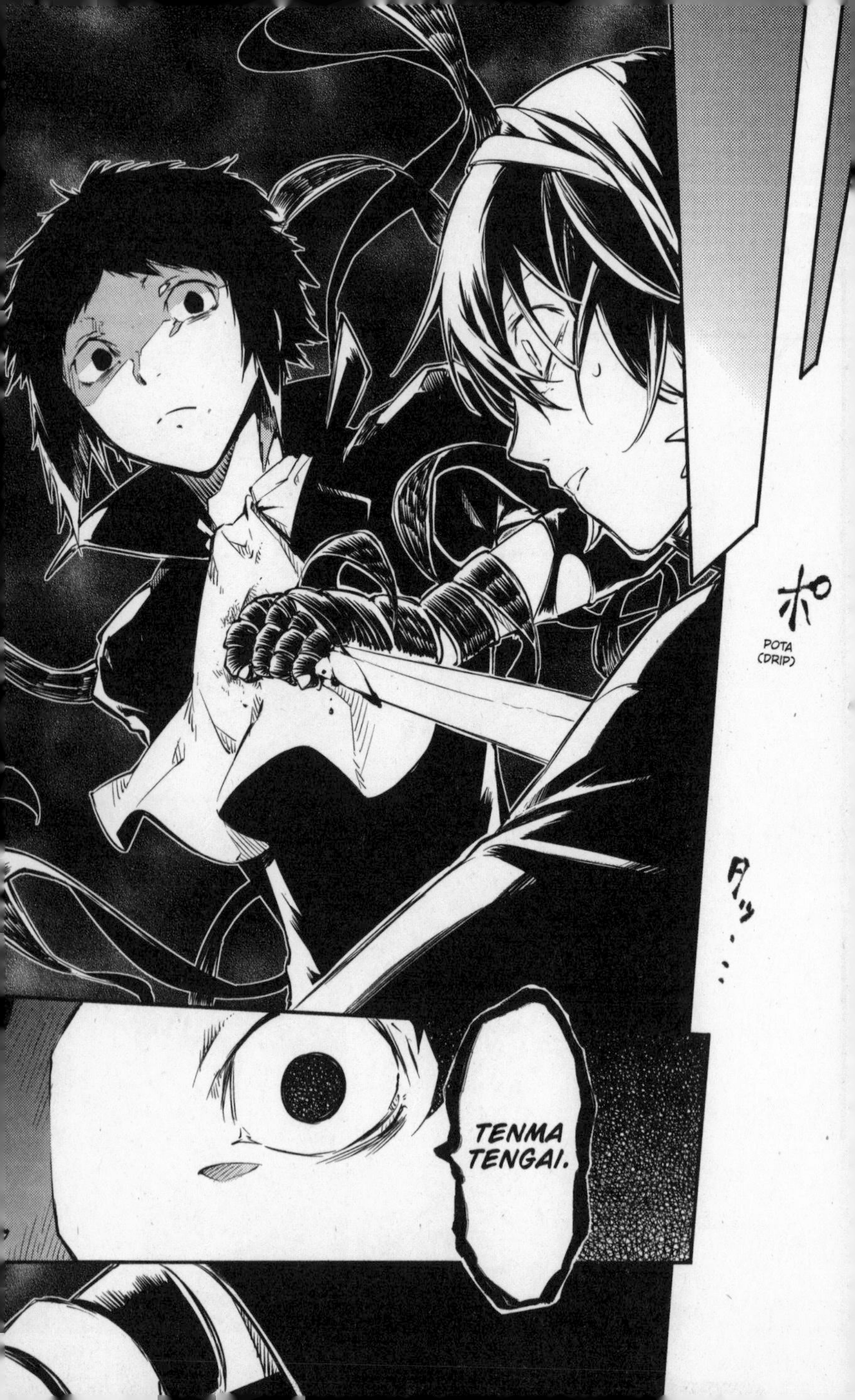
ポ
POTA (DRIP)
TENMA TENGAI.

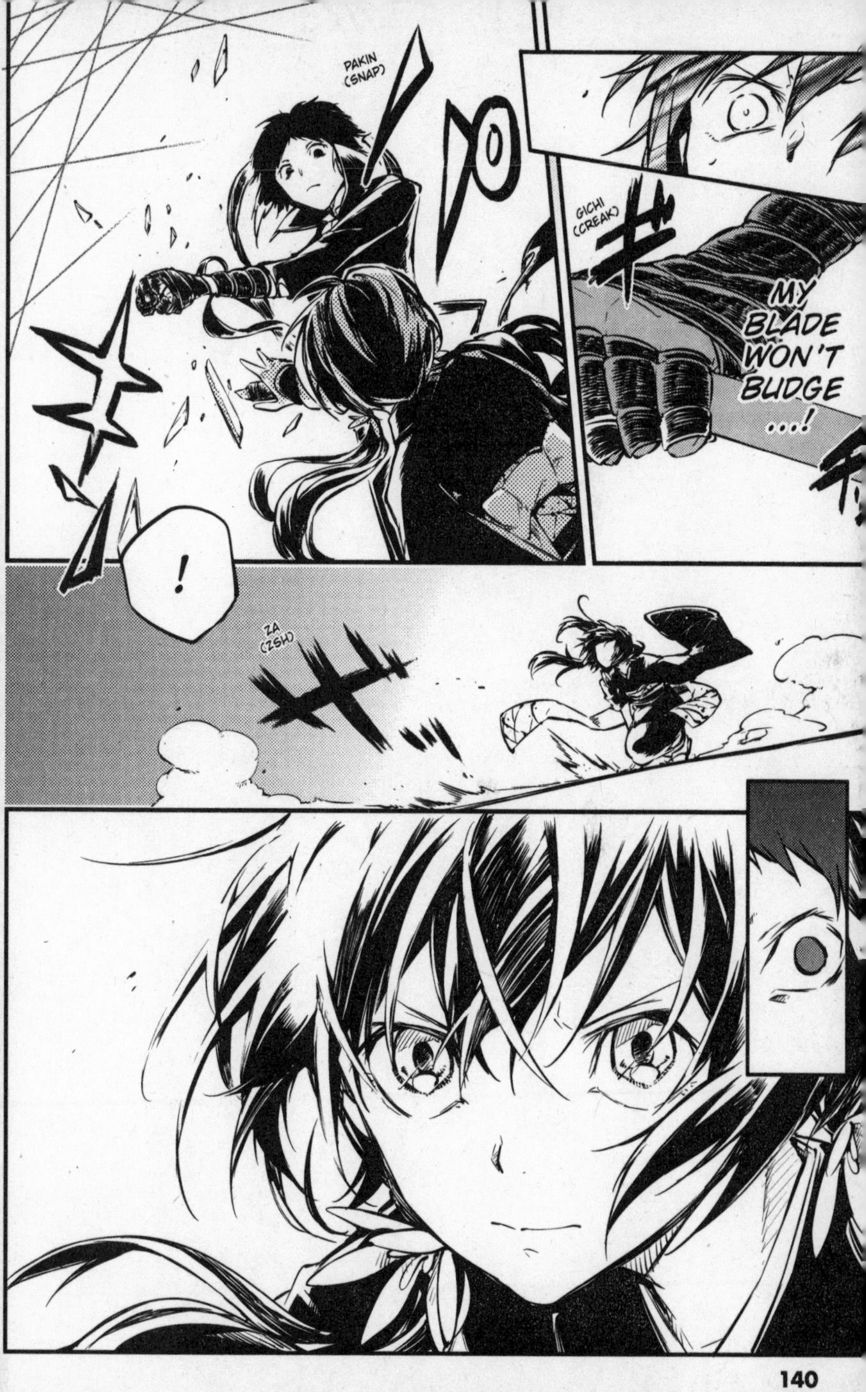
GICHI (CREAK)
MY BLADE WON'T BUDGE ...!
PAKIN (SNAP)
!
ZA (ZSH)

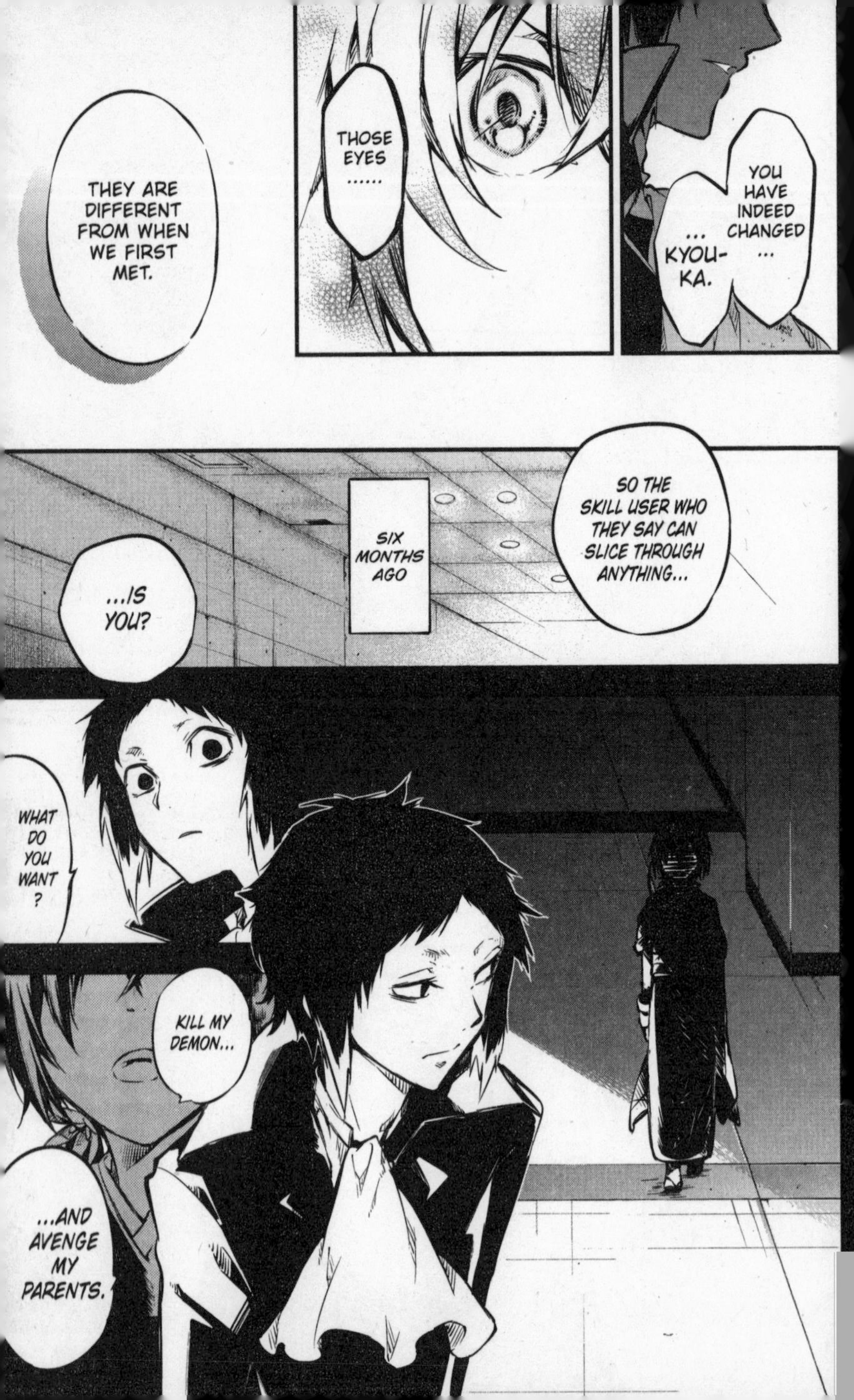
YOU HAVE INDEED CHANGED ...
... KYOU-KA.
THOSE EYES ......
THEY ARE DIFFERENT FROM WHEN WE FIRST MET.
SO THE SKILL USER WHO THEY SAY CAN SLICE THROUGH ANYTHING...
SIX MONTHS AGO
...IS YOU?
WHAT DO YOU WANT ?
KILL MY DEMON...
...AND AVENGE MY PARENTS.

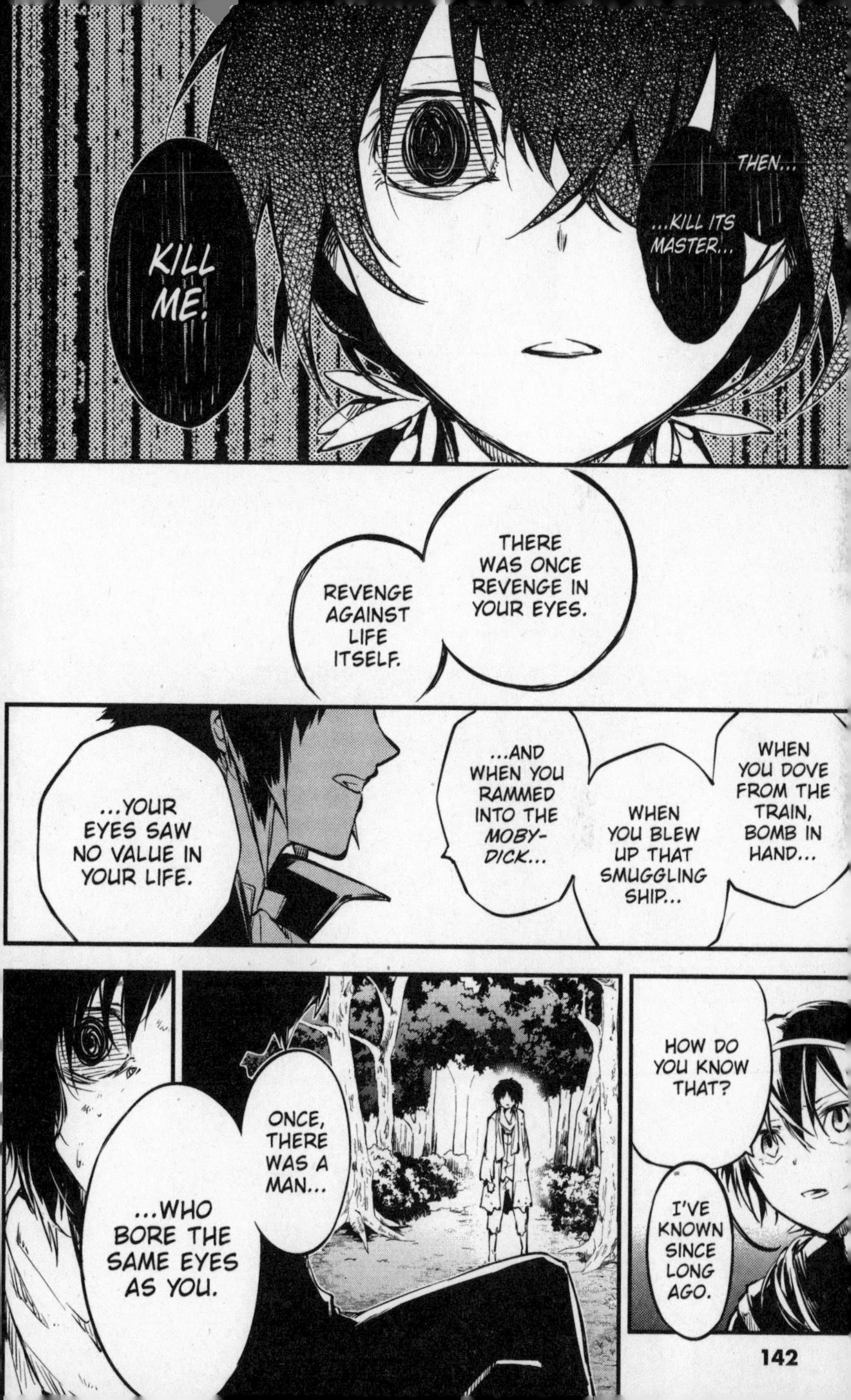
THEN...
...KILL ITS MASTER...
KILL ME.
THERE WAS ONCE REVENGE IN YOUR EYES.
REVENGE AGAINST LIFE ITSELF.
WHEN YOU DOVE FROM THE TRAIN, BOMB IN HAND...
WHEN YOU BLEW UP THAT SMUGGLING SHIP...
...AND WHEN YOU RAMMED INTO THE *MOBY-DICK*...
...YOUR EYES SAW NO VALUE IN YOUR LIFE.
HOW DO YOU KNOW THAT?
I'VE KNOWN SINCE LONG AGO.
ONCE, THERE WAS A MAN...
...WHO BORE THE SAME EYES AS YOU.

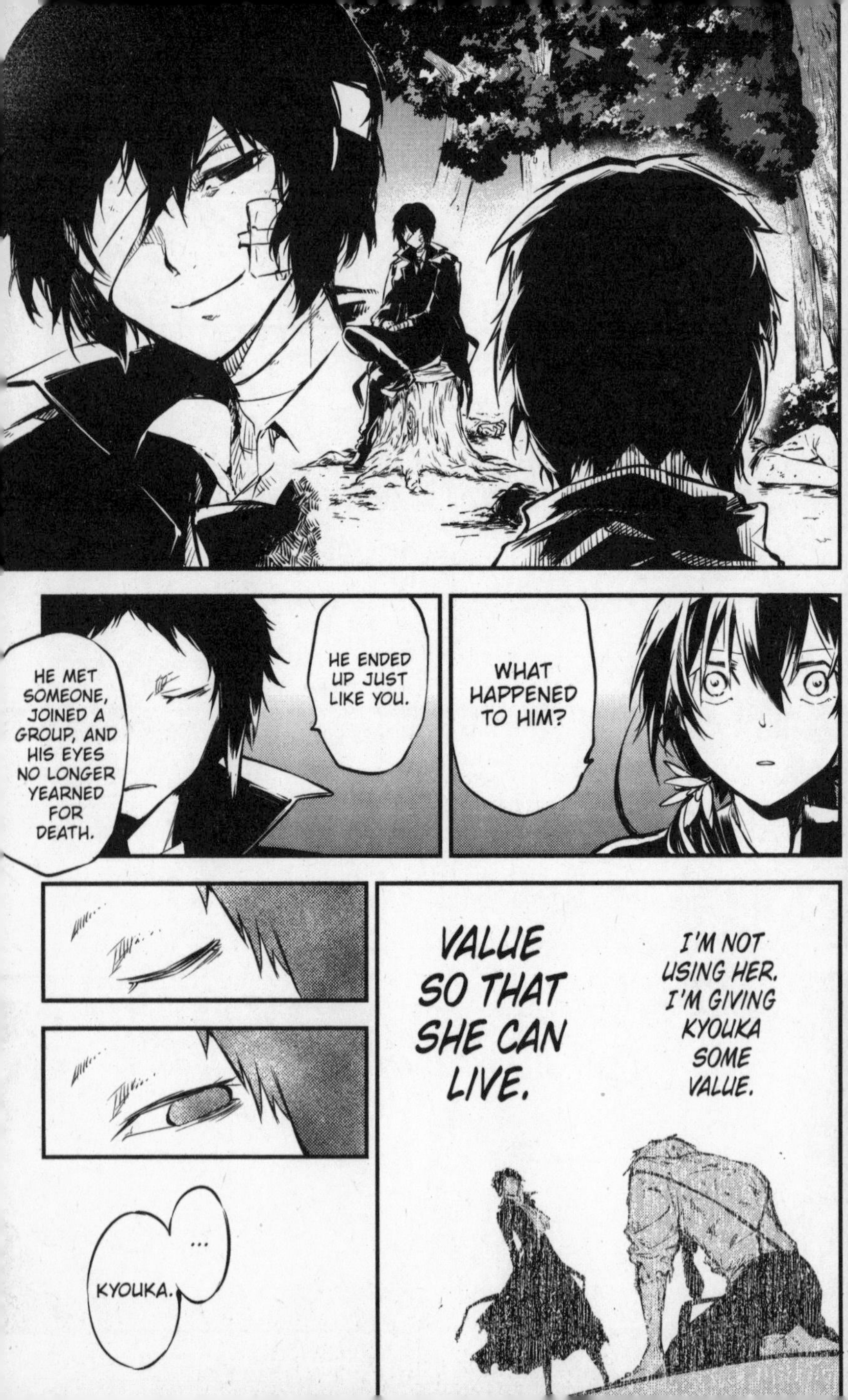
WHAT HAPPENED TO HIM?
HE ENDED UP JUST LIKE YOU.
HE MET SOMEONE, JOINED A GROUP, AND HIS EYES NO LONGER YEARNED FOR DEATH.
I'M NOT USING HER. I'M GIVING KYOUKA SOME VALUE.
VALUE SO THAT SHE CAN LIVE.
...
KYOUKA.

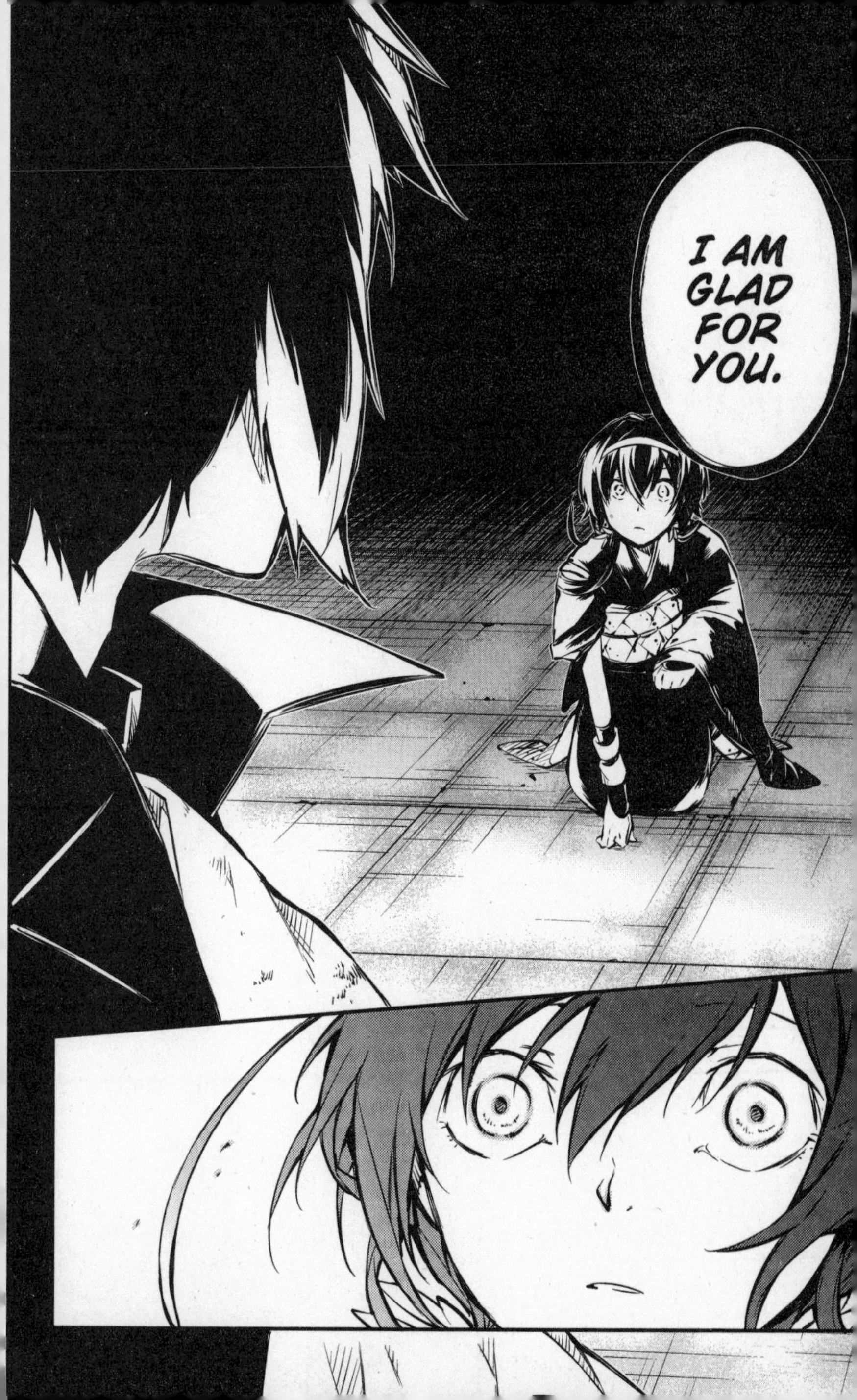
I AM GLAD FOR YOU.

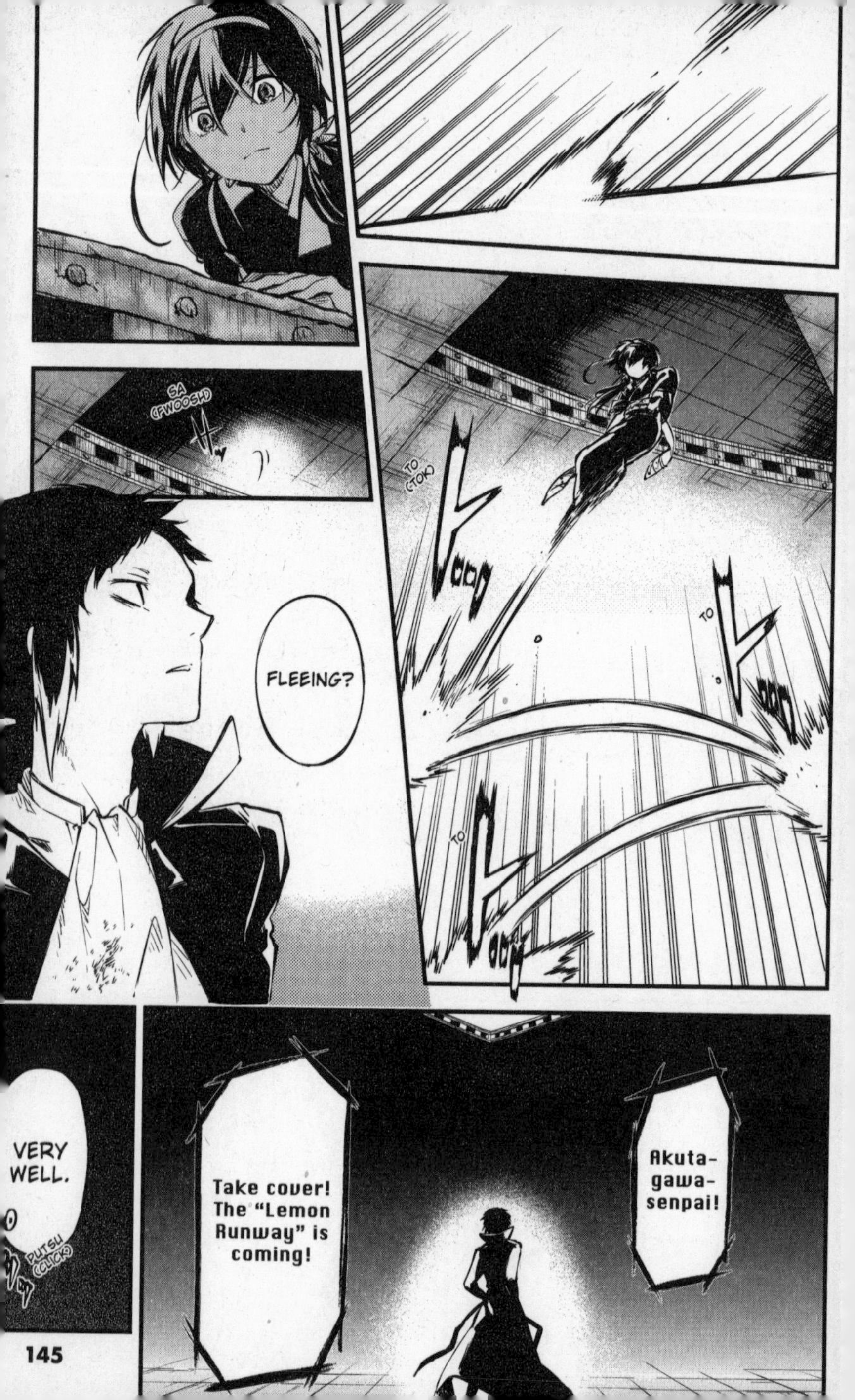
TO (TOK)
TO
TO
SA (FWOOSH)
FLEEING?
Akuta-gawa-senpai!
Take cover! The "Lemon Runway" is coming!
VERY WELL.
PUTSU (CLICK)

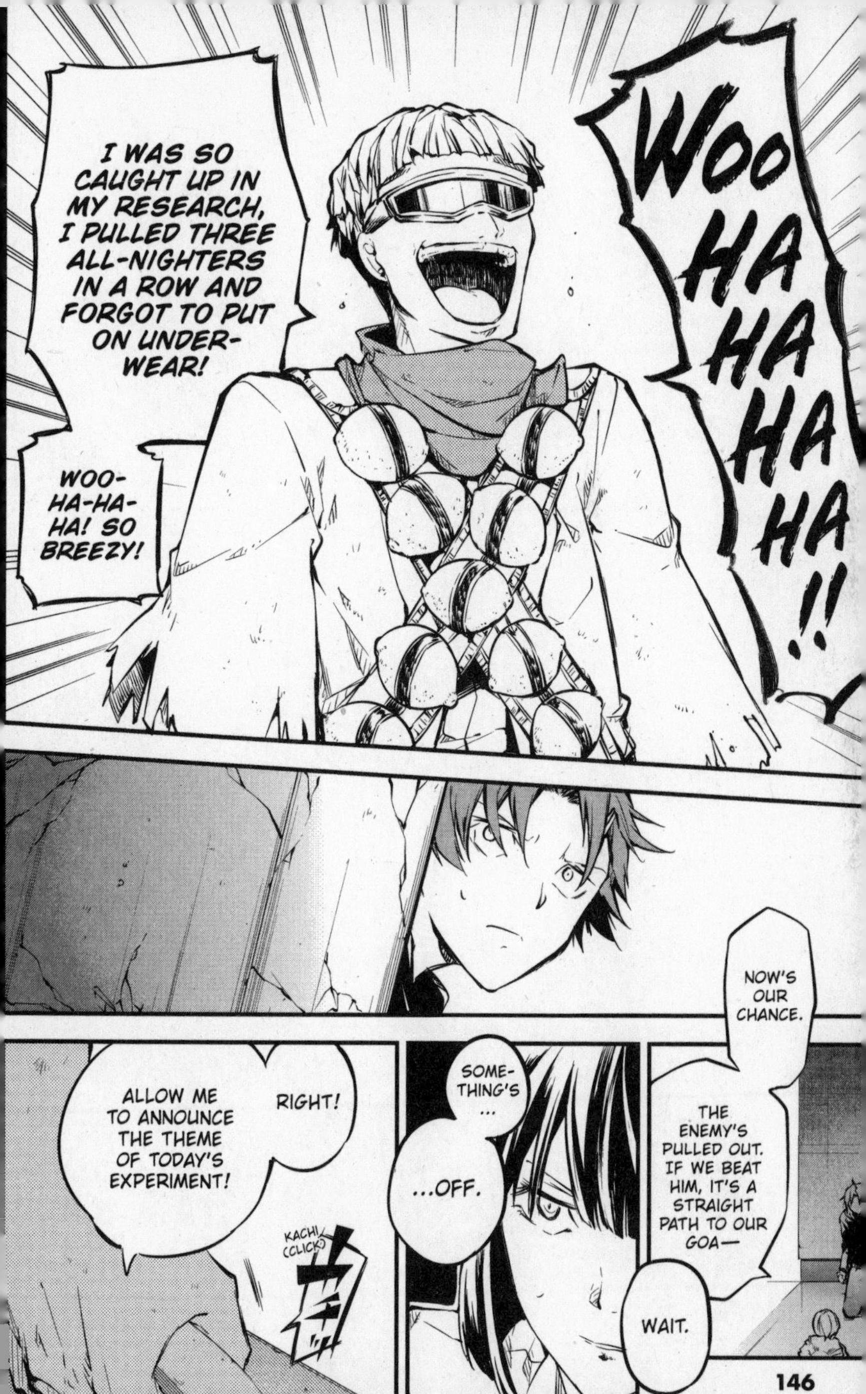

WOO HA HA HA HA HA HA!!
I WAS SO CAUGHT UP IN MY RESEARCH, I PULLED THREE ALL-NIGHTERS IN A ROW AND FORGOT TO PUT ON UNDER-WEAR!
WOO-HA-HA-HA! SO BREEZY!
NOW'S OUR CHANCE.
THE ENEMY'S PULLED OUT. IF WE BEAT HIM, IT'S A STRAIGHT PATH TO OUR GOA—
WAIT.
SOME-THING'S ...
...OFF.
RIGHT!
ALLOW ME TO ANNOUNCE THE THEME OF TODAY'S EXPERIMENT!
KACHI (CLICK)

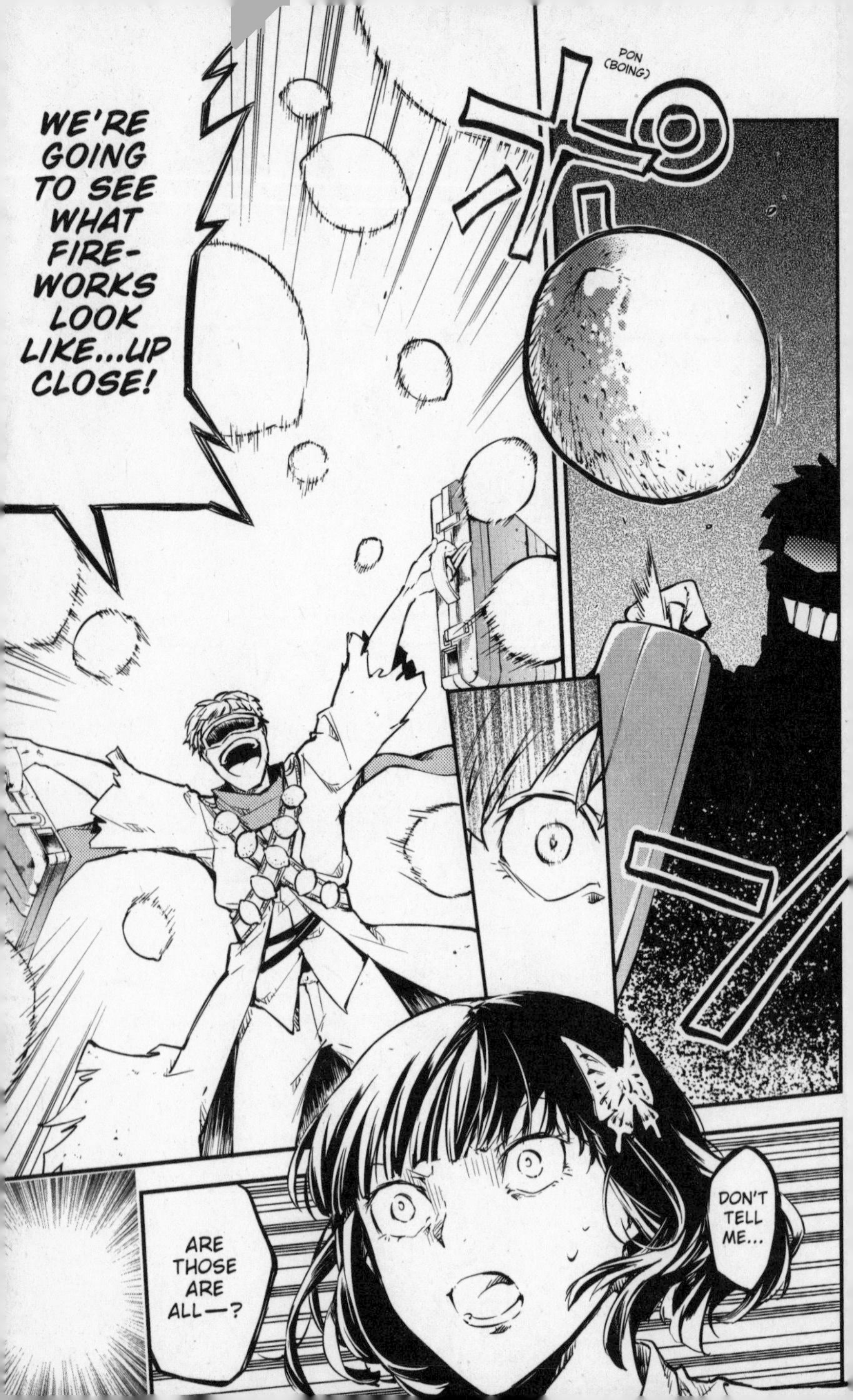
PON (BOING)
WE'RE GOING TO SEE WHAT FIRE-WORKS LOOK LIKE...UP CLOSE!
DON'T TELL ME...
ARE THOSE ARE ALL—?

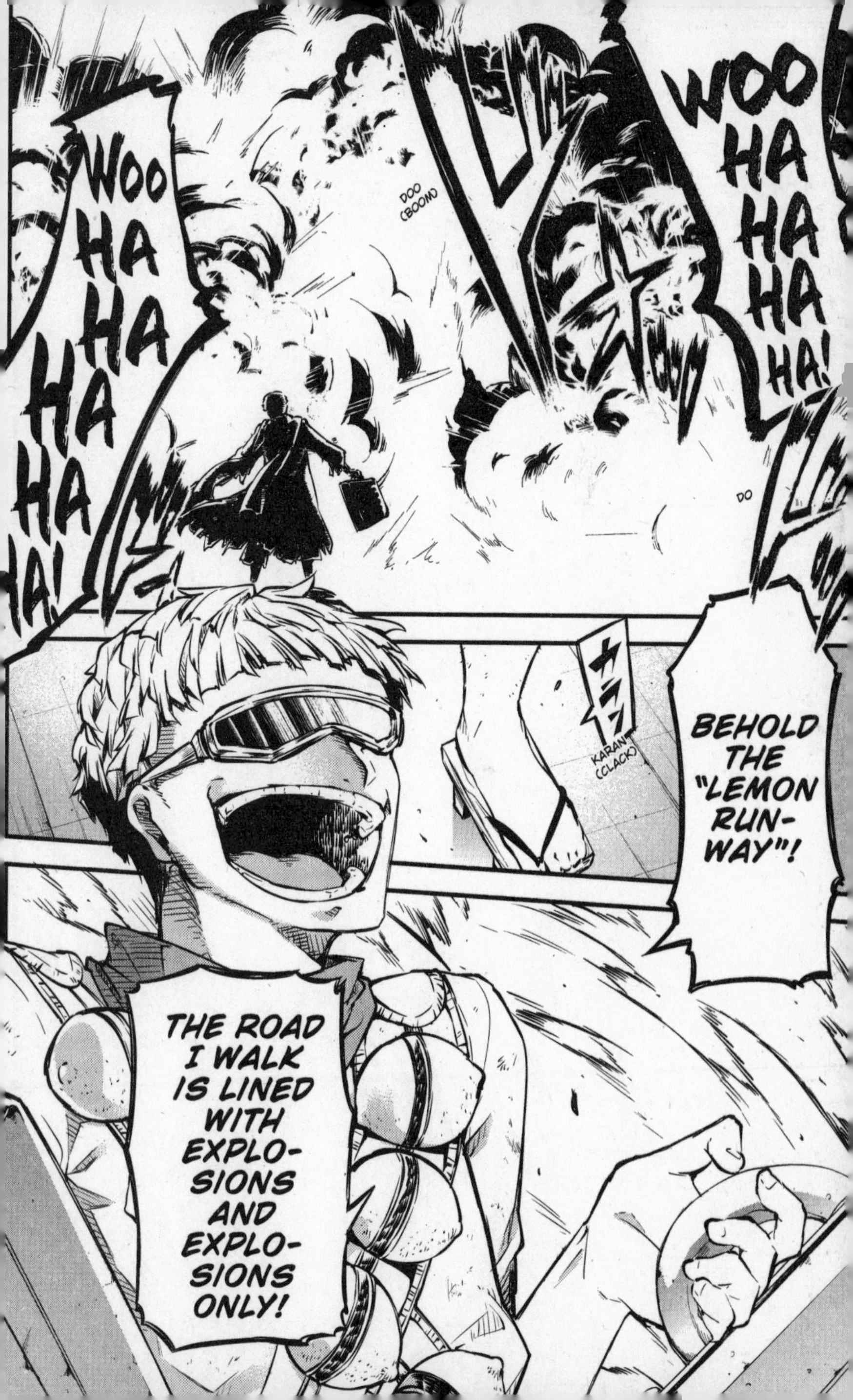
WOO HA HA HA HA HA!
DO
DOO (BOOM)
WOO HA HA HA HA HA HA!
BEHOLD THE "LEMON RUN-WAY"!
KARAN (CLACK)
THE ROAD I WALK IS LINED WITH EXPLOSIONS AND EXPLOSIONS ONLY!

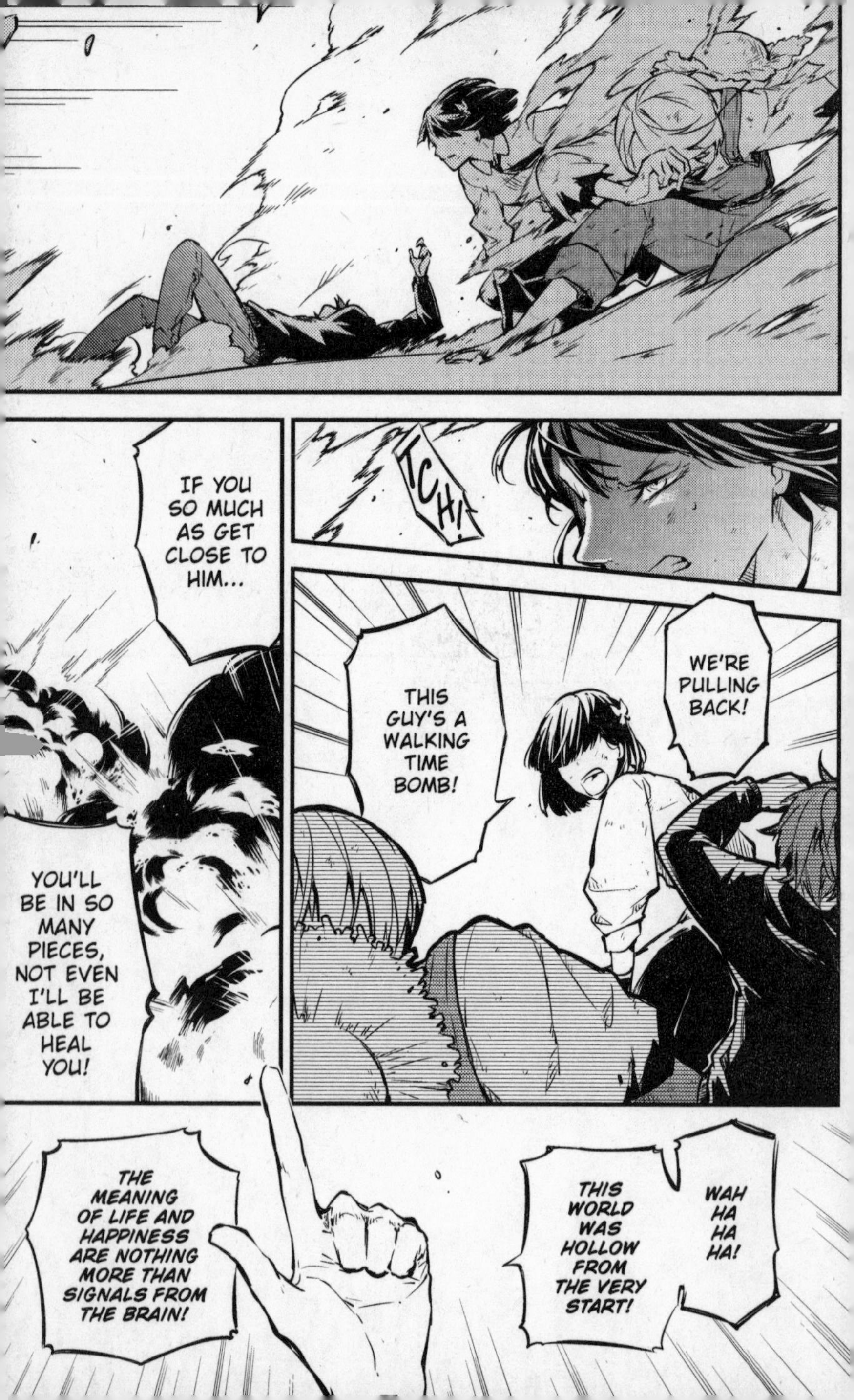

TCH!
WE'RE PULLING BACK!
THIS GUY'S A WALKING TIME BOMB!
IF YOU SO MUCH AS GET CLOSE TO HIM...
YOU'LL BE IN SO MANY PIECES, NOT EVEN I'LL BE ABLE TO HEAL YOU!
WAH HA HA HA!
THIS WORLD WAS HOLLOW FROM THE VERY START!
THE MEANING OF LIFE AND HAPPINESS ARE NOTHING MORE THAN SIGNALS FROM THE BRAIN!

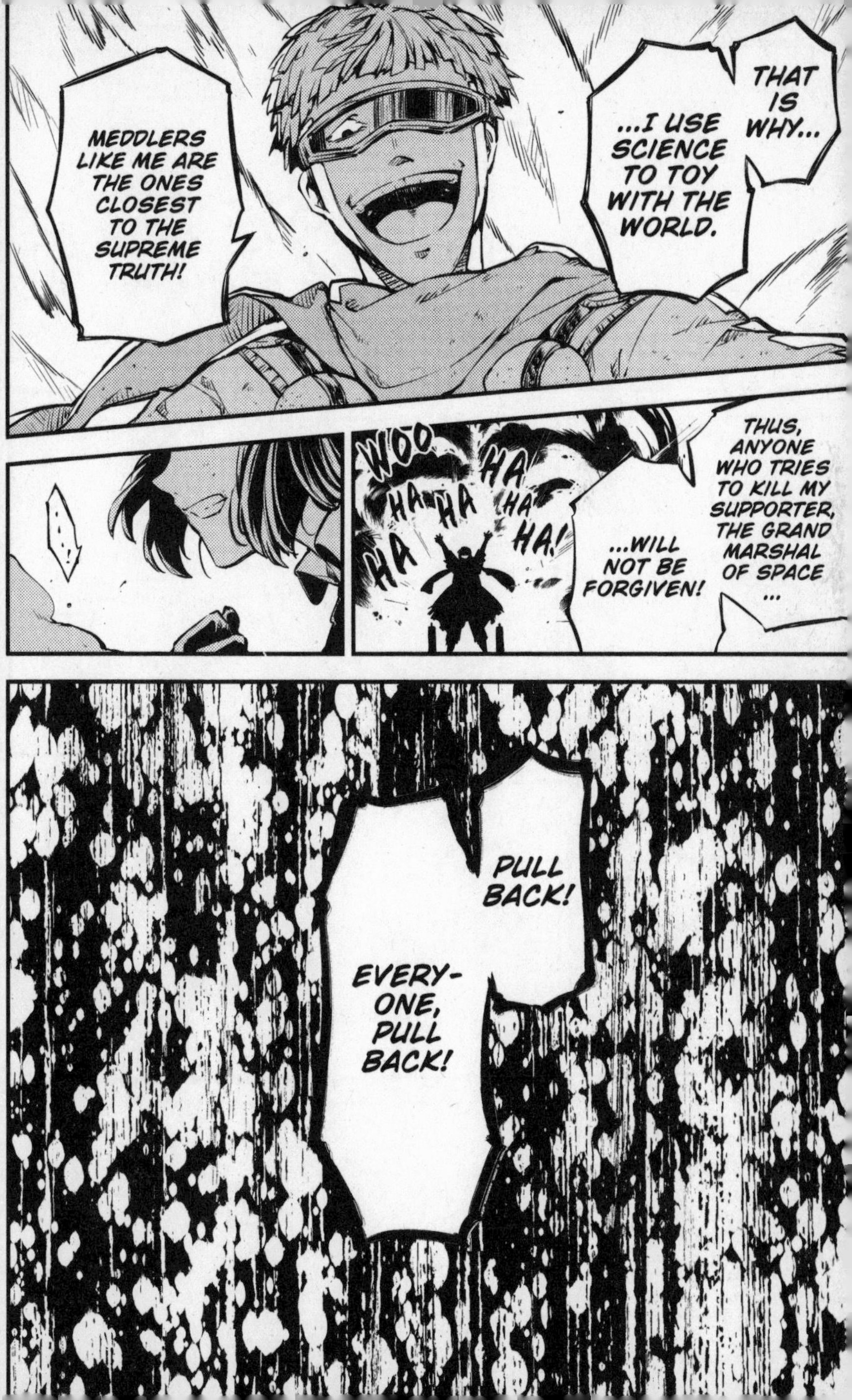
THAT IS WHY...
...I USE SCIENCE TO TOY WITH THE WORLD.
MEDDLERS LIKE ME ARE THE ONES CLOSEST TO THE SUPREME TRUTH!
THUS, ANYONE WHO TRIES TO KILL MY SUPPORTER, THE GRAND MARSHAL OF SPACE ...
...WILL NOT BE FORGIVEN!
WOO HA HA HA HA HA HA HA!
...!
PULL BACK!
EVERY-ONE, PULL BACK!

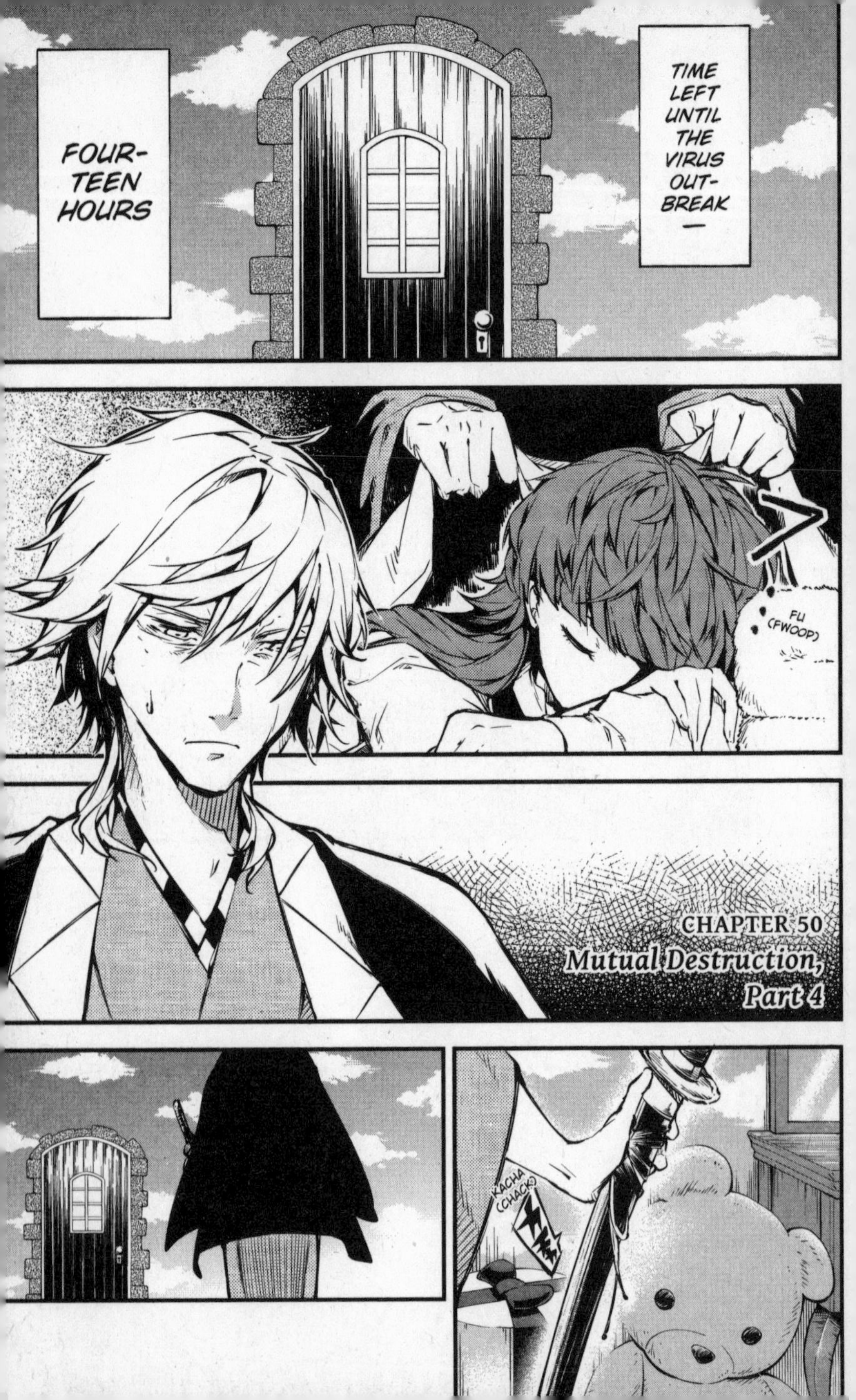
TIME LEFT UNTIL THE VIRUS OUT-BREAK —
FOUR-TEEN HOURS
FU (FWOOP)
CHAPTER 50
Mutual Destruction, Part 4
KACHA (CHACK)

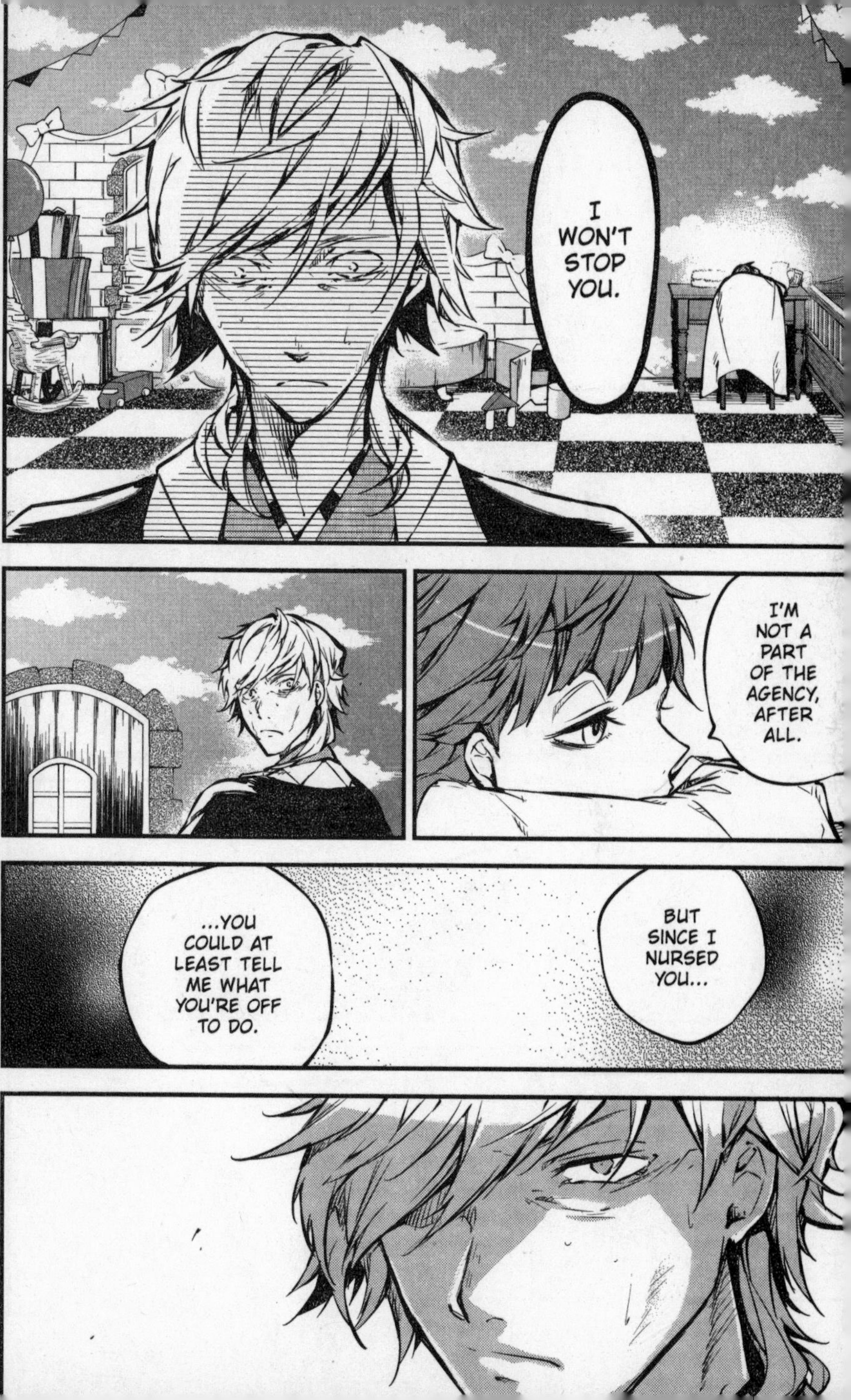
I WON'T STOP YOU.
I'M NOT A PART OF THE AGENCY, AFTER ALL.
BUT SINCE I NURSED YOU...
...YOU COULD AT LEAST TELL ME WHAT YOU'RE OFF TO DO.

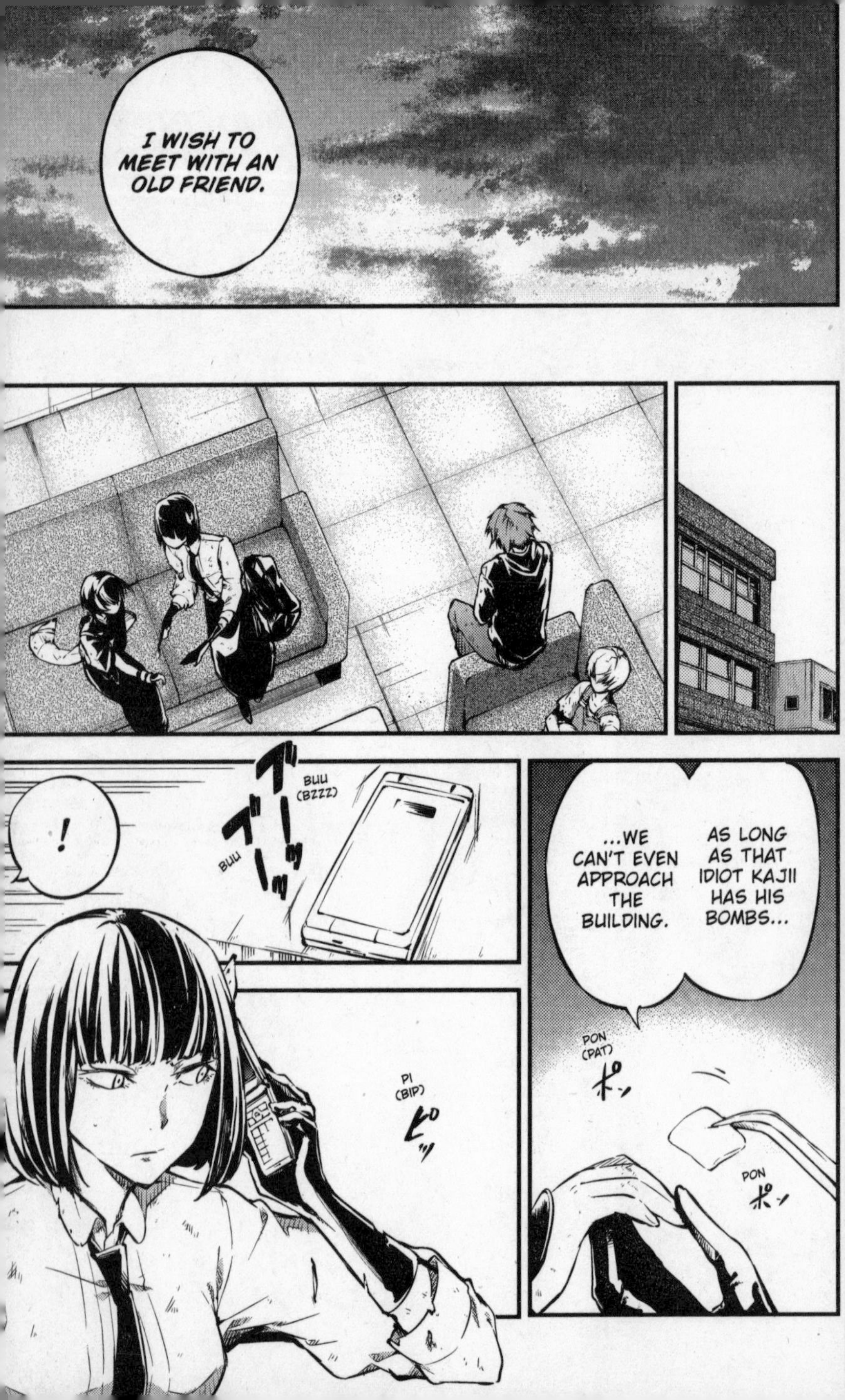
I WISH TO MEET WITH AN OLD FRIEND.
AS LONG AS THAT IDIOT KAJII HAS HIS BOMBS...
...WE CAN'T EVEN APPROACH THE BUILDING.
PON (PAT)
PON
BUU (BZZZ)
BUU
!
PI (BIP)

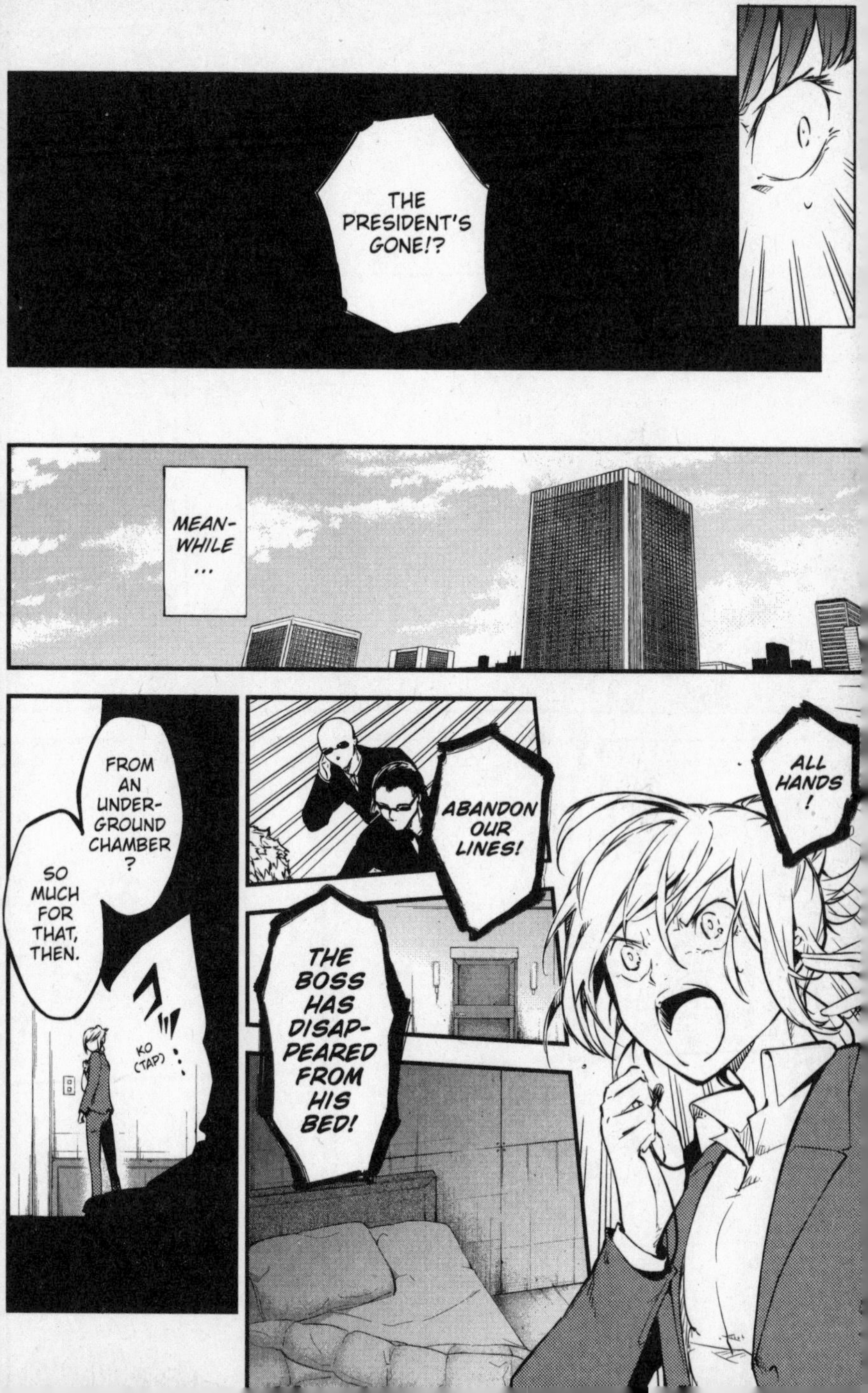
THE PRESIDENT'S GONE!?
MEAN-WHILE...
ALL HANDS!
ABANDON OUR LINES!
THE BOSS HAS DISAP-PEARED FROM HIS BED!
FROM AN UNDER-GROUND CHAMBER?
SO MUCH FOR THAT, THEN.
KO (TAP)...

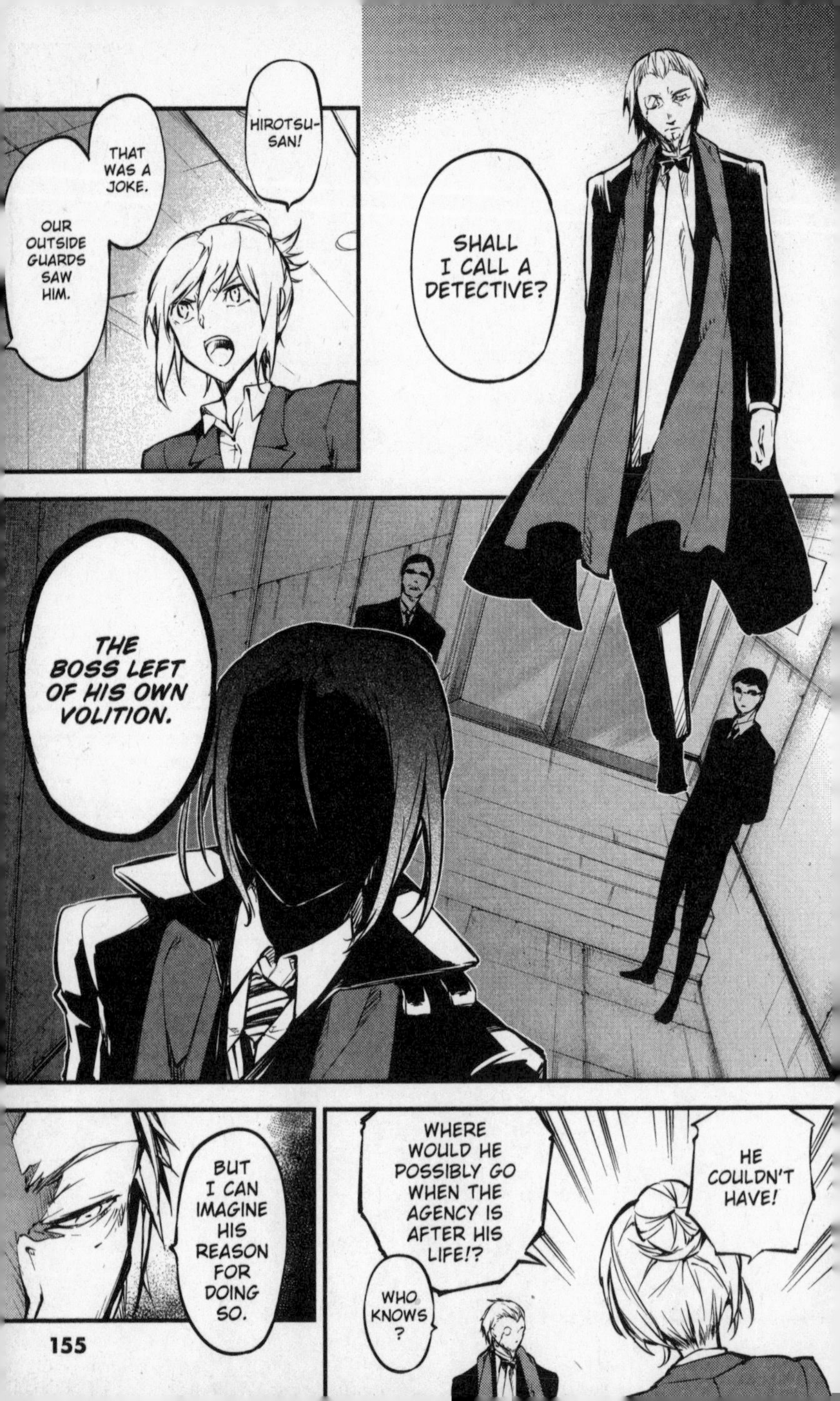
SHALL I CALL A DETECTIVE?
HIROTSU-SAN!
THAT WAS A JOKE.
OUR OUTSIDE GUARDS SAW HIM.
THE BOSS LEFT OF HIS OWN VOLITION.
HE COULDN'T HAVE!
WHERE WOULD HE POSSIBLY GO WHEN THE AGENCY IS AFTER HIS LIFE!?
WHO KNOWS?
BUT I CAN IMAGINE HIS REASON FOR DOING SO.

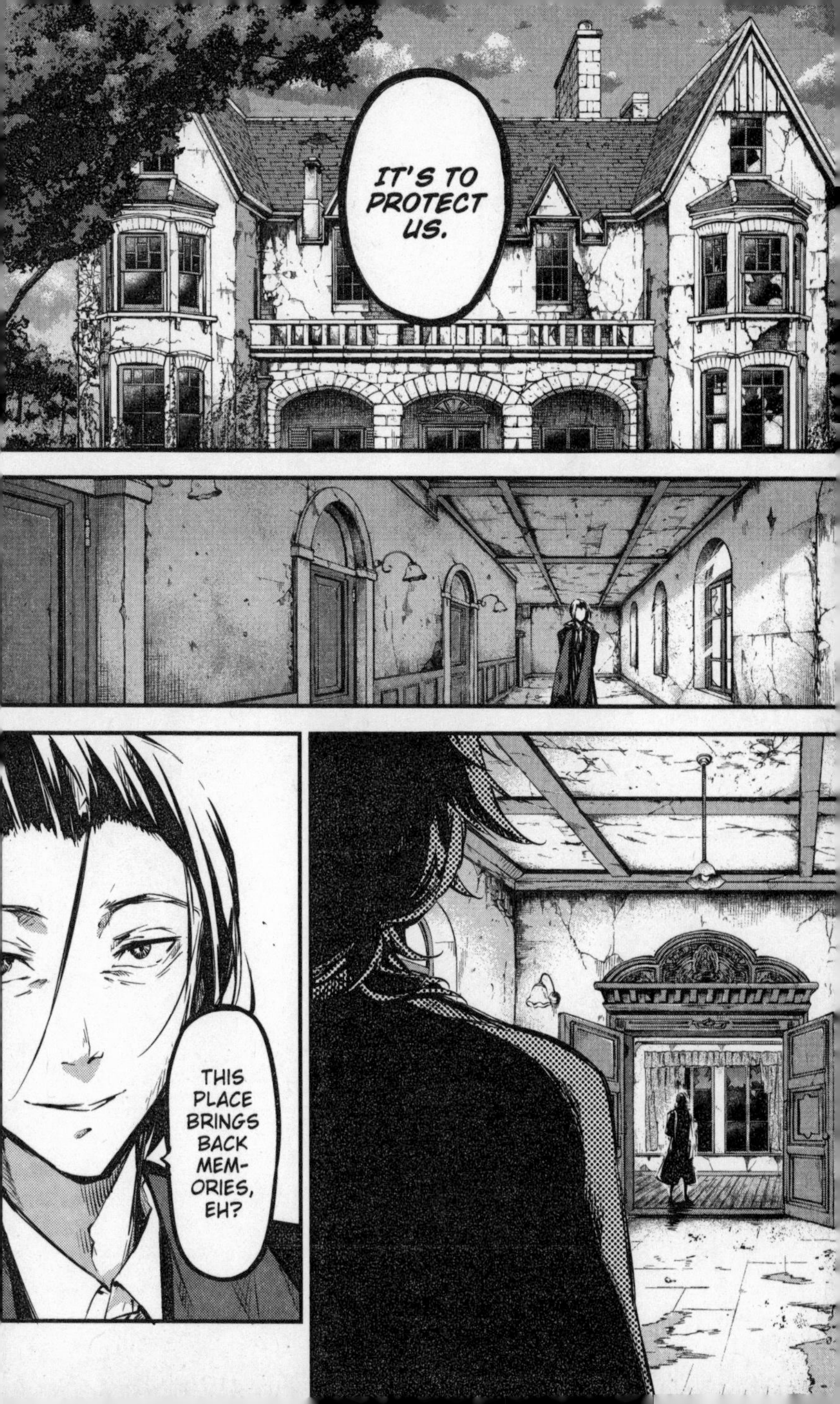
IT'S TO PROTECT US.
THIS PLACE BRINGS BACK MEM-ORIES, EH?

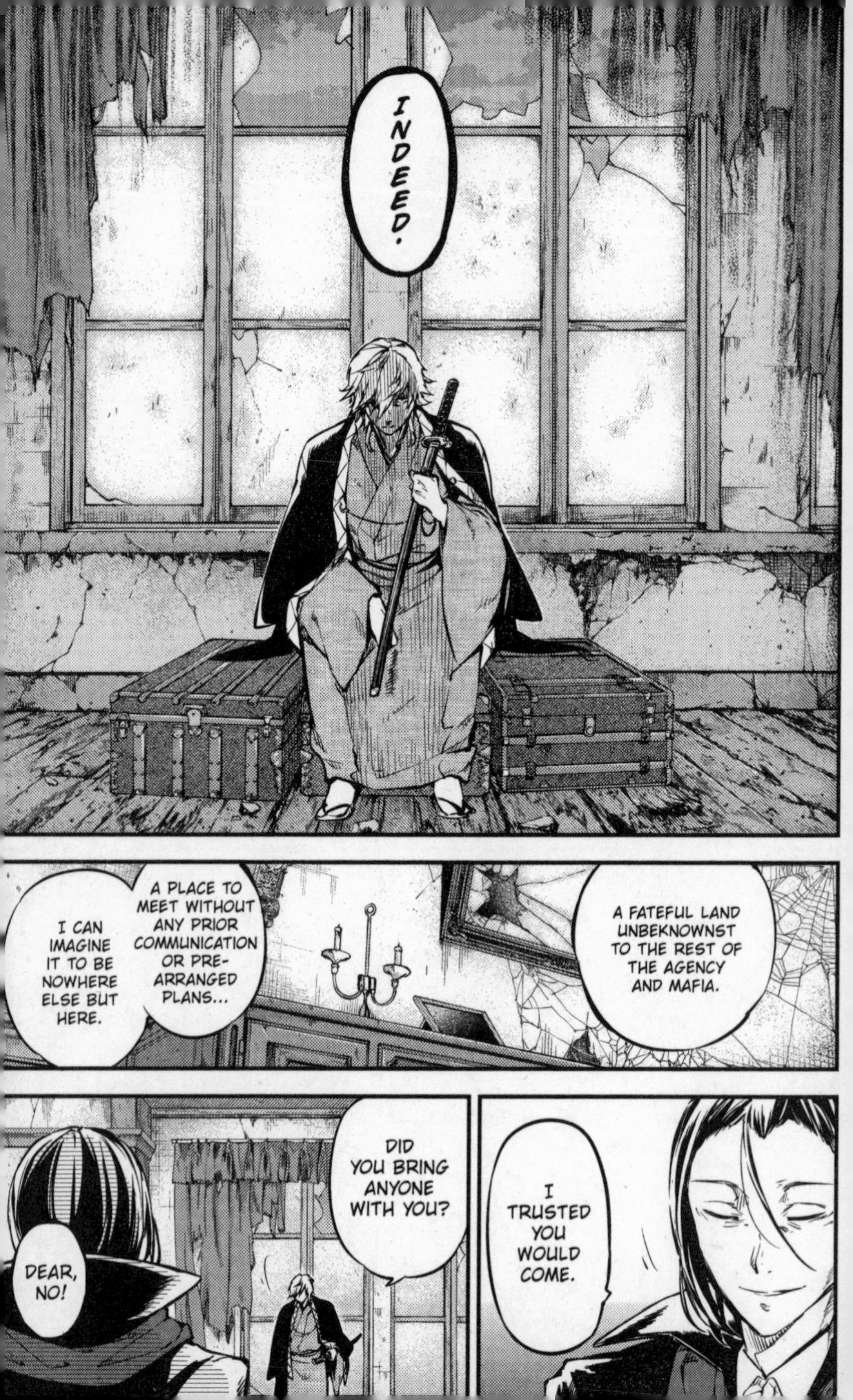
INDEED.
A FATEFUL LAND UNBEKNOWNST TO THE REST OF THE AGENCY AND MAFIA.
A PLACE TO MEET WITHOUT ANY PRIOR COMMUNICATION OR PRE-ARRANGED PLANS...
I CAN IMAGINE IT TO BE NOWHERE ELSE BUT HERE.
I TRUSTED YOU WOULD COME.
DID YOU BRING ANYONE WITH YOU?
DEAR, NO!

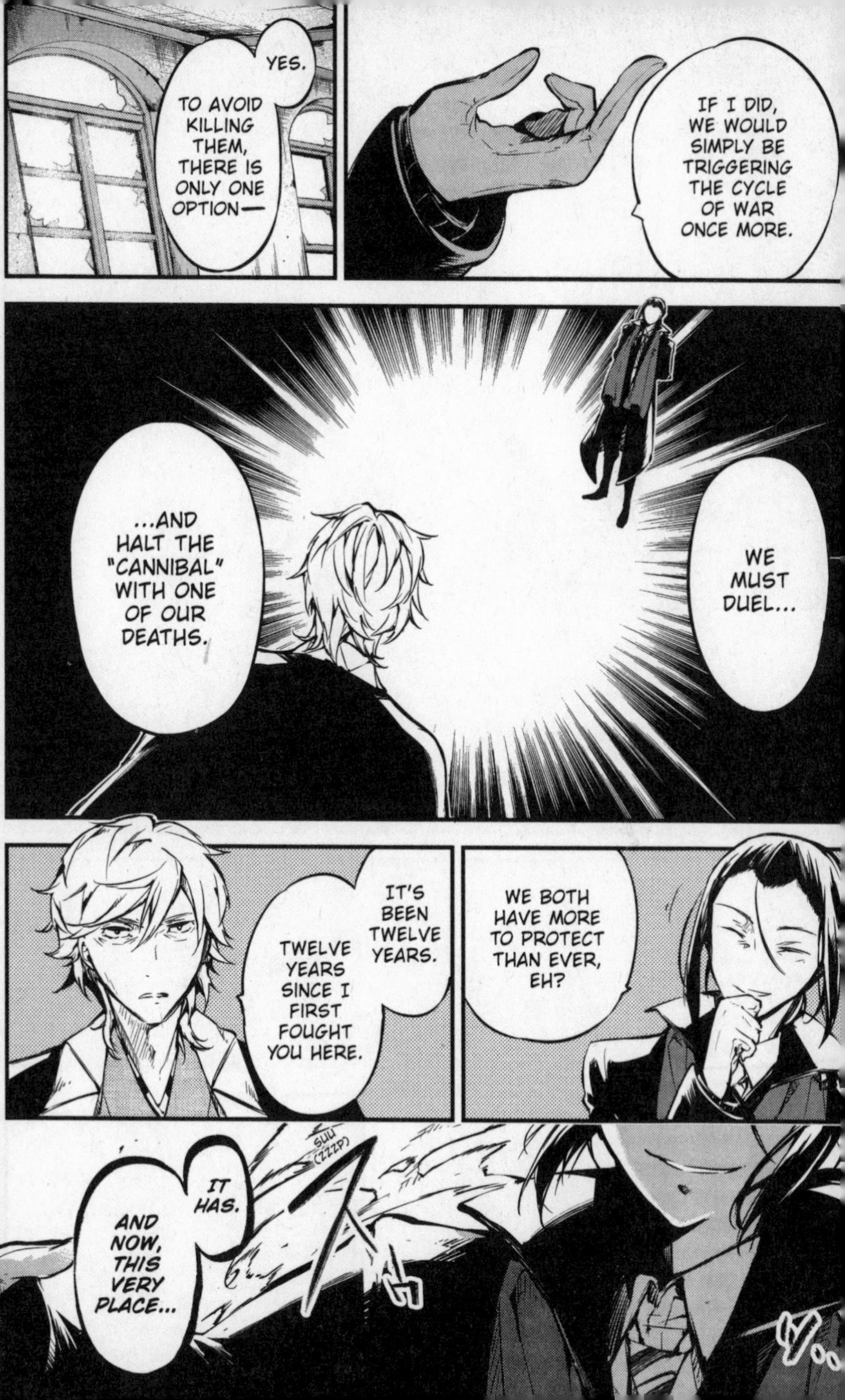
IF I DID, WE WOULD SIMPLY BE TRIGGERING THE CYCLE OF WAR ONCE MORE.
YES.
TO AVOID KILLING THEM, THERE IS ONLY ONE OPTION—
WE MUST DUEL...
...AND HALT THE "CANNIBAL" WITH ONE OF OUR DEATHS.
WE BOTH HAVE MORE TO PROTECT THAN EVER, EH?
IT'S BEEN TWELVE YEARS.
TWELVE YEARS SINCE I FIRST FOUGHT YOU HERE.
SUU (ZZZP)
IT HAS.
AND NOW, THIS VERY PLACE...

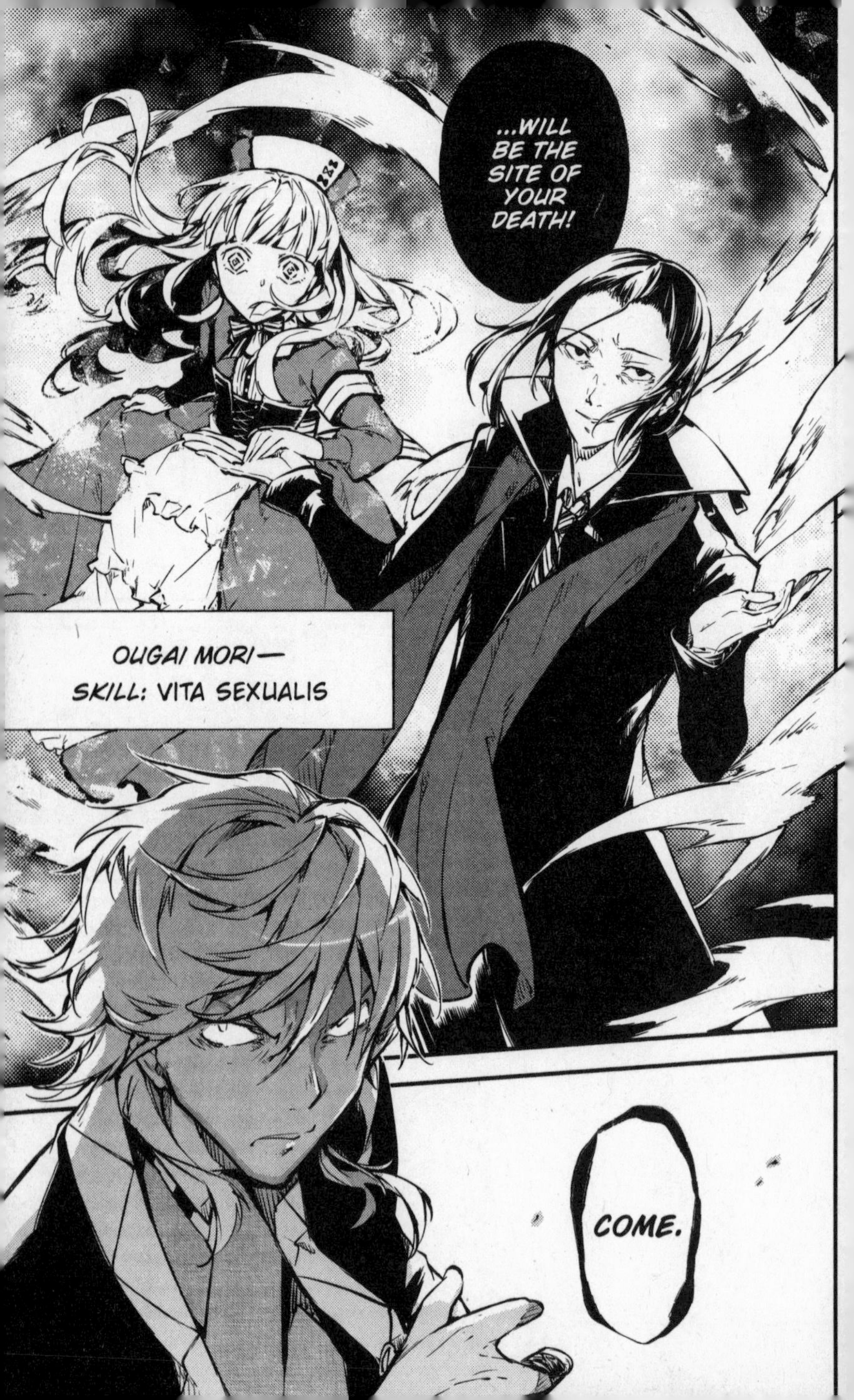
...WILL BE THE SITE OF YOUR DEATH!
OUGAI MORI— SKILL: VITA SEXUALIS
COME.

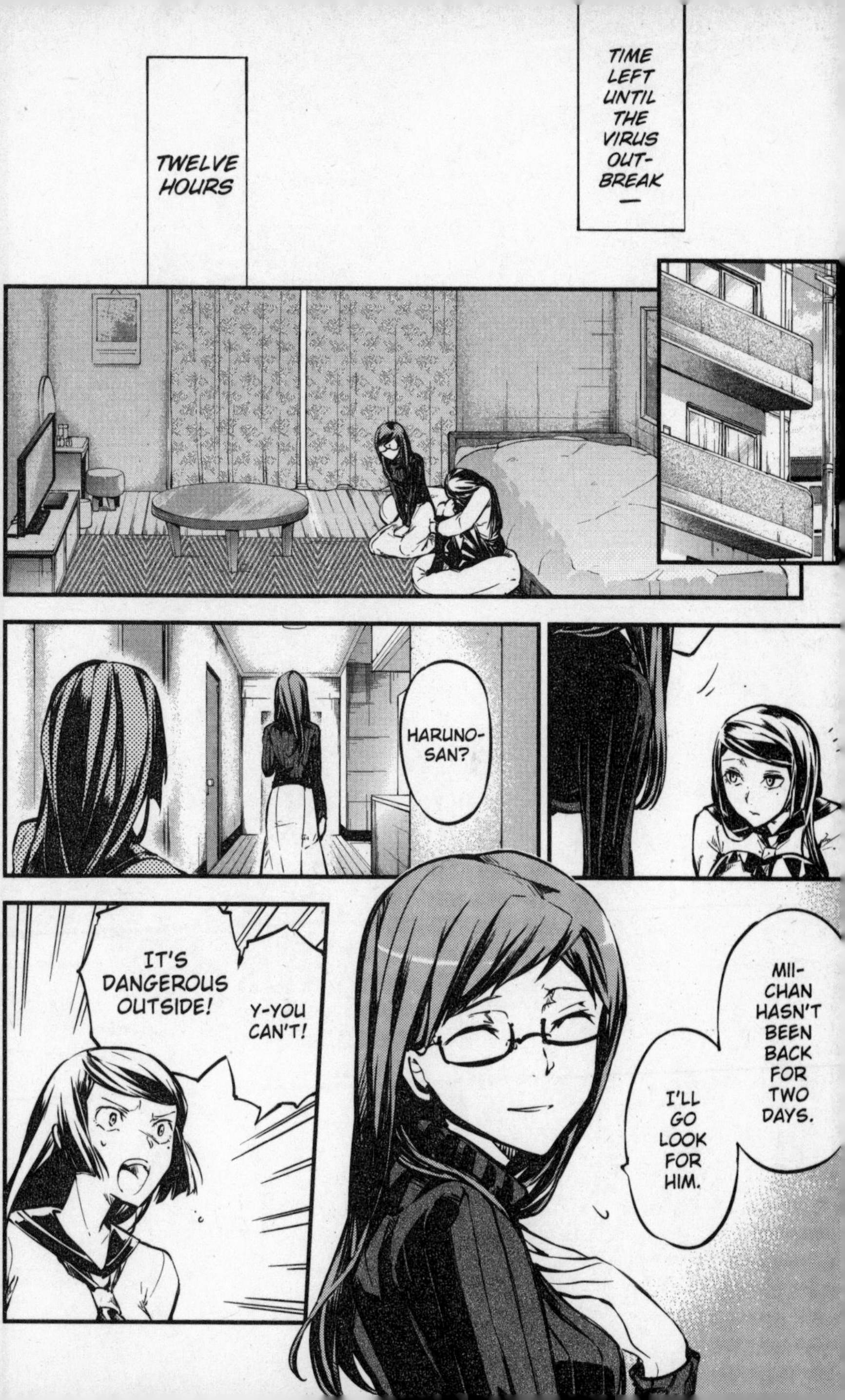
TIME LEFT UNTIL THE VIRUS OUT-BREAK —
TWELVE HOURS
HARUNO-SAN?
MII-CHAN HASN'T BEEN BACK FOR TWO DAYS.
I'LL GO LOOK FOR HIM.
Y-YOU CAN'T!
IT'S DANGEROUS OUTSIDE!

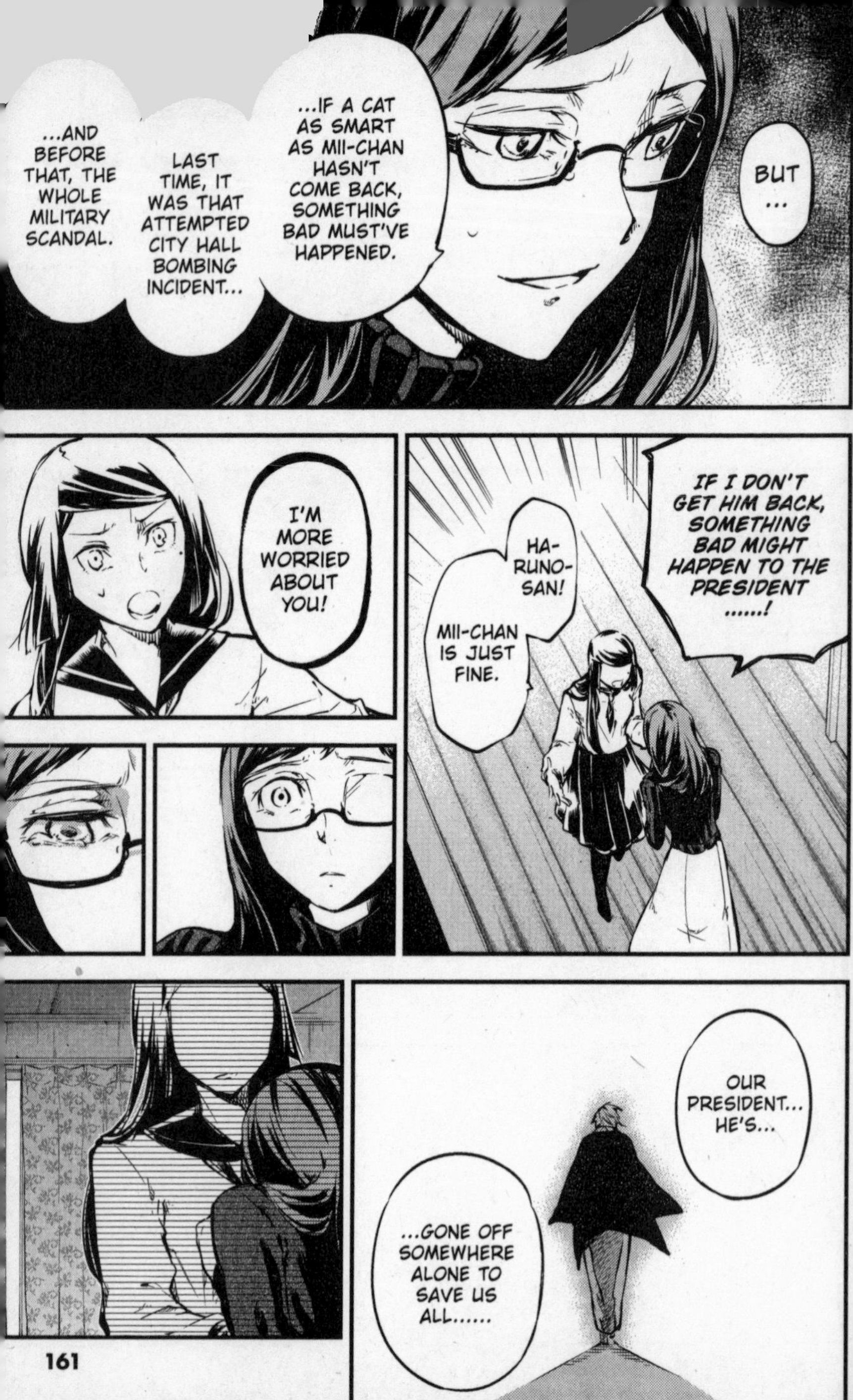
BUT ...
...IF A CAT AS SMART AS MII-CHAN HASN'T COME BACK, SOMETHING BAD MUST'VE HAPPENED.
LAST TIME, IT WAS THAT ATTEMPTED CITY HALL BOMBING INCIDENT...
...AND BEFORE THAT, THE WHOLE MILITARY SCANDAL.
IF I DON'T GET HIM BACK, SOMETHING BAD MIGHT HAPPEN TO THE PRESIDENT ......!
HA-RUNO-SAN!
MII-CHAN IS JUST FINE.
I'M MORE WORRIED ABOUT YOU!
OUR PRESIDENT... HE'S...
...GONE OFF SOMEWHERE ALONE TO SAVE US ALL......

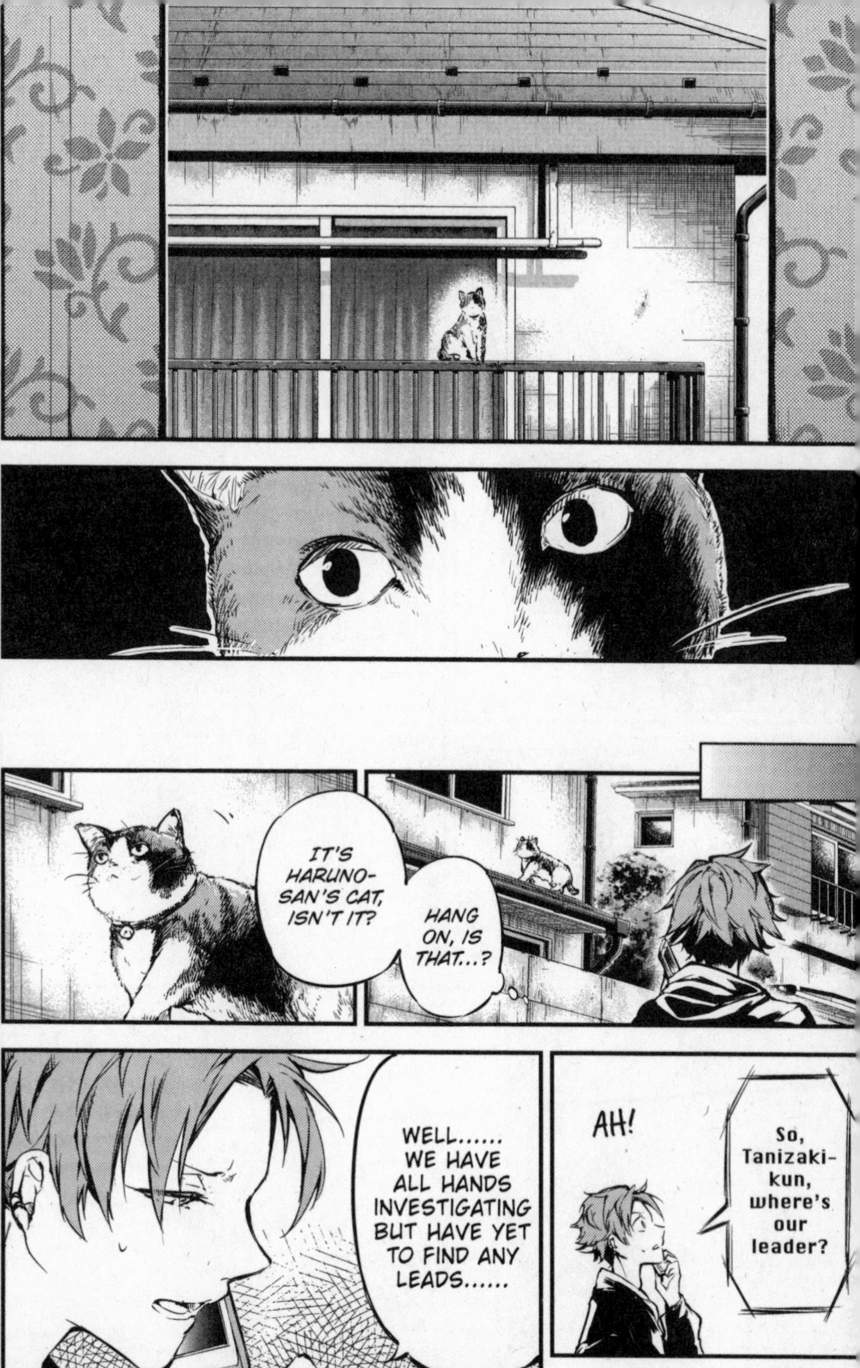
HANG ON, IS THAT...?
IT'S HARUNO-SAN'S CAT, ISN'T IT?
So, Tanizaki-kun, where's our leader?
AH!
WELL...... WE HAVE ALL HANDS INVESTIGATING BUT HAVE YET TO FIND ANY LEADS......

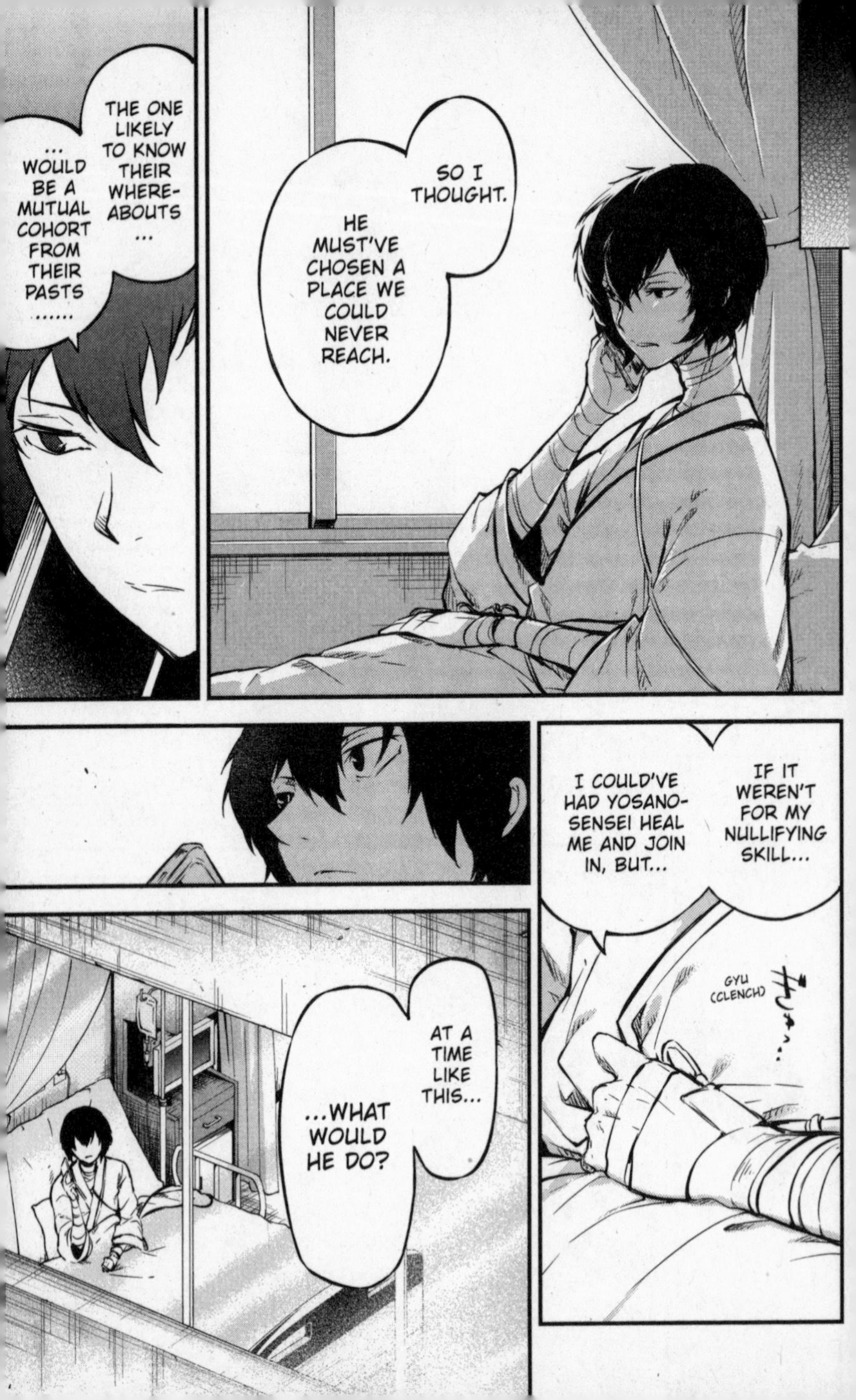
SO I THOUGHT.
HE MUST'VE CHOSEN A PLACE WE COULD NEVER REACH.
THE ONE LIKELY TO KNOW THEIR WHERE-ABOUTS...
...WOULD BE A MUTUAL COHORT FROM THEIR PASTS.......
IF IT WEREN'T FOR MY NULLIFYING SKILL...
I COULD'VE HAD YOSANO-SENSEI HEAL ME AND JOIN IN, BUT...
GYU (CLENCH)
AT A TIME LIKE THIS...
...WHAT WOULD HE DO?

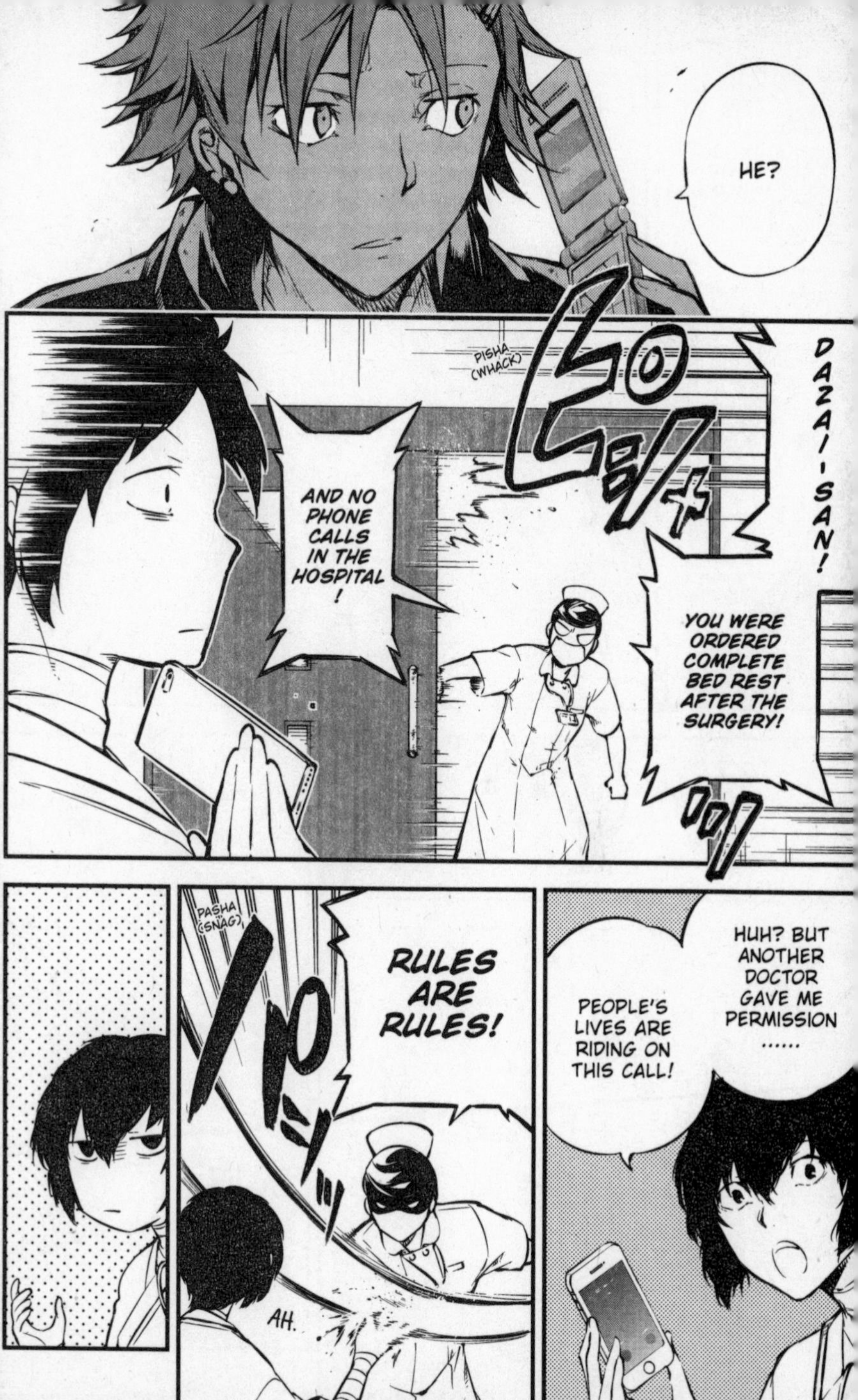
HE?
DAZAI-SAN!
YOU WERE ORDERED COMPLETE BED REST AFTER THE SURGERY!
PISHA (WHACK)
AND NO PHONE CALLS IN THE HOSPITAL!
HUH? BUT ANOTHER DOCTOR GAVE ME PERMISSION ......
PEOPLE'S LIVES ARE RIDING ON THIS CALL!
PASHA (SNAG)
RULES ARE RULES!
AH.

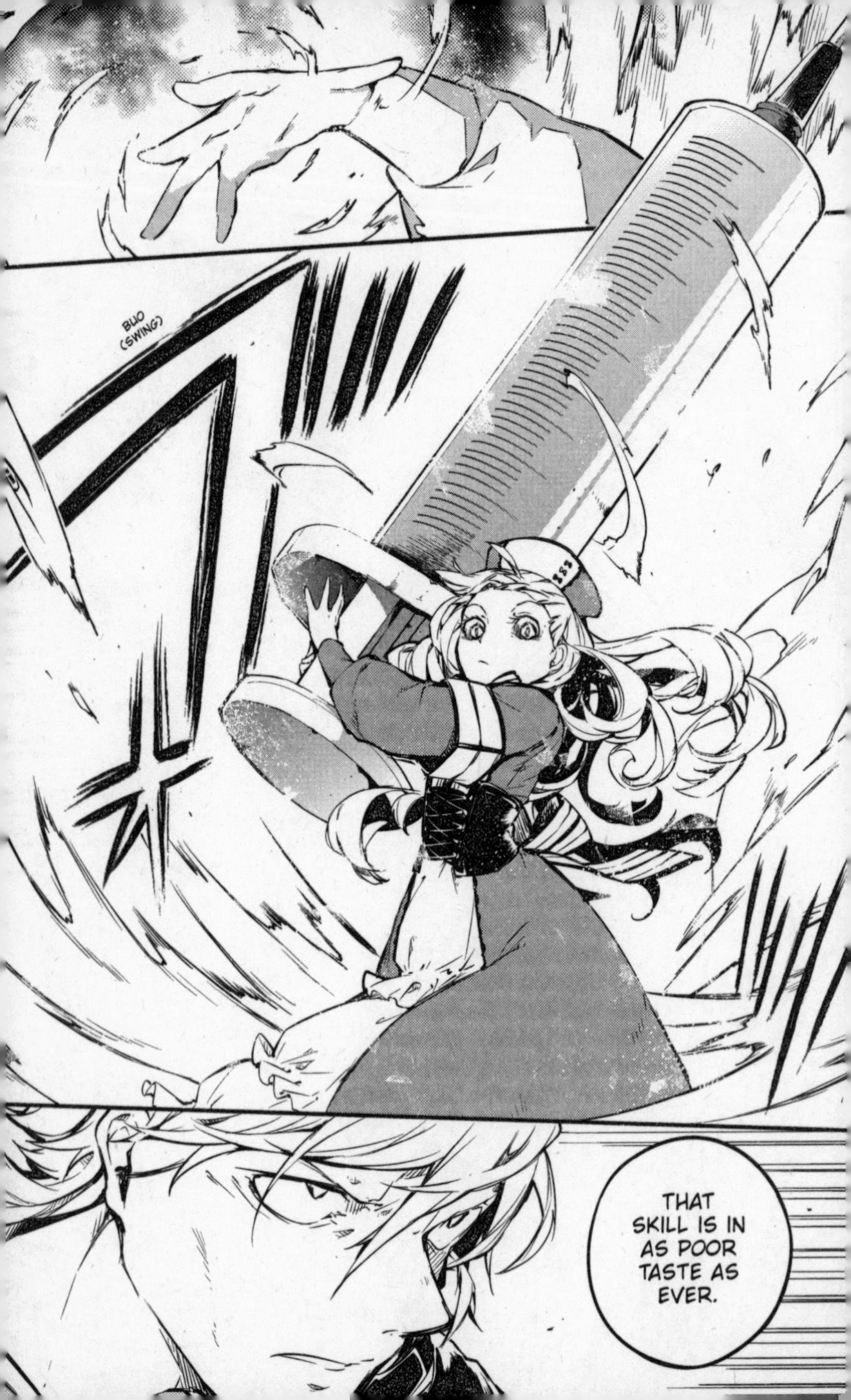
BUO (SWING)
THAT SKILL IS IN AS POOR TASTE AS EVER.

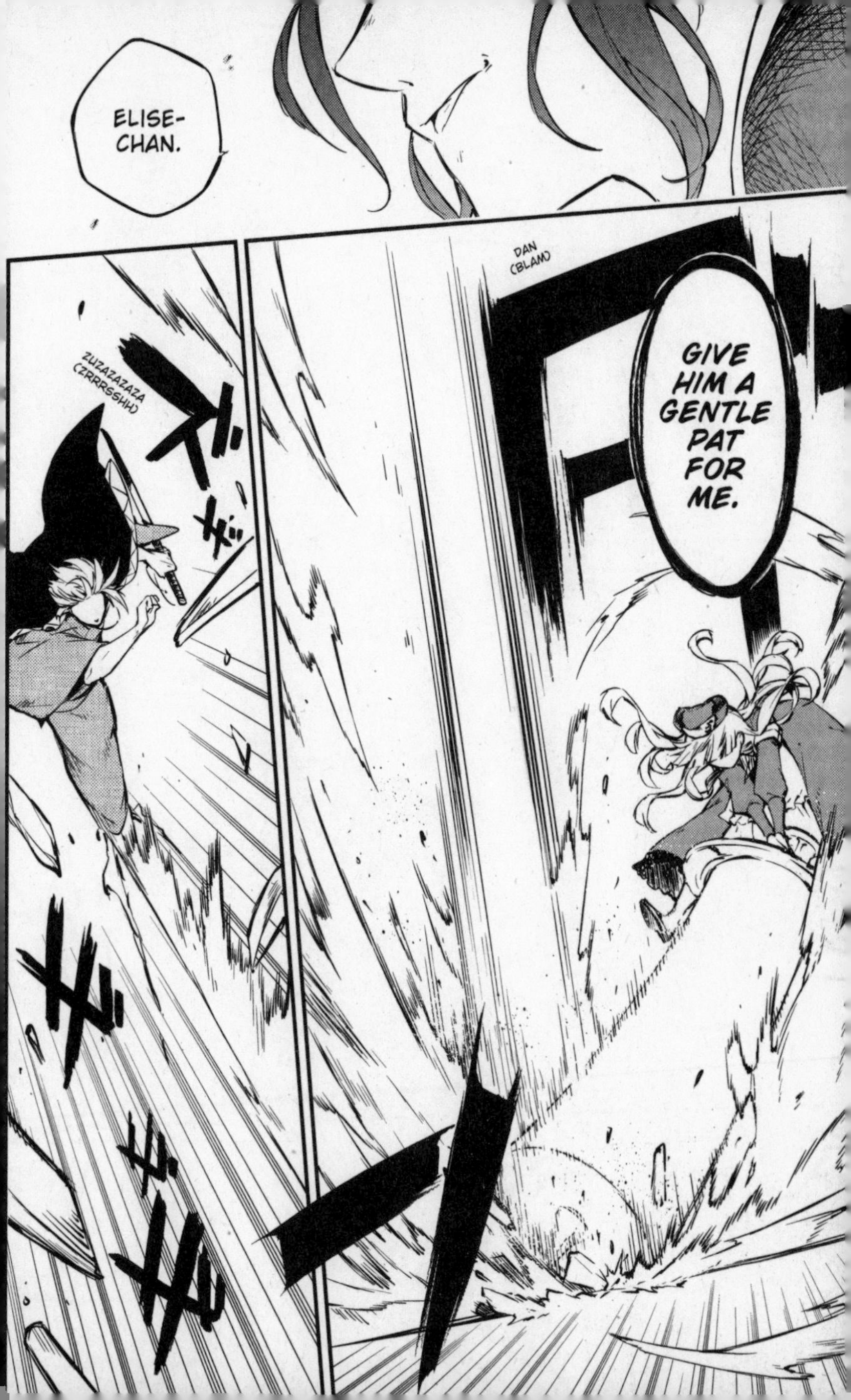
ELISE-CHAN.
DAN (BLAM)
GIVE HIM A GENTLE PAT FOR ME.
ZUZAZAZAZA (ZRRRSSHH)

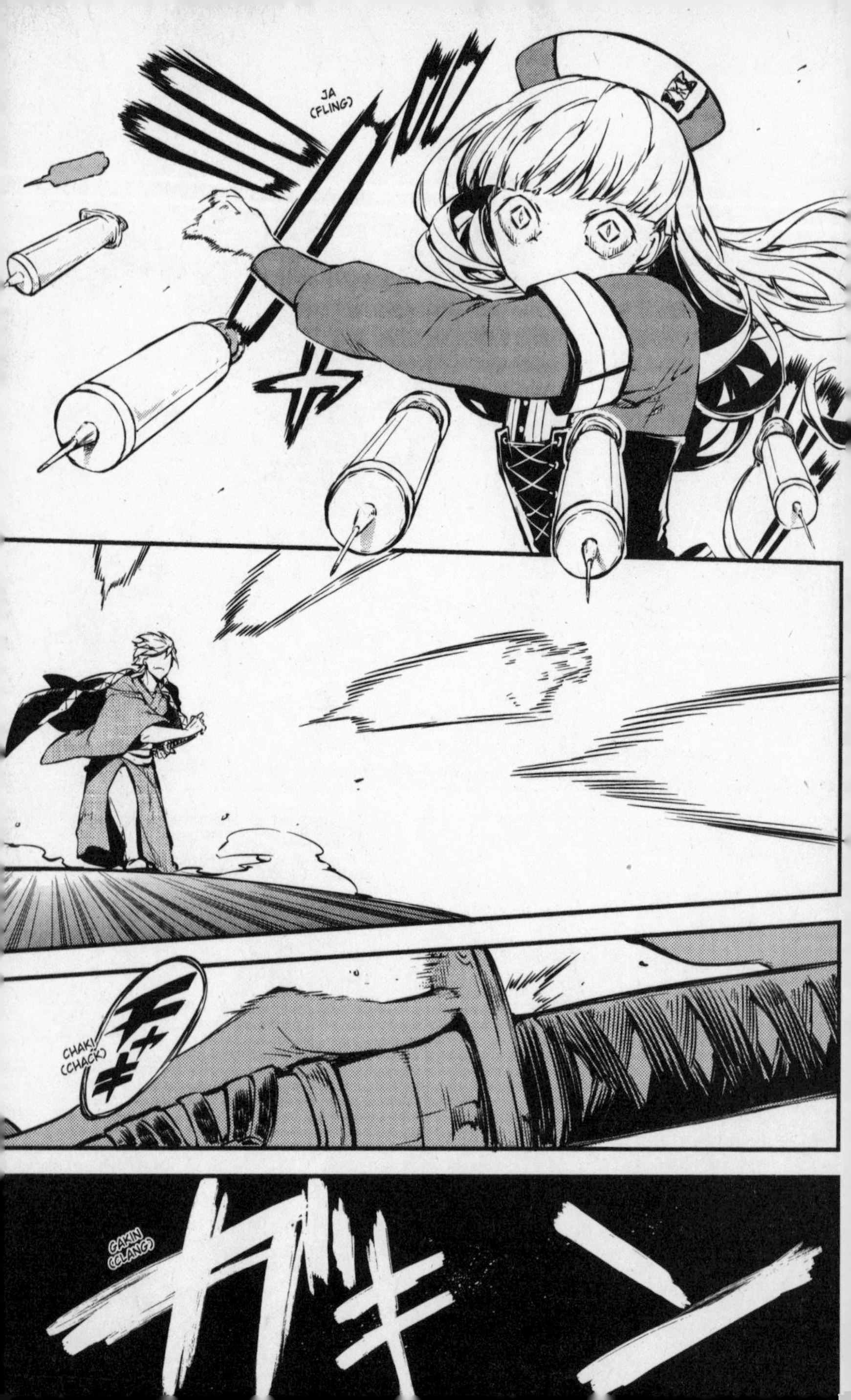
JA
(FLING)
CHAKI
(CHACK)
GAKIN
(CLANG)

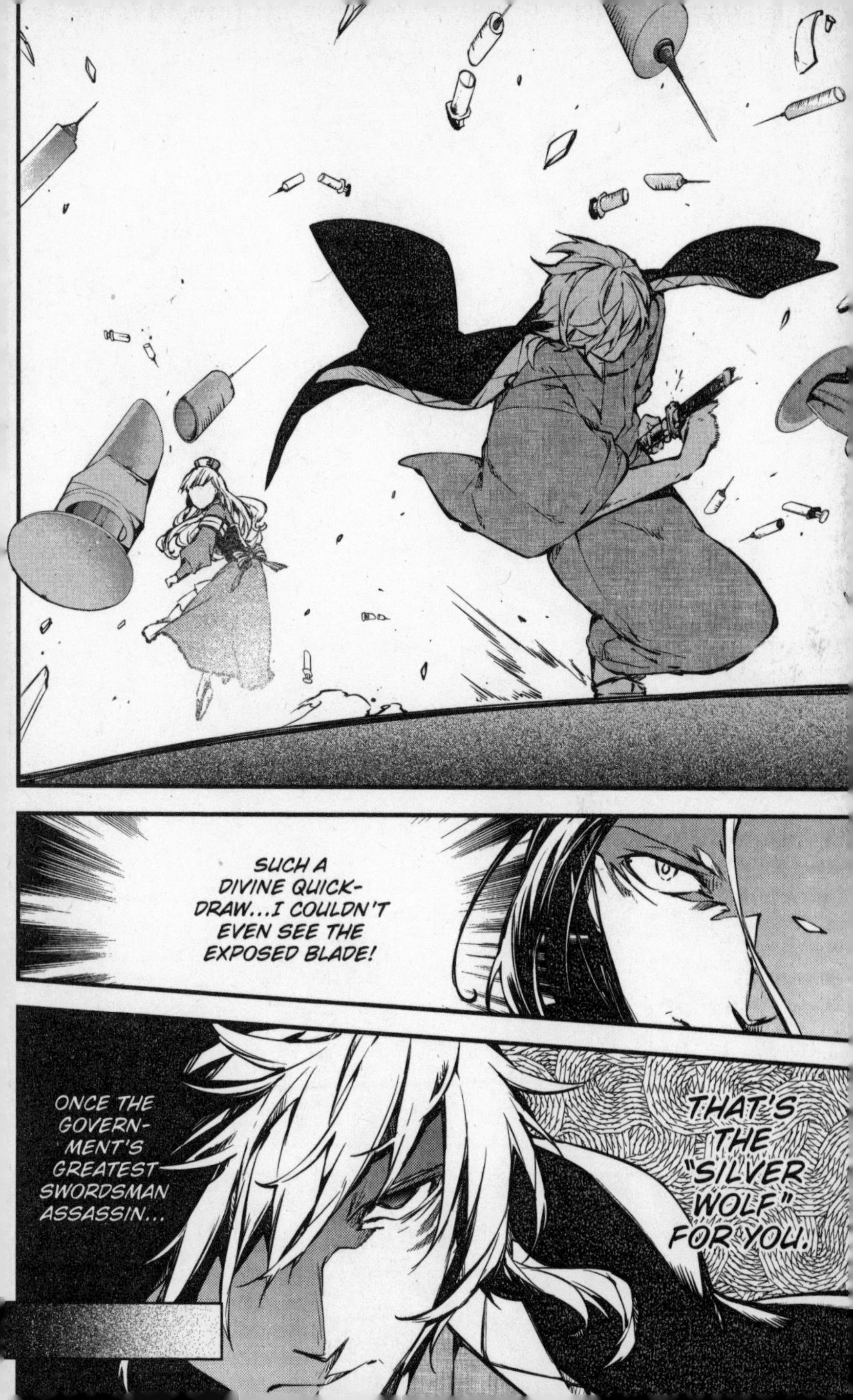
SUCH A DIVINE QUICK-DRAW...I COULDN'T EVEN SEE THE EXPOSED BLADE!
THAT'S THE "SILVER WOLF" FOR YOU.
ONCE THE GOVERNMENT'S GREATEST SWORDSMAN ASSASSIN...

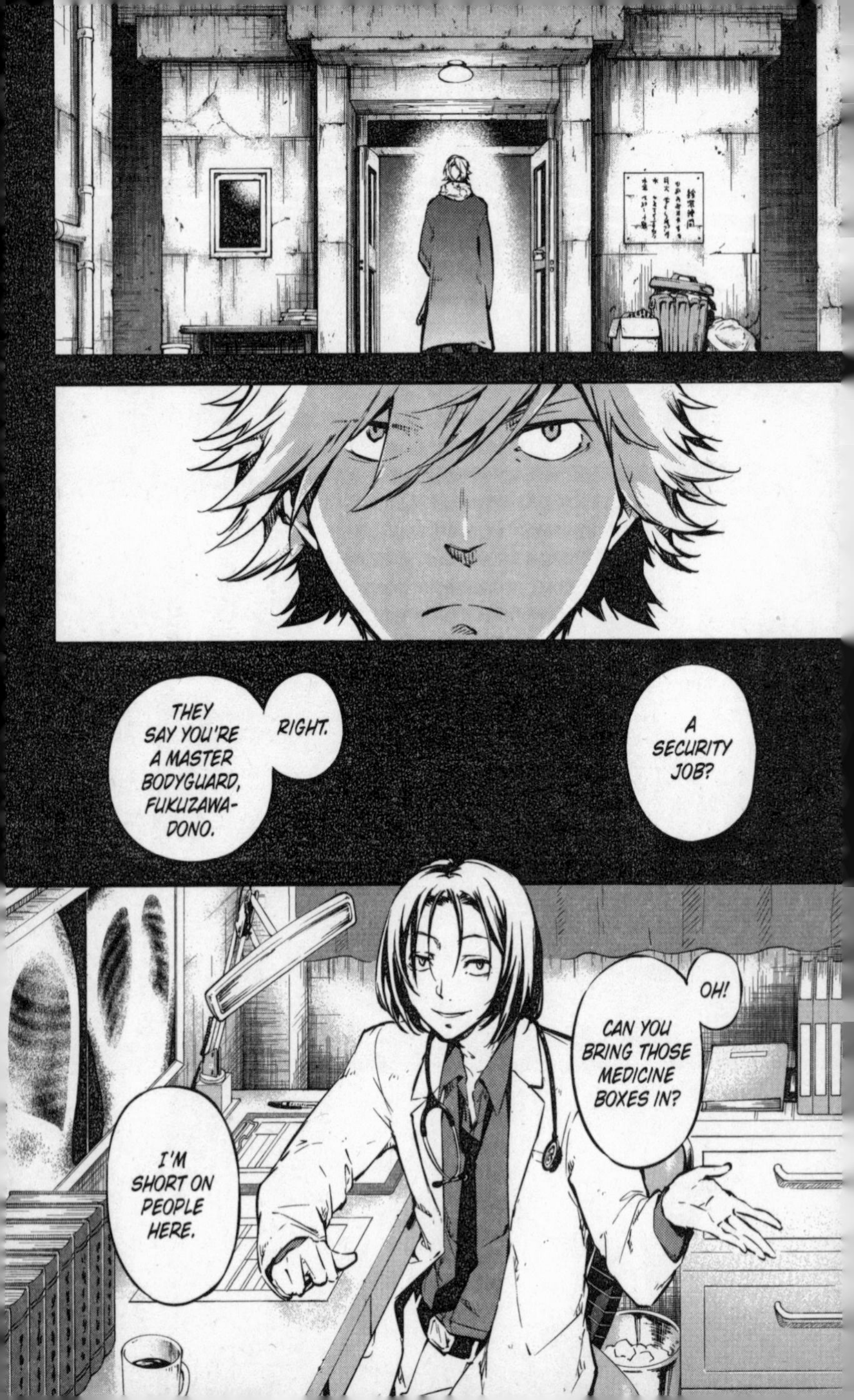
A SECURITY JOB?
RIGHT.
THEY SAY YOU'RE A MASTER BODYGUARD, FUKUZAWA-DONO.
OH!
CAN YOU BRING THOSE MEDICINE BOXES IN?
I'M SHORT ON PEOPLE HERE.

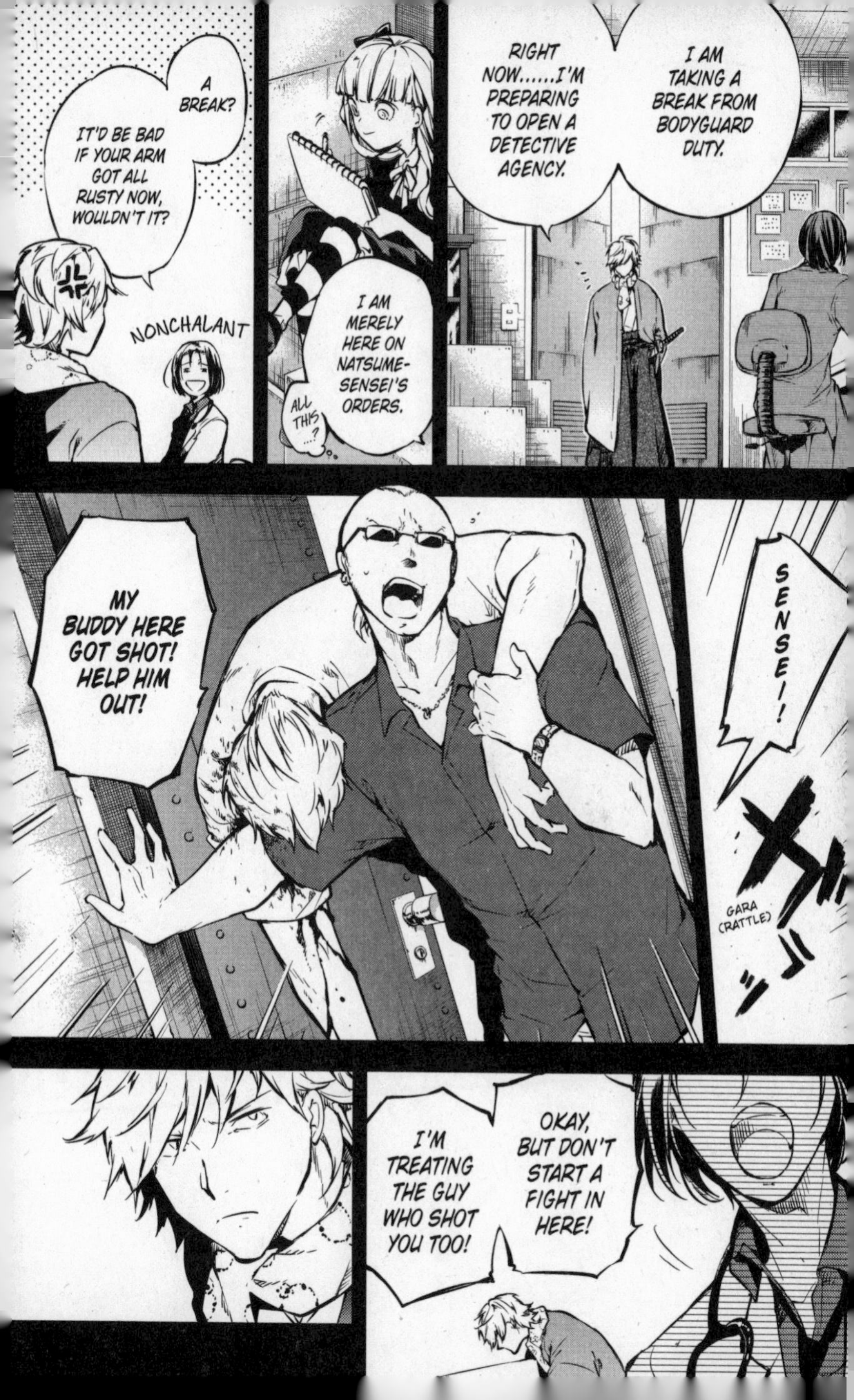
I AM TAKING A BREAK FROM BODYGUARD DUTY.
RIGHT NOW......I'M PREPARING TO OPEN A DETECTIVE AGENCY.
I AM MERELY HERE ON NATSUME-SENSEI'S ORDERS.
ALL THIS ...?
A BREAK?
IT'D BE BAD IF YOUR ARM GOT ALL RUSTY NOW, WOULDN'T IT?
NONCHALANT
SENSEI!!
GARA (RATTLE)
MY BUDDY HERE GOT SHOT! HELP HIM OUT!
OKAY, BUT DON'T START A FIGHT IN HERE!
I'M TREATING THE GUY WHO SHOT YOU TOO!

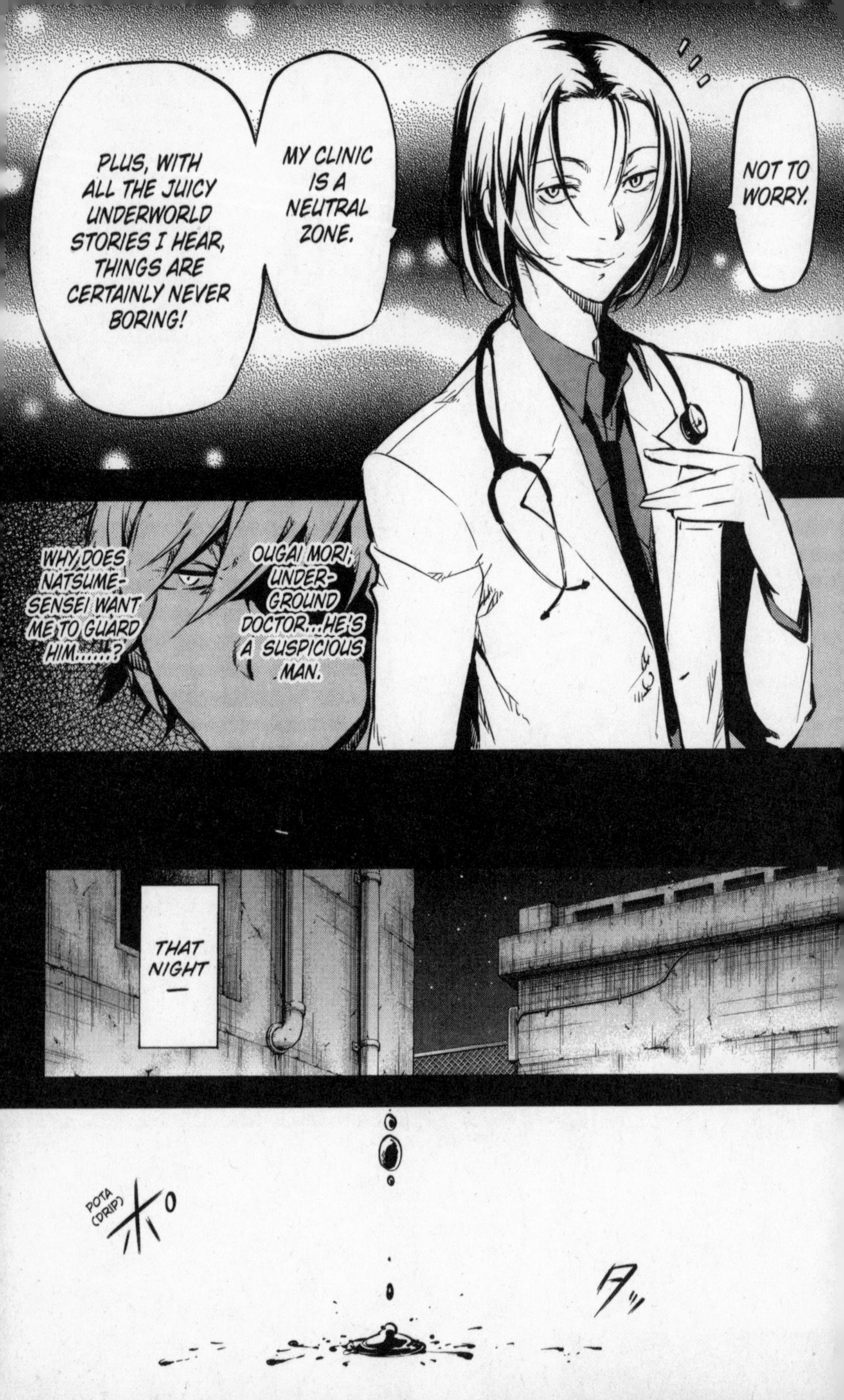
NOT TO WORRY.
MY CLINIC IS A NEUTRAL ZONE.
PLUS, WITH ALL THE JUICY UNDERWORLD STORIES I HEAR, THINGS ARE CERTAINLY NEVER BORING!
OUGAI MORI, UNDER-GROUND DOCTOR...HE'S A SUSPICIOUS MAN.
WHY DOES NATSUME-SENSEI WANT ME TO GUARD HIM......?
THAT NIGHT —
POTA (DRIP)

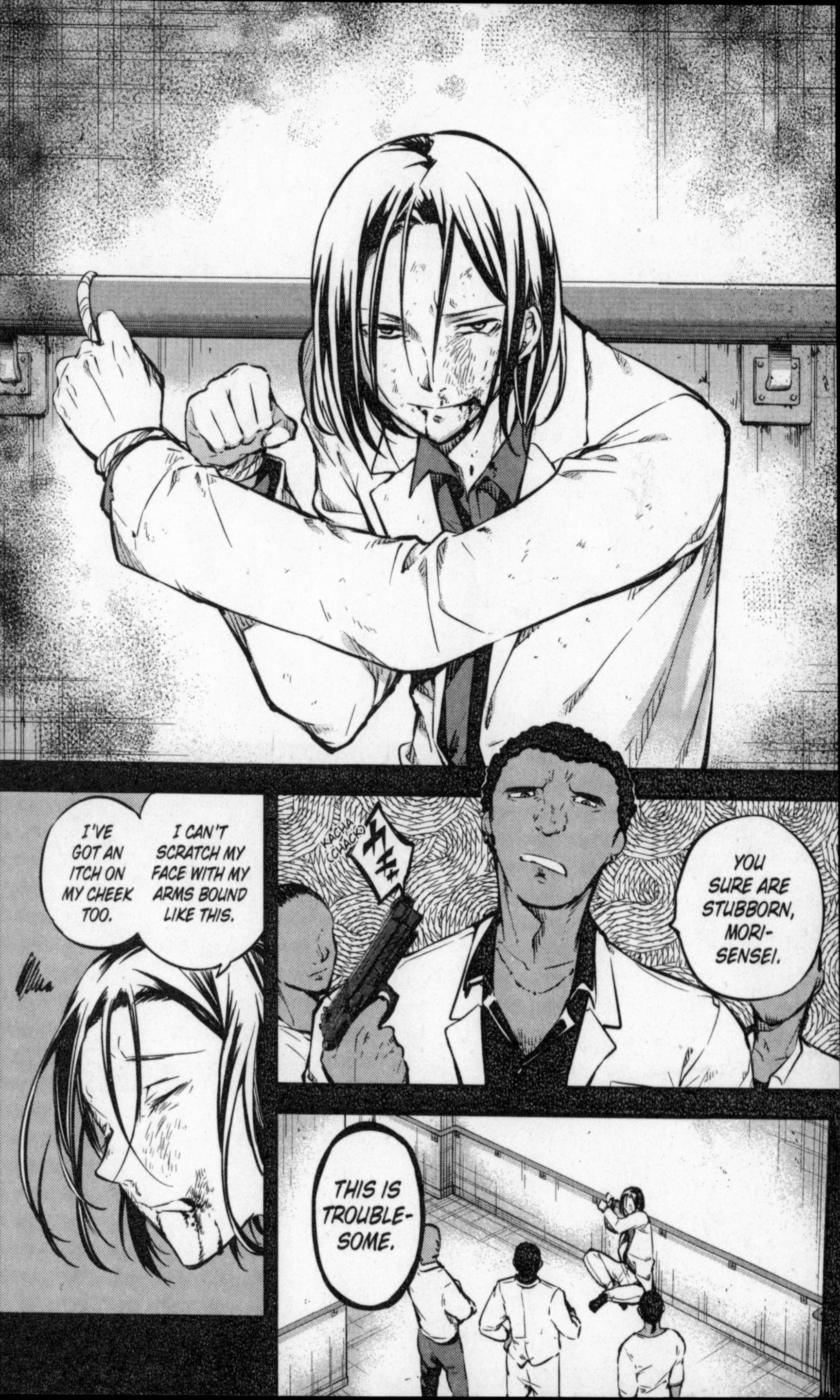
KACHA (CHACK)
YOU SURE ARE STUBBORN, MORI-SENSEI.
THIS IS TROUBLE-SOME.
I CAN'T SCRATCH MY FACE WITH MY ARMS BOUND LIKE THIS.
I'VE GOT AN ITCH ON MY CHEEK TOO.

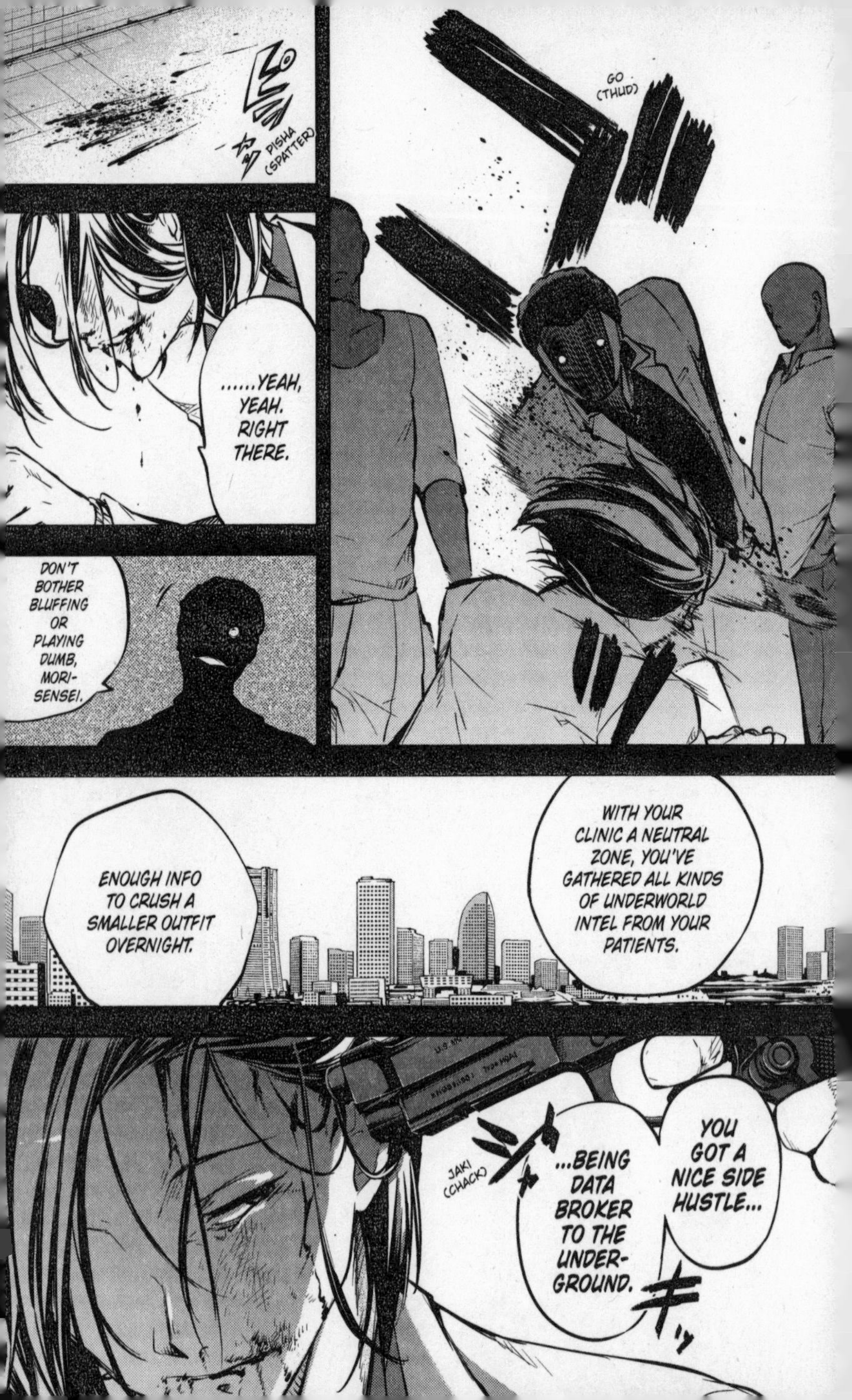
GO (THUD)
PISHA (SPATTER)
......YEAH, YEAH. RIGHT THERE.
DON'T BOTHER BLUFFING OR PLAYING DUMB, MORI-SENSEI.
WITH YOUR CLINIC A NEUTRAL ZONE, YOU'VE GATHERED ALL KINDS OF UNDERWORLD INTEL FROM YOUR PATIENTS.
ENOUGH INFO TO CRUSH A SMALLER OUTFIT OVERNIGHT.
YOU GOT A NICE SIDE HUSTLE...
...BEING DATA BROKER TO THE UNDER-GROUND.
JAKI (CHACK)

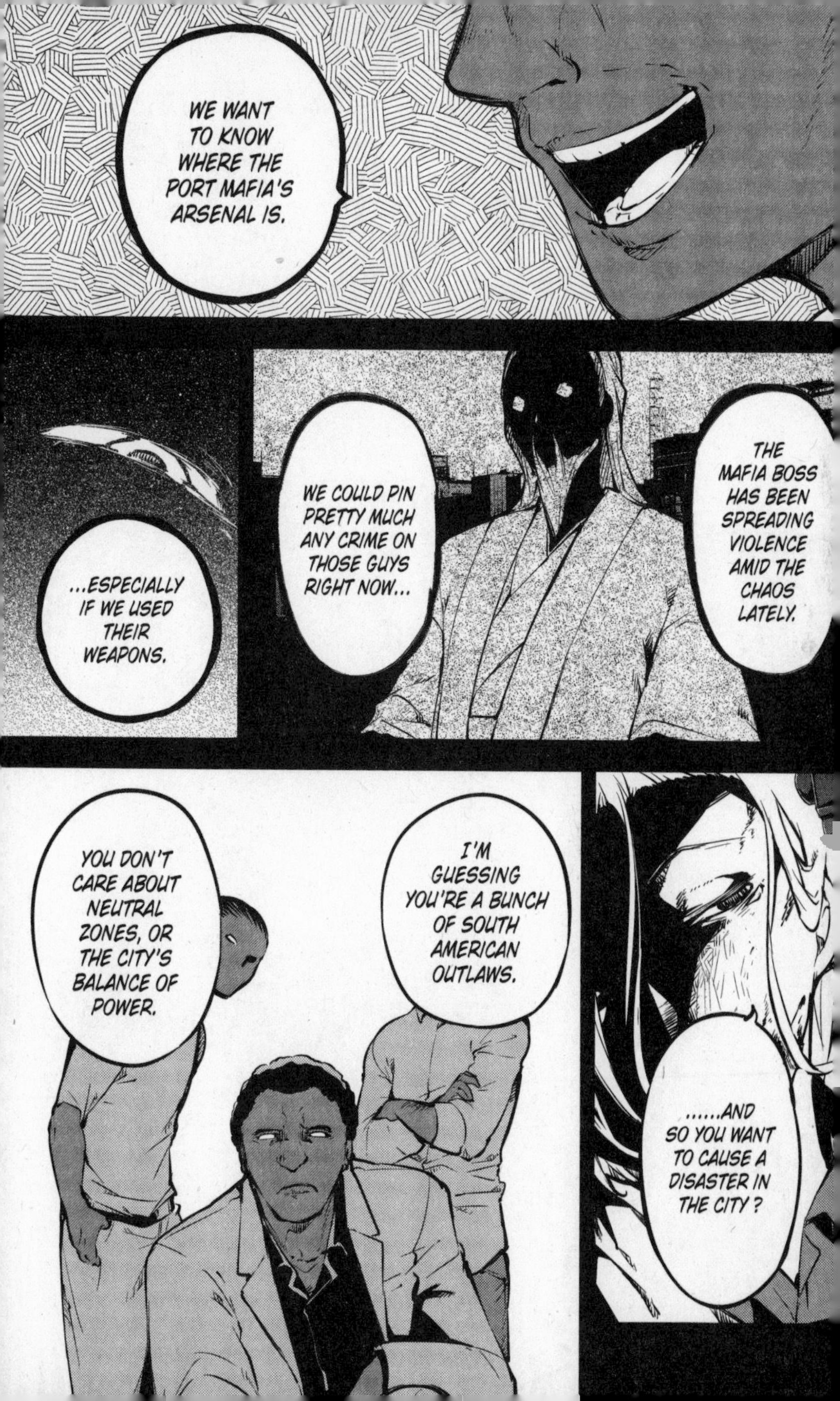
WE WANT TO KNOW WHERE THE PORT MAFIA'S ARSENAL IS.
THE MAFIA BOSS HAS BEEN SPREADING VIOLENCE AMID THE CHAOS LATELY.
WE COULD PIN PRETTY MUCH ANY CRIME ON THOSE GUYS RIGHT NOW...
...ESPECIALLY IF WE USED THEIR WEAPONS.
......AND SO YOU WANT TO CAUSE A DISASTER IN THE CITY?
I'M GUESSING YOU'RE A BUNCH OF SOUTH AMERICAN OUTLAWS.
YOU DON'T CARE ABOUT NEUTRAL ZONES, OR THE CITY'S BALANCE OF POWER.

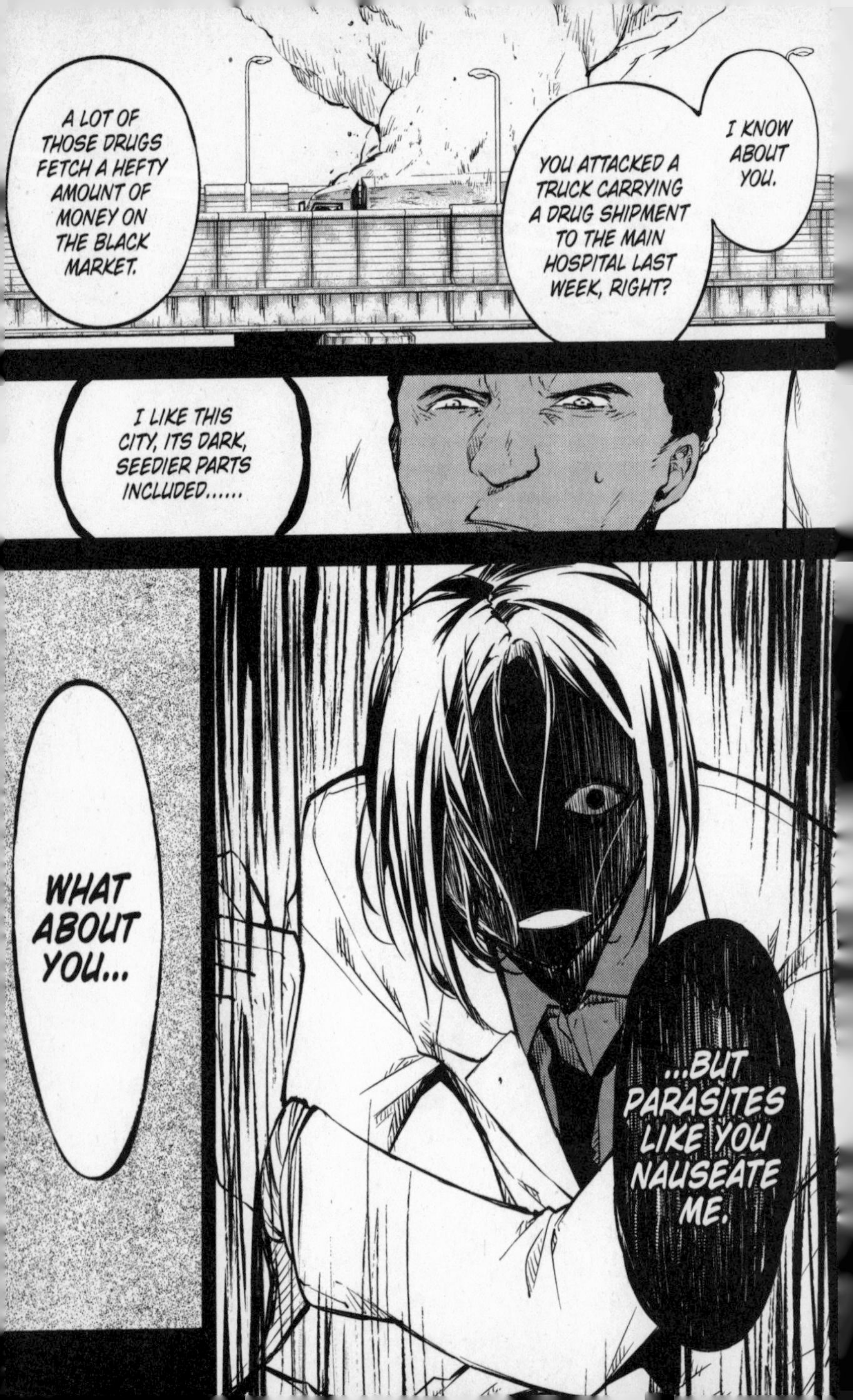
I KNOW ABOUT YOU.
YOU ATTACKED A TRUCK CARRYING A DRUG SHIPMENT TO THE MAIN HOSPITAL LAST WEEK, RIGHT?
A LOT OF THOSE DRUGS FETCH A HEFTY AMOUNT OF MONEY ON THE BLACK MARKET.
I LIKE THIS CITY, ITS DARK, SEEDIER PARTS INCLUDED......
...BUT PARASITES LIKE YOU NAUSEATE ME.
WHAT ABOUT YOU...

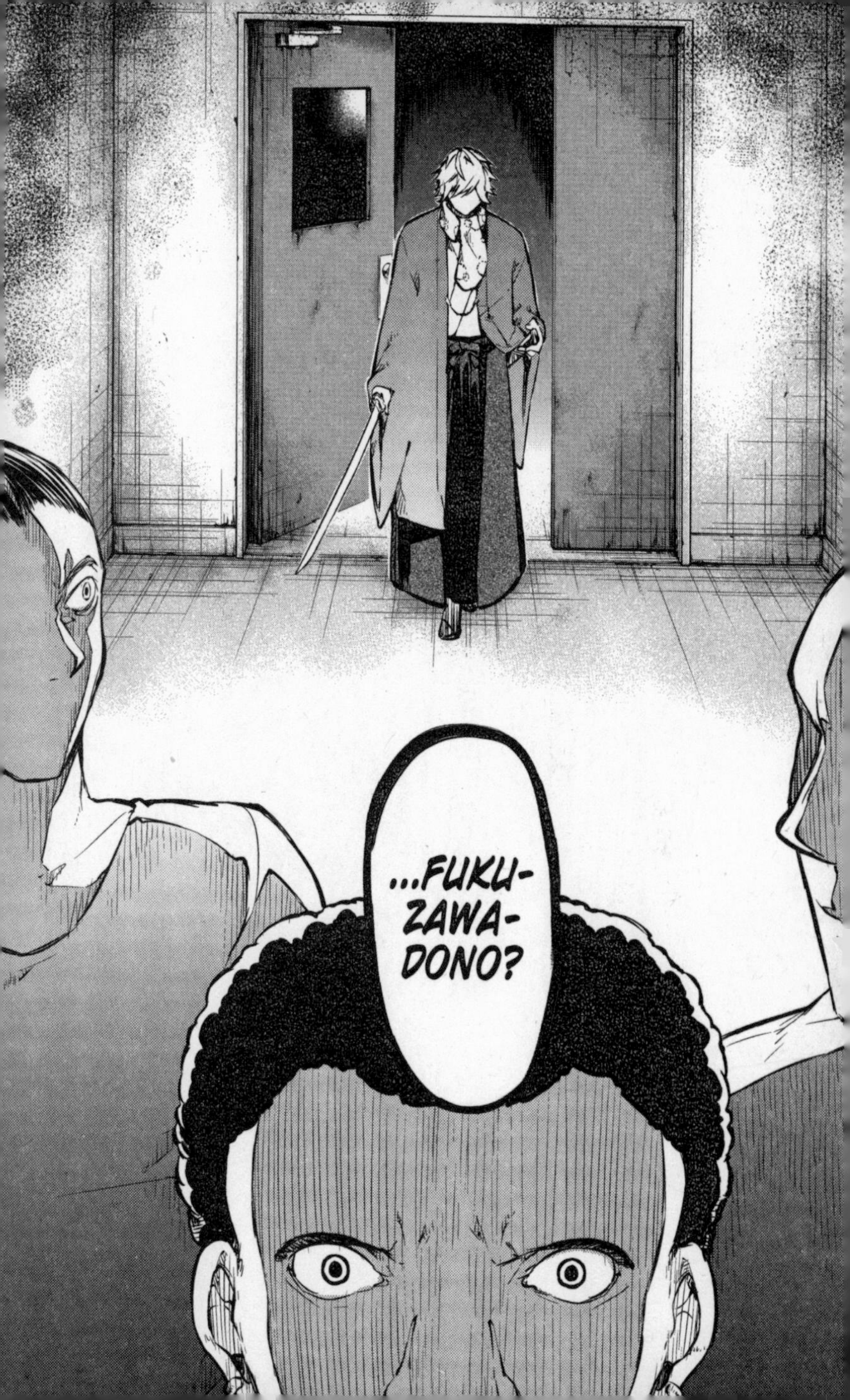
...FUKU-ZAWA-DONO?

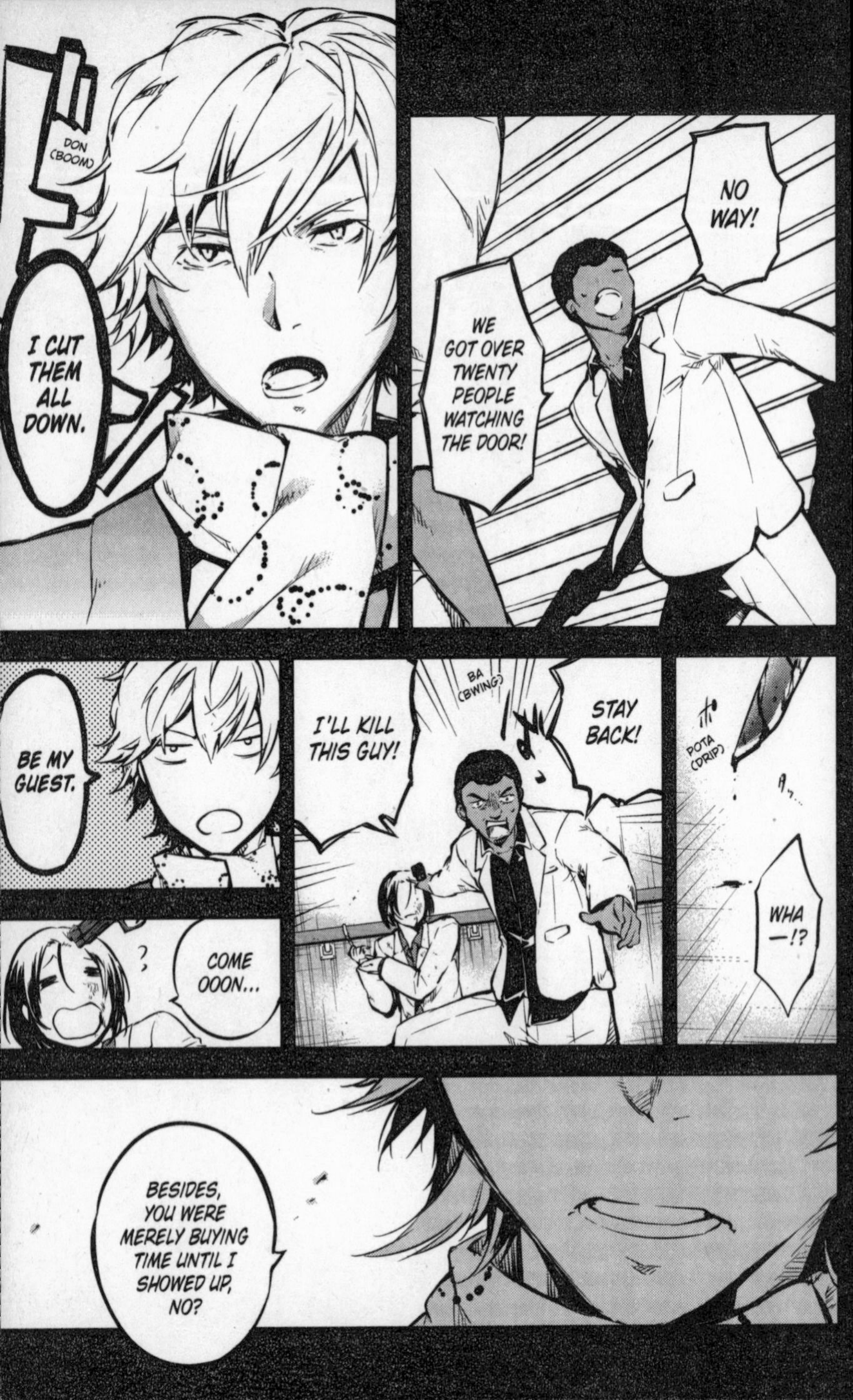
NO WAY!
WE GOT OVER TWENTY PEOPLE WATCHING THE DOOR!
DON (BOOM)
I CUT THEM ALL DOWN.
POTA (DRIP)
WHA—!?
BA (BWING)
STAY BACK!
I'LL KILL THIS GUY!
BE MY GUEST.
?
COME OOON...
BESIDES, YOU WERE MERELY BUYING TIME UNTIL I SHOWED UP, NO?

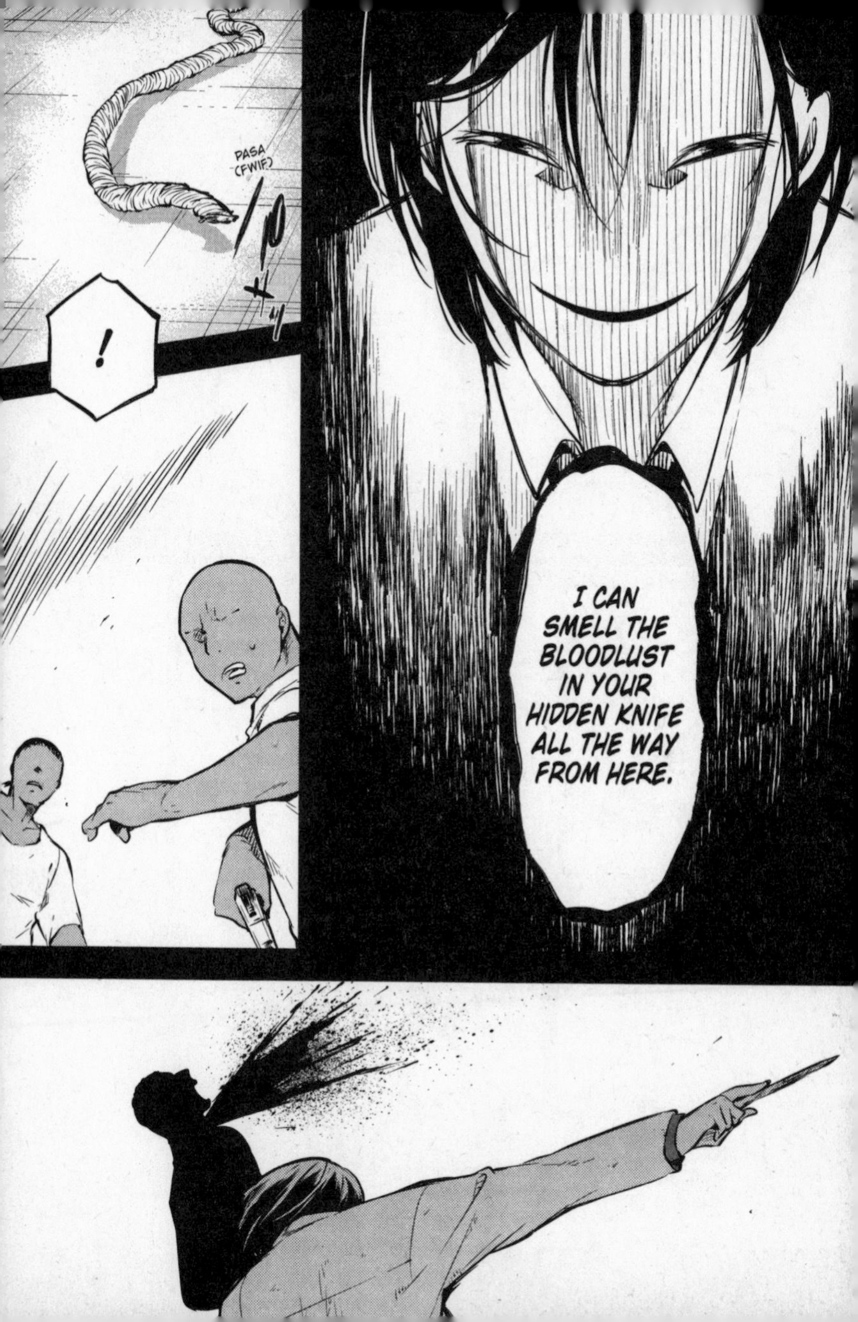
I CAN SMELL THE BLOODLUST IN YOUR HIDDEN KNIFE ALL THE WAY FROM HERE.
PASA (FWIP)
!

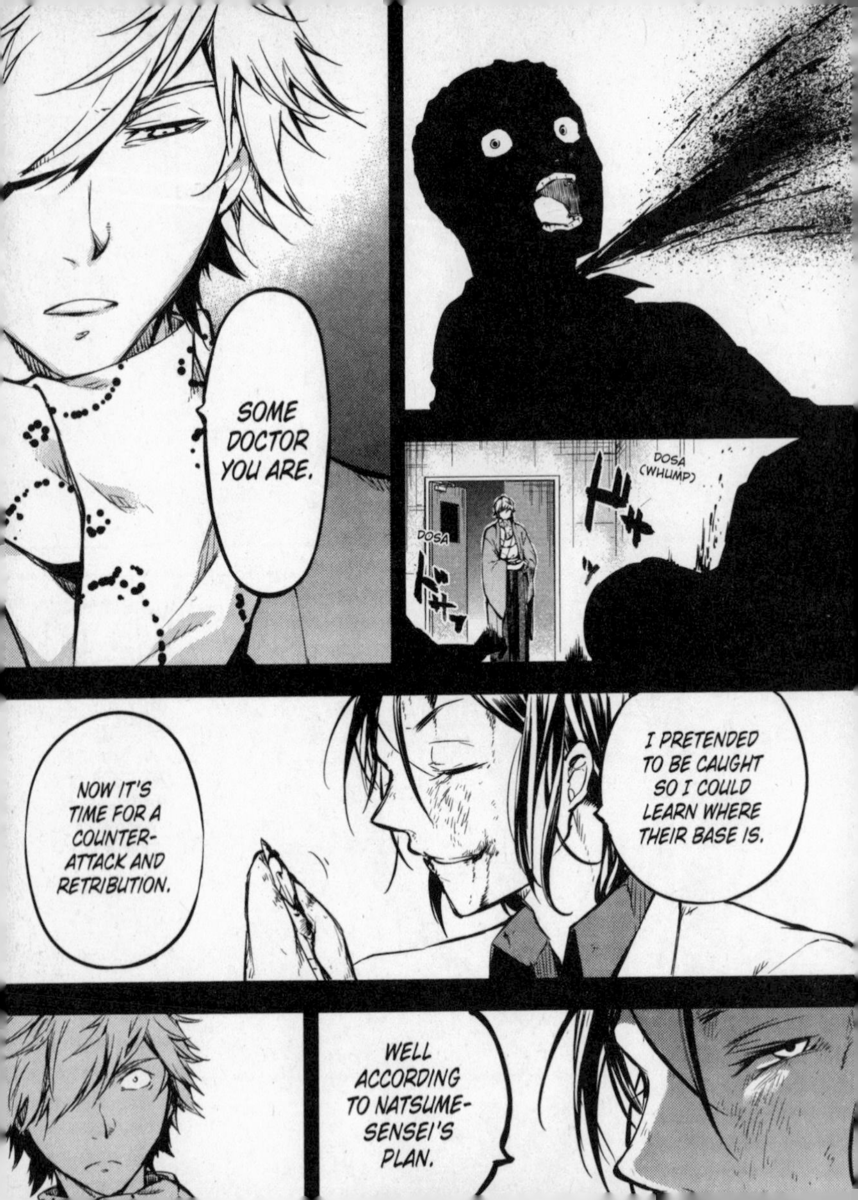
DOSA (WHUMP)
ドサッ
DOSA
ドサッ
SOME DOCTOR YOU ARE.
I PRETENDED TO BE CAUGHT SO I COULD LEARN WHERE THEIR BASE IS.
NOW IT'S TIME FOR A COUNTER-ATTACK AND RETRIBUTION.
WELL ACCORDING TO NATSUME-SENSEI'S PLAN.

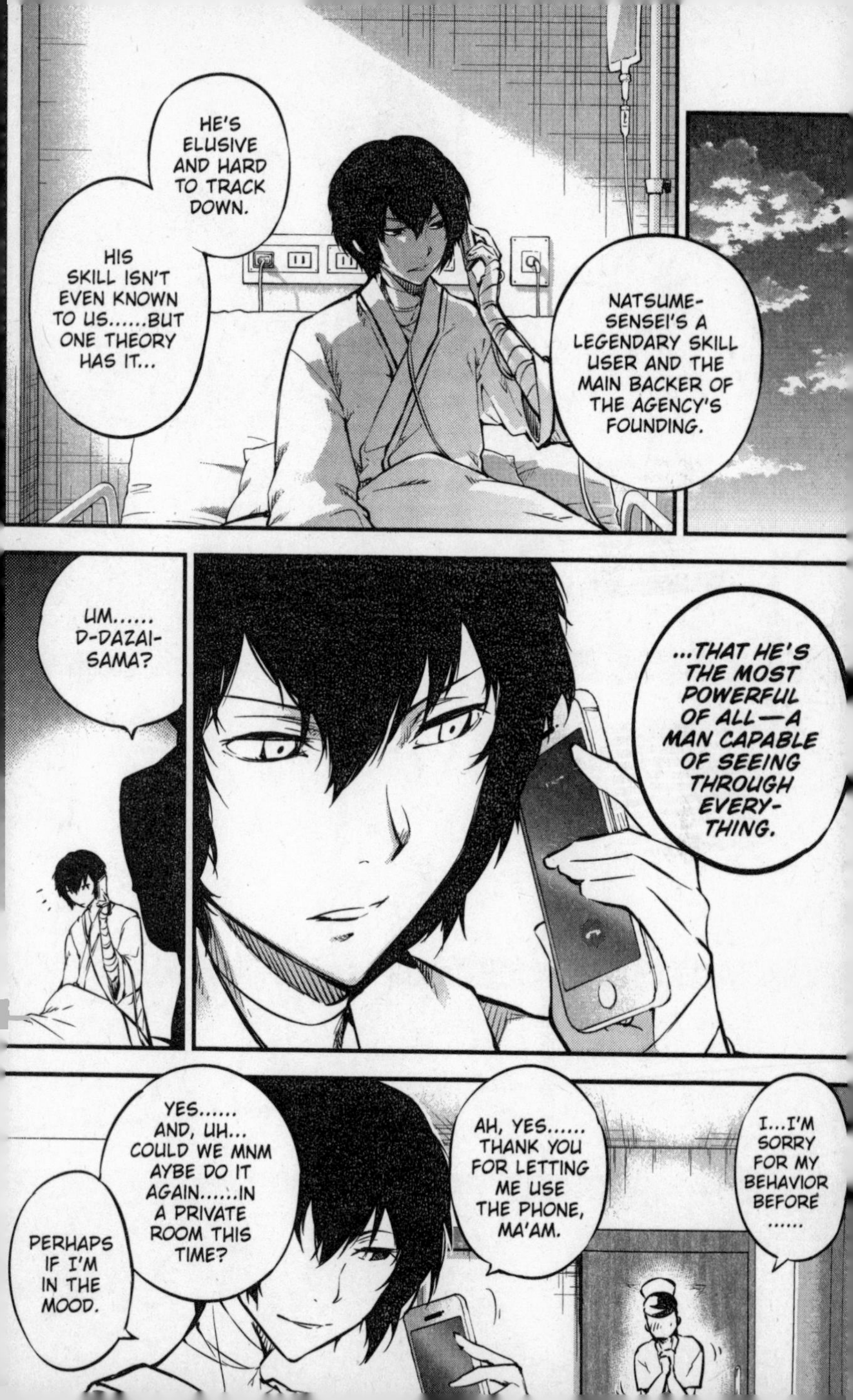
NATSUME-SENSEI'S A LEGENDARY SKILL USER AND THE MAIN BACKER OF THE AGENCY'S FOUNDING.
HE'S ELUSIVE AND HARD TO TRACK DOWN.
HIS SKILL ISN'T EVEN KNOWN TO US......BUT ONE THEORY HAS IT...
...THAT HE'S THE MOST POWERFUL OF ALL—A MAN CAPABLE OF SEEING THROUGH EVERY-THING.
UM...... D-DAZAI-SAMA?
I...I'M SORRY FOR MY BEHAVIOR BEFORE ......
AH, YES...... THANK YOU FOR LETTING ME USE THE PHONE, MA'AM.
YES...... AND, UH... COULD WE MNM AYBE DO IT AGAIN......IN A PRIVATE ROOM THIS TIME?
PERHAPS IF I'M IN THE MOOD.

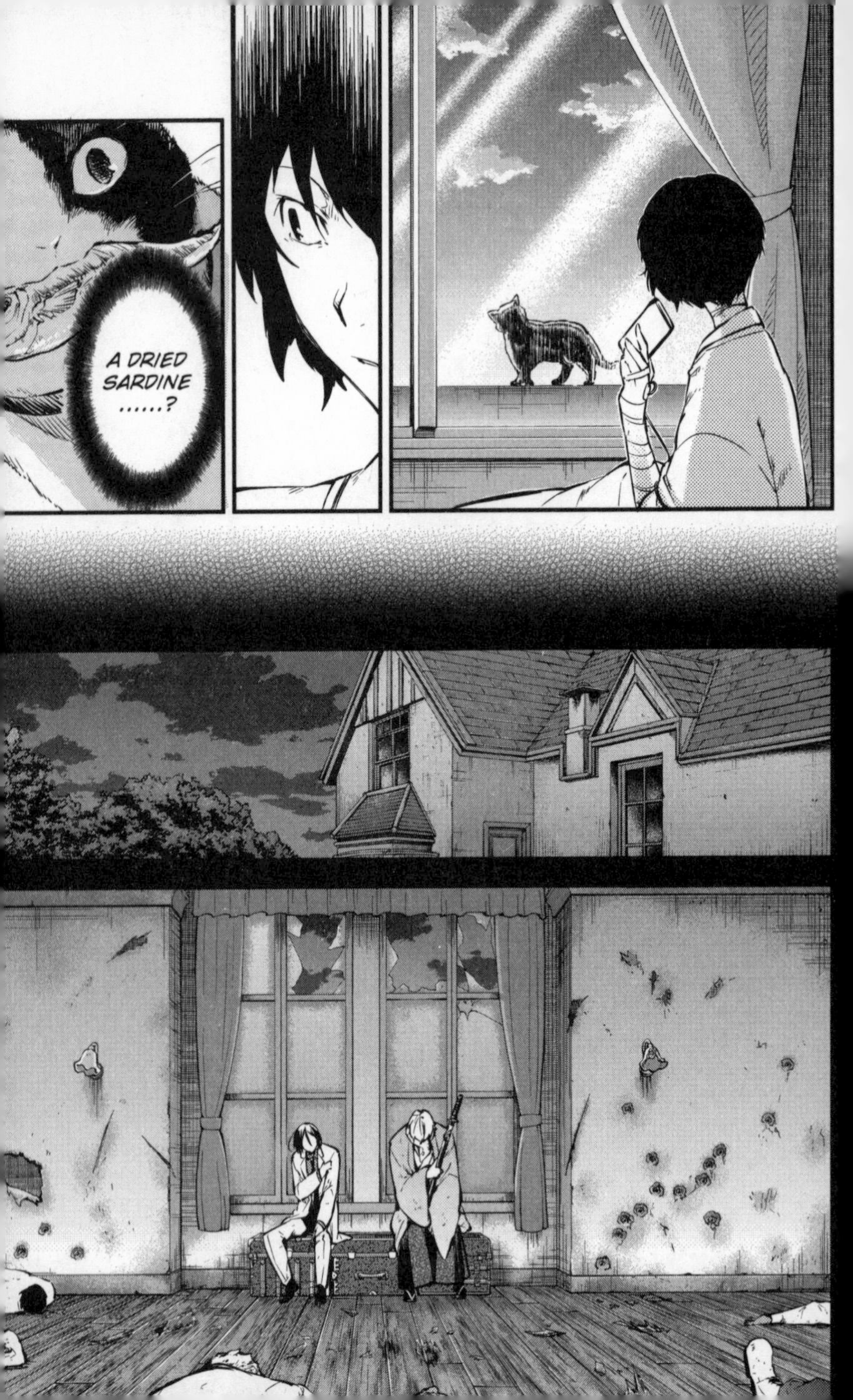
A DRIED SARDINE ......?

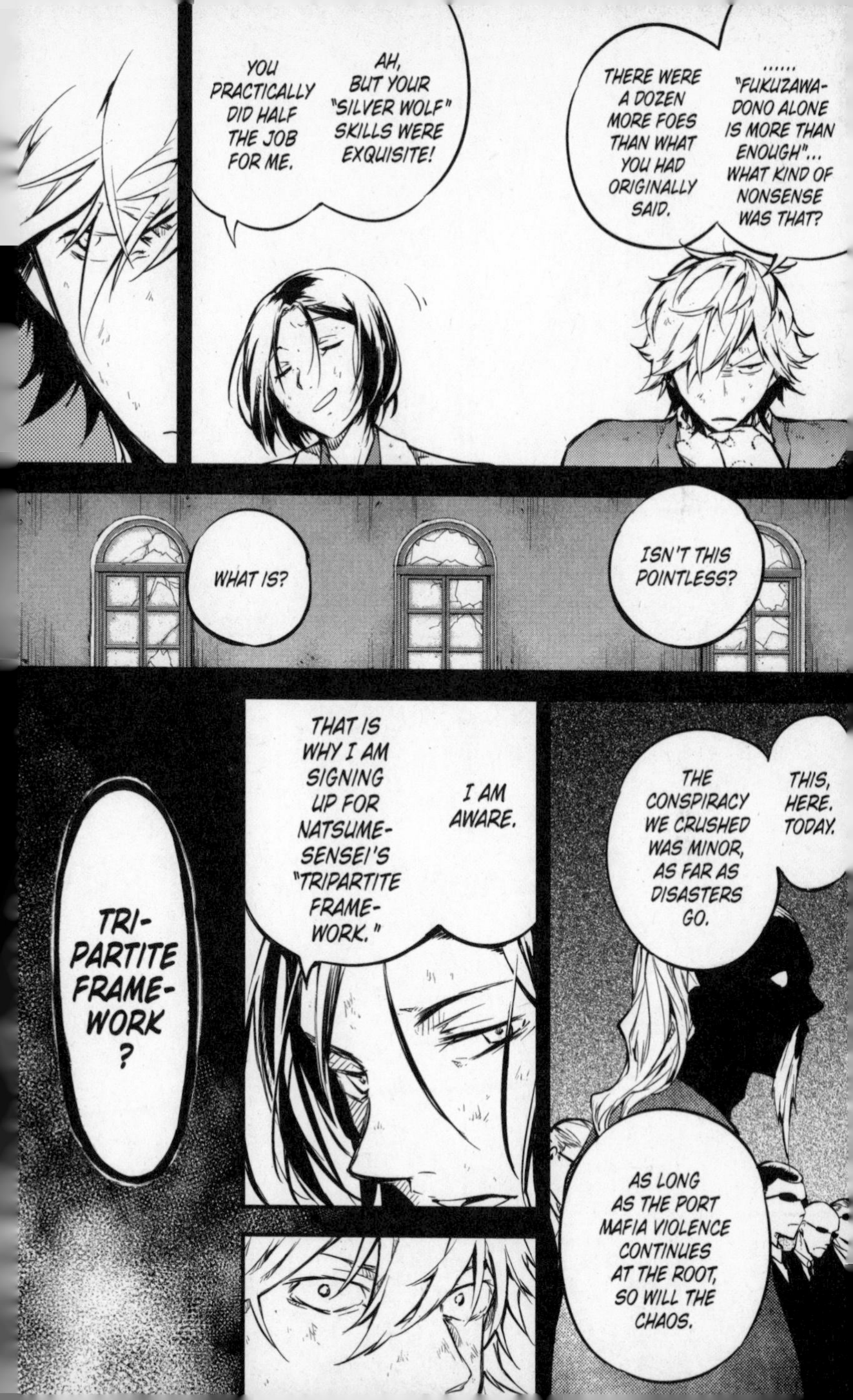
......
"FUKUZAWA-DONO ALONE IS MORE THAN ENOUGH"... WHAT KIND OF NONSENSE WAS THAT?
THERE WERE A DOZEN MORE FOES THAN WHAT YOU HAD ORIGINALLY SAID.
AH, BUT YOUR "SILVER WOLF" SKILLS WERE EXQUISITE!
YOU PRACTICALLY DID HALF THE JOB FOR ME.
ISN'T THIS POINTLESS?
WHAT IS?
THIS, HERE. TODAY.
THE CONSPIRACY WE CRUSHED WAS MINOR, AS FAR AS DISASTERS GO.
AS LONG AS THE PORT MAFIA VIOLENCE CONTINUES AT THE ROOT, SO WILL THE CHAOS.
I AM AWARE.
THAT IS WHY I AM SIGNING UP FOR NATSUME-SENSEI'S "TRIPARTITE FRAME-WORK."
TRI-PARTITE FRAME-WORK?

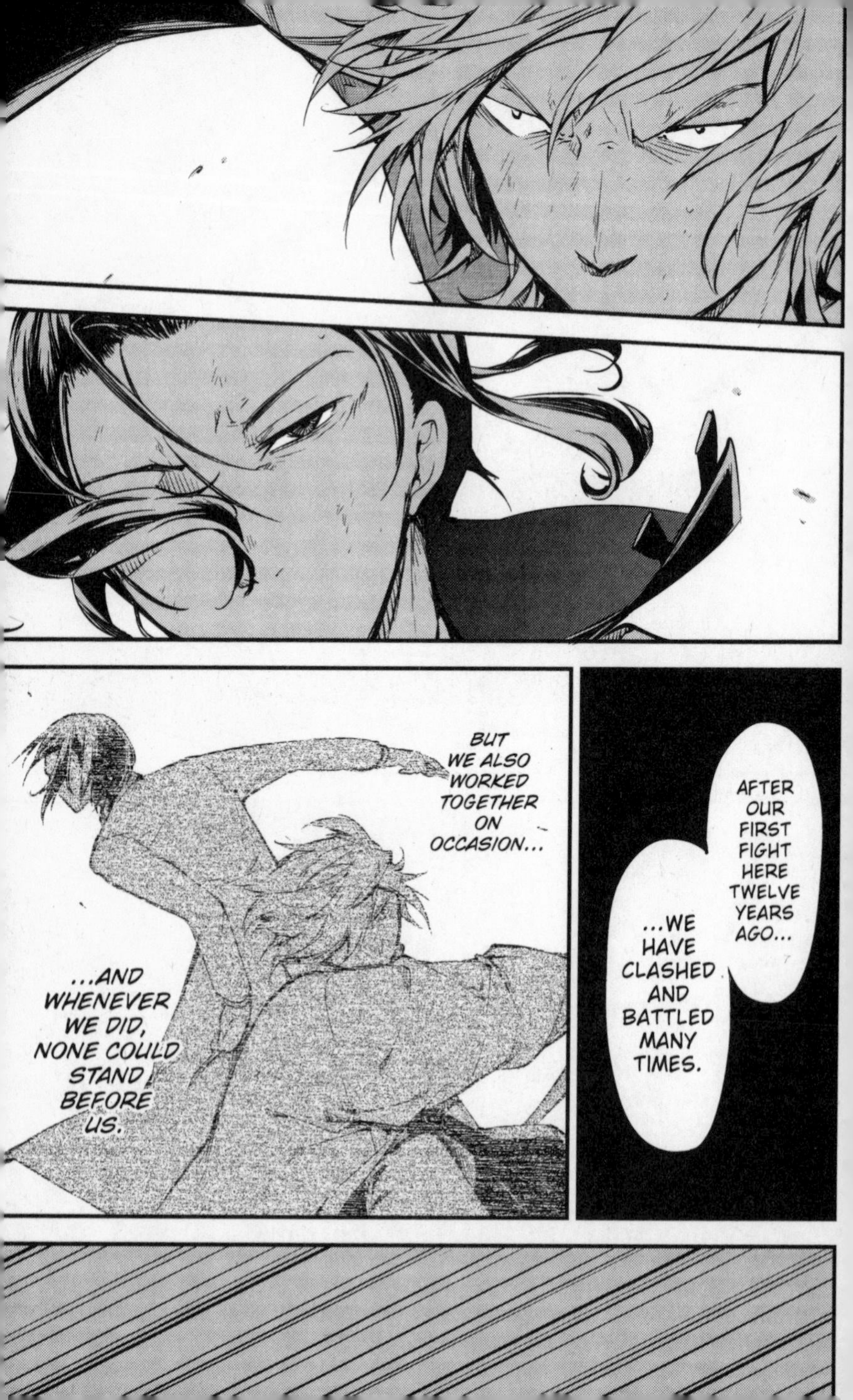
AFTER OUR FIRST FIGHT HERE TWELVE YEARS AGO...
...WE HAVE CLASHED AND BATTLED MANY TIMES.
BUT WE ALSO WORKED TOGETHER ON OCCASION...
...AND WHENEVER WE DID, NONE COULD STAND BEFORE US.

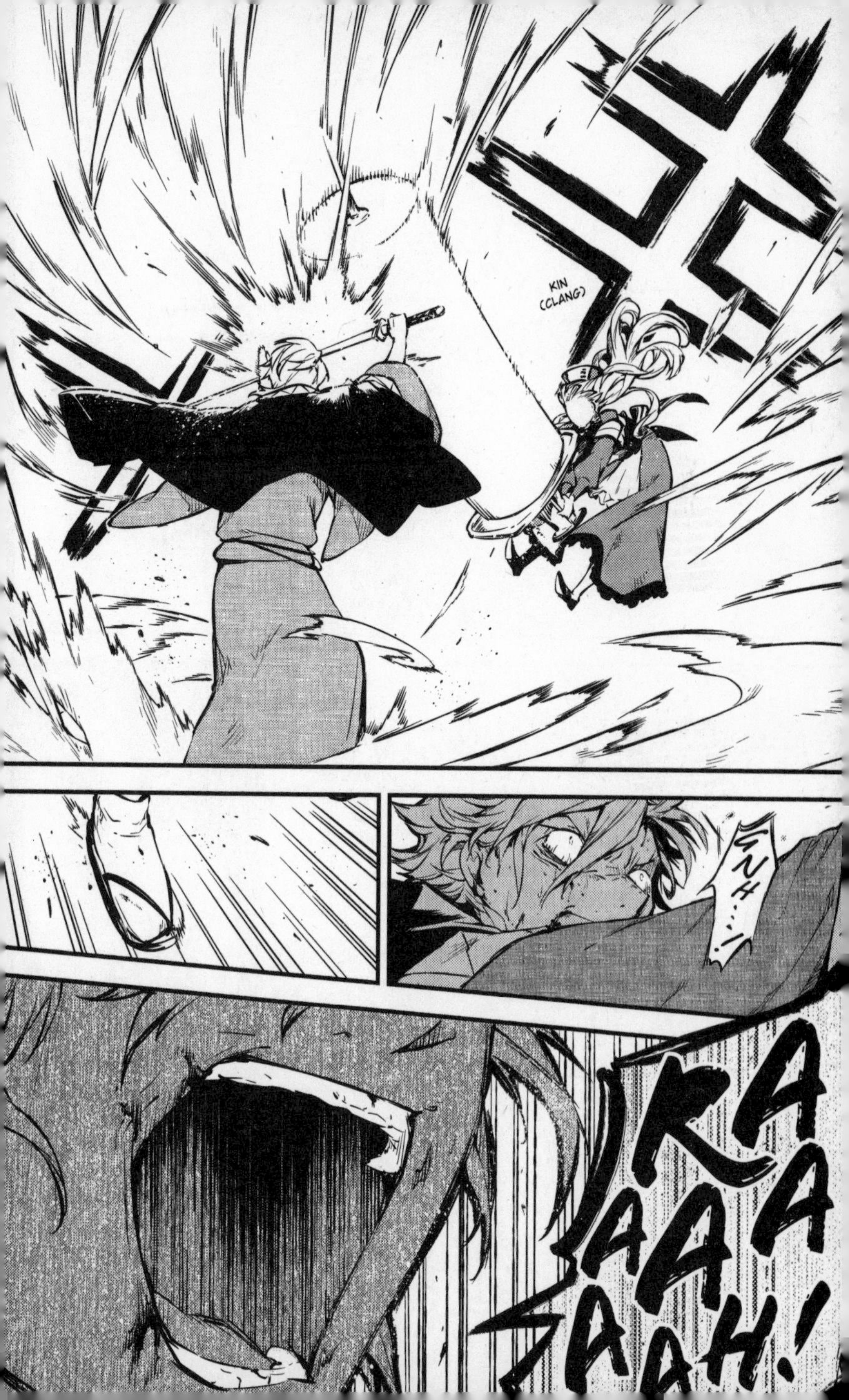
KIN
(CLANG)
GNH...!
KAAAAAAAH!

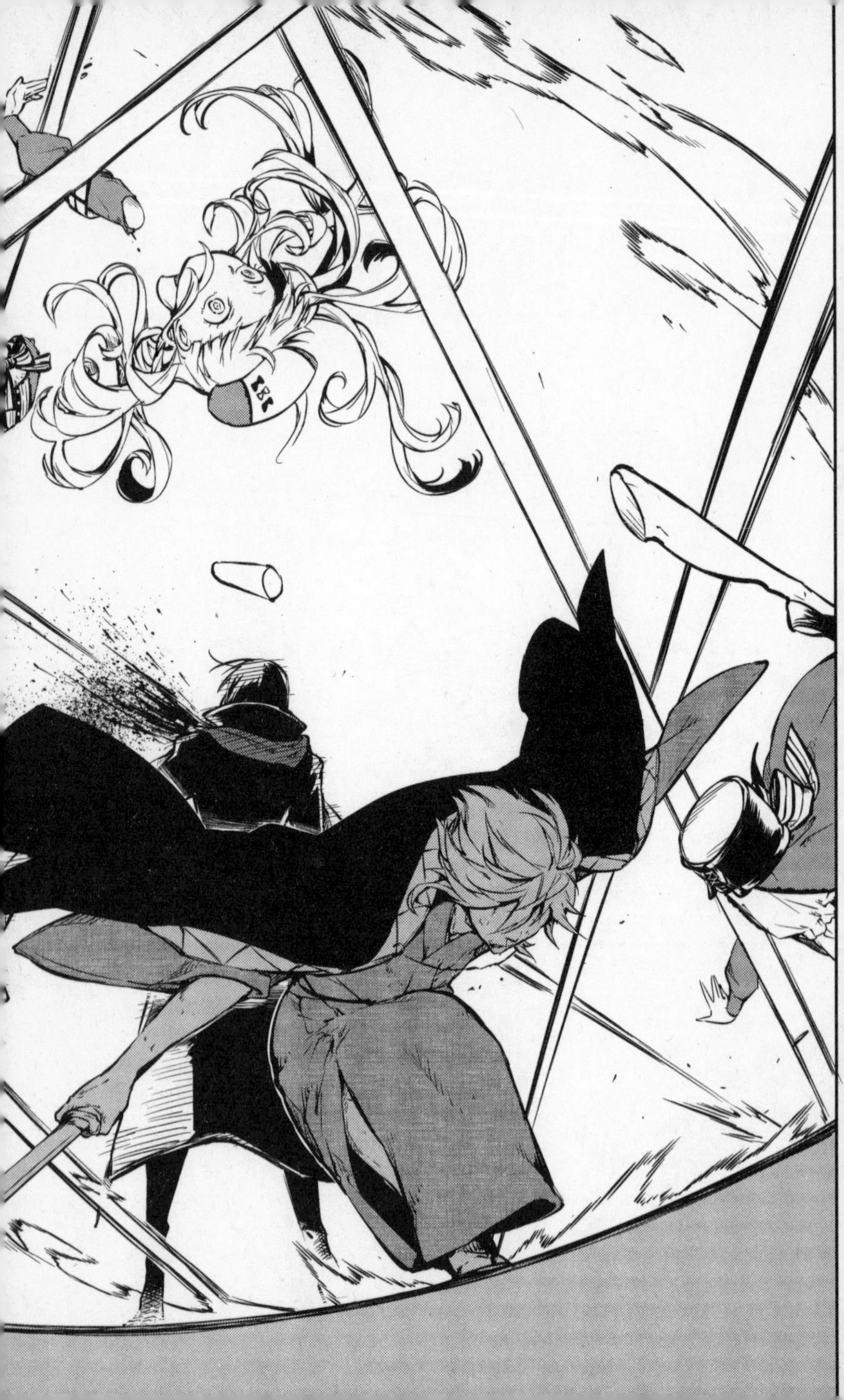

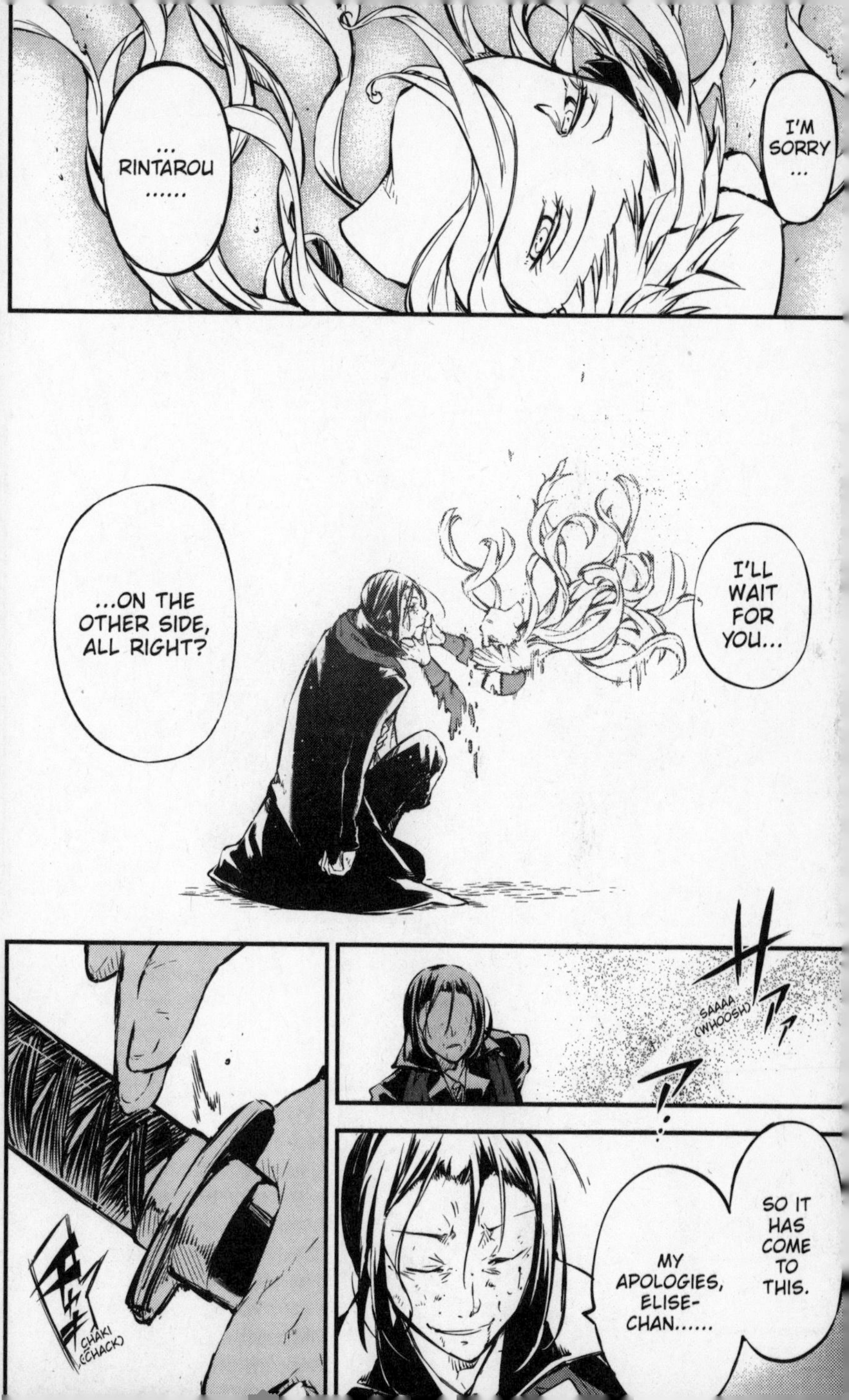
I'M SORRY ...
... RINTAROU ......
I'LL WAIT FOR YOU...
...ON THE OTHER SIDE, ALL RIGHT?
SAAAA (WHOOSH)
SO IT HAS COME TO THIS.
MY APOLOGIES, ELISE-CHAN......
CHAKI (CHACK)

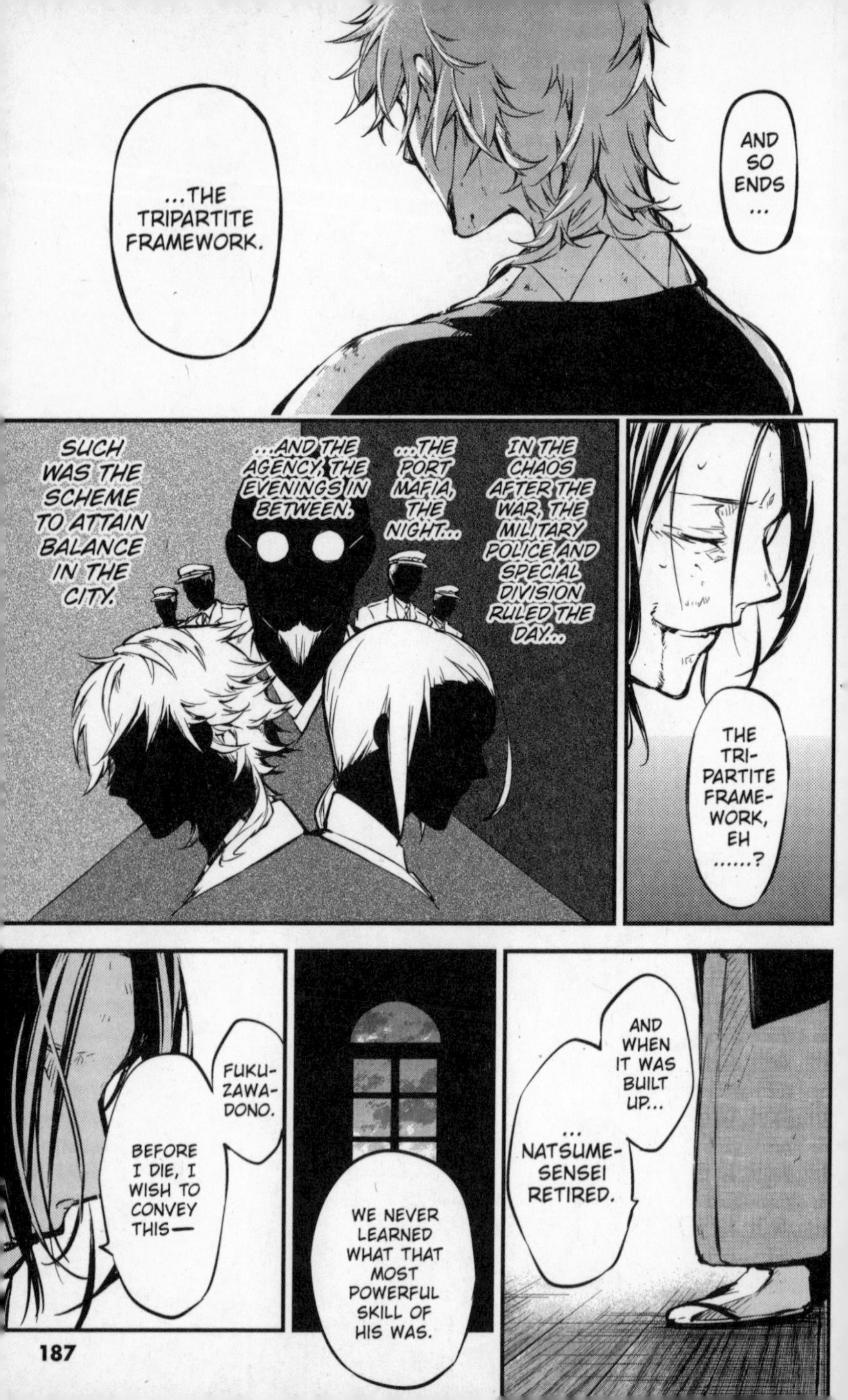
AND SO ENDS...
...THE TRIPARTITE FRAMEWORK.
THE TRIPARTITE FRAMEWORK, EH ......?
IN THE CHAOS AFTER THE WAR, THE MILITARY POLICE AND SPECIAL DIVISION RULED THE DAY...
...THE PORT MAFIA, THE NIGHT...
...AND THE AGENCY, THE EVENINGS IN BETWEEN.
SUCH WAS THE SCHEME TO ATTAIN BALANCE IN THE CITY.
AND WHEN IT WAS BUILT UP...
...NATSUME-SENSEI RETIRED.
WE NEVER LEARNED WHAT THAT MOST POWERFUL SKILL OF HIS WAS.
FUKUZAWA-DONO.
BEFORE I DIE, I WISH TO CONVEY THIS—

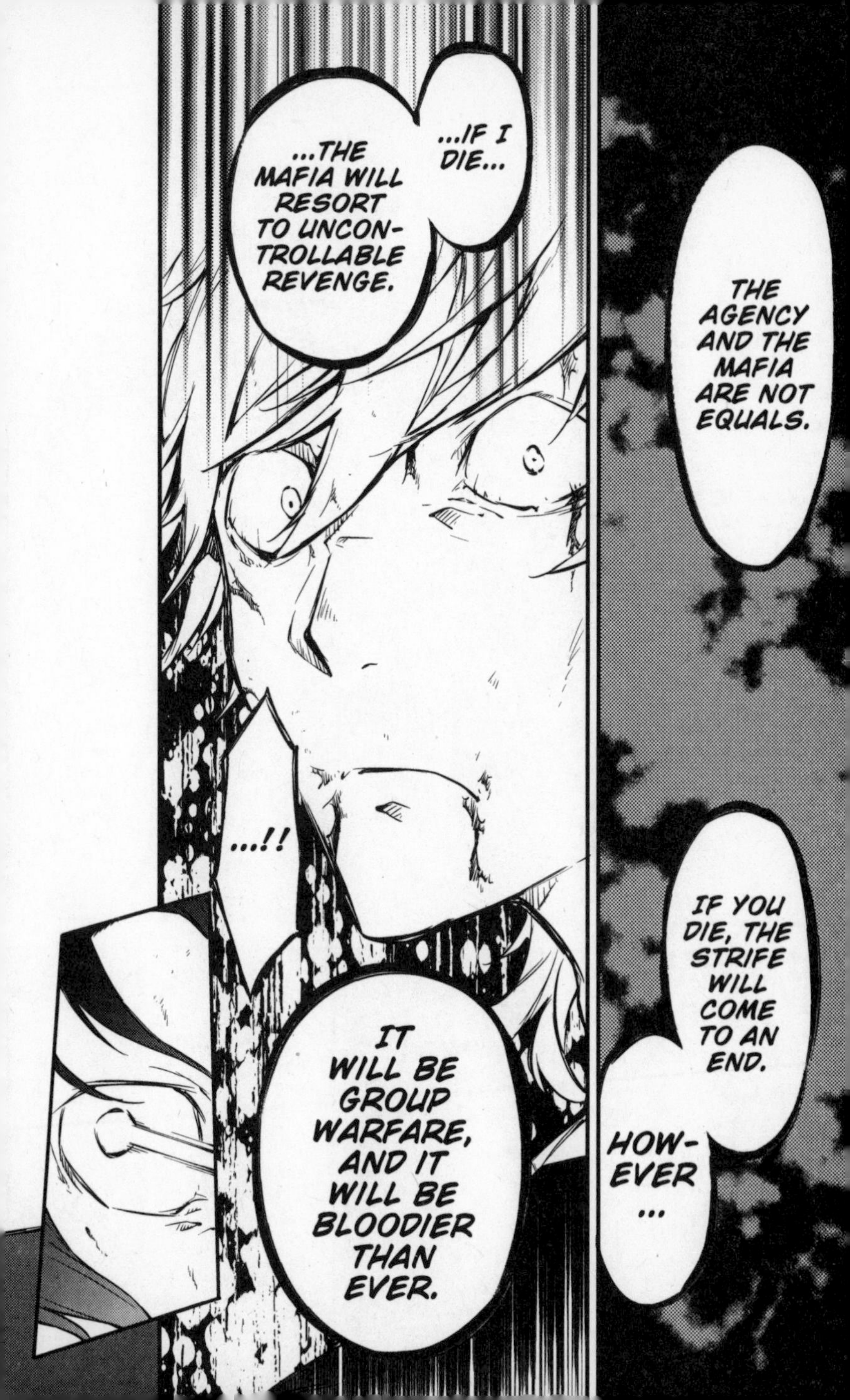
THE AGENCY AND THE MAFIA ARE NOT EQUALS.
IF YOU DIE, THE STRIFE WILL COME TO AN END.
HOW-EVER...
...IF I DIE...
...THE MAFIA WILL RESORT TO UNCON-TROLLABLE REVENGE.
...!!
IT WILL BE GROUP WARFARE, AND IT WILL BE BLOODIER THAN EVER.

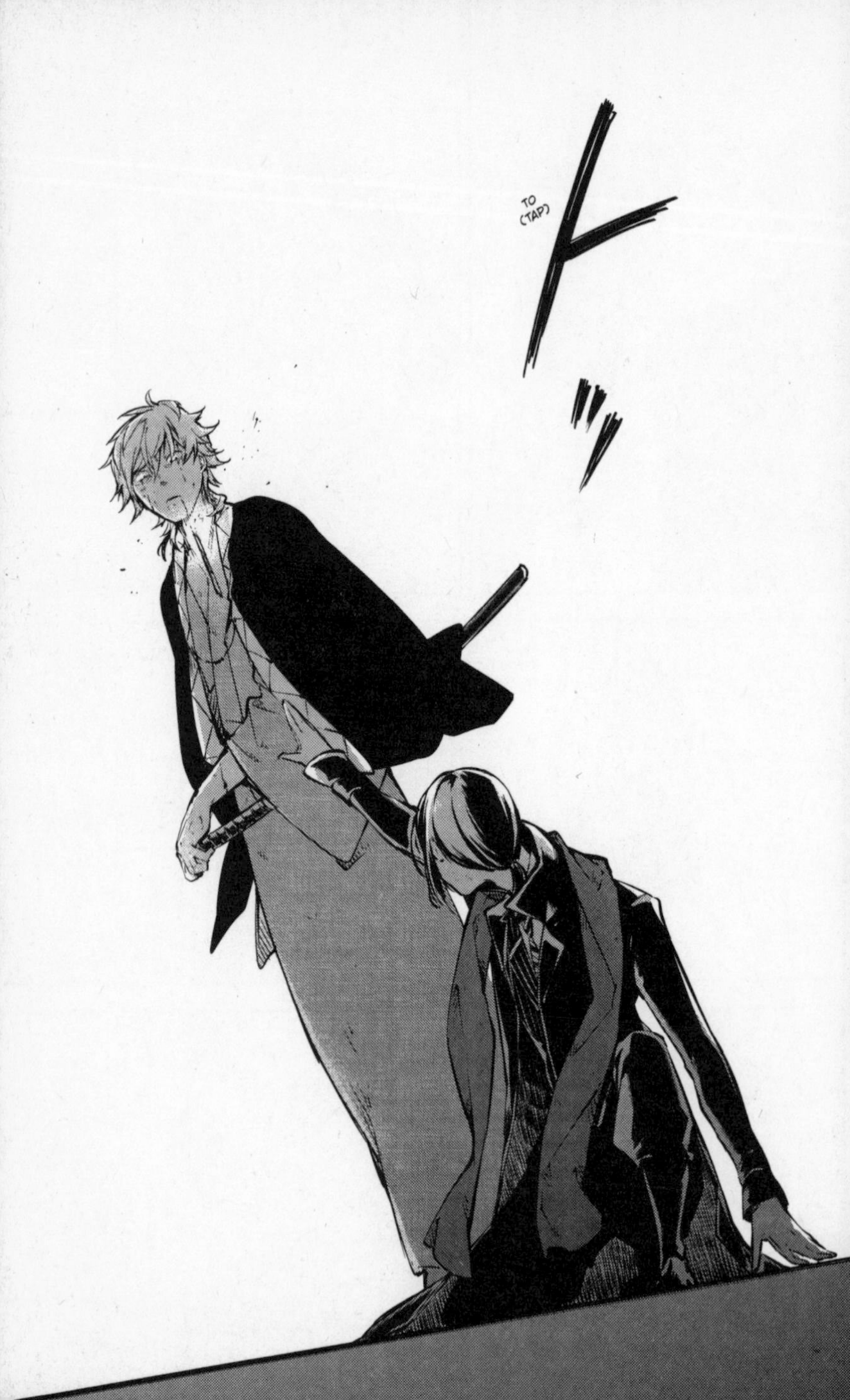
TO
(TAP)

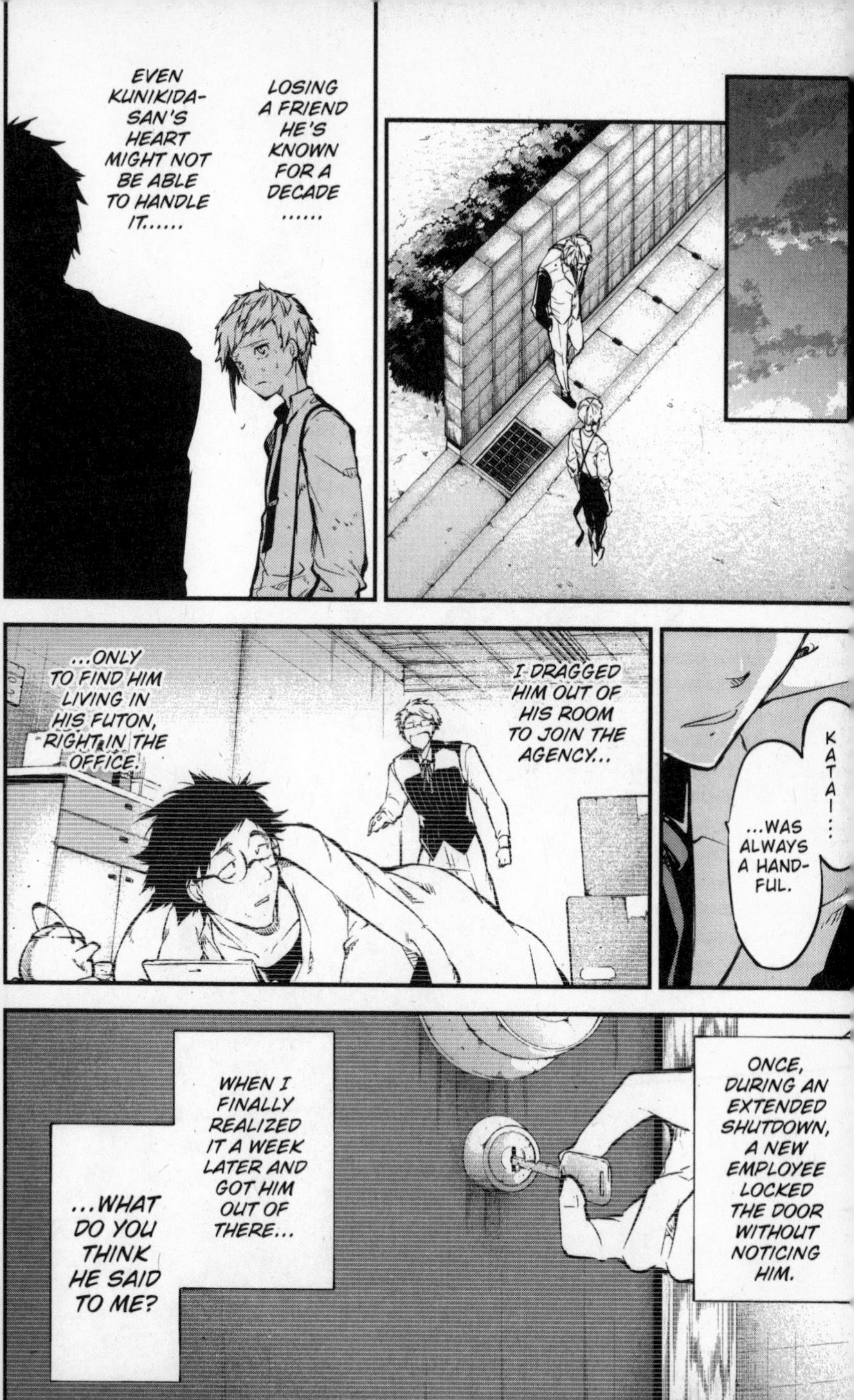
LOSING A FRIEND HE'S KNOWN FOR A DECADE......
EVEN KUNIKIDA-SAN'S HEART MIGHT NOT BE ABLE TO HANDLE IT......
KATAI...
...WAS ALWAYS A HAND-FUL.
I DRAGGED HIM OUT OF HIS ROOM TO JOIN THE AGENCY...
...ONLY TO FIND HIM LIVING IN HIS FUTON, RIGHT IN THE OFFICE.
ONCE, DURING AN EXTENDED SHUTDOWN, A NEW EMPLOYEE LOCKED THE DOOR WITHOUT NOTICING HIM.
WHEN I FINALLY REALIZED IT A WEEK LATER AND GOT HIM OUT OF THERE...
...WHAT DO YOU THINK HE SAID TO ME?

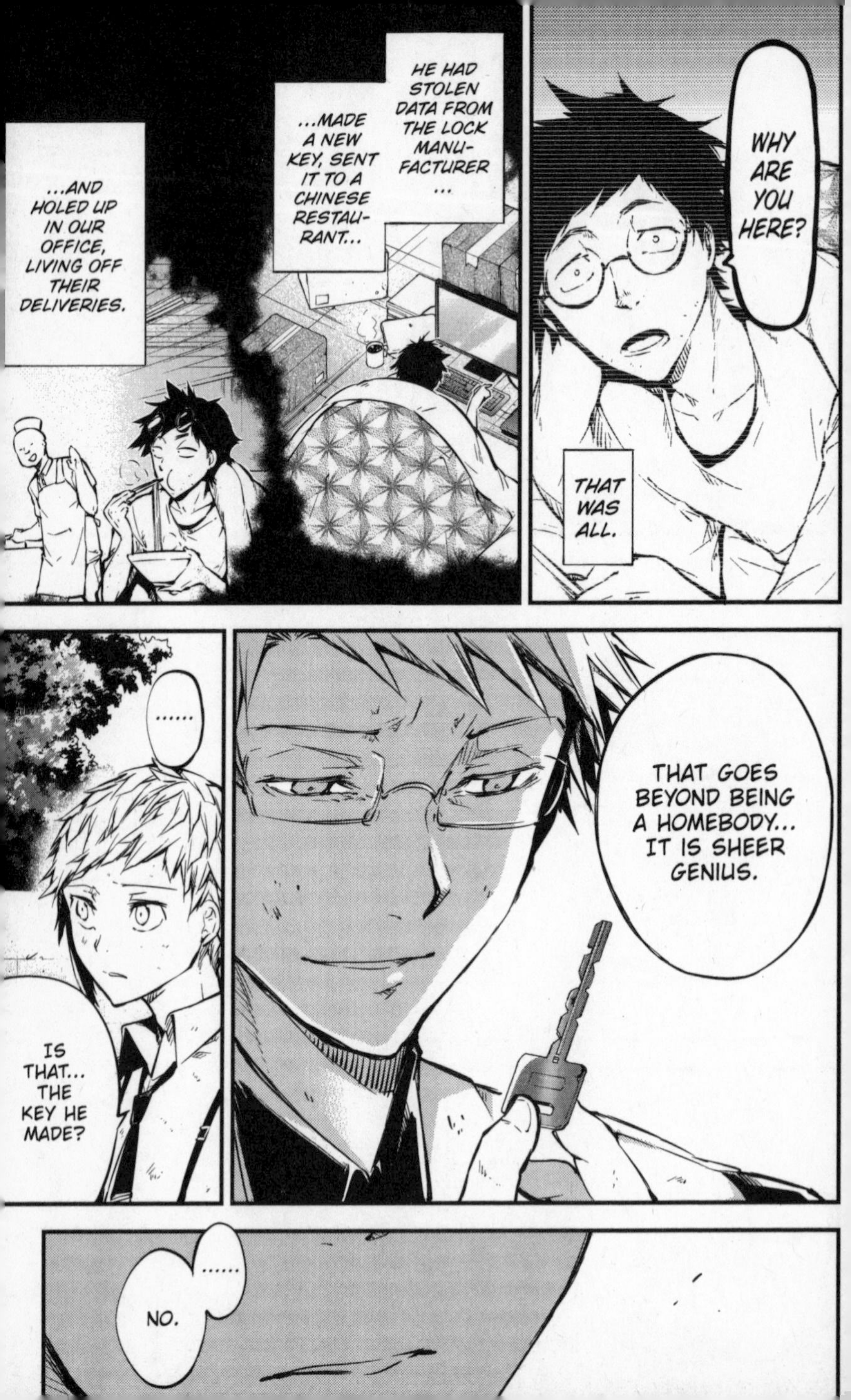
WHY ARE YOU HERE?
THAT WAS ALL.
HE HAD STOLEN DATA FROM THE LOCK MANUFACTURER ...
...MADE A NEW KEY, SENT IT TO A CHINESE RESTAURANT...
...AND HOLED UP IN OUR OFFICE, LIVING OFF THEIR DELIVERIES.
THAT GOES BEYOND BEING A HOMEBODY... IT IS SHEER GENIUS.
......
IS THAT... THE KEY HE MADE?
......
NO.

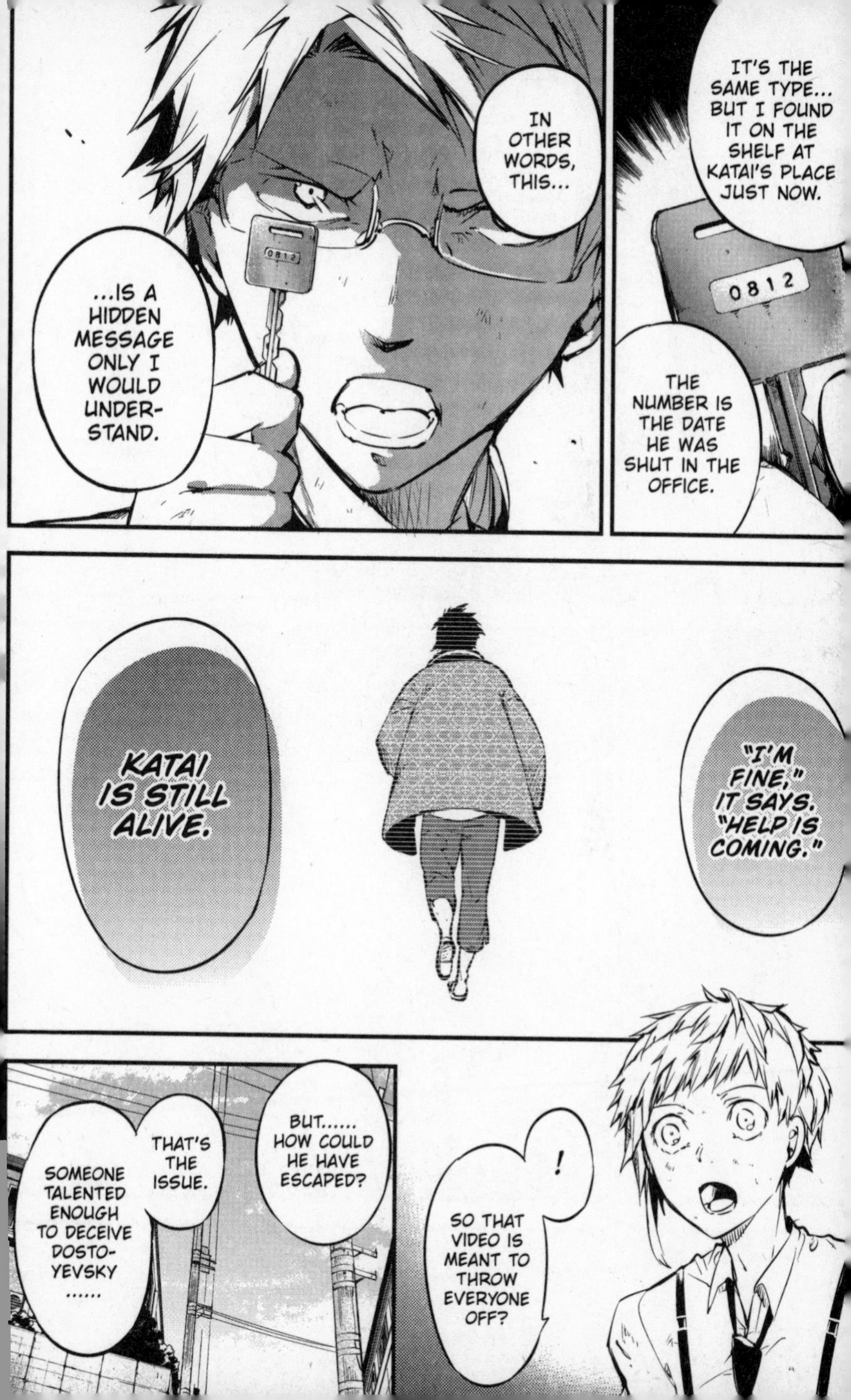
IT'S THE SAME TYPE... BUT I FOUND IT ON THE SHELF AT KATAI'S PLACE JUST NOW.
0812
THE NUMBER IS THE DATE HE WAS SHUT IN THE OFFICE.
IN OTHER WORDS, THIS...
0812
...IS A HIDDEN MESSAGE ONLY I WOULD UNDER-STAND.
"I'M FINE," IT SAYS. "HELP IS COMING."
KATAI IS STILL ALIVE.
!
SO THAT VIDEO IS MEANT TO THROW EVERYONE OFF?
BUT...... HOW COULD HE HAVE ESCAPED?
THAT'S THE ISSUE.
SOMEONE TALENTED ENOUGH TO DECEIVE DOSTO-YEVSKY ......

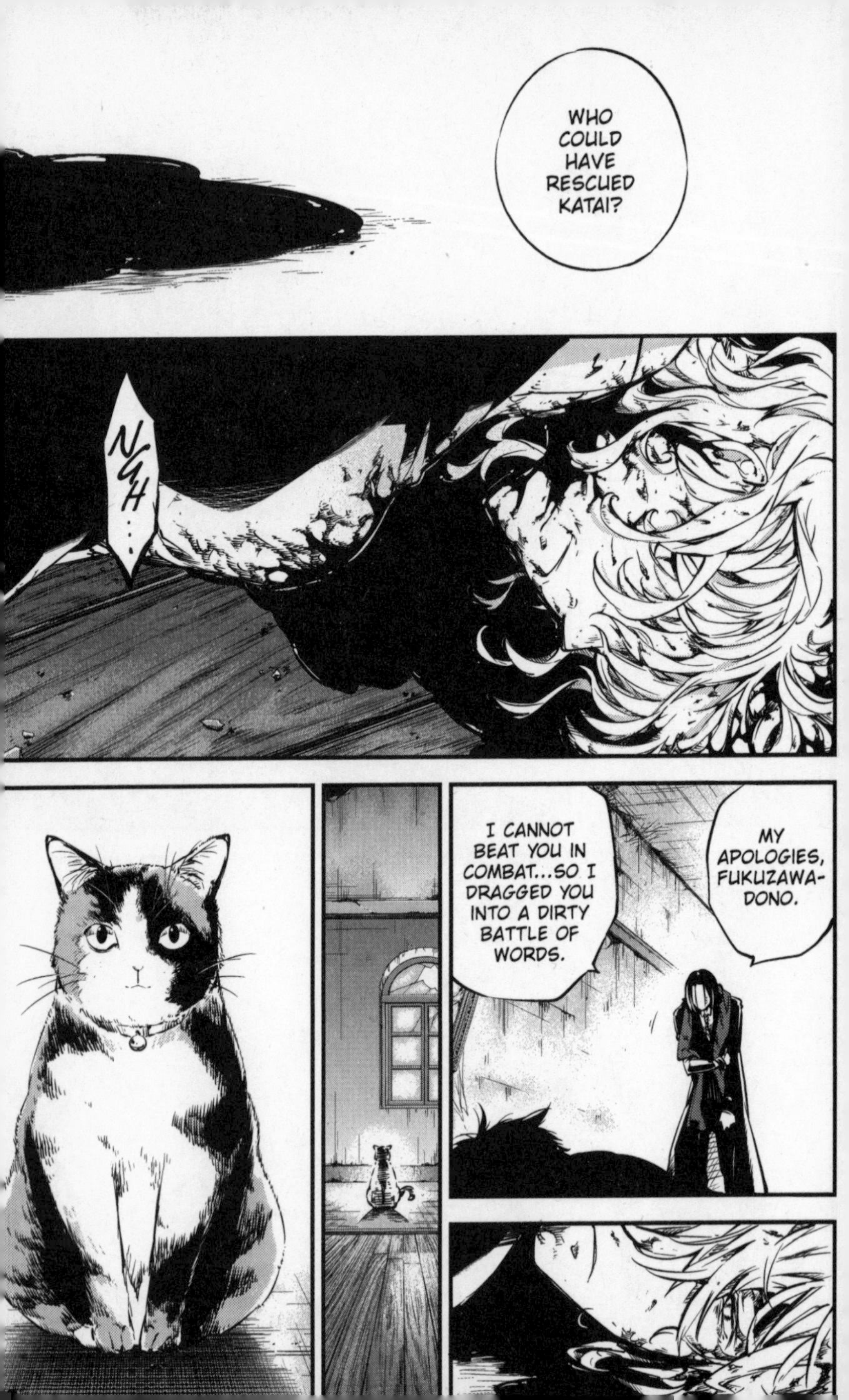
WHO COULD HAVE RESCUED KATAI?
NGH...
MY APOLOGIES, FUKUZAWA-DONO.
I CANNOT BEAT YOU IN COMBAT...SO I DRAGGED YOU INTO A DIRTY BATTLE OF WORDS.

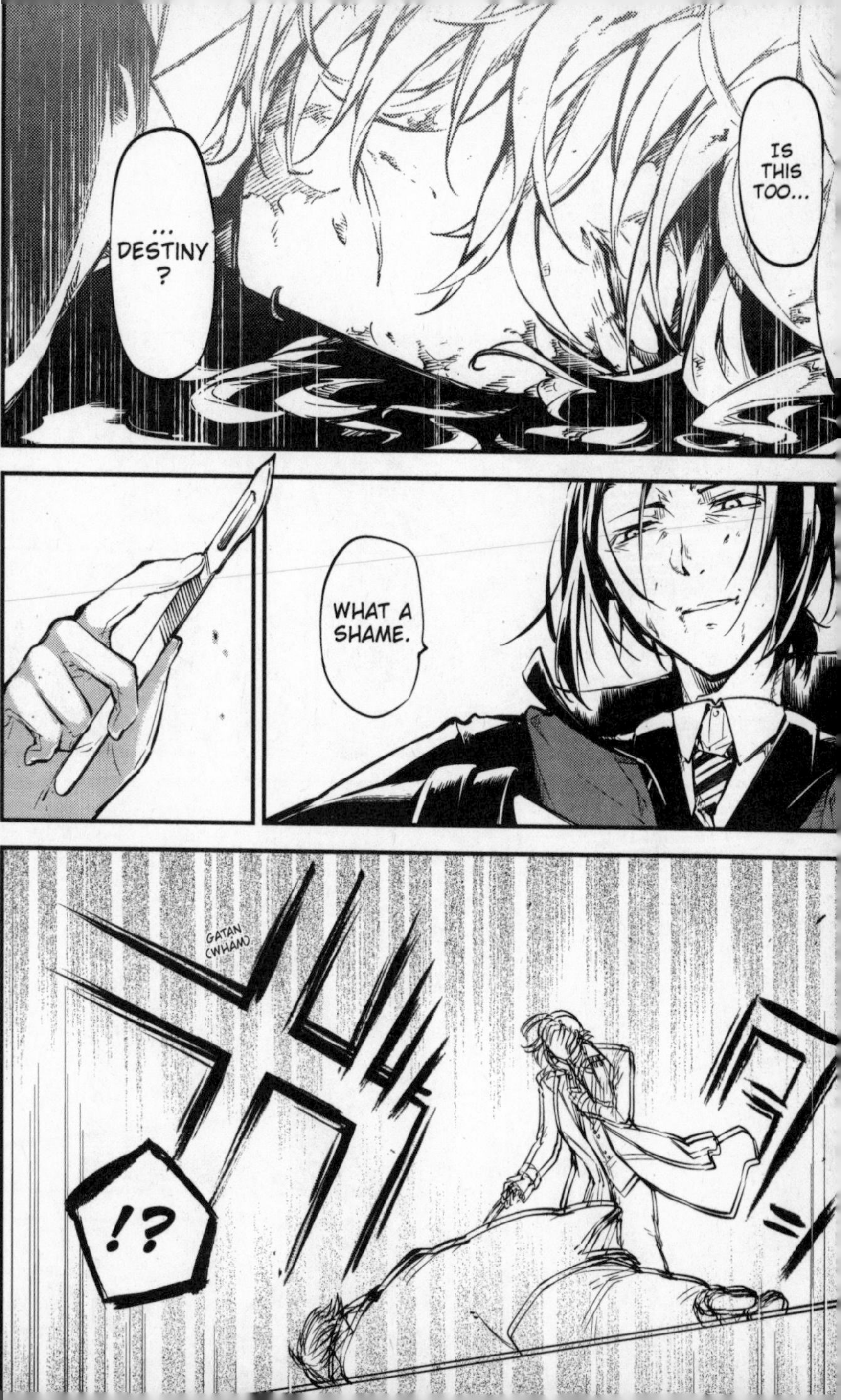
IS THIS TOO...
...DESTINY?
WHAT A SHAME.
GATAN (WHAM)
!?

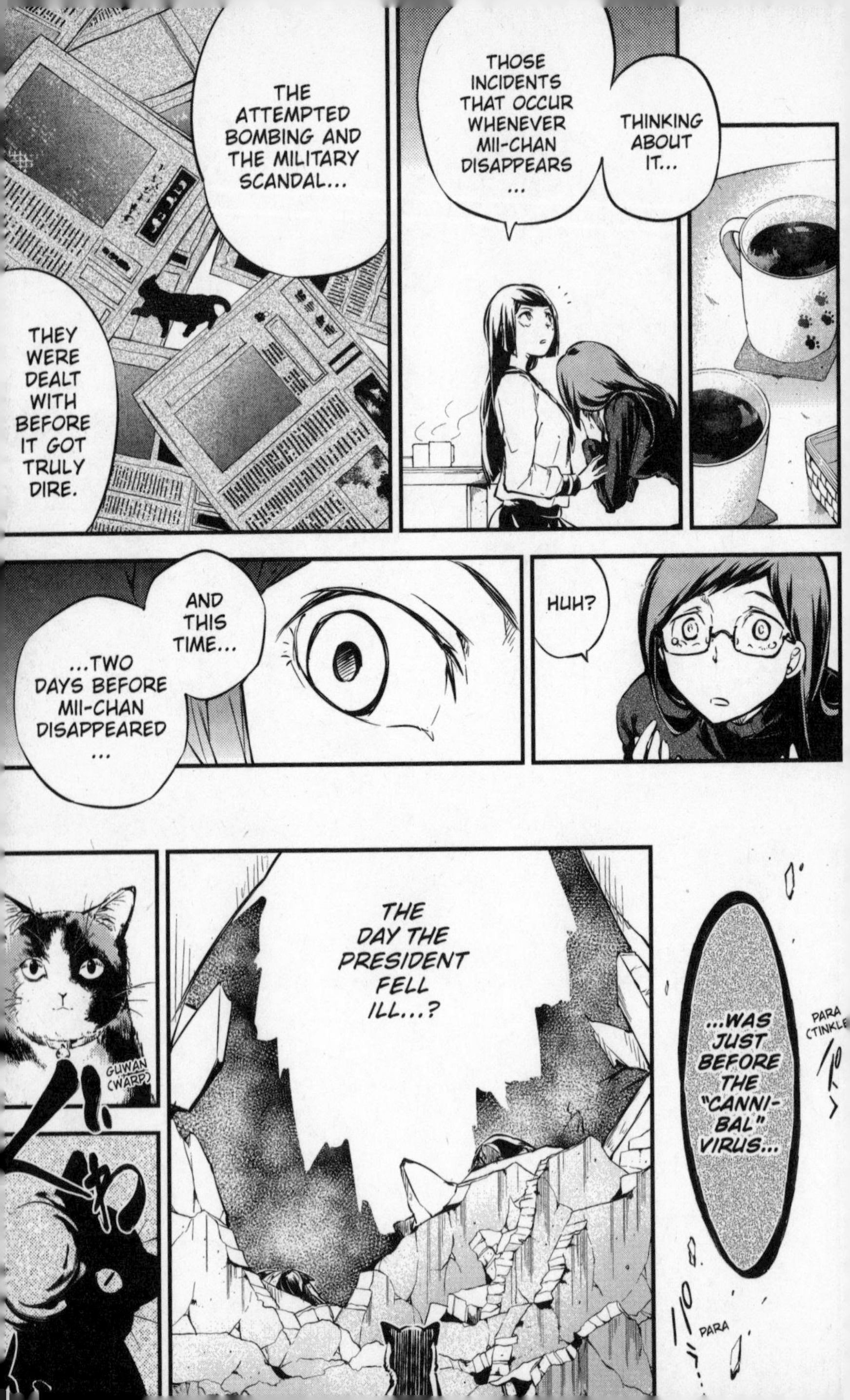
THINKING ABOUT IT...
THOSE INCIDENTS THAT OCCUR WHENEVER MII-CHAN DISAPPEARS...
THE ATTEMPTED BOMBING AND THE MILITARY SCANDAL...
THEY WERE DEALT WITH BEFORE IT GOT TRULY DIRE.
HUH?
AND THIS TIME...
...TWO DAYS BEFORE MII-CHAN DISAPPEARED...
PARA (TINKLE)
THE DAY THE PRESIDENT FELL ILL...?
...WAS JUST BEFORE THE "CANNIBAL" VIRUS...
PARA
GUWAN (WARP)

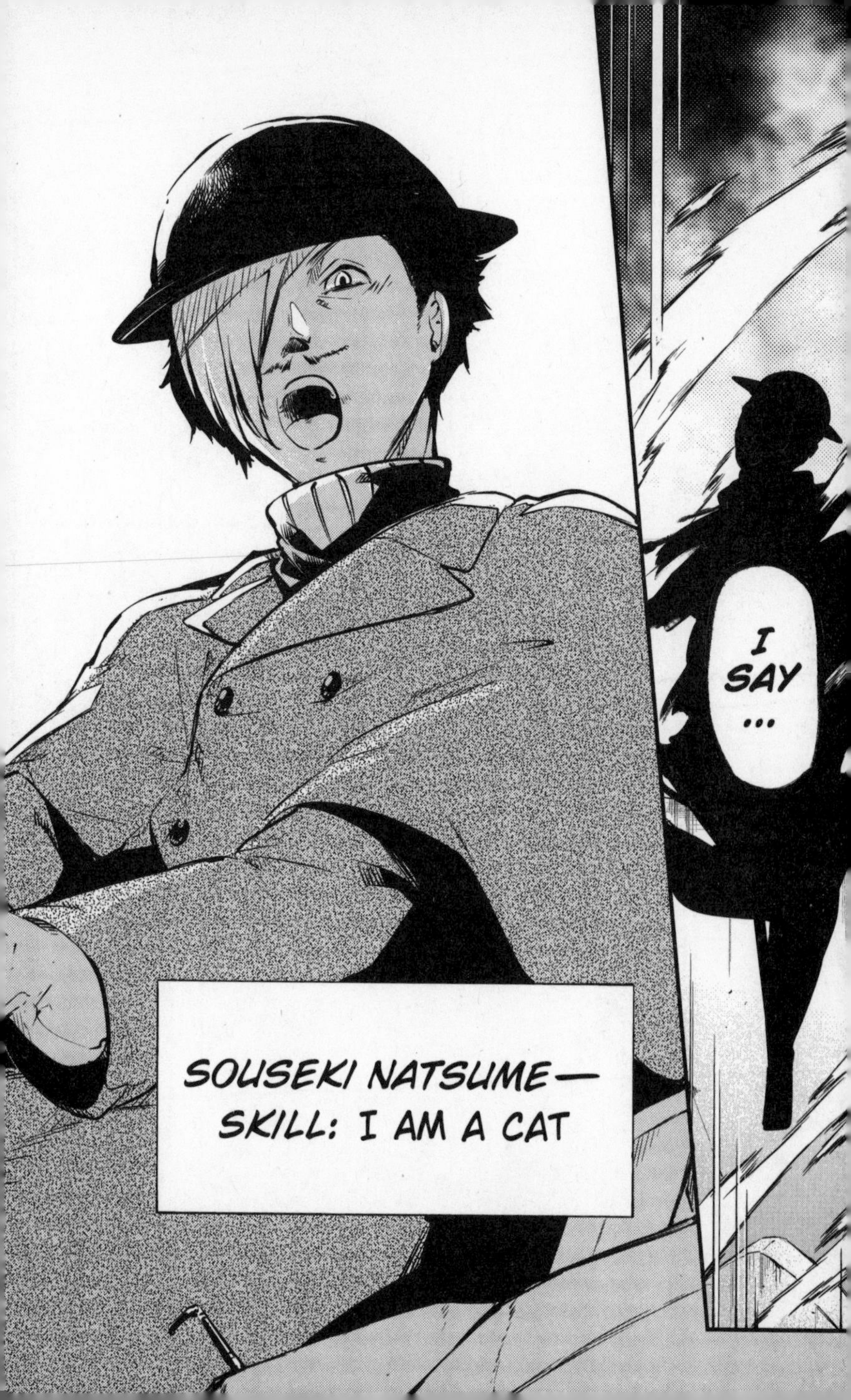
I SAY...
SOUSEKI NATSUME—
SKILL: I AM A CAT

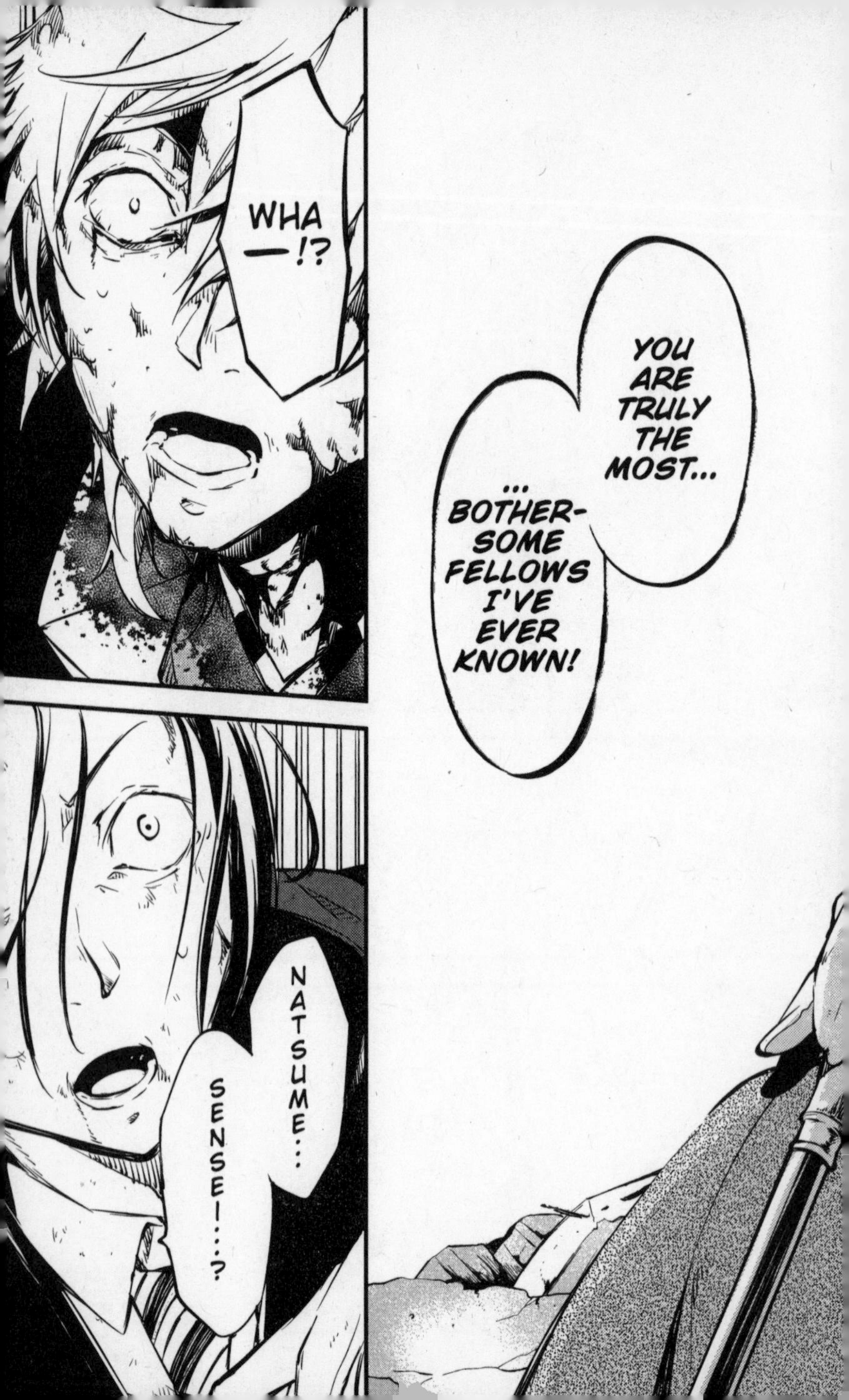
YOU ARE TRULY THE MOST...
...BOTHER-SOME FELLOWS I'VE EVER KNOWN!
WHA—!?
NATSUME... SENSEI...?

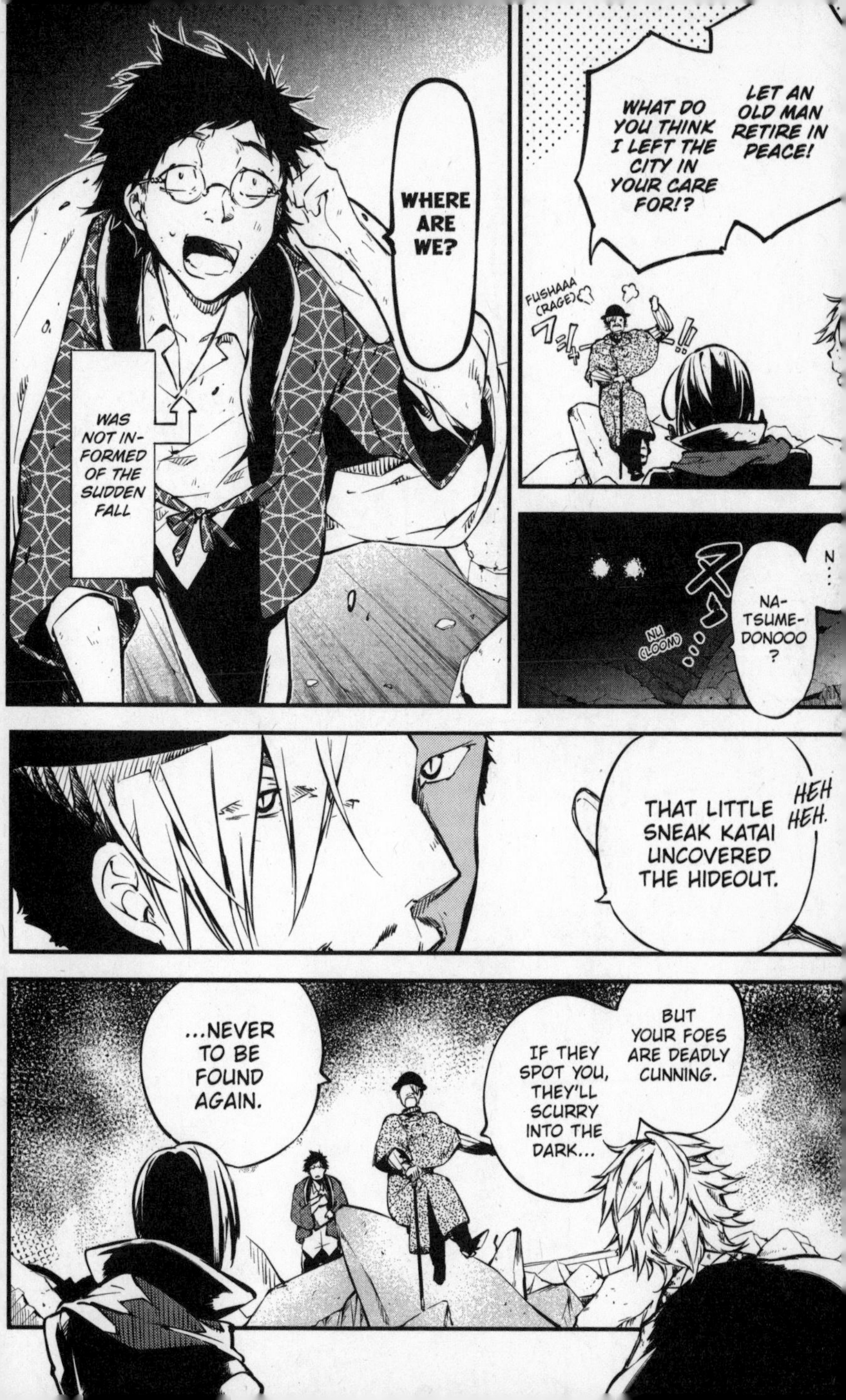
LET AN OLD MAN RETIRE IN PEACE!
WHAT DO YOU THINK I LEFT THE CITY IN YOUR CARE FOR!?
FUSHAAA (RAGE)
N... NA-TSUME-DONOOO?
NU (LOOM)
WHERE ARE WE?
WAS NOT INFORMED OF THE SUDDEN FALL
HEH HEH.
THAT LITTLE SNEAK KATAI UNCOVERED THE HIDEOUT.
BUT YOUR FOES ARE DEADLY CUNNING.
IF THEY SPOT YOU, THEY'LL SCURRY INTO THE DARK...
...NEVER TO BE FOUND AGAIN.

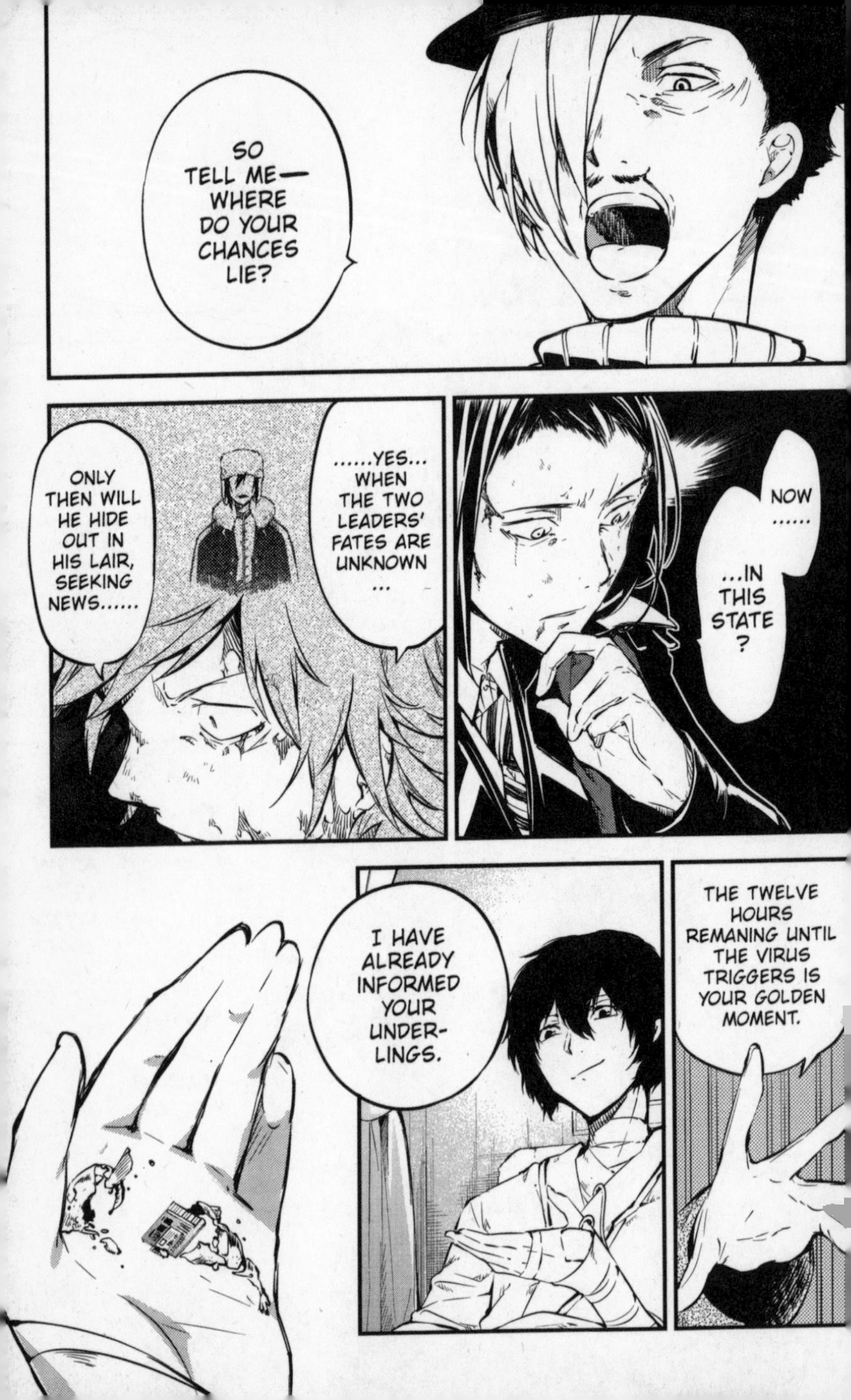
SO TELL ME— WHERE DO YOUR CHANCES LIE?
NOW ......
...IN THIS STATE?
......YES... WHEN THE TWO LEADERS' FATES ARE UNKNOWN ...
ONLY THEN WILL HE HIDE OUT IN HIS LAIR, SEEKING NEWS......
THE TWELVE HOURS REMANING UNTIL THE VIRUS TRIGGERS IS YOUR GOLDEN MOMENT.
I HAVE ALREADY INFORMED YOUR UNDER-LINGS.

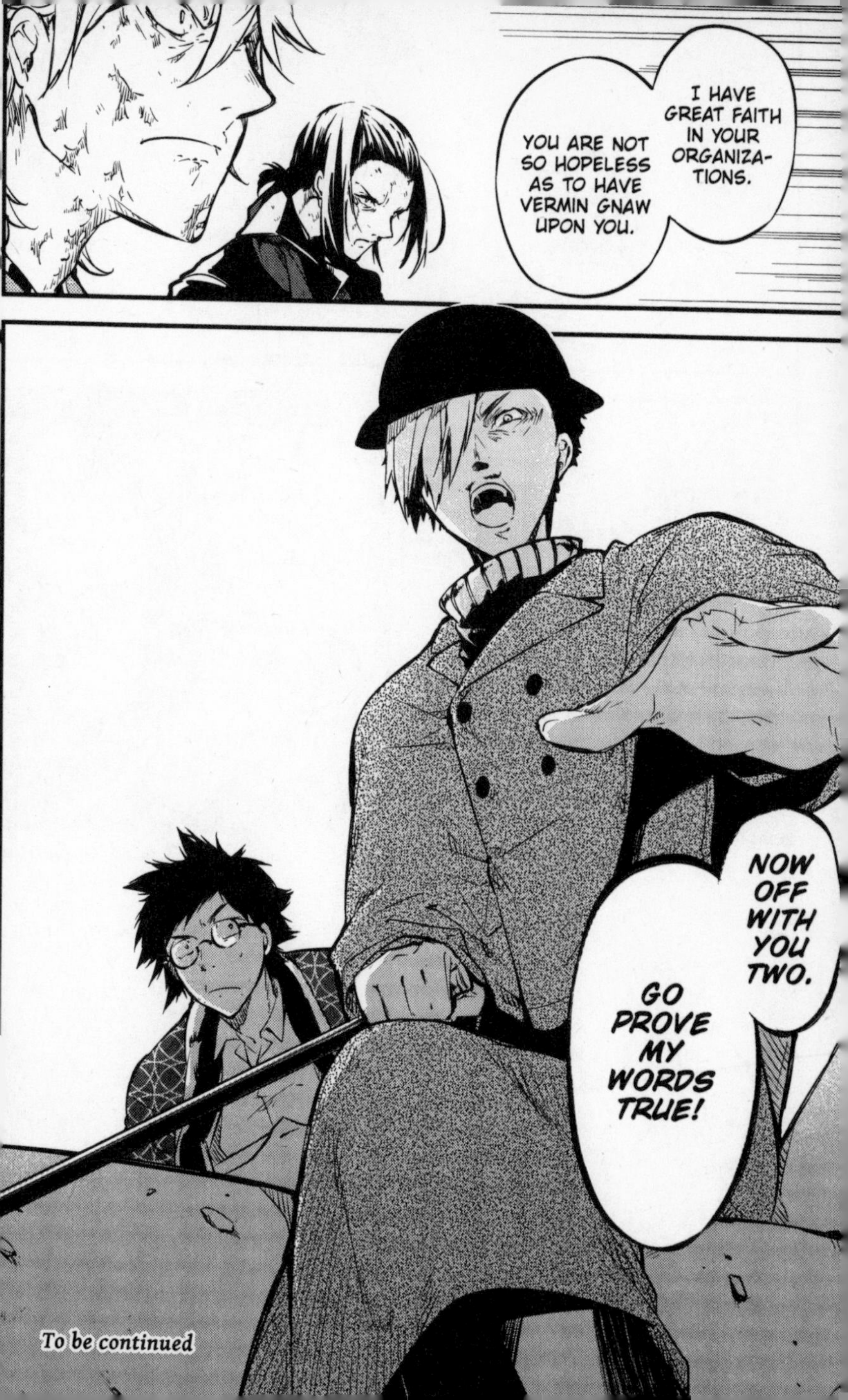
I HAVE GREAT FAITH IN YOUR ORGANIZATIONS.
YOU ARE NOT SO HOPELESS AS TO HAVE VERMIN GNAW UPON YOU.
NOW OFF WITH YOU TWO.
GO PROVE MY WORDS TRUE!
To be continued

BUNGO
STRAY DOGS

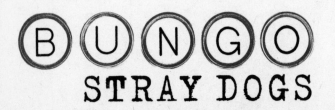

BUNGO STRAY DOGS

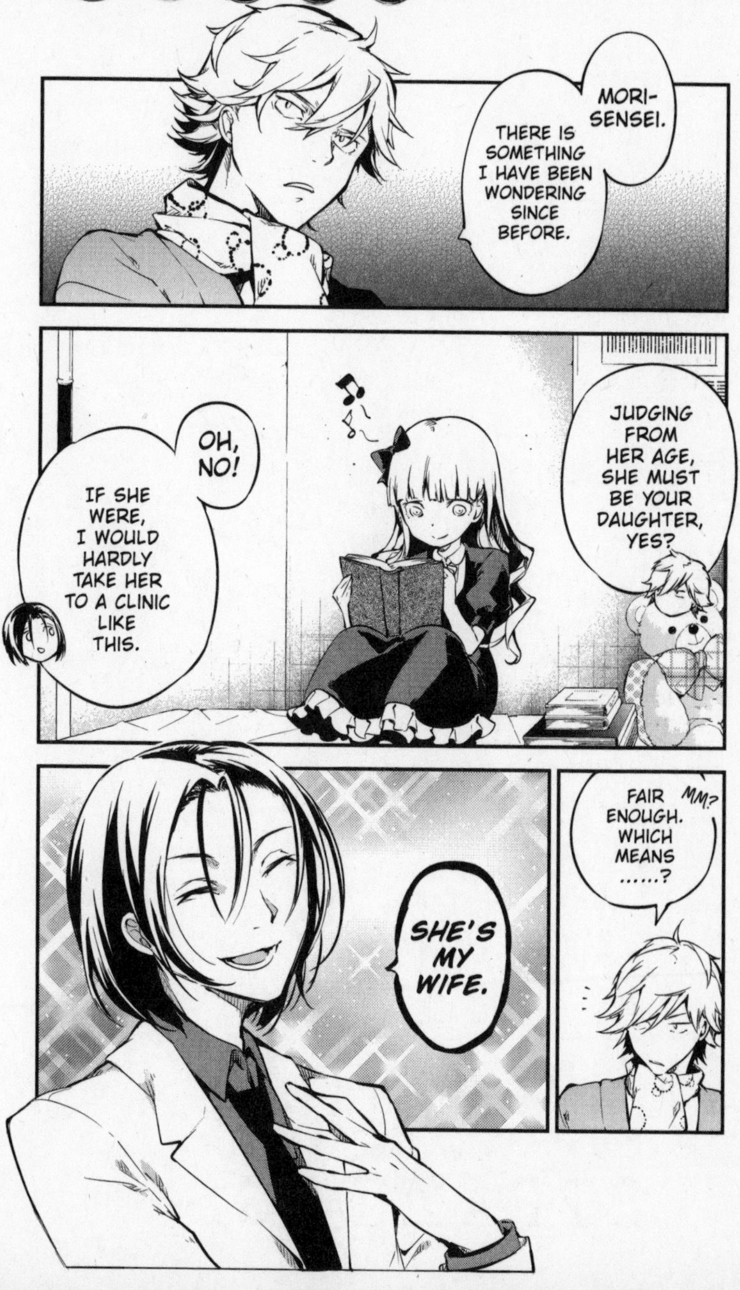
MORI-SENSEI.
THERE IS SOMETHING I HAVE BEEN WONDERING SINCE BEFORE.
JUDGING FROM HER AGE, SHE MUST BE YOUR DAUGHTER, YES?
OH, NO!
IF SHE WERE, I WOULD HARDLY TAKE HER TO A CLINIC LIKE THIS.
MM?
FAIR ENOUGH. WHICH MEANS ......?
SHE'S MY WIFE.

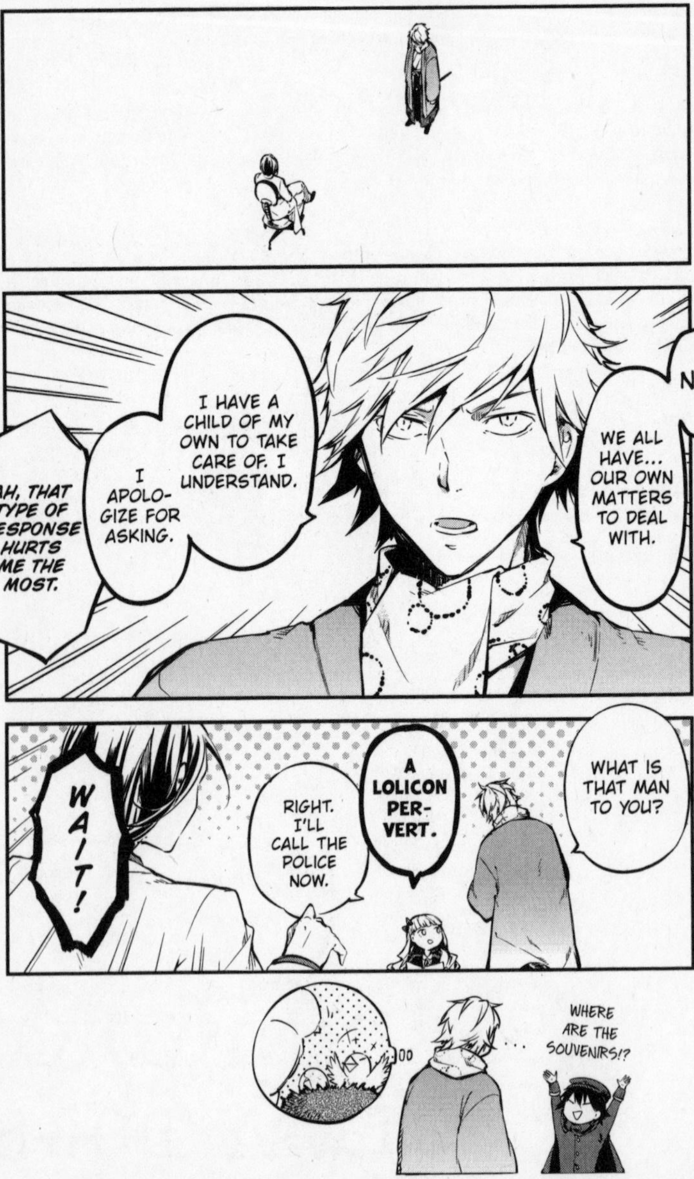
NO.
WE ALL HAVE... OUR OWN MATTERS TO DEAL WITH.
I HAVE A CHILD OF MY OWN TO TAKE CARE OF. I UNDERSTAND.
I APOLOGIZE FOR ASKING.
AH, THAT TYPE OF RESPONSE HURTS ME THE MOST.
WHAT IS THAT MAN TO YOU?
A LOLICON PERVERT.
RIGHT. I'LL CALL THE POLICE NOW.
WAIT!
WHERE ARE THE SOUVENIRS!?
...

Translation Notes

Page 6
Yosano uses the word **fate**, or *innen* in Japanese, to refer to Fukuzawa and Mori's shared predicament. *Innen* was derived from the Sanskrit word *nidana*, which is a Buddhist term to describe the individual stages that form the cycle of life and death.

Page 27
Meursault is a character from *The Stranger*, a novel by French author Albert Camus that was published in 1942. The book is about a emotionally detached, apathetic man who is charged with murder and whose life is threatened due to his lack of remorse. Meursault is also the name of a place in eastern France famous for its wine.

Page 98
In Japanese, the phrase **sinister mind behind the curtain** is *kuromaku*—literally "black curtain." It refers to the black curtain used in *kabuki* (a type of traditional Japanese theatre) to indicate a change in setting or nighttime. It can also mean "wire-puller," or someone who operates behind-the-scenes for highly influential figures and political officials in particular. This can also be translated as "mastermind."

Page 111
A *futon* is a rollable, cotton-filled mattress that is commonly used in Japan. It is often laid on top of a tatami floor.

Page 139
Tenma Tengai means "demon of the sixth heaven wearing armor."

BUNGO STRAY DOGS

AUTHOR GUIDE (PART 5)

The characters of *Bungo Stray Dogs* are based on major literary figures from Japan and around the world! Here's a handy guide to help you learn about some of the writers who inspired the weird and wonderful cast of this series!

KATAI TAYAMA (1872-1930)

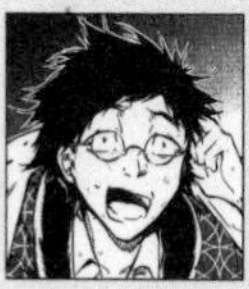

Born into a samurai family, Tayama later moved to Tokyo and began his journey as an aspiring writer, rubbing elbows with the likes of Kouyou Ozaki and Doppo Kunikida. His works paved the way for Japanese autobiographical I-novels and were inspired by his turbulent love relationships, his main work *Futon* detailing a middle-aged author's attraction toward a younger student.

LUCY MONTGOMERY (1874-1942)

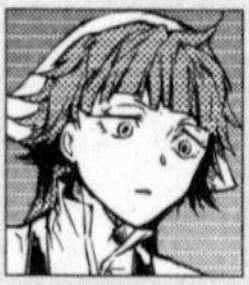

Best known for her book *Anne of Green Gables*, Montgomery first wrote the book in 1905 and sent it to multiple publishers only to be rejected. It was accepted three years later and soon went on to become a huge bestseller, prompting the creation of the well-loved series we are familiar with today. The book follows the adventures of a young orphan girl who is mistakenly sent to the wrong home but in the end is given a chance to live with her new family in the town of Green Gables.

FYODOR DOSTOYEVSKY (1821-1881)

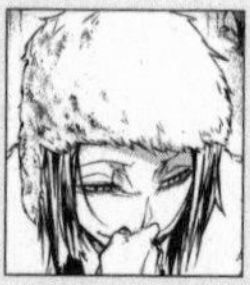

A Russian novelist whose mega-popular works explore human emotions, psychology, and existentialism, Dostoyevsky was influenced by fictional works and fairytales from a young age. Some of his key works include *Notes From the Underground*, *Crime and Punishment*, and *The Idiot*. Much of his stories include dark, philosophical themes such as imprisonment and extreme brutality in his semi-autobiographical novel *The House of the Dead*.

AGATHA CHRISTIE (1890-1976)

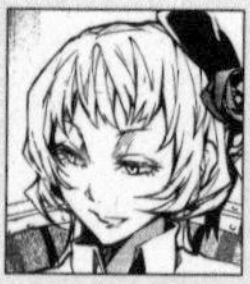

A fan of mystery and detective novels like Sherlock Holmes, Christie was a prolific English writer who specialized in murder mysteries and thrillers. A few of her well-known works include *And Then There Were None*, *Murder on the Orient Express*, and *Death on the Nile*. Her first official foray into writing was due in part to her sister, who said she wouldn't be able to write a decent mystery novel, thereby leading Christie to write one just to prove her wrong.

SOUSEKI NATSUME (1867-1916)

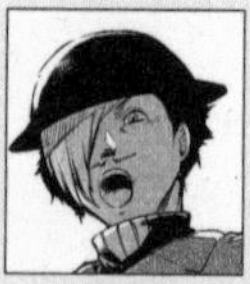

As one of the most well-known and influential Japanese writers, Natsume has a handful of works that have become a central part of the modern literature repertoire in Japan such as *I Am a Cat*, *Kokoro*, *Sanshirou*, and *Botchan*. *I Am a Cat* is a novel narrated by a cat who tells the life stories of various middle-class people during the Meiji period when Japan was experiencing post-war westernization.

Two girls, a new school, and the beginning of a beautiful friendship.

Kiss & White Lily for My Dearest Girl

In middle school, Ayaka Shiramine was the perfect student: hard-working, with excellent grades and a great personality to match. As Ayaka enters high school she expects to still be on top, but one thing she didn't account for is her new classmate, the lazy yet genuine genius Yurine Kurosawa. What's in store for Ayaka and Yurine as they go through high school...together?

Yen Press

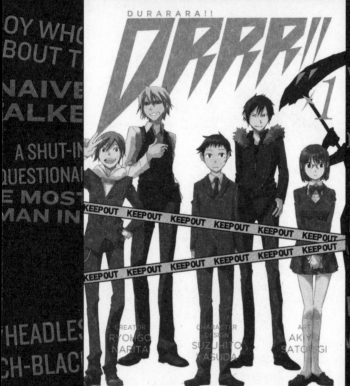

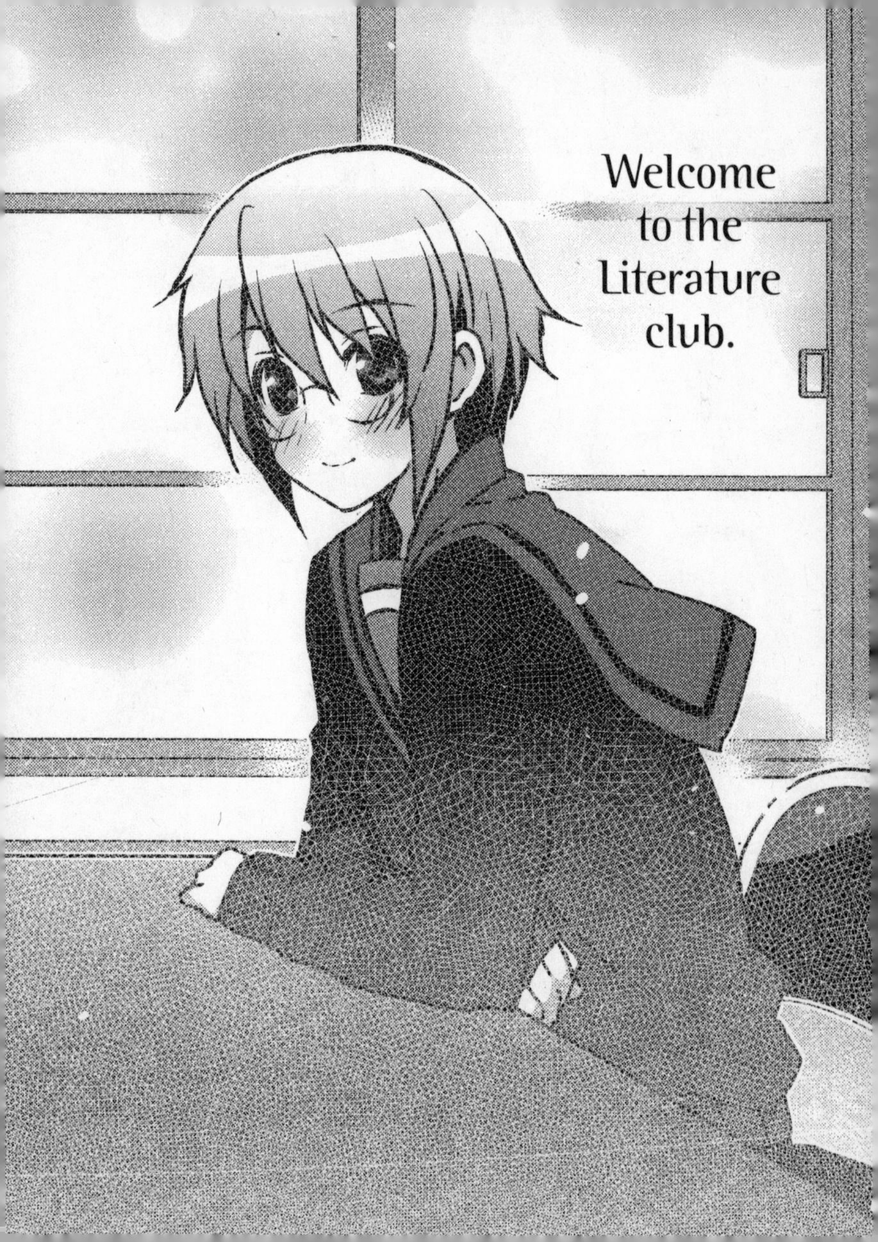
Welcome to the Literature club.

BUNGO STRAY DOGS

Story: Kafka Asagiri   Art: Sango Harukawa

Translation: Kevin Gifford   †   Lettering: Bianca Pistillo

BUNGO STRAY DOGS Volume 12
©Kafka ASAGIRI 2017
©Sango HARUKAWA 2017
First published in Japan in 2017 by KADOKAWA CORPORATION, Tokyo.
English translation rights arranged with KADOKAWA CORPORATION, Tokyo through TUTTLE-MORI AGENCY, INC., Tokyo.

English translation © 2019 by Yen Press, LLC

Yen Press
150 West 30th Street, 19th Floor
New York, NY 10001

Visit us at yenpress.com
facebook.com/yenpress
twitter.com/yenpress
yenpress.tumblr.com
instagram.com/yenpress

First Yen Press Edition: September 2019

Yen Press is an imprint of Yen Press, LLC.
The Yen Press name and logo are trademarks of Yen Press, LLC.

Library of Congress Control Number: 2016956681

ISBNs: 978-1-9753-0452-2 (paperback)
       978-1-9753-0453-9 (ebook)

10 9 8 7 6 5 4 3 2 1

WOR

Printed in the United States of America